NEW GILL HISTORY OF IRELAND 2

Sixteenth-Century Ireland:
The Incomplete Conquest

NEW GILL HISTORY OF IRELAND

1. *Medieval Ireland: The Enduring Tradition*
   Michael Richter

2. *Sixteenth-Century Ireland: The Incomplete Conquest*
   Colm Lennon

3. *Seventeenth-Century Ireland: The War of Religions*
   Brendan Fitzpatrick

4. *Eighteenth-Century Ireland: The Long Peace*
   Eamon O'Flaherty

5. *Nineteenth-Century Ireland: The Search for Stability*
   D. George Boyce

6. *Twentieth-Century Ireland: Nation and State*
   Dermot Keogh

The Gill History of Ireland originally appeared in eleven paperback volumes between 1972 and 1975. It was immediately acknowledged as the most authoritative multi-volume history of Ireland. Now, because of the continuing evolution in the writing of the Irish history, it is being succeeded by the NEW GILL HISTORY OF IRELAND. The format is different—six longer volumes, rather than eleven short ones—but the intention is the same: to offer the general reader an accessible and up-to-date survey of Irish history.

NEW GILL HISTORY OF IRELAND
2

Sixteenth-Century Ireland: The Incomplete Conquest

COLM LENNON

GILL & MACMILLAN

Published in Ireland by
Gill & Macmillan Ltd
Goldenbridge
Dublin 8
with associated companies throughout the world

www.gillmacmillan.ie

© Colm Lennon 1994
0 7171 1622 0 (hard cover)
0 7171 1623 9 (paperback)
Index compiled by Helen Litton
Print origination by
Carrigboy Typesetting, Co. Cork
Printed by ColourBooks Ltd, Dublin

A catalogue record is available for this book from the British Library.

3   5   4

For Margaret

Contents

List of maps

Acknowledgments

Introduction   1
The natural environment about 1500   1
The political environment: the lordship of Ireland   10
  as framework

1. Town and County in the English Part of Ireland, *c.* 1500   20
Towns and their ruling groups   22
Cultural and economic functions of towns   27
The meshing of manor and market   32

2. Society and Culture in Gaelic Ireland   42
Peasants and landlords in Gaelic society   43
Gaelic lords and overlords   50
Law and learning among the Gaelic population   57

3. The Kildares and their Critics, 1500–20   65
The basis of Kildare family power   68
The Earls of Kildare and Gaelic Ireland   74
Kildare's apogee and the rise of Old English reformers   77

4. Kildare Power and Tudor Intervention, 1520–35   87
The Surrey expedition and its significance   89
The rotating governorship in the 1520s:
  Fitzgerald and Butler in balance   93
Causes and course of the Kildare rebellion   104

5. Religion and Reformation, 1500–40   113
The pre-Reformation church among the English of Ireland 116
Religion in Gaelic Ireland in the late middle ages   124
The early Reformation under Henry VIII   134

6. Political and Religious Reform and Reaction, 1536–56   144
   Options for reform: the failure of Lord Deputy Grey   145
   Accommodation and assimilation: St Leger's initial success 152
   Militarism and modification of policy in the
      mid-century years   164

7. The Pale and Greater Leinster, 1556–88   177
   Ambitious lord deputyships and Leinster, 1556–79   179
   Coexistence and conflict among Old English,
      Gaelic Irish and New English   187
   Crisis in the Pale, 1580–86   202

8. Munster: Presidency and Plantation, 1565–95   208
   English activity and native reaction, 1565–73   210
   Desmond, the presidency and rebellion, 1573–83   216
   The planning and practice of plantation   229

9. Connacht: Council and Composition, 1569–95   237
   The establishment of the presidency council   239
   The Composition and communal relations within
      Connacht, 1585–95   249

10. Ulster and the General Crisis of the Nine Years' War,
    1560–1603   264
   Sussex, Sidney and Shane O'Neill   266
   Colonial schemes and their aftermath   274
   The rise of Hugh O'Neill   283
   The Nine Years' War   292

11. From Reformation to Counter-Reformation, 1560–1600   303
   Structural weakness of the church and problems of
      evangelisation   305
   Communal responses to the Reformation   311
   Religious conviction and political identity in a time
      of crisis, 1579–1600   315

References   326

Bibliographical Guide   352

Index   361

Maps

The lordship of Ireland in the early sixteenth century   19

The region of Dublin in the early sixteenth century   31

The leading families of Ireland in the sixteenth century   41

Sixteenth-century Irish dioceses   116

Elizabethan Ireland   176

NOTE ON CURRENCY AND DATING

Sums of money in Irish currency are specifically denoted as such throughout the book; sums in sterling are not so denoted. The Irish pound was generally reckoned as the equivalent in value of 13s 4d (or one mark) sterling.

In contrast to the practice of some contemporaries, the year is reckoned as beginning on 1 January. All precise dates after 5 October 1582 are given according to the old-style or Julian calendar.

Acknowledgments

OF all the periods covered by the New Gill History of Ireland, the sixteenth century is perhaps the one whose historiography has been most transformed in the past two decades. The work of Margaret MacCurtain and Kenneth Nicholls, who were directly concerned with this era in the first series, pointed the way towards research in many fields, and scholars are indebted to them for their example. The task of writing the present volume would have been impossible without a plenitude of writings of many historians. I have great pleasure in acknowledging the generosity of the scholarly fraternity, friends and family by which I have benefited while writing this book. It may not be invidious to single out Dr Ciaran Brady, whose perceptive writings and stimulating company have helped enormously in the shaping of the volume. Dr Raymond Gillespie, happily now a colleague, deserves mention for his selflessness in providing ideas and materials. Among those who sent me copies of their work or whose conversation encouraged fruitful lines of inquiry are Brendan Bradshaw, Nicholas Canny, Vincent Carey, Art Cosgrove, Bernadette Cunningham, Steven Ellis, Alan Ford, Gráinne Henry, Rolf Loeber, Hiram Morgan, James Murray, Mary O'Dowd, Helga Robinson-Hammerstein and Anthony Sheehan. I would like to pay tribute to Professor Vincent Comerford, my colleagues and students in the Department of Modern History and other staff members at St Patrick's College, Maynooth, for providing a supportive academic environment. I am very grateful to Peter Lennon for his cartographic work, and to Marian Lyons, who read a draft of part of the work and made some very useful comments. My principal debt is to my wife, Margaret, who has helped me in so many ways, both by her unfailing interest in and commitment to the project and by her practical assistance in facilitating the research and writing.

Introduction

The natural environment about 1500

FOR most people in early sixteenth-century Ireland the world was narrowly confined to locality. They drew their concepts of space and time from direct experience of the environment. Nature, pristine and primeval, framed the lives of a great number of the inhabitants, although forest clearances, bog reclamations and nucleated villages had brought some adaptation of geography for settlement during the medieval centuries. For all, in whatever location in the island, or age group or station in society, high mortality rates cut ties of family and friendship with sad regularity. The implacable forces of famine and disease were frequent influences upon lifespans. In 1500 the taming of the physical environment and the overcoming of its attendant perils were scarcely dreamed of. As other maritime countries in Europe embarked upon overseas explorations, Ireland was itself a land for discovery and eventual colonisation by newcomers. The plantation estate and the purpose-built town of the early seventeenth century entailed the shaping of the countryside and the harvesting of its resources in a way which was still inconceivable one hundred years earlier. Even further in the future lay the breakthroughs in agriculture and science which were to affect fundamentally the recurrence of famine and plague.

Whereas the majority of Irish people may have had a world-view which was sharply delimited by familiar physical features, the small educated elite scarcely visualised the island more clearly. Most accounts of the country and its inhabitants were to be found in the tales of foreign pilgrims to St Patrick's Purgatory in the north-west or else were based on the three-hundred-year-old *Topographia Hiberniae* of Gerald of Wales. That no native chorographical overview existed about 1500 was due to the lack of those antiquarian and historical studies being pioneered by the humanists in countries influenced by the Renaissance. One of the few outsiders to describe

Ireland even cursorily about that time was Polydore Vergil, an Italian scholar who lived in England, and his perspective (like Gerald of Wales's) was that of the sophisticated cosmopolitan writing about the less advanced periphery. In the later sixteenth century the topographical unveiling of much of the island took place in the context of English governmental reform proposals. Meanwhile, among native scholars, the Gaelic bards revealed a poetic rather than a scientific view of the landscape, and the territorial views of writers from anglicised regions were subsidiary to their ideas for political reform.[1]

There were no accurate or detailed maps of the island's interior to guide travellers in the early sixteenth century. Here also Ireland lagged behind those countries in which a Renaissance-inspired study of ancient geography was giving rise to more scientific cartography. Ireland did appear on maps of Europe, but with few of its inland features revealed. There were many coastal maps of the country, known as portolan charts, then in circulation. These provided details of the shoreline to guide mariners and traders in their navigation. Mostly of Italian origin, the portolans bear testimony to the vitality of trade between the Mediterranean and other continental regions and Ireland, and especially its western and southern ports. But accurate navigation was a different matter to sound geographical knowledge, as witness the continental merchant who inquired of a Galwegian: 'In what part of Galway does Hibernia stand?' As with chorographical accounts, the impetus for surveying and mapping the remoter regions of the island came with the thrusting reform schemes and military ventures of administrators after the mid-century, and also with the planning of organised settlements of new proprietors. The expanding outreach of the English government is illustrated by ever more detailed maps of the country whose contours could not be pictured in the early 1500s.[2]

In 1570 Abraham Ortelius produced the most detailed map of Ireland which had appeared down to that time. It was part of his splendid new atlas of the world, revealing the major advances in geographical knowledge in the era of exploration and discovery. An expanding market was developing among educated lay people as well as merchants for the technically and artistically accomplished works of Dutch and Flemish cartographers, and also for the published accounts of travels to little-known or unknown places throughout the world. By the end of the century Ortelius and his illustrious contemporary, Gerardus Mercator, had further refined the map of Ireland, including in their work the names and locations of its political elites. For an interested readership in the later sixteenth century the revelation of Ireland in such detail was a novelty, though the island was established as a reasonably well-known destination for Europeans during the late middle ages. In spite of being poorly served by native or visiting chorographers in the sixteenth century, Ireland could be described to mapmakers such as Ortelius and Mercator by members of the growing community of Irish *émigrés* in the Low Countries.[3]

The island of Ireland has a comparatively greater variety of terrains than many larger countries, including England. Within relatively small spaces plains can give way to undulating land and steep mountainous areas, and the soil changes from fertile to forested or boggy. Natural frontiers of mountain, bog and forest enclosed many communities in territories in a way which reinforced cultural distinctiveness. Before the axes and engines of the civil and military organisers began to subdue it to some extent, landscape proved to be protective of traditional lifestyles, such as that of the Kavanagh clan in the heavily wooded Blackstairs Mountains.[4] The sheer size and near-impenetrability rather than the beauty of those features of mountain, forest and bog would have caused them to bulk large in any contemporary description of Ireland. The forbidding nature of the almost unbroken chain of highlands ringing the island was compounded by their slopes being covered by dense woods, most notably in Antrim, Cork and Kerry, and Wicklow. These and other forest areas consisting of deciduous trees such as hazel, oak, ash, yew and willow extended over an eighth of the land of Ireland in 1500. Among the best-known woods in the sixteenth century were the great forest of Glenconkeyne, north-west of Lough Neagh, and the Dufferin, the Fews and Kilwarlin woods in Down, the Munster highland forests of Kerry, Cork and Tipperary, the forests in the basins of the south-eastern rivers, most notably the Slaney, Barrow and Suir, and those on the mountain slopes of southern Leinster, including the great woods of Shillelagh and Glencree. Clearances of these stout stands of timber did not take place at an accelerated rate until the final decades of the century, and so they remained custodial of human and animal habitation. The bogs too, covering about a quarter of the land mass, provided habitats, particularly in the central lowlands. Although unfitted for tillage, these stretches of bogland and scrub have been identified as providing conduits for the passage of ideas at many times in Irish history, up to and including the sixteenth century.[5]

Thus, while uplands, boglands and woodlands presented formidable obstacles to travellers, they sheltered a native, albeit thinly dispersed, population. Only the highly motivated outsider ventured from the coastline to the interior in the late middle ages. Arteries of travel and communication did exist throughout the island, however, as they had done since ancient times, but only native inhabitants were thoroughly familiar with them. A network of roads, highways, pathways and toghers (or causeways through marshes) crisscrossed even the remotest areas, many of them possibly linking with the old great roads through the Celtic provinces. The first accurate surveys drawn of sixteenth-century Leix and Offaly, for example, show the persistence of these old routeways even through the most inhospitable terrain. To natives these upland and lowland ways were efficient corridors of communication for commercial and social intercourse, but strangers found them difficult to traverse without local knowledge or accurate maps, especially in afforested or marshy territory.[6]

Rivers were used as an important means of internal travel, particularly in those regions which were inaccessible by road, though progress could be hazardous where galleried forests overhung steep valleys. In the absence of effective wheeled transport, the sending of goods by water was essential for internal trade. Hence, for example, bills presented to the Irish parliament for the care of rivers marked the concern of merchants and gentry to maintain the waterways free from obstructions such as weirs and wrecks. The most notable riverine routes would have been along the Nore, which had inland harbours, the Suir, Barrow and Slaney, all of which were navigable for long stretches, the Lee and the Munster Blackwater, the Shannon and some of its tributaries, and the Bann, Erne and Lagan. In the heart of the eastern region the rivers Liffey and Boyne were conduits for commodities and culture into the heart of the island. Sixteenth-century rivers were rarely banked with man-made wharves, and the consequent danger of flooding rendered them unsuitable for travel in very wet seasons.[7]

Overland or water-borne travel by officials of central government in the sixteenth century required some local knowledge and control of certain nodal points where routes converged. One of the preoccupations of governors of Ireland from the 1520s onwards was the cutting of passes through forests and the laying of causeways through bogs. Engineers and masons were included in the expeditionary sorties of Lord Deputy Grey in the later 1530s, for instance, as he sought to make permanent the ways he forged into thitherto little-traversed regions. Natural passes and fording-places were defensible by natives, as the crucial struggle for the Moyry Pass south of Newry in the Nine Years' War was to show. The occasional ill-judged choice of a fording-place or a mountain pass for the route of a marauding force could make that place synonymous with disastrous folly, as, for example, with the Pass of the Plumes (where English troops fled from the army of Owney O'More, leaving their finely feathered helmets behind), or the Ford of the Biscuits (where another discomfited band of English soldiers was routed without time to gather their scattered provisions). Small wonder, therefore, that the preference of central and local government officials was for the maintenance of stone-bridged crossing-points such as Leighlin Bridge over the Barrow in Carlow, which was a vital channel of communication between the southern Pale and that area of the English lordship in Ormond territory and Wexford. By contrast, O'Brien's Bridge over the Shannon, a Gaelic wooden structure, was regarded by successive governors as a target for demolition, as it facilitated raids from the O'Brien lordship of Thomond into the lordships of north Munster.[8]

Tudor officials in the early sixteenth century may have preferred to travel by coastal routes between ports and havens. Certainly the coasting trade was a feature of the voyaging of those natives who ventured outside their own immediate environs. The aforementioned portolan charts attest the existence of a chain of harbours, large and small, which were visited by Irish and other merchants in every part of the island, though the northern shoreline as shown on these charts had fewer havens. The evidence of records of marital and social connections of merchant bodies in different ports tends to confirm the importance of this coastal faring. In sixteenth-century Dublin, for example, there were matrimonial alliances forged between leading patrician families and their counterparts in Dundalk, Drogheda, Arklow, Wexford, Waterford and Limerick, as well as English towns and regions. The Irish ports were places of resort of traders from Scotland, Brittany, France, Flanders, Italy, Portugal and Spain, and so the populations were open to cultural as well as commercial intercourse.[9]

Piracy and storms were cited by Robert Ratcliffe, a Chester mariner who owned the post-boat to Dublin, as being responsible for losses sustained by him in 1589. Ratcliffe served as postmaster on the Dublin–Chester route, despite the existence of a shorter route to Holyhead, which allowed for a sixty-five-hour passage in the late sixteenth century, given favourable winds. Some merchants preferred to undertake the extra overland journey with packhorse from Holyhead to Chester, the main entrepôt for goods in the Anglo-Irish trade. The existence of a post-bark in the later part of the century attests the importance of communications between the two islands. The extremely regular two-way flow of correspondence between Dublin and London for most of the sixteenth century was achieved in the face of the potential disruptions. Letters from Dublin to London were taking nine days to reach their destination in good travelling conditions at the end of the century, and twelve days in the opposite direction, against the prevailing westerly winds. Cork was on average ten days distant in communication terms from London, though return correspondence could take up to twenty-four days. Exceptionally, the news of Queen Elizabeth's death was known in the east of Ireland within three days of its occurrence, with significant political implications for the concluding of the peace of Mellifont in 1603. Unseasonal weather could cause major delays, as in 1582 when the queen's missive to her Lord Deputy in Dublin took six weeks and two days to arrive. A worse fate befell Sir Henry Sidney's new administration in 1566 when the treasure ship upon which he was depending sank in the Irish Sea. Internal communications suffered because of the poor system of inter-regional roads, but as passes were cleared and fords and bridges constructed more widely the transmission of news between places within Ireland was speeded up.[10]

While the conquest of terrestrial space lay some way in the future and travelling speeds remained unchanged throughout the early modern period, the measurement of time was being accorded more importance. Rural communities still tended to mark the passage of time in terms of festivals of the church year which ordained seasons of devotion and recreation, the rhythm of the seaons which dictated agricultural work, and meal-times which structured daily activity. Even in towns and cities, the working day and year were divided along similar lines: industrial time was measured by the variable daylight hours, from sunrise to sunset. Chronometry was proceeding apace, although clocks were a comparative novelty in the sixteenth century. Dublin, for example, had public timepieces erected at prominent locations, such as the Castle and St Patrick's Cathedral, and civic clock-keepers were appointed to maintain the orology. Certain feasts of the pre-Reformation church such as St Anne's Day and Corpus Christi which had been public holidays may not have been recognised any longer after the Reformation, but Barnaby Rich, a retired English soldier living in Ireland, deprecated the inordinate number of public festivals observed there in the early seventeenth century.[11]

While the accurate measurement of time may have become possible with the use of more sophisticated clocks, the fragility of the human life-cycle was pitifully manifest in the high mortality rates which affected all age groups. It has been established that Ireland was comparatively underpopulated in the early sixteenth century and that rapid demographic growth did not take place as it did elsewhere in Europe during that period. A recent well-informed estimate put the population of the island at perhaps a good deal less than half a million at the end of the fifteenth century, with no increase registered until the seventeenth. There is no doubt that the great demographic crisis of the mid-fourteenth century affected Ireland just as badly as it did other countries, with the more densely peopled Anglo-Norman regions sustaining more losses than the Gaelic ones. Recovery of population to levels attained before the Black Death of 1348–51, evident in other countries by the late fifteenth century, did not take place in Ireland for over a hundred years thereafter. In the absence of scientific studies of birth and death rates in the island for the sixteenth century, one can only guess that the deleterious effects of famine and dearth, infectious diseases and warfare there were not outweighed by birth rates. Ireland shared with its European counterparts the phenomena of low life expectancy (28 for males at birth, and 34 for females), very high rates of infant mortality (with perhaps up to a quarter of babies dying before their first birthday) and relatively high ages for first marriages (mid-twenties for brides and grooms). Centenarians were not unknown in the sixteenth century: two bishops, Miler Magrath of Cashel and Eugene O'Harte of Achonry, lived for over a hundred years, while Katharine, Countess of Desmond, was reputed to have lived for almost 140 years. In Dublin the average age at death of the members of the privileged aldermanic class was about fifty years.[12]

The vagaries of climate rendered people extremely vulnerable to sudden misfortune in the early modern period. As mentioned, adverse weather conditions severely affected communications by land

and sea in an age of tenuous links between regions. More grievous, however, if related, was the impact of unseasonal climatic conditions in the growing season. The information drawn from annalistic and other allusions suggests that no major change in meteorological patterns occurred until the very end of the sixteenth century, when Ireland may have begun to be affected by the 'little ice age'. With the exception of years such as 1496–7, 1505, 1520–21 and 1545, the period down to the mid-century seems to have been climatically benign. In the years mentioned, however, very wet and cold growing seasons were harmful enough to cause famine, but dearths could occur in regions and localities even when normal patterns were only moderately disturbed, especially as the surpluses of food were comparatively rare in most parts. Normal climatic conditions in wintertime precluded efforts at relief of shortages, particularly in remoter areas. From the 1540s onwards a qualitative change may have set in in Irish weather patterns, though extreme cold such as was experienced by other European countries, for example about 1564 (the worst winter since 1430), was a comparative rarity in the island. The metereological turbulence of the mid-1570s may have caused dearth and disease, and there can be little doubt that the sequence of appalling summers and autumns in the 1590s gave rise to mortality on a large scale owing to failure of food supplies.[13]

Closely allied to intemperate weather as a harbinger of death for sixteenth-century people was disease. Plague was only the most virulent form of morbidity which struck at local, regional and sometimes national level. There are references to plagues visiting large areas in 1519–20, 1534, 1536, 1575, 1597 and 1602–4. Although Ireland was not as badly affected by acute visitations during the century as other places, numbers of inhabitants carried off by such outbreaks could be considerable, as in 1575, for instance, when chroniclers estimated that 3,000 persons died in Dublin alone, and in 1602 and 1604, when up to ten per cent of the population of the country may have perished. Numerous other forms of illness, including the 'sweating sickness' and the 'English disease', were recorded as bringers of sickness and death at frequent intervals. Also the occurrence of dearth or even famine could weaken a community and render it especially susceptible to infections, as happened in 1575 and 1597, for example. The problems of political and military planners may have been compounded by the fact that Ireland seems to have constituted a separate 'disease environment'.

Thus unseasoned soldiers serving in Ireland could succumb very quickly to what was called the 'country disease'. The rate at which newly arrived personnel, including viceroys, were debilitated by illness is notable, the general health hazards of the time being compounded by the perils of a hostile environment. Conversely, newcomers were feared by natives as bringers of infections. For all, the facilities for medical care were scanty if not non-existent. Hospitals did function in towns, some under religious care, others run by municipalities, and some funded by private philanthropy. Outbreaks of plague, however, occasioned panic measures of pest-houses and quarantines, and for more mundane ailments the barber-surgeon and the apothecary were to hand to apply their crafts. Gaelic medical knowledge did not appear to have progressed beyond these skills.[14]

Warfare, both internecine and external to lordships, increased in destructiveness as the century progressed, bringing disease, violent death and food shortages. Reference has been made to the links between campaigning soldiers and infections, but this phenomenon of large non-native troop movements through regions of the island was not a notable feature until the last three decades or so. Down to the Elizabethan period (and beyond) the most common form of bellicose activity was the internal raid and counter-raid. But certain changes in the nature of warfare in Ireland caused increased harm to human and natural resources. The construction of stone castles on a large scale by Gaelic lords resulted in the introduction of siege warfare with heavier engines of war directed at static garrisons (as opposed to retreating raiding parties). Another result was the extension of the war-making season beyond the thitherto common span of the summer months. Scottish mercenary forces were imported to complement the galloglas bands of warlords from the mid-fifteenth century onwards. And by 1500 the use of guns was becoming widespread, particularly among the Gaelic footsoldiers, the kerne.[15]

Obviously factors such as climate, disease and demographic fluctuations had a bearing on the nature of economic activity and social development, but it is clear that geography had the greatest influence on the pattern of settlement. The area of Ireland which had attracted most colonial settlement through the centuries lay east of a line from Strangford Lough to Bantry Bay. The most recent incursus, by the Normans, had been principally within this extended region of Ireland, including the triangular area with Louth as its apex and Kerry and Wexford as its base limits. Socio-economic changes were most notable in this zone, while northern and western districts were slowest to feel the impact of urbanisation and rural transformation. The Norman impress upon the chosen colonial area (which itself became a core to the native periphery) was chiefly in the form of boroughs, nucleated villages and manorial estates. Some deforestation occurred in the three centuries down to 1500 at a limited pace, especially in the river valleys of the south. The terrain (the mountainous part of south Leinster and east and north Munster being excluded) was ideal for the typical village-centred, strip-divided farms with their hierarchical communities of lords, head tenants and labourers. The colony needed towns, and these were designated in the Viking-founded ports and inland centres. The effects of the proximity of Wales, for long the nurturing bridgehead for colonists in Ireland, were most evident in the Europeanised feudalism of towns, villages and farms in Leinster and east Munster. Significant Gaelic lordships did survive within the zone of most intensive colonisation, those of the O'Byrnes, O'Tooles and Kavanaghs in Wicklow and Carlow, and the O'Connors, O'Mores and O'Carrolls in the midlands of Leix and Offaly being among the most important. The existing natives were pressured to a large extent into inhabiting the more afforested or mountainous areas or the more inhospitable region to the west and north. A form of pastoralism was forced on the Gaelic or pre-existing population by their being excluded from prime lands.[16]

The political environment: the lordship of Ireland as framework

The diversity of social, economic and cultural interrelationships between those of English and Welsh origin and the native population suggests that the geographical barriers which determined the pattern of Norman settlement were less relevant by 1500. One aspect of the 'Gaelic recovery' from the fourteenth century onwards was the migration of Gaelic peasant families to lands in English colonial districts where they were needed to maintain levels of population. Gaelic chiefs also absorbed manorial settlements and began slowly to change their economic orientation towards agriculture and market trading. In the borderlands between Gaelic and English regions, known as the marches, the overlapping of pastoral and arable systems was evident—in the west of Meath and parts of

Tipperary and Cork, for instance. Here the Norman settlers had come under the influence of Gaelic social and economic customs. Practical co-operation and interchange—in trade, labour, marriage, law and learning—may have helped to soften the ethnic differences, but outside observers such as Polydore Vergil were more impressed by the contrasting characteristics of the English and Gaelic inhabitants of Ireland. The residents of the Pale, the colonial core of the eastern region, comprising the counties of Louth, Meath, Kildare and Dublin, could be taken as exemplars of English civility in Ireland. The most imperviously Gaelic areas of the island were perhaps to be found in the remoter regions of Ulster. Between these extremes of Gaeldom and Englishry there was a great variety of forms of cultural cross-fertilisation.[17]

Reflected in the division between the mixed farming of the more anglicised areas and the pastoralism of the marches and Gaelic territories was the political and constitutional separateness of English and Gaelic. Ireland had been constituted a lordship of the Kings of England since the twelfth century, and the early Anglo-Norman settlers had attempted to make good the claim by conquering as much of the island as they could. By the fourteenth century, however, it was clear that in practice the king's Irish lordship was a reality in at best just over half of Ireland's expanse. In the areas of successful Norman and English settlement the authority of the English monarch as Lord of Ireland was recognised, and outside of these the political, legal and landholding systems remained autonomous, dominated by the traditionally sovereign Gaelic rulers. In order to normalise political and legal relations between colonials and their Gaelic neighbours in the mid-fourteenth century, a body of legislation was drawn up in the colony's parliament, culminating in the famous Statutes of Kilkenny of 1366. A system of dual government was thereby established, with differing approaches being adopted by the English administration in Ireland to the feudal or legally held territories on the one hand, and the territories held by non-feudal tenure, either by Gaelic principles of tenure or corruption of the original grant of feudal tenure, on the other. The policy of coexistence was complemented by one of consolidating the borders of the colonial area by more active deployment of English personnel and resources in Ireland in the later fourteenth century. Although the momentum of that supportive action for the colony was lost in the earlier fifteenth century, the designation of the Pale as a priority area for administrative reform was symbolic of the policy of realistic recognition of actual capabilities without prejudice to ultimate ambitions.[18]

The reach of the administration of the English lordship in 1500, then, far outstripped what it could actually grasp. Although operating in a very different political environment from the kingdom of England, the institutions which had developed during the medieval period were designed to cater for the governance of the entire island should the ambition of generations of English colonials become a reality. Meanwhile the jurisdiction of the English king as Lord of Ireland was strongly effective in the Pale and south-eastern regions, and with varying degrees of force in areas which retained residual structures of feudalism from the time of the Anglo-Norman advance. As the place of residence of old-established English families, the eastern shires were the mainstay of the colony, and leading members of the community played an active part in staffing its agencies. These elites in town and county also took the lead in pressing mainly through parliamentary representation for reform of flagging English governmental institutions, complaining of the poverty of their holding in the land. The main targets of their criticism were the neglectful English kings of the late middle ages and the domineering Anglo-Norman magnates who lived mostly outside the Pale. The family heads of the three earldoms of Kildare, Ormond and Desmond were at the apex of this ascendancy, and the dynasts asserted their control over the southern Pale and its marches, the south-eastern river valleys, and north-west and south Munster respectively. Bred to sturdy self-reliance during the fifteenth century, the earls had evolved their own military and judicial regimes in an environment of power struggles among internal and pan-provincial factions. Despite the manifest dynastic particularism within these and the other regions of Norman settlement such as eastern Connacht and a small enclave in north-east Ulster, the authority of the English crown flowed with varying degrees of efficacy through them. The Anglo-Norman magnates had been relied upon by the administration for the maintenance of the colonial presence in their bailiwicks, and these natural leaders of the colony outside the Pale co-operated by allowing English common law to function and crown revenues to be collected therein.[19]

At the head of the administration of the English lordship of Ireland was the chief governor who, in the absence of the king, represented him for his subjects in Ireland. For most of the first third of the sixteenth century the position was held by one of the three Irish earldom families—that of Kildare. The highest title of honour was that of Lord Lieutenant, but the holder, normally a prince of the blood in England, seldom came to Ireland. The governorship therefore was effectively in the hands of the lieutenant's deputy, or Lord Deputy, who enjoyed a fulness of power within the lordship commensurate with his being delegated royal powers in relation to Ireland. As head of the civil and military establishment, the governor (or viceroy, as he is sometimes called) supervised the full range of governmental functions wherever they had effect throughout the island, and was committed to defending the colonial area, especially the Pale, against attack. From the 1490s the authority of the Lords Deputy was more circumscribed, and, in practice, the rule of the Earls of Kildare represented a compromise, the government of Ireland being carried on with the minimum of expense for the new Tudor monarchy and the Fitzgerald lords enjoying many perquisites. Generally the Geraldine deputyship of the early decades of the century presided over a revival of crown institutions in the lordship, as the earls ruled in what they could claim were the interests of the king.[20]

The king's Irish council operated in conjunction with the governor, advising him and performing administrative and judicial functions. The council which was active in the early sixteenth century comprised approximately seven key office-holders in the central administration. The privileged coterie normally included the Lord Chancellor, who came to act as president of the council in the Lord Deputy's absence, the Vice-Treasurer, the Chief Justices—of the Courts of King's Bench and Common Pleas—and the Chief Baron of the Exchequer as well as the Master of the Rolls. The importance of this inner circle of councillors was underscored by their appointments being reserved more fully to the king instead of the governor from 1479. This was designed to curb the autonomy of the Lords Deputy. Otherwise the incumbent—from then on, with few breaks, the Earl of Kildare—could prefer his own clients and supporters to the detriment of conciliar independence. The dominance of the earls over the council while they held the deputyship, however, masked the real changes that were taking place in its role and functions. From about 1520 onwards a Privy Council of select members could be said to have existed, and this body asserted itself to act in the absence of the Lord Deputy under the Chancellor on many occasions in the 1520s and 1530s. The old medieval great council, of magnates and bishops, continued to meet on occasion, but executive powers, long vested in the council, were now being exercised more fully by its members.[21]

The forum for the presentation of communal grievances, as well as for the association of the political community with government policy, came more and more to be parliament. The assembly met with regularity in the late fifteenth century, and it represented, in three separate houses, the peers and bishops, the gentry and merchants, and the lower clergy. By 1500 parliament, like the council, had almost ceased to be peripatetic, meeting nearly always in Dublin or Drogheda, though itineration continued to be used by the governors when they wanted to display English institutions in the remoter colonial areas. The functions of parliament traditionally included the assenting of members to taxation, most notably the subsidy payable on landownership, regulation of administration matters, passage of new laws or changing of existing ones, and the resolution of private plaints. As the century began, however, the balance of responsibilities was changing. The passage of the famous Poynings' Law in 1494 under the English-born Lord Deputy of that name circumscribed the power of the Irish parliament. Thenceforth the Irish council had to request permission from London for the holding of an assembly, and it had to transmit to the English king and his Privy Council there the bills which it intended to pass in the Irish legislature. Only when the bills were returned in the approved form to Dublin could parliament be asked to go ahead and pass them into law. The effects on the Irish parliament were profound and far-reaching, going way beyond the curbing of governmental power on the ground in Ireland. In the short term at least, the parliament was summoned much less frequently, and its role as a court arbitrating between private parties in dispute was less relevant. More and more the parliament came to be an agency for acquiescence in legislative plans and taxation demands, its status overshadowed by the claims of the English counterpart to override it and legislate on its behalf.[22]

The main tax for the English administration at the turn of the century was the subsidy, the most lucrative source of colonial revenue down to the 1530s. It was charged on each ploughland (120 acres) of cultivated land, and its collection had been streamlined in the last years of the fifteenth century, particularly through the institution of five- or ten-year levies. As well as the subsidy, the crown income included the customs duties, which were increasing around the turn of the century. More efficient management of the royal estates and manors augmented the rental income of the exchequer, and other feudal incidents and profits of justice amounted to more than £1,600 Irish in about 1500. On the expenditure side, the main items were the salaries and fees of royal officials and the defence of the colony and its inner core, the Pale. At that time the governors were allowed to receive the royal revenues without account, and could manage their administration by assigning income from crown sources without their having to pass through the exchequer. Out of the annual income, as well as official salaries which totalled about £650 Irish, the governors had to fund the cost of the army. If, as was the case for most of the early decades of the century, the viceroy was native-born, he could use his own resources for raising and maintaining an armed force, but an English-born governor invariably needed subsidies from England to keep the soldiers in pay. Thanks to reforms undertaken in the system of maximising the revenues and cutting costs from the 1490s onwards, the Irish revenues were not unhealthy down to 1534, but the procedures of the exchequer were in dire need of an overhaul.[23]

In the eyes of the residents of the colonial area, the main function of the administration was their protection and defence from damaging raids and encroachments. In the circumstances of English subventions for the lordship of Ireland being withdrawn, it was the responsibility of the local community under the viceroy's leadership to organise its own defences, and this was carried out in a number of ways in the early sixteenth century. During the tenure of office of the Earls of Kildare the governor had a household force of about 120 horse. The local residents were obliged to contribute to the household retinue by purveying produce at fixed rates. With the consolidation of the Pale and its marches in the later fifteenth century, other sources of defence were needed, such as the Brotherhood of Arms, a force of less than 200 archers and horse very much under the Earl of Kildare's control. The mainstay of the defence of the lordship were the general or local hostings or levies of troops, to which the landowners of the region were expected to contribute according to means. The terms of such hostings, including specific dates, length of service and cartage of provisions, were agreed by the council afforced with local magnates, and they could rally over 1,000 soldiers, archers, pikemen, horse, and even galloglas and kerne which were quartered on the magnates' own lands. In the remoter areas such as the Ormond and Desmond lordships local defence was organised by the magnates, usually with the agreement of the gentry and freeholders of the areas.[24]

In order to wean the Irish lords away from aggressive methods in the settling of their disputes, the government of the lordship had consistently tried to encourage recourse to the royal courts. From the 1490s onwards there were signs that the reorganisation of the system of justice was achieving some success at the levels of both central and local jurisdictions. The principal courts of the lordship— King's Bench, Common Pleas, Exchequer and Chancery—were modelled on their English counterparts, though their processes were more antiquated. Ideally appointments of justices and other staff to these courts were supposed to be made more on the basis of judicial expertise than on clerical experience, although there was no educational structure in Ireland for the training of lawyers. Students of law from Ireland had to attend the Inns of Court in London, admission to the bar being forbidden for those who had not completed terms there after 1541. The criminal law was the jurisdiction mostly of the Court of King's Bench, as well as that of Exchequer, with death penalties being handed down for many felonies. Revenue matters occupied the Exchequer court also, and the King's Bench dealt with crown pleas. From the early sixteenth century onwards the equity jurisdiction of the Court of Chancery developed apace, litigation involving disputes over lands and titles being heard before it, and the Court of Common Pleas was thus overshadowed. Parliament's judicial role was more limited after the early 1500s, but the king's council in Ireland continued to exercise functions in relation to equity disputes between magnates and others, a foreshadowing of the formal prerogative Court of Castle Chamber raised on the foundations of conciliar justice in the 1560s.[25]

Local courts continued to flourish throughout the lordship, sometimes in competition with the central courts but usually supplementing their activities. There were sheriffs' tourns held in the baronies of the counties, manorial and municipal courts, as well as liberty jurisdictions. Within the Pale and other shires judges went on circuit, bringing royal justice into the localities, and in the outlying shired areas such as Kilkenny and Waterford commissioners were regularly appointed, some of them resident and others on an *ad hoc* basis, comprising judicial officers as well local worthies. The linch-pins in the meshing of royal and local systems of justice were the county sheriffs, who played a variety of parts. They were administrative agents of central government, levying revenues, proclaiming statutes and ordinances, and serving writs. Militarily they organised the martial levies of the shires and led the *'posse comitatus'*, making 'roads' into Gaelic districts. And as judicial figures, they heard cases involving lesser crimes in the barony courts and presided over the county courts. While the shrievalties in the Pale were changed annually among leading local gentry, the out-lying shires saw the offices dominated by powerful landed families who monopolised the office, the Powers in Waterford and the Burkes in Connacht being examples. By and large, the recourse of inhabitants to the local courts was cheaper and safer, and the central courts' work tended to be dominated by plaintiffs and litigants from the inner Pale shires.[26]

The king's writ ran in theory throughout the late medieval lordship except within the enclaves of private jurisdiction, the local liberties and palatinates. One such exempted area was the liberty of St Sepulchre outside the walls of Dublin, which was under the private jurisdiction of the Archbishops of Dublin. The liberty court of the archbishop had powers which excluded the authority of both municipal and state courts. There were also privileges attached to the trading of goods within its franchises. More extensive were the great liberties of Anglo-Norman magnates—the Earl of Shrewsbury in Wexford, the Earl of Desmond in Kerry, the Earl of Ormond in Tipperary, and the Earl of Kildare in his home county. These juris-dictions had well-developed judicial systems with designated law officers conducting regular sessions, and they also had acquired other political, economic and military exemptions. These franchisal liberties were popular with litigants and plaintiffs because they were conveniently local and pre-empted the need for recourse to the distant and expensive Dublin courts. From the administration's perspective, palatinates, liberties and franchises were a guarantee of some kind of order and administration in the localities, and in the difficult march conditions the very survival of ordered government was a priority. Accordingly, for example, municipalities were empowered to use customs revenues and fee-farm rents due to the crown as murage, or revenue for the repair of walls and civic utilities.

Local privileges could be asserted on many fronts, and prisage rights claimed by the Earls of Ormond as a hereditary perquisite were stoutly resisted by the leading towns down to the sixteenth century. We now turn to the myriad forms of local and regional rights asserted in the English and Gaelic areas of Ireland.[27]

N

Carrickfergus

Sligo

Ardglass

Carlingford

Dundalk

LOUTH

Blackwater

Kells Drogheda

Athboy Navan

Mullingar MEATH Trim

Boyne Liffey

Athlone Dublin

Galway Athenry DUBLIN

Naas

KILDARE

Wicklow

Barrow

Nore Carlow

Kilkenny CARLOW Arklow

Limerick TIPPERARY KILKENNY

Cashel Callan

LIMERICK Fethard Carrick WEXFORD

Maigue Kilmallock Clonmel Suir on Suir New Ross

KERRY Waterford Wexford

WATERFORD Fethard

Dingle CORK Dungarvan Dunmore East

Cork

Kinsale

Rosscarbery

Baltimore

0   30   60
                    km
0   20   40
                    miles

The lordship of Ireland in the early sixteenth century

Town and County in the English Part of Ireland, *c.* 1500

TOWNS and their hinterlands were a vibrant aspect of early sixteenth-century Ireland. Urban centres of varying size had been foci of social, cultural and economic development within the island since the arrival of the Normans and even before. Agrarian manor and town were inextricably linked, as most Irish commerce, both domestic and foreign, was based on the productivity of farm-lands. The older port towns, such as Dublin, Waterford and Cork, owed their vitality to the Vikings with their far-flung trading net-work, while the newer centres (sometimes revitalised older ones) such as Clonmel and Kilkenny grew under seignorial patronage as boroughs on fertile manors. While some boroughs may have lapsed into marcher outposts, cut off from once productive hinterlands, they retained vestigial market functions. Antipathy to Gaelic clans and institutions was frequently expressed by citizens and compellingly manifested in their hostings and 'roads' into Gaelic districts. This was partly a reflection of the European town-dwellers' rejection of non-settled pastoralism and oppressive militarism. Yet despite offi-cial municipal disavowal of ties with Gaelic clanspeople, there were very many points of contact, not just for goods but of personnel and ideas, and in this context the semi-strangulated manorial boroughs no less than the more thriving municipalities were significant.[1]

Recent historical writings on later medieval Ireland have acknowl-edged the importance of the role of towns, with their hinterlands, in much of Ireland. Although perhaps not as numerous or as large as in the earlier Anglo-Norman period, urban centres are seen to have had well-ordered polities, clusters of wealthy families which profited from trade and rents, thriving spiritual institutions, and the dynamism to draw into their nexus through markets and fairs the people and produce of the vicinities. During the later middle ages the central administration came to rely heavily on the towns and cities as cynosures of Englishness. The citizens spoke English, dressed in English style and lived in houses designed in the fashion of dwellings in cities in England. Not only were the customs and institutions of towns modelled closely on those of the mother country, but the prevailing mentality of the inhabitants within urban precincts was civic and commercial. For close to the heart of most substantial towns was the merchant guild with its strict rules for trade, expressive ritual and powerful personnel who were inter-changeable with the ruling city councillors.[2]

While about 250 urban settlements may have been founded or refurbished down to the fourteenth century, there were only fifty towns of some size around 1500. Many of the medieval boroughs never prospered, failing to attract burgesses or suffering inordinately from the effects of warfare or plague. Others may have attained the status of large villages with populations of a few hundred. Although the exact size of the towns in the early sixteenth century cannot be known with certainty, the number suggested here would perhaps yield an urban population of at least fifty thousand. Accepting Kenneth Nicholls's estimate of a total population of the island of half a million at most, it can be posited that ten per cent of the inhab-itants were urban-dwellers, a figure in line with the proportion for England and other European countries at that time. As the lowlands and river valleys in Leinster and Meath were the most urbanised as well as the most densely peopled areas of the country, the economic, social and cultural functions of towns influenced a large section of the entire population. Connacht and Ulster had comparatively few towns, but even in these provinces there were commercial con-nections between ports such as Galway, Sligo, Carrickfergus and Carlingford and the interior through proto-urban settlements and lesser havens. In certain regions groups of towns, such as Drogheda, Dundalk and Ardee in north Leinster, and Waterford, Carrick and Clonmel in Ormond country, had close trading links.[3]

In order to qualify for the appellation 'town', centres of at least several hundred inhabitants needed to have exhibited some or all of these features: corporate administration, topographical complexity (including walls and defensive works and perhaps suburban growth), market functions, institutions of spiritual and secular care such as hospitals or poorhouses, and interplay with rural vicinages of vary-ing extents. In common with towns in contemporary England, Irish boroughs seem to have been passing through a phase of relative decline in the late middle ages: Dublin castle was ruinous in 1521, for example, the bridge at Drogheda had collapsed in 1472, and fires in Dundalk (in 1430, 1444 and 1452), Navan (in 1539), Athboy (in 1443), Clonmel (in 1516) and Sligo (on many occasions) retarded urban growth. Many walls and fortifications, symbols of urban pride as well as protective bastions, were the subject of special grants and remissions through the fifteenth and early sixteenth centuries. Within these enclosures (varying from under twenty acres in some of the small Ormond boroughs to over 140 acres in the case of Dublin) shrinkage of streetscapes had occurred from the mid-fourteenth century, and population losses had never been made good. Yet although major public construction works fell victim to scarcity of municipal funds, private wealth fostered the building of residences and chantry chapels. And despite the decay of commercial facilities such as bridges, harbours and wharves in some centres, and the diminution of direct control over immediate vicinities, townspeople could extend their trading and cultural hinterlands by imaginative enterprises over varying distances and sensible accommodation with potentially hostile neighbours.[4]

Towns and their ruling groups

The growth of Irish medieval towns had been fostered by royal and aristocratic grants, but in 1500 most major urban centres aspired to self-government, with varying degrees of success. The old Viking ports of Drogheda, Dublin, Wexford, Waterford, Cork and Limerick, along with Galway, had developed quasi-autonomous powers after three centuries of royal beneficence in the form of charters and statutory regulations. The main aims of the royal or seignorial benefactors of urban settlements were to support trade through establishing settled market centres and fairs and to advance manufacture and crafts. Administrative and judicial institutions complemented economic ones. While many small boroughs failed to grow into towns through population failure or wastage due to war, those which did, such as Thurles, County Tipperary, and Kells, County Meath, evolved into sizeable centres, accumulating additional grants from the crown or local lords. In towns, even of the first rank such as Limerick and Galway, which had to contend with overweening local nobles—the O'Briens and the Clanricard Burkes respectively in those cases—municipal privilege compromised with local powers, especially when remote from the centre of English power. For the most part, however, petitions from urban centres to the crown for relief of municipal distress were received sympathetically at the royal court in London.[5]

The most common grants to importunate boroughs in the late fifteenth century were of the remission of all or part of the fee-farm rent payable by the larger towns to the crown, and of murage, enabling civic communities to make use of customs and tolls on trade for paving streets and repairing walls and utilities. Both forms of concession attest the reality of civic privilege and responsibility in the late middle ages. The principal features of citizenship in Ireland as elsewhere were the privilege of trading within the borough franchises on preferential terms and the freedom from feudal levies and taxes. Concomitant was the communal right to self-regulation in legal and other matters. The highly prized order of citizenship entailed the responsibilities of paying rent in the form of fee-farms or burgage, contributing to civic cesses and levies, upholding the monopolies and rights of the guilds, and generally participating in the administration of the borough. While admission to citizenship in the smaller settlements may not have involved a formal procedure, entry into the ranks of freemen of larger towns was strictly regulated through apprenticeship in the guilds, marriage to a citizen, heredity or special grace and favour. The leading municipalities such as Waterford or Drogheda had fairly rigidly defined barriers between the free and the unfree, the latter dwelling within the franchises on sufferance. Above all, however, the municipal advancement of the late fifteenth-century Irish town is reflected in the nature of its conciliar government.[6]

The six principal boroughs reached the summit of their municipal autonomy in the decades around 1500. A series of charters of privileges had brought *de facto* incorporation, which meant that the ruling councils were recognised by the crown as proper corporations. The bigger the municipality the more complex were the conciliar structures. Twenty-four aldermen, forty-eight sheriffs' peers and ninety-six guildsmen or 'numbers' formed the tiers of the common council in the borough of Dublin, and twenty-three aldermen and fourteen commons made up the ranks of that body in Drogheda. In the cities the senior councillors or aldermen monopolised power by 1500 at the expense of the commons, who usually represented the non-mercantile craft guilds. Municipal courts, comprising the senior councillors with their legal appointees, or the sheriffs or provosts, adjudicated on all cases involving citizens, except for a few charges reserved to the central courts. The profits of justice, as well as rents from civic properties, fines for admission of citizens to the franchises, and tolls on trade, made up the bulk of civic revenues, while the principal expenses were stipends and salaries for city officials, public works and the fee-farm rent to the crown (varying from 200 marks (£134 13s 4d) per annum for Dublin to £10 for Naas). The ceremonial regalia used on public occasions symbolised the devolution of power by the crown to the civities: the king's sword in the cases of Dublin, Drogheda, Waterford and Limerick, and the maces, borne by special bearers. The processions of civic dignitaries in their hats and liveries in order of importance marked the privileged orders apart within their communities.[7]

The stratification of the corps of civic officials and the range of their duties depended on the size of the population of the urban centre. At its most basic, the borough administration had at its head a sovereign, provost, portreeve (reeve) or mayor, usually elected annually. In the major towns there were two bailiffs or sheriffs to implement the courts' decisions and to carry out a range of administrative functions. In Dublin the mayor, who normally received an annual stipend of £30, had many responsibilities: he was clerk of the markets, justice of labourers, justice of the peace and of jail delivery, justice of weights and measures, assizer of bread and ale, justice of taverners and escheator during his busy year of office. In the other cities the mayors had some or most of these responsibilities. Civic order rested on the implementation of by-laws passed at regular meetings of common councils. These addressed the gamut of urban-dwellers' concerns, including the supply of food to the markets or shambles, the piping in of pure water, the maintenance of standards of hygiene in public places, the provision of services for the poor or homeless, the punishment of crime, the protection of the town from internal disaster such as fire, and the provision for defence against external attack. Diverse officials carried out these functions, from important appointees such as town clerks, recorders and constables, down through the ranks of water-bailiffs, beadles of the poor, gatekeepers and clock-keepers to casual labourers such as porters or carters.[8]

The small ruling groups of patricians in the major boroughs by 1500 comprised affluent merchant families. As the crown devolved more and more governing powers to the corporations, these leading citizens were best positioned to benefit politically and economically. In the two largest cities, Dublin and Waterford, with perhaps the widest trading networks, the number of families achieving elevated civic office over a two- to three-generational span was comparatively high: up to thirty or forty in the sixteenth and early seventeenth centuries, indicating a fair degree of openness of the ruling coteries. By contrast, the smaller cities—Galway, Drogheda, Limerick, Cork and Kilkenny—were dominated by elites of twelve to fifteen families. In all cases, however, the men and women of the patriciates were closely linked through intermarriage. Marital alliances between the leading families provided the social axes of the higher stratum: alliances between Sedgrave and Ball family members, Rothes and Shees, Arthurs and Creaghs, Sherlocks and Walshes were very common in Dublin, Kilkenny, Limerick and Waterford respectively. Such consolidation of political power and mercantile wealth tended to strengthen the fabric of urban life, even in times of economic or political difficulty. Where new families came into the nexus, usually through trade or migration, they were absorbed into the larger civic communities. By contrast, some towns were dominated and given commercial identity by one family: the Creans in Sligo, for example, and the Pettits in Mullingar. Besides tightening social bonds within cities, nuptial arrangements fostered close ties between county gentry families in the hinterlands and the urban elites.[9]

To achieve political office at the highest level was nearly impossible for those who were not of the wealthiest group in urban society, and this was more or less exclusively mercantile. An office-holder had to make good from his own pocket any monetary losses incurred during his term. The ascendancy of affluent merchants in civic government was institutionalised in the large boroughs where the merchant guilds dominated councils as well as markets. The wealth of this elite group, protected both by their guild privileges and the chartered rights granted by the crown, is attested not only by intermarriage with the gentry but also by the lavish domestic furnishings listed in inventories of, say, the Blakes of Galway or the Stanihursts of Dublin. But private wealth may not always have betokened municipal prosperity. In the later fifteenth century major civic projects in the large towns were scarce, while smaller centres such as Thurles, Trim and Naas found it hard to retain their urban identity. Although there were signs of architectural vigour in Kilkenny with the construction of the tholsel and in Galway with the building of the church of St Nicholas, most new building projects were undertaken for private patrons, such as the James Rice chapel in Waterford or the Burnell bequest in Dublin. Towns had very small budgets and could easily be overshadowed by other corporations such as guilds, chantries or monasteries. Thus while private wealth in the hands of rich patricians was accumulating rapidly in the late middle ages, most borough corporations were appealing plaintively to the crown for the alleviation of their distress.[10]

The royal government was prepared to countenance these pleas from the corporations of Ireland because it wished to ensure ordered local administration in the hands of reliable and worthy patricians. The principal families played a leading part in forging civic cohesion and identity through their marriages, their business partnerships and their participation in the annual round of urban rituals. In late medieval cities the wealthiest citizens lived in the central areas, influencing the design of streetscapes with their stone or cagework residences. The most prominent were commemorated in the naming of large houses or inns, such as Blakeney's Inns and Preston's Inns in Dublin. In marcher towns, such as Carlingford, Ardee, Trim, Naas, Newcastle Lyons and Dalkey as well some Ormond centres, merchant families in the fifteenth century built castellated homes, the equivalent of the rural tower-houses. These defensive properties were more than decorative, as attested by the high number of burnings of urban settlements in that era. Attachment to parish was embodied in the church monuments such as tombs and wall plaques which were inscribed with the names of patricians and their family connections. Street, parish and ward—in which the patricians as senior councillors organised tax payment, defence and law enforcement—these were the arenas in which the socially ascendant lorded it over the less privileged. These included apprentices, humbler artisans, manual labourers and the band of beggars and unattached. Out from the centre—and outside the walls in the suburbs of the larger towns—the wooden dwellings and other insubstantial structures indicated the areas of urban impoverishment and lack of privilege.[11]

As with many of their counterparts elsewhere in Europe, late fifteenth-century Irish towns needed an influx of migrants to maintain the urban population at a sufficiently high level to run institutions such as corporations, guilds and other bodies. Thus newcomers to apprenticeships within the guilds and as marital partners for existing families were encouraged, but poor immigrants and those of Gaelic origin were not. Civic by-laws attempted to prevent the entry of those latter groups, with varying degrees of success and commitment. At times of difficulty in the rural economy the attractions of the town were manifest: freedom from seigneurial exactions, opportunities for advancement through the guild system, and the availability of at least minimal welfare institutions. To city authorities, charged with defending the community against physical assault and infection, the checking of strangers at the gates was a matter of urgency. The official anti-Gaelic regime was no doubt motivated by the threat of attack, while fear of the plague and other diseases accounted for the general defensiveness. Boroughs of all sizes during the medieval period had their leper-houses, usually outside the walls (if any), while the larger centres had hospitals and almshouses, most of them before the 1530s attached to religious houses. Cities such as Dublin even had special officials to deal with the poor and destitute, beadles of beggars, for example, doubling up as keepers of swine. At times of particular crisis, for example during severe visitations of plague, special measures were taken to ensure the isolation of victims and the burial of the dead. Careful monitoring of possible sources of infection, such as tainted food or water supplies, was a constant preoccupation.[12]

Cultural and economic functions of towns

Urban solidarity was well characterised by municipal and private philanthropy which was directed at alleviating deprivation and suffering. Leper-houses were maintained by boroughs with the aid of levies on citizens, wardens usually being appointed by the town authorities. The period also witnessed a trend towards more private endowment of almshouses and hospitals. In 1480 the Dean of Waterford linked the establishment of his chantry in the cathedral to the financing of a hostel for poor men, and in this venture he was joined by James Rice, a prominent citizen. In Dublin one Redman took over the decaying hospital at St John's, Newgate, and provided some forty beds for patients. Primary and secondary schools were another cultural asset of towns, helping to foster civic identity and attracting scholars from outside. Religious foundations were also active in education, some of the cathedrals and at least one nunnery providing schooling for girls and boys from the towns and their hinterlands. While elementary teaching may have been undertaken by domestic tutors in the homes of the wealthy, and apprenticeships served the less privileged, a growing tendency in the sixteenth century was for municipal authorities or private benefactors to found and maintain schools. For example, Dublin had its municipal school by the 1560s, while in Waterford and Kilkenny flourishing grammar schools were founded under the patronage of the Butlers. Many merchant families were sorely conscious of the need to establish a university in the country to prevent young people having to travel abroad at great expense. Many unsuccessful schemes were mooted for the founding of a college down to the later sixteenth century. Failure to set up an Irish university before the 1590s was offset to an extent by overseas migration of scholars for education, but the effects were detrimental to the advancement of learning in Ireland in the period.[13]

Ritual and processions on days of civic festivity and public ceremony offered the citizens the opportunity to display the urban orders in their sequence of precedence, and also gave each, no matter how humble, the feeling of belonging to the body corporate. Religious and secular rites punctuated the civic year. On station days and ceremonial occasions, such as the riding of the franchises in Dublin and the formal procession to St Saviour's, Waterford, by the newly elected mayor and bailiffs, the municipal authorities revealed their ascendancy within the civic ranks, dressed in their liveries and bearing their regalia of office. Dramas were enacted on religious festivals, usually by the guilds. In Kilkenny and Dublin, for example, there were sequences of mystery plays which involved large numbers of citizen actors and spectators. A popular time for these enactments was Corpus Christi, a day of special significance for towns, signifying as it did another body corporate—the church. In the later sixteenth century when the Reformation devalued these popular shows, secular pageants such as that of St George substituted and professional troupes of players visited towns to put on plays. The guilds, both secular and religious, made a notable contribution to the fund of civic ritual. As part of their public celebrations on patronal days, craft or trade guilds held processions to their chapels in parish churches. The religious guilds provided a yearly round of liturgical services and rituals for members and associates. Both types of institution were also important in forging bonds of civic fellowship through their provision of mutual aid, material and spiritual.[14]

The basic economic functions of the towns as laid down in the foundation charters were to provide a regular market for the exchange of goods between citizens and rural-dwellers, and to hold a fair at least annually with the purpose of attracting commerce over longer distances. Markets and fairs had helped to confirm the urban status of the more successful boroughs of the late middle ages, but in the less successful these institutions were frequently forestalled by illegal trading. In addition to these vital agencies, burgesses or natives were conferred with the privilege of freedom to trade exclusively within the franchises of the borough. In the case of crown grants to the cities, these chartered rights empowered the merchants' guilds to organise and regulate urban commerce. The 'companies of merchants' were traditionally recognised by the crown as the mainstays of the cities in their battle to survive as cultural and trading centres. Gradually they came to enjoy a monopoly of retailing and wholesaling within the franchises, the state authorities relinquishing even minimal rights of inspection of native merchants' cargoes. Crucially the central concerns of the merchants' guilds came to be identified with those of the civic corporations. This convergence of interests redounded to the benefit of the councillors, as urban order was better assured in the extensive rules concerning apprentices, the detailed ordering of retailing and wholesaling in the franchises through the guildhall, the strict banning of illegal strangers, and punishment of infringers of the regulations.[15]

In the major chartered boroughs the municipal councils had appropriated rights to tolls and levies with which the commerce of merchant 'strangers' was mulcted. As the international trade of the principal cities had expanded during the medieval period, government regulation had become more stringent. The establishment of a customs regime by the early fourteenth century was testimony to this. The great custom of wool and wool-related produce was to be levied, but not on the goods of merchant guildsmen. The establishment of staple ports—namely Dublin, Drogheda, Waterford, Cork and Limerick—was intended to control the export of wool and hides and the import of salt and iron. Regulation of wine imports came in the form of prisage, granted in the twelfth century to the Butlers of

Ormond, but this levy of one tun in twenty was evaded successfully by port authorities or else employed to municipal benefit. While the other forms of government toll—the petty custom and the tax of poundage (introduced at the end of the fifteenth century)—were less lucrative to the state than was hoped, by 1500 a decline in customs revenues had been reversed. But with the development of merchant guild monopolies, a complex set of structures had evolved to enable native city merchants to avoid the inquiries of the few customs officials who were appointed, and indeed in some cases the officials were citizens appointed by the municipalities.[16]

The aggrandisement of the merchant fraternities in the later fifteenth century may be contrasted with the erosion of the position of the craft guilds. While trade in exports of the produce of hinterlands and imports from Britain and the continent flourished in the period, native manufacture, based on Irish raw materials, stagnated or declined. Accordingly, the craft guilds were in a weak position relative to the great merchant guilds. This is borne out in the municipal representation of the craft guilds on the councils of cities such as Dublin and Waterford in the 1490s: the lesser guildsmen were heavily outnumbered by the members of the merchants' bodies. Internal and external reasons may be adduced for the failure of manufacturing based on the boroughs. The hopes of the Anglo-Norman town-founders that burgesses would create active manufacturing centres based on the woollen industry, particularly in the south-eastern river valleys, did not materialise. By 1500 the quantity of cloths being woven for purposes other than mere local consumption was comparatively small. The population decline in the fourteenth century may have adversely affected internal demand, and Irish cloth, with the exception of rugs, mantles and friezes, fared badly in competition with other European manufactures. Also the demand from abroad for highly valued raw wool and linen yarn from Ireland was growing very strongly into the sixteenth century. So, notwithstanding state and local efforts to prohibit the export of unworked or semi-worked materials in order to foster native industry, and despite individual enterprises such as that of Piers Butler, Earl of Ossory, who set up model factories in Kilkenny, the decay of Irish manufacturing continued throughout the period. Accordingly, urban and rural manufacture was on a small scale for the most part, only the tanning of hides perhaps providing some dynamism with state encouragement. Otherwise the brewers, dis-

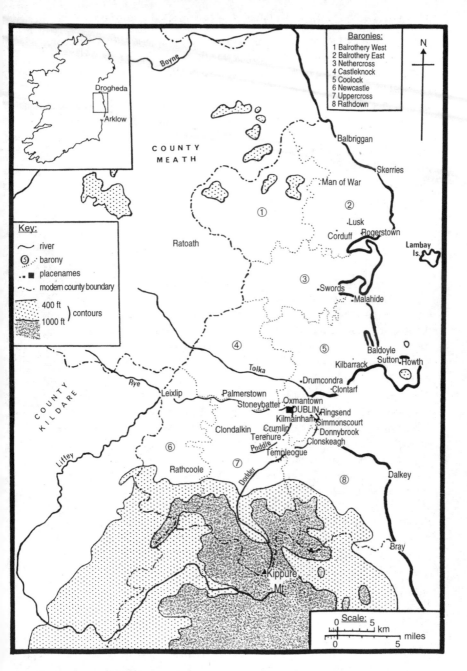

The region of Dublin in the early sixteenth century

tillers, millers, tailors, shoemakers and carpenters, among others, were producing for strictly local needs, while the great merchant companies satisfied demands for basic manufactures and luxuries through imports.[17]

The accumulated wealth of the merchants not only provided scope for overseas trading ventures and advancing of loans, but also allowed for investment in leases and land in the neighbouring countryside. County seats of successful municipal families dotted the hinterlands of Dublin, Drogheda and (to a lesser extent) Waterford. Marriages of patricians to gentry spouses led to their upward mobility, and mercantile elites in the different port cities co-operated with one another, especially in times of threat to municipal liberties, to form a powerful lobby. In view of this ascendancy, it is a surprise to read the impassioned pleas of authorities in cities—and towns—in the late fifteenth century for relief of communal poverty and distress. The explanation must be sought in the shrinking of the physical or 'cultural' hinterlands of urban communities. For undoubtedly cities, in the south and west especially, were environed by ever-diminishing safe areas for marketing of goods, and overbearing lords who wished to dictate the terms of commerce within their jurisdictions. The inland Pale towns had suffered very badly in this respect, and only Dublin and Drogheda could command trading zones of a reasonable radius. And even the merchants of these two east-coast ports had to come to terms with an economic and social world not geared to the market system. Thus the '*béal bocht*' affected by councils around 1500 was a response to challenges to liberties and also a kind of insurance policy to complement practical accommodations with non-civic elements who threatened disruptive activities such as banditry, pillage, piracy and forestalling. Irish municipalities were not alone in demanding special favours to bolster urban institutions against seignorial rivalry: English boroughs were seeking similar concessions at the same time. But the Irish boroughs had to deal with a very different kind of trade with their hinterlands, and their complaints had a fair amount of validity.[18]

The meshing of manor and market

The success of the substantial merchants rested solidly upon the meshing of the manorial economy with the urban market. From the earliest arrival of the Anglo-Normans it was recognised that the towns would be outlets for the surpluses of agrarian manors, and that towns themselves would stimulate productive use of the soil. The number of boroughs which remained predominantly agricultural and non-urban serves to stress that the essential roots of borough and manor development were in the soil. The medieval period saw a steady development in the agrarian economy, matching that of southern and central England. The manors were divided into the infield and outfield, rights to the use of which were held by the manorial population. The arable land was ploughed by teams of horses with the up-to-date ploughs and harrows of the time. The typical Norman manor in the south and east followed the three-crop rotation system, with two fields in use in a growing year and the third one fallow. Wheat, barley and oats were the principal cereals grown, and down to the early fourteenth century surpluses were produced for export through the towns. Yields of crops were low as was usual in contemporary Europe, averaging about four parts of produce to one of seed, but colonisation and cultivation of land were extensive before the demographic and political difficulties of the fourteenth century. Manure was available in limited quantities from the animals maintained on the pastoral parts of the outfield (the ratio of pasture to arable before the mid-fourteenth century being one to nine). Manors also had domestic animals and fowl, and gardens and orchards in proximity to the residences. By the late thirteenth century Irish manors were contributing to a highly successful export market in agricultural produce, particularly cereals.[19]

Thereafter the amount of land under the plough shrank, direct cultivation of demesne lands declined, and a switch of emphasis from arable farming to animal husbandry took place. Animal products such as skins, hides, woolfells and tallow, along with beef, butter and wool, were exported in increasing abundance from the manors through the ports in the fifteenth century. These items became the staples of Irish overseas trade, along with fish, during the sixteenth century. Cereal production did not decline substantially in certain areas, such as the Fingal region of the Pale, but the shrinkage in the production of wheat is notable in the later fifteenth century, to judge by the petitions in parliament in 1471, for instance, for the banning of exports of grain to prevent famine and dearth. Ireland had ceased to become a net exporter of corn by the sixteenth century. Population decline on the manors in late medieval Ireland was both a cause and a symptom of agrarian change. Without an abundant supply of labour, landlords were forced to revert to two-crop rotation in certain areas or yield up ploughed land to pasture or scrub. More fundamentally, a transition to leasing of demesne land instead of direct cultivation was forced on many manorial estates. A complex interplay of factors—depopulation due to famine and plague, unsettled conditions on manors in the south-east due to warfare, the absenteeism of major landholders such as the Earl of Shrewsbury and the fragmentation of succession to other estates among heiresses—all combined to make for less stability for tenurial communities. The flight of English tenants from the more exposed manors to the eastern seaboard of north Leinster and to England and Wales has been noted. Undoubtedly a reason for this development, as is evident from the commissioners' reports in the south-east in the 1530s and the complaints of the Tipperary freeholders to the Earl of Ormond in 1542, was the failure of strong local or central authority to protect the rural community from destructive raiding. What was at stake was the traditional village structure with its institutions and orders, all of them vulnerable in consequence of the subversion of the rules of the market.[20]

Peasant communities in the rural hinterlands of the towns about 1500 varied in degrees of freedom and prosperity and in ethnic background. Those of English origin tended to be the more substantial, affluent and free. Conversely, in the marcher areas of the Leinster and Ormond Pales particularly, the lowest grade of peasant, the betagh, was likely to be of Gaelic origin. The free tenants and farmers, mostly of English origin, leased lands from the lord, most being bound to sue at the lord's court and some to supply labour services at ploughing and harvest times. Under them were the gavillers (not so common in the later fifteenth century), who held their lands at shorter terms and had variable amounts of land. The cottagers were smallholders who supplied most labour services on the estates and held little more than a small plot. Some of this rank were of Gaelic origin. The betaghs, as mentioned, were mainly of Gaelic origin and were equivalent to English villeins. By the end of the fifteenth century they were mostly free of the soil, owing services to their lords and farming as few as five acres with their families. Owing to the shortage of labour in the fourteenth and fifteenth centuries, the status of the betaghs was improving. Overlying the gradations of tenantry on the manors were the chartered rights of burgesses, granted by the magnates to borough-dwellers. These privileges were conferred in the hope of generating markets and fairs, and possibly local industry. The nucleus of rural communities was the clustered habitation of the village or hamlet which, despite the dispersal of individuals' lands throughout many fields, was a focus for local identity and loyalties.[21]

While declining social and economic circumstances around 1500 worsened conditions for some manor-dwellers of inferior rank, the lords of the estates and head tenants were in a position to capitalise on commercial opportunities. This rank included aristocrats such as the Earls of Ormond, Desmond and Kildare, the county gentry and merchant rentiers who had invested in rural property. Members of the latter group tended to exploit estates more intensively, by enclosing commons land for pasture, for example, and by imposing heavy dues and restrictions on the now sparser manorial populations. Also in the category of lords were leading ecclesiastical authorities and the crown itself. Evidently rural lords were enjoying prosperous lifestyles, to judge by their castle-building, church endowments and investments in leases and real estate. While major nobles were not cultivating their demesnes directly as in the past, church authorities and merchant rentiers still tended to do so. The most frequent complaint heard from traders in city and town was that non-urban magnates were flouting the regulations for commerce laid down in statutes and charters since the twelfth century. Those city patricians who were involved in landholding as head tenants of lords such as the Archbishop of Dublin and as proprietors in their own right could uphold the civic principles of retailing and wholesaling. But outside the privileged boroughs and their environs, the *ad hoc* nature of trade and exchange could not be controlled by the guilds without the co-operation of the magnates. As long as traditional manorial officials such as the reeve, bailiff and steward were active there was some guarantee of the proper economic nexus being upheld, but it is not known to what extent these were operating in the sixteenth century.[22]

Trade and its regulation were the essential connectors between towns and their hinterlands. The facilitating of commercial contacts was, of course, inherent in the constitutions of the towns. Charters upheld the freedom of the enfranchised citizens to trade without the burdens of taxes such as murage, pontage and lastage, while imposing these upon non-natives. Town by-laws further identified the rights of native traders and craftspeople *vis-à-vis* outsiders. Guilds had specific rules for retailing and wholesaling within and outside the franchises of towns, and upheld the monopoly privileges of the native merchants against all-comers. In particular forestalling, the undercutting of the market, and regrating or hoarding were outlawed. Central government weighed in with customs and staple regulations which were designed in principle to give an impetus to town commerce, and any burdensome elements were evaded by citizen traders. Very precise rules governed markets and fairs, fixed by date in foundation charters, with special courts to enforce their business. State grants and parliamentary measures were deployed to cope with trading problems as they arose, such as corn shortages and failures in manufactures of raw materials. Co-operation between towns in garnering the produce of extended hinterlands was not uncommon, though competition between some towns in the same region was very evident in the early sixteenth century, as in the case of Galway and Limerick, and Waterford and Ross. Thus there was an impressive battery of instruments for chaining the producers in the hinterlands to the urban trading system.[23]

Town markets and guild monopolies were vitiated by logistical and jurisdictional hindrances. Townspeople had had to come to terms with difficulties in transport during the late middle ages. There is evidence for a fairly extensive network of roads in the hinterlands of some towns, such as Dublin and the Ormond boroughs, and some landlords were assiduous in maintaining and building bridges and clearing highways. As has been seen, water-borne travel was regarded as safer than land-based, and thus the navigable rivers were arteries of commerce. The river system of the south-east was particularly important for centres such as Kilkenny, Ross and Waterford in times of disorder in the vicinities. But road transport of goods by horse and pack and riverine or coasting transport by barge and boat were subject to severe disruption, as is seen by the evidence of townspeople from Clonmel, Carrick, Fethard, Wexford, Kilkenny and Waterford. Highway robbery was common, and kidnappings and unofficial levies were perpetrated by restless rural-dwellers, some of them of aristocratic or gentry status. Piracy at sea and weirs for blocking river trade were hazards for water-borne trade. Perhaps a more insuperable barrier to the effective exchange of goods was the fragility of money-based trading. Currency was in short supply among the inhabitants of all but the more urbanised areas, and barter was therefore a feature of commercial dealings in many parts. The lack of a banking system was not a handicap, as loans in the form of stock or seeds or even capital equipment were made by merchants to foster agriculture and crafts, and a mortgage system did develop in English as well as Irish areas during the sixteenth century.[24]

Also obstructive of the commercial market were forestalling activities linked directly to the exercise of seignorial and state power. In gaelicised hinterlands of some boroughs the system of coign and livery cut across the market, as did the purveyance system (of compulsory purchase at fixed rates for the supply of the governor's household and troops) even in the core English areas in the later sixteenth century. Just as fee-farms and burgage rents were payable by citizens to their town lords for their privileged trading conditions, 'black rents' were necessary for municipal survival, as in Cork and Limerick for example. These were annual payments made to an overpowering neighbouring lord to ensure protection from his raiding and plundering. The absence of authority of the central administration at local level was thereby glaringly obvious. Trading conditions for merchants were unsafe outside the walls of even some of the largest towns and cities, and the arbitrary exactions and levies of ambitious lords hindered the fair exchange of goods. Some magnates connived with illegal traders to undercut the town markets by selling at below-market rates, away from approved stalls. If the lords of the manors themselves were circumventing the markets and fairs of the boroughs, the frustration of merchants was understandable. Once manorial social and economic organisation was dispensed with, the unofficial intercourse of manorial and non-manorial dwellers was facilitated. It was at this interface between the official producers and traders and the unofficial (possibly not money-based) that the means of keeping up supplies of agricultural produce for internal and external distribution were ensured.[25]

The abuse of the market system is also attested by the phenomenon of the 'grey merchants' (so called perhaps because of the dustiness of their clothes from travelling country roads), who were the agents of town merchants for trading with rural producers, both English and Gaelic Irish. As their activities were outside the scope of guild regulation, they were the subject of much punitive legislation, not only civic but parliamentary as well, as, for example, in the 1541–3, 1560 and 1585–6 assemblies. These measures fit into a wider pattern of exclusions from apprenticeship, citizenship and residence, already in being since the Statutes of Kilkenny, most but not all directed against Gaelic people. One purpose was to prevent the dilution of civic culture, but the key factor was the commercial well-being of the boroughs. In the fifteenth and early sixteenth centuries there were scores of examples of protectionist by-laws, backing up the parliamentary statutes of 1431 and 1450, for instance. Ordinances of the Dublin civic assembly of 1454 and 1455 banned Irish traders, particularly 'holtaghys' or Ulstermen, evidently commonly engaged in commerce with citizens. Limerick, Kilkenny and Waterford were among other cities to pass anti-Gaelic laws referring specifically to trade, and many of the concessionary charters granted to these boroughs were in recompense for the privations suffered as a result of Irish assaults on city traders. A series of laws passed by Waterford corporation from 1461 to 1492 was especially penal, culminating in a code of English dress for citizens. At a later stage similar guidelines were laid down for Galwegians in 1536–7. The repetition of these time-worn measures indicates that their force was blunted in practice. Evidence from many centres shows that people of Irish race were playing a bigger role in urban affairs, not necessarily in the political life of the franchises, but rather as workers in humbler capacities and as rural-dwellers in the vicinages, sometimes called 'Irishtowns'.[26]

The reality of the trading nexus of the towns was very different to what was being reflected in the laws and by-laws. In a myriad of ways accommodations were being made between merchants and non-urban magnates, Anglo-Norman and Gaelic. The much-maligned 'grey merchants' were obviously flouting the rules of retailing and wholesaling established by the guilds, but they were agents of individual town merchants. In this respect they were part of an organised system of forestalling which was the price that urban-dwellers had to pay to ensure a satisfactory supply of marketable goods. Institutions such as the staple were also endangered by the employment of illegal agents. The system of head ports did not become established until legislation of 1570, and small creeks and havens were used by non-urban magnates to run their own trade with foreign merchants. The activities of the O'Driscoll lords of west Cork were contentious right through to the mid-sixteenth century. In order to control the production and supply of agricultural produce to the towns, magnates were involved in intimidating merchants, as in Fethard, Clonmel and some of the other south-eastern towns. Some products such as timber had to come from Gaelic zones, given the afforested nature of the habitats, and thus the Dublin merchants were heavily engaged in trade with Wicklow clansmen. In the late fifteenth century the pattern of legalised exemptions to trade with the banned Irish was becoming stronger. Barely a year after passing the most stringent laws Waterford corporation, along with Cork, Limerick and Youghal, was in 1463 empowered to trade with the Irish. In the same decade Dublin corporation was forced to admit to the reality of Gaelic trade, and gradually Galway and Ross were to exempt trade with Gaelic natives of the hinterlands from guild bans. Much of this trade would have involved barter at some point in the transactions, as the Gaelic economy was still non-monetary for the most part, but the evidence suggests that complaisant lords, mostly Anglo-Norman, were the facilitators, in return for handsome rewards. In the fluid circumstances of the marchlands within which many towns were absorbed, the whole system of protections, cuttings and spendings would have merged with trading arrangements for the profit of the lords and their urban counterparts, at the expense of rural producers and dwellers in the lesser boroughs. The decay of the market towns of the western Pale is testimony to this trend.[27]

The flourishing overseas trade of the ports in the late middle ages shows how interdependent were the town merchants and the producers and consumers in the extended hinterlands. The exporters in the towns garnered from the Anglo-Norman and Gaelic producers the commodities which were most in demand in markets in England and on the continent: hides, wool, fish, flax and furs. In return, as importers, they offered to the residents of the hinterlands essential items such as salt, wine, iron and fine cloth. Adaptation and resilience on the part of mercantile and agrarian communities, already noted in relation to production and regulation of commerce since the mid-fourteenth century, are also a feature of the foreign trade of Ireland around 1500. Down to the end of the thirteenth century wool, grain and hides produced by the manorial economy were marketed widely through ports from the Baltic to the Bay of Biscay and the Mediterranean, and native and foreign merchants brought back to Ireland wine, salt and luxury goods. Different trends in the following two hundred years resulted from the economic changes within the country and disruptions of overseas commercial routes.

Most outgoing trade by 1500 was in products associated with fish, cattle and sheep, while the roll of imports remained unchanged. While many of the southern and western ports retained their links with the continent, a considerable amount of traffic in goods into and out of Ireland was through England and Wales. The port towns of the Pale, Drogheda and Dublin, were versatile in their commercial connections, with cross-channel ports such as Chester and Liverpool, with Brittany, Spain and Scotland, and with the other Irish littoral towns to the north and south in the vital coasting trade.[28]

The fisheries of the Irish Sea contributed to the prosperity of merchant communities in ports and harbours of the Pale and north-east Ulster during the late fifteenth century. By contrast, the great herring shoals off the south-west and west coasts tended to enrich directly the non-urban lords whose territories were maritime. These fisheries attracted fleets of hundreds of foreign fishing vessels, mostly from Spain, whose crews used havens and creeks along the coastline as anchorages where they could process the catch. Lords such as O'Sullivan Beare and O'Driscoll in west Cork derived very large income from levies on these activities and goods exchanged for fish. Of the other varieties of fish, salmon was the most highly prized, and it was through the port of Bristol that very lucrative Irish salmon exports reached the English market. Next to fish, hides of cows and calves were the most important Irish export in the late fifteenth century. The great bulk of hides originated in the Gaelic and gaelicised areas where the lords possessed vast herds of cattle. Town merchants from all over Ireland gathered in the hides from wide catchment areas, some dealing directly with Gaelic suppliers and others gathering consignments from smaller markets. The wills of Blake family members in Galway suggest that hides may even have been used as units of exchange with both Gaelic herdsmen and outside traders. The main continental market for Irish hides was Flanders, whence they were channelled into the great European trading routes. Flemish ports also received quantities of Irish wool and woolfells, but exports from Ireland may have declined in the fifteenth century. The Irish frieze or rough, napped serge-cloth and mantle, the capacious garment of rough wool characteristic of Gaelic dress, were the most popular forms of cloth imports from Ireland among continentals, as well as linen textiles. Wine, fine cloth, iron, salt and other manufactured items formed the bulk of imports into Ireland.[29]

N

O'Doherty
MacQuillan
MacDonnell
MacSweeney
O'Cahan
O'Boyle
O'Neill
Clandeboye
MacSweeney
O'Donnell
O'Neill
Maguire
Magennis
O'Connor
Sligo
O'Dowd
MacMahon
O'Hanlon
Barrett
MacDonagh
O'Rourke
O'Hara
O'Reilly
Plunket
O'Gara
MacDermot
Nugent
MacCostello
Burke
O'Connor
O'Malley
O'Farrell
MacMorris
Delamere
The
Pale
Bermingham
Dalton
O'Flaherty
O'Kelly
Dillon
Blake
O'Connor
O'Madden
O'Molloy
Earldom of Kildare
Burke
(Clanricard)
O'Dunne
O'Connor
O'Carroll
O'Dempsey
O'Toole
O'Brien
O'Kennedy
O'More
Fitzgerald
O'Byrne
MacNamara
MacGillapatrick
Burke
Butler of Ormond
MacMurrough
O'Dwyer
Fitzmaurice
Fitzgerald
Roche
Power
Earldom of Desmond
Fitzgerald
MacCarthy Mor
Barry
O'Sullivan Mor
MacCarthy (Muskerry)
O'Sullivan Beare
MacCarthy Reagh
O'Driscoll

0   30   60
                        km
                        miles
0   20   40

The leading families of Ireland in the sixteenth century

Society and Culture
in Gaelic Ireland

Irish people are very religious but do not regard stealing as
sinful, nor is it punished as a crime. They hold that we
[foreigners] are uncivilised because we keep the gifts of
fortune for ourselves, while they live naturally, believing
that all things should be held in common. This accounts for
the number of thieves: you are in peril of being robbed or
killed here if you travel the country without a strong
bodyguard. I have heard that in places farther north people
are more uncivilised, going about nude, living in mountain
caves and eating raw meat.

THESE words were written by Francesco Chiericati in a letter
to the Duchess of Mantua, Isabella d'Este, in 1517. A priest and
humanist who acted as papal nuncio to England, Chiericati had
toured Ireland in a direction north-westwards of Dublin that year.
As a sophisticated cosmopolitan from a Renaissance court, he
observed the state and manners of the Gaelic natives of south Ulster
keenly. His testimony is of great interest because it is one of the
earliest of the many surviving depictions of Gaelic society in the
sixteenth century. Chiericati came to Ireland as a sightseer, but
most of the later observers were committed to action in relation to
the polity and society they reported on as officials and servitors of
the English crown. Whether they advocated reform by peaceful or
violent means, these commentators were inevitably motivated by
political bias in their anatomising of Gaelic people and their mode
of life. Such criticial yet compelling writings have influenced the
rendition of early modern Gaelic Ireland in later historiography.
Because of the paucity of rich veins of internal documentation,
undue emphasis has been given to accounts by hostile outsiders.
Thus the representation of Gaelic Ireland as primitive, warlike, poor
and semi-nomadic has persisted down to comparatively recently.[1]

Thanks to the research of experts in the past twenty-five years, a more balanced picture of sixteenth-century Gaelic Ireland has emerged. Using a variety of documents, including annals, poems, administrative records (mostly of non-Gaelic origin), monastic, episcopal and papal registers and other tracts, historians have skilfully and painstakingly pieced together a version of Gaelic economic, political, military, social and cultural activity in the late medieval and early modern periods. Although professing the tentativeness of this new framework, they have modified significantly the older one in a number of crucial areas. Far from being anarchic, chaotic and chronically disordered, Gaelic society in these latest accounts is seen as a complex and organised system of institutions with its own principles and rules of arrangement. Although rooted in tradition, this organism was not static or moribund in the Tudor period, but capable of changing internally and adapting to outside influences. Nor were Gaelic regions totally isolated and self-contained: wide-ranging contacts were maintained, most especially with the Scottish economic and cultural zone, and also with the Iberian countries, France, Flanders and Italy. The natives of Gaelic Ireland showed an infinite capacity to adapt to and absorb a variety of external impulses, and they in turn influenced newcomers to the country. Indeed, the quality and extent of Gaelic influences have been revised in the context of the study of the island's history in the period. Almost everywhere there were to be found greater or lesser signs of Gaelic civility, and not just in the areas traditionally associated with the great Gaelic families. Certainly purer forms of Gaelic institutions existed in the remoter parts where Anglo-Norman penetration had been less intense, but the interface between the civilisations was elusive and shifting and cannot be defined with absolute surety.[2]

Peasants and landlords in Gaelic society

Remarkably, entire Gaelic social systems had survived even in the heart of the region of most intensive Anglo-Norman settlement. In 1500 integrated clan living could be found most notably in the Wicklow, Carlow and north Wexford region of Leinster, as well as in the midlands, the west Cork and north Tipperary regions of Munster and the Iveagh region of south-east Ulster. On the other hand, as we have seen, the territory normally considered to be

coextensive with Gaelic Ireland contained areas where English institutions persisted. On balance, however, it was the Gaelic population
which inhabited the less hospitable terrain which was more suitable
for pasture than for tillage, especially in circumstances of low
population density and low intensity of land usage. The natives'
landholding and social systems evolved in response to the general
patterns of settlement which had emerged over the centuries.
Certainly most sixteenth-century commentators stressed the attachment of Gaelic people to stock-raising, non-village community
forms and mobility through the countryside. But generalisations
were apt to be erroneous: there was much cultivation in Gaelic areas,
while parts of the older colonial zone, and not just those inhabited
by Gaelic clans, exhibited pastoral features. And in the regions
where the two ethnic groups interlocked there were hybrid economic
systems which facilitated commercial activity and a limited amount
of manufacture.[3]

Many contemporaries emphasised the wandering style of Gaelic
pastoralism. Edmund Spenser, for example, while recognising its
importance in the Irish economy, execrated such nomadism as he
saw it because it provided a shield for law-breakers and scope for
licentiousness. Certainly the custom of 'booleying', that is, migration
of communities from winter grazing lands to summer pasture and
back again, was widespread in Connacht and Ulster. It has been
shown, however, that this transhumance was orderly, and limited
by the pattern of sowing and reaping of crops in spring and autumn.
Large herds were the real symbol of wealth in Gaelic society, some
chieftains numbering their cows in thousands. These were guarded
against the *creach* or raiding of hostile persons by longer-range
migration in times of warfare, involving whole populations. The
caoraidheacht or 'creaght' involved either groups of refugees driving
cattle with them or the use of herds in battle, and continued into a
much later period. In the early 1570s in Clandeboye, for instance,
creaghts were deployed skilfully by Sir Brian MacPhelim O'Neill
to defeat the expeditionary force of Thomas Smith. Conversely,
there are many instances from the same period and later of the
seizure of Irish lords' herds by English soldiers or Gaelic rivals to
undermine their economies or to prevent cows being used to pay
mercenaries, as was the custom of the time.

Normal cattle-raising conditions were fostered in the standing
herbage of meadows. As cows did not have winter hay or housing,

the animals were very vulnerable to mortality during harsh winters. The typically small black cows produced enough milk to make five gallons of butter per annum. Cows could be rented by poor folk in return for agreed amounts of butter and buttermilk payable to the landowner. As well as providing foodstuffs, in the form of meat, dairy products and a jelly-like compound of cow's blood and butter, cattle were also the source of Ireland's most important export commodity—hides. Sheep and pigs were also a significant part of Irish pastoralism: mutton was consumed, and pork was highly prized as a delicacy at feasts. Wool, woolfells and sheepskins were valuable as exports. Among the kinds of horses kept were mares for breeding purposes, hobbies or small riding-horses, pack-horses for transport, and 'garrans' for ploughing. In a society which was so dependent on agricultural produce for its survival, let alone prosperity, the care and feeding of animals was of paramount importance.[4]

Some cultivation of lands was necessary for the production of food for animals and humans, but it has been shown that tillage was not just marginal to the Gaelic areas, as was once thought. Although unlikely to have been organised on a manorial infield and outfield basis, crop-growing was carried on extensively, with every scrap of cultivable land being worked. There is compelling evidence of abundant corn harvests in the lordships of, for example, the O'Shaughnessys in Galway, the O'Byrnes in Wicklow, the O'Neills in Tyrone and the O'Connors in Offaly. The long fallow system, that is, the leaving of land untilled for a considerable length of time, was used more commonly than the three-crop rotation which was usual in older colonial areas. Land was fertilised with sand and, in some maritime areas, with seaweed. Fields were open and unenclosed, surrounded by fences of stakes and wattles, while townland boundaries, of some political significance, were encompassed by hedges and ditches. Land was ploughed by horses, mainly pulling the light plough by the tail, though heavy ploughs pulled by harnessed horse or ox teams were also used. The principal crops grown were oats (for feeding both people and animals), barley (for beer-making), wheat and flax—the latter a notable cash-crop which was exported with success. Winnowing of the crops was carried out by burning of the straw and chaff to leave the grain, and grinding was done by means of quern-stones. The diet of the agricultural community had butter and oatcakes as staples, indicating this concentration on pastoral and arable economic activity, while favoured beverages were ale and buttermilk. Fisheries were intensely exploited for internal consumption and for exports, though fish was not a favourite food of the Irish. Herbs and vegetables helped to balance the high-protein foods, and there is evidence also for some orchards in Gaelic parts.[5]

Among the peasantry in Gaelic Ireland there were gradations of wealth and influence. While there were no serfs or unfree bondsmen in the feudal sense, the vast majority of cultivators were heavily oppressed by the landowners, possessing few rights and having no recourse to local estate courts. The contractual arrangements of tenancy might allow for the lending of stock, seed or equipment by the landowner to the tenant in return for a proportion of the produce. Some cultivators with a modest base of stock possession could seize opportunities for betterment by acquiring land on pledge from declining landowners and become renting middlemen themselves, and some were members of influential though landless clans who lived as substantial tenants on the extensive demesne lands of some lord or powerful clan. Most peasants, however, were economically depressed, subject to a wide variety of exactions from their landlords. In the sixteenth century when rural workers were scarce, landowners attempted to impose labour services such as a number of days' ploughing, reaping or sowing. But the Gaelic peasantry had one source of economic power: they could migrate from one territory to another at set times of year in search of better conditions for themselves and their families. Despite the endeavours of landowners to stunt such mobility, there are many reports of migration, such as that of Bishop Lyon of Cork, who complained in 1597 that the tenants 'continue not three years in a place, but run roving about the country like wild men fleeing from one place to another', and that of Sir Richard Bingham in Connacht in 1591, who lamented that 'the tenants do shift their dwellings every year at May'. Migration from Gaelic socio-political zones to the anglicised regions, including the Pale, was extremely common in the early sixteenth century, and movement in the opposite direction, to Tyrone in the 1560s for example, attested the tendency of the tenants in all parts of Ireland to vote with their feet.[6]

Gaelic landholding was undoubtedly characterised by some impermanence. Because of the low population, there was a correspondingly low-intensity use of land. Migration of subject groups from one territory to another for economic improvement posed difficulties for the landholders of Gaelic society. They were in competition for labouring folk in circumstances of demographic shortage, and, despite having access to wide expanses of under-utilised land, proprietorial control over people was what was most prized. As a consequence of the mobility fostered by an essentially pastoral lifestyle and migratory tenancy patterns, habitation in the Gaelic areas could be transitory. The houses of the unprivileged classes were constructed of vegetative materials, such as wood, mud and straw, and those of the higher orders were scarcely more durable. Tenants' houses were usually round and one-roomed, often without chimneys and requiring little skill to build. Although town-living had little appeal for Gaelic people, there may have been a tendency in the late medieval period for small settlements of tenants to cluster around the tower-houses of the landholders. The building of these structures by members of the Gaelic elite in the fifteenth and sixteenth centuries marked an aspiration to more settled living. Normally stone-built of three or four storeys, tower-houses con-tained a main hall and dining area on the top floor, with chambers and living quarters, perhaps for two or three families, on the others. They served not only defensively but perhaps also as social and commercial foci also.[7]

Although most Gaelic families preferred to live outside towns, producers in the pastoral, agrarian and maritime economies were involved in the urban commercial nexus. Obviously there was steady migration of Gaelic people to the towns in the late medieval period, to judge by the frequency of anti-Irish laws passed by municipal councils. There are cases of Gaelic merchant families such as the Creans in Sligo, the Dorseys (or Darcys) in Galway, the Ronaynes in Cork and the Malones in Dublin successfully ascending to the rank of urban patricians. In the case of Cavan, town development was sponsored by the O'Reilly lords of east Breifne, and the MacBrady merchants based there had business interests in the northern Pale. Most trade involving Gaelic personnel was conducted away from town markets, however. The representatives of the Old English town merchants, the 'grey merchants', travelled to the sources of production in Gaelic areas, paying taxes on their com-mercial dealings to the lord of the territory. The chiefs normally enjoyed monopoly and pre-emptive rights over the agricultural produce and domestic manufactures such as linens and mantles within their lordships. The wills of city merchants, most notably those of the Blake family of Galway, reveal extensive dealings with Gaelic farmers in the hinterlands, and the Dublin timber trade depended on the suppliers of the Gaelic Wicklow region. Along the northern and western seaboards, away from the port cities, a flourishing trade took place between local Gaelic producers and overseas merchants, untrammelled by municipal strictures. Strong commercial links existed between the west of Scotland and Gaelic Ulster, while the creeks and small harbours of Munster and Connacht attracted Spanish and Breton shipping.[8]

Aristocratic modes of inheritance could be detrimental to settled landholding. Although there were considerable variations in the practice within territories and families, the division of lands took place among the males of the clan (as understood in one of the most important of its corporate functions, the occupation or ownership of land). The common practice of partible inheritance by the males was seen simplistically by sixteenth-century English observers as the Irish version of the Kentish 'gavelkind' custom. On the death of a landholding member of the family, all the lands owned or occupied by the family were redistributed among the surviving co-heirs, normally the brothers of the deceased. In some parts of the country redistribution of shares took place at the behest of the eldest of the clan every year on Mayday, with consequent benefits in terms of size of proprietorship to a lord such as the O'Callaghan in Munster, for example. In other regions it was the duty of the most junior of the co-heirs to make the partition into shares from which the entitled beneficiaries would then choose in order of seniority. After a number of partible sharings over generations, divisions tended to become permanent, though disagreements took place between sitting occupiers and claimants who hoped to benefit from another redistribution. In the absence of a uniform law of land inheritance, local customs might be referred to in disputes, but these were not always adhered to in practice. The periodic reapportionment of lands was a disincentive to their productive development, and in practice it may have rarely occurred in some areas. Here circumstances such as premature deaths might lead to a modification of inheritance customs by the individual family.[9]

Ownership of land in Gaelic Ireland was vested in the ruling lineage groups or clans within the politicial entities known as lordships. In some of these, where the power of the chief and his immediate family was in the ascendant, most landholding was confined to his lineal branch, the other family branches holding disproportionately smaller estates. On the other hand, where power was more evenly shared among the septs of the ruling family there was a more even split in landowning, perhaps into several *cómhranna* or segments. Obviously linked to the question of redistribution under the system of partible inheritance already discussed, continuity of ownership was normally a manifestation of stable political lordship, whereas the landholding system of lordships in which there had been major upheavals in the disposal of political authority was marked by discontinuity. As well as these ruling lineages, the other landholding families were those which had hereditarily served the lords' clans in some capacity. These included mercenary soldiers, notably galloglas families, literary and legal clans, ecclesiastical families, some commercial families, for example the Creans of Sligo, and also families which had formerly been of greater political importance within the lordship but which declined in political esteem and proportionately in landholding as the new ruling family expanded. Within each landowning network were to be found the mensal lands of the chief of the name, these being an estate appropriate to the chieftaincy and occupied by the household families, traditional retainers of the ruling house who provided rent in the form of produce. In addition, each landlord had his demesne lands, which very often he cultivated himself.[10]

On the basis of this demesne cultivation in many parts of Ireland, convincing proof has been adduced for there being no rigid division of Gaelic society into two classes, landowners and cultivators. Share-cropping labourers or *bothaigh* helped the landowning clans with the cultivation of their lands. Proprietors also set part of their own estates for rents, which included labour dues such as ploughing or reaping. Substantial gentlemen with many dependants could be cultivators, either functioning as actual landowners themselves or renting land in tenancy to have greater stocks of grazing cattle or labour resources. Thus a middleman or rural capitalist class was present at least embryonically in sixteenth-century Gaelic Ireland, taking advantage of opportunities for renting lands with their stock and labour potential, little heeding the question of title or proprietorship. In a society where family fortunes waxed and waned with great frequency, there was considerable change in landownership in any case, and certain estates could have double claims to legal ownership. Land which was waste could be legitimately taken over by the principal owner for the grazing of his herds, a valuable perquisite in that pastoral society. In cases where economically depressed families failed to pay exactions imposed on lands by aggressive lords, the owner could seize part thereof and enjoy the fruits until the original occupier was in a position to take back the plot. The other main means of transfer of land was through the pledge or mortgage which was entered into by the mortgagee on the basis that the land passed from his control to that of the mortgagor. The original occupier could remain on in the capacity of tenant, hoping for but rarely realising the objective of winning back control over his land. Accordingly, layers of ownership lay upon certain territories, rendering it extremely difficult for common lawyers to disentangle claims under Irish land law.[11]

Gaelic lords and overlords

Owing to the overlapping of rent for land and levies imposed for chiefry or lordship rights, it is not surprising that the relationship between landownership and political authority was confounded both then and subsequently. Chiefly jurisdiction in the earlier medieval period entailed the protection and representation of the inhabitants of a territory, the personal possession of which was not necessary for kingship. By the sixteenth century political control increasingly meant the personal headship of the dominant kin-group and the absorption of all the subject territory as the lord's demesne. The inhabitants were then more than just subjects, becoming tenants also, even when technically freeholders. Certainly hereditary ruling clans of greater and lesser status were normally the possessors of the land to the exclusion of almost all others. Leaving aside temporarily the clan aspect with its corporate rights, the situation within the smaller lordships was akin to the English one in terms of politico-proprietorial authority. What made a fundamental difference in the eyes of contemporary observers was the question of political over-lordship and its maintenance. There were in Gaelic (and Anglo-Norman) Ireland dozens of lordships, variously called 'nations' and 'countries', ruled over by lords of varying standing. These lords attained the headship or chieftaincy of their clans or ruling lineages, and they proceeded to assert their authority over their own kin-group branches and traditional subject families who performed special services for them, and also, to as great an extent as possible, over neighbouring lords whom they would regard as their vassals. The greater the share of the territory of a region or province that a lord could control, the more secure his authority was, and the nearer he approached to paramountcy in the region. Down through the lesser ranks of chieftain, the same drive to overlordship of putative vassals was evident, successfully sustained only through the exaction of rights and tributes.[12]

The proliferation of ruling dynasties, partly fostered by the relaxed approach of the Gaelic Irish to sexuality, ensured the expansion of the dominant dynasty, and also provided candidates for intrusion into the headship of subject lordships. But the existence of a number of contenders for the headship of a clan gave an added competitiveness to the succession stakes within lordships. For succession under Irish law was by election, technically from an extended four-generation family group, the *derbfine*. Theoretically the election of the chief and the *tánaiste*, or second in command, took place at an assembly of the vassal nobility or gentry of a lordship, the choice falling upon 'the eldest and worthiest' of those qualified to succeed. Once nominated, the chieftain-designate was inaugurated with various rituals at a hallowed place in the presence of vassal chieftains, heads of ecclesiastical and learned families, and, where applicable, the overlord. The key part of the ceremony of ordination of the new chief was his being named by surname title only, 'O'Neill', for example, in the case of the Tyrone clan. Despite the fixation of English commentators with the title of *tánaiste*, coining from it the generic word for Irish succession practice, 'tanistry', the holder did not always succeed to the chieftaincy. Sometimes he predeceased the lord, or a stronger challenger emerged from within the ruling dynasty. In practice, the best-placed to succeed a dead chief was his eldest son, a *de facto* system of primogeniture coming into vogue in lordships such as those of MacCarthy More in south-west Munster and Maguire in Fermanagh. Mutations of the system occurred when a more distant kinsman with a sufficient following took over, and the *mac ríogh*, or king's son, had to be content with his specially designated lands, military command and residual political eminence. The son of a *mac ríogh* could compensate for the ousting of his immediate family by the cadets of a succeeding dynast by casting off dependency on the new chief and developing a new sub-lordship with its own chain of inheritance within the main ruling clan. Through such a process emerged the autonomous lordships of O'Neill of Clandeboye, O'Neill of the Fews, and the clan of Philip Maguire in western Fermanagh.[13]

If real economic power lay in the number of potential labourers over whom a landlord had sway, political prestige was measured by the number of clients or vassals a lord held in submission. By the early sixteenth century the drive towards provincial overlordship on the part of some Irish magnates—of both Gaelic and Anglo-Norman origin—was a salient feature of politico-military affairs throughout the island. Apart from the direct clientship of the hereditary families dwelling on the *lucht tighe* or mensal lands of a chieftain, an extreme form of dependency was that of a chieftain whose very election was at the behest of an overlord: the MacSweeney lords of Fanad, for example, were regularly appointed by O'Donnell of Tyrconnell and paid a gifts of cows for the favour. The new, more demanding lord–vassal relationship depended very much on the deployment of force and the exaction of military support in return for protection. One kind of collective tutelage was that in which the marcher lands of the Pale and colony were held by neighbouring warlords to whom were paid 'black rents', a form of protection money. Vassalage could be extended through forceful means such as the cattle-raid or by diplomacy in supporting a winning contender in a succession dispute. The bond of clientship thus contracted entailed the payment of tributes in money or kind and the performance of military service on the part of the vassal or *uirrí* in return for his overlord's *slánuigheacht* or security. A lesser chief could buy his *slánuigheacht* from a greater, even if he were nominally the territorial subject of another: for instance, in the late fifteenth century Brian O'Reilly of east Breifne, technically under the overlordship of O'Neill, opted for the protection of O'Donnell instead. This fostering of a network of supporters on a non-territorial basis parallels the growth of systems of retainers by English and Anglo-Norman aristocrats in the period.[14]

The challenging of old concepts of kingship in the practices of sixteenth-century overlords reflects the changing nature of political hegemony. An early, purer form of vassalage and submission in Gaelic society involved the proferring of hostages by the underling and his acceptance of a *tuarastal*, or ceremonial gift, from the superior as a symbol of abjectness. In early sixteenth-century parlance, the term *tuarastal* had come to refer to wages paid usually to mercenary soldiers. The ancient concept of the *enech* or honour of the overlord (which could be besmirched for non-fulfilment of his promise of protection to his vassals) became less important than the notion of his *onóir*, signifying esteem or obedience. The imposition of the *riar* or will of the paramount chief on subject territories beyond the traditional contracted dues was mirrored in the new stress on straight-forward spending by clients for the offer of protective overlordship. Such expansionism is best exemplified in the early sixteenth century in the large number of clients of English and Gaelic background who paid a considerable aggregate sum for the protection of the Anglo-Norman magnate, the Earl of Kildare. In the north Connacht region another pattern of tiered overlordship is evident. There the O'Connor Sligo had come to exert a loose sway over lesser chiefs such as the O'Haras, O'Garas and MacDonaghs, maintaining a castle in each of their territories and exacting military support. By the early sixteenth century the O'Connors had succumbed to the superior power of the O'Donnell of Tyrconnell, who made good his claims in Lower Connacht by subjecting all the clans there to his suprem-acy. This involved levying men for military service, victuals and wages for galloglas, money tributes and the customs from Sligo town. This O'Donnell overlordship was without land in north Connacht, and it required the chief's annual personal itineration of the lordships to collect tribute and quash opposition.[15]

As the more ambitious Anglo-Norman and Gaelic lords of early sixteenth-century Ireland aspired to paramountcy, using increasingly forceful methods, their administrations might be expected to have become more professional and complex. This was certainly the case with the feudal magnates, but the native Irish lords did not foster bureaucratic reform in the way that other contemporary European rulers did. Contracts and agreements concerning land and authority were usually unwritten. Lord Deputy St Leger complained that Conn O'Neill and Manus O'Donnell, the lords of Tyrone and Tyrconnell, could produce nothing but 'old parchments, confirmed by no seal . . . as are composed by vain poets' when he attempted to arbitrate their disputes in 1543. By that time the Gaelic lords no longer used the services of chancellors and seneschals as household officials, but relied very heavily on *maoir*, the gatherers of tributes and rents, and marshals who arranged the billeting and cessing of troops on their countries. Previously the hereditary functionaries of the chiefs had been drawn exclusively from the ranks of the noble families dwelling on the mensal lands. In the sixteenth century some of the principal administrators were heads of hereditary service families, the O'Donnellys continuing to serve O'Neills as marshals, for example, and the O'Connollys the MacMahons. *Maoir* were probably chosen by the chiefs, however, on the basis of professional prowess rather than heredity. Marshals, whether hereditary or not, were key figures in making ready the chiefs' war-machines and were well remunerated: the O'Donnellys were paid one soldier's allowance in forty and got the heads and hides of all cattle killed to provide feasts for O'Neill. The household troop comprised a small permanent force of 'kerne' or footsoldiers in the lord's pay, most of whom were mercenaries and not hereditary vassal chieftains. Thus, while Irish lords adapted their administrations to take account of trends elsewhere in the selection of non-noble servitors, the end towards which that service was directed was the sustaining of the war-state and forced overlordship.[16]

The basis of Gaelic political authority was the system of exactions which contemporaries referred to as 'coyne (or coign) and livery'. A conjunction of the Gaelic word for free 'guesting' or billeting of soldiers and servants (*coinnmheadh*) and the Anglo-Norman word for purveyance, the term indicates the universality of the system throughout the island. A sixteenth-century lord's power was measured by the extent of his ability to impose this form of exaction, involving both customary and arbitrary dues demanded by intimidation. To be a successful warlord meant, in other words, having as widespread a network of subjects and retainers as possible to lodge, feed and pay mercenary troops. Comprising many different kinds of levy of varying antiquity and regionality, the system of coign and livery was extremely oppressive for taxpayers, and its abolition was to be integral to Tudor reform schemes. Some aspects were of long standing in Gaelic society. Traditionally the chieftain's household was supplied with produce by the hereditary lineages dwelling on the mensal lands or *lucht tighe*, literally 'household'. The MacManus clan, members of which were called *biataigh*, or food-providers, performed this function for the Maguires, upon whose mensal lands they resided. Also traditional were the chiefry tributes exacted from the subject territories by lords and overlords: these comprised dues in the form of money or food—beeves, oats and butter, for instance—labour services such as a fixed number of days' ploughing, sowing or reaping, and also military levies. As land rights within territories in Gaelic Ireland became more dependent on the will of the lords, freeholding dwellers therein came to be regarded more as tenants-at-will of the lords and were subjected to more exacting burdens than the traditional tributes. Tracts of land could be doubly charged both with the local lord's dues and the overlord's, the aggregate load pressing heavily on the taxpayers.[17]

The custom of 'cuddies' (*cuid oíche*, or a night's portion of food and drink), the duty of providing one or two nights' feasting for one's lord, was long-established and universal. It was almost identical to the custom of *cóisir* or 'coshery', which required of certain vassals the laying on of banquets for their masters. In the sixteenth century the 'cuddies' seem to have increased in elaborateness as large trains of attendants, reflecting the overlords' enhanced powers, had also to be catered for. By the end of the period the exaction was so common that it was converted into a fixed charge in kind or money: MacCarthy More, the Earl of Clancarty, could take his refection at the taxpayer's house, or have it sent, in the form of meat, drink, honey and flour to the value of £4 8s 8d per annum, to his own residence. Closely linked to the system of cuddies or coshery was that of *buannacht* or 'bonaght', the billeting of soldiers (known as 'bonaghts') by a lord on his subjects. The Irish custom of quartering of troops had been taken over by the Anglo-Normans, and the compound system of *buannacht* was employed universally in late medieval Ireland for the cessing of the galloglas on the country. In addition to billeting, the lords claimed extensive rights for all manner of expenses. Provisions for horses and hounds were levied by magnates such as the Earls of Kildare and Ormond and chiefs such as O'Dunne, and a range of servants was entitled to free entertainment. These included craftworkers, for example the masons and labourers engaged on building projects for Piers Roe Butler, Earl of Ossory. The effects of the composite charges, recouped mostly in kind, on society and economy are difficult to measure, but the equilibrium between supply and demand could be upset in time of war when large-scale provisioning was needed, or by the influence of markets where surplus quantities of food collected from taxpayers could be exchanged for cash or non-perishable goods.[18]

The duty to serve in the general hosting or rising-out (*gairm sluaigh*) was universal in sixteenth-century Ireland, and it was a substantial part of the fulfilment of the vassal lord's obligations to his superior. The more affluent landowning classes liable to hereditary obligations (such as the O'Hagans, Quinns and Devlins, known as his 'horsemen' on O'Neill's mensal lands) provided the backbone of the cavalry, responding to summonses for service which might last for several weeks of every year. Riding without stirrups on a saddle of stuffed cushions, the horseman carried a javelin, dagger and sword, was attired with helmet and mail-shirt or jacket of quilted leather, and was accompanied on journeys by at least two horse-boys. Also making up the complement of the *sluaigheadh* were the kerne, lightly armed and light-footed infantry, who were normally able-bodied freemen and bore arms as a matter of course. Without armour, the kerne had as weapons either sword and targets, bows and arrows or javelins. As mentioned, some lords had bands of professional kerne under hereditary captains. The occasions for the use of the summoned horsemen and kerne were more numerous during of the period under review as private wars proliferated and contracts between individual chieftains and the state formally entailed a commitment to military service. Failure on the part of a sub-chief to meet the requirement of providing soldiers resulted in punitive fines, Maguire, for example, having to give O'Neill a cow for every man missing out of his due hosting of two hundred. By the second half of the century vassal chiefs such as O'Sullivan Beare, under MacCarthy More as superior, were employing regular standing armies of galloglas and kerne to be deployed when summoned.[19]

Most ambitious lords were by then using mercenary soldiers in their forces to supplement the rising-out of horsemen and kerne. Originally a minor feature of the Gaelic military establishment, the mercenary bands had a central role to play in Irish warfare. Induced by Gaelic marital connections between the Ulster and western Scottish aristocracy, the galloglas came to settle in the northern part of the country and were contracted to fight by Irish lords. Some heads of galloglas families such as the MacSweeneys of Fanad became chieftains in their own right, in their case as vassals of O'Donnell of Tyrconnell, but elsewhere the galloglas received scattered estates rather than coherent holdings. Everywhere, however, they were accorded billeting rights for themselves and their followers. Physically extremely impressive, the galloglas were armed with their distinctive long-handled axe and also great two-handed swords, as well as spears. Well ensconced in Ulster and Connacht by 1500 where hereditary bonds had developed between them and particular Irish lordships, the galloglas were only then beginning to become common in Munster and Leinster, where they were employed by Anglo-Norman magnates and, in time, the English government. Another feature, again occurring first in Ulster, was the employment of migrant fighters, called 'redshanks', from the Western Isles of Scotland on short-term contracts.[20]

The military requirements of most lords in early sixteenth-century Ireland were still determined by the small-scale, if persistent, nature of inter-clan warfare. Most hostilities were caused by lords attempting to assert supremacy over vassals. To that end, the driving of cattle, the most valuable resource, and the harrying of the population by plundering and burning were normal ploys in order to enforce subjection, and the light-footed, lightly armed kerne, backed up by the mounted levies, were best suited to the raids. Skirmishes which followed the pursuit of the raiders by the plundered took place, with the retreating lightly armed subordinates sent ahead with the booty, and the cavalry or galloglas, if present, forming a protective rearguard. The numbers engaged in such local forays were comparatively small, but the recruitment of substantial numbers of mercenaries by the more affluent lords had already made more elaborate martial activities feasible. The warding and besieging of stone castles was frequent in the fifteenth century. In 1420, for example, Brian O'Connor Sligo built Bundrowes castle, and O'Donnell responded by constructing a castle at Ballyshannon in 1423. Besides the existing siege-engines, the use of artillery, first introduced by the Earls of Kildare in the later fifteenth century, began to spread into Gaelic districts by the earlier sixteenth. Smaller firearms were also being employed in many places by this time, the kerne becoming quite adept in the handling and firing of guns. The introduction of more powerful weaponry and the escalation of hostilities due to the larger numbers of fighting men being deployed on all sides resulted in the increased violence and destructiveness of Irish warfare in the later sixteenth century.[21]

Law and learning among the Gaelic population

For the peaceful arbitration of disputes, the Gaelic chieftains had judges or brehons, usually hereditary, who administered the Irish legal system, the brehon law. Curators of the arcane knowledge of the ancient legal texts, the brehons had as their basic function to adjudicate in cases involving the territorial ruler, or, as became more frequent, in matters of common concern between his subjects. Both parties in a dispute agreed to submit themselves to the arbitration of the brehon beforehand. Awards made included a fee of about one-eleventh of the sum or damages in question for the brehon, as well as a fee to the lord of the territory for overseeing justice. The successful plaintiff in most cases would be forced to seek compensation from the defendant by 'private distress', the seizure of goods or cattle as a 'pledge for justice'. Traditionally there was no criminal law as such in Gaelic Ireland, and offences such as theft, murder and arson were simple torts to be resolved by the payment of damages to the injured party. A fine called an *éiric* was imposed on the kin-group of a murderer, the sum exacted usually payable in the form of a substantial number of cows, varying according to the social status of the victim. A convicted thief had to pay a recompense of several times the value of the stolen goods. A proportion of fines went to the chieftain of the plaintiff, the profits of justice helping to swell his income considerably. The system was based on the principle of *cin comhfhocuis* or 'kincogish' whereby the corporate family was responsible for the actions of its members. Thus the whole of the MacCoghlan/Delvin clan were considered liable for the huge *éiric* of 340 cows which the Earl of Kildare exacted in 1554 for the slaying of his foster-brother by one of its members.[22]

Adaptability of the law and its practitioners is a marked feature in all parts of Ireland down to the later sixteenth century. Relatively soon after its establishment in the twelfth century the colonial government had begun to recognise the use of brehon law among the Gaelic Irish. Anglo-Norman magnates adapted features of the brehon law to the common law in a hybrid system known as 'march law'. The Earls of Ormond employed hereditary brehon families such as MacClancy and MacEgan in the later middle ages, and the 'legally ambidexterous' Earl of Kildare used both English and brehon law, 'whichever he thought most beneficial, as the case did require'. By the early sixteenth century a balance between the legal systems had been struck, with even colonial shire areas employing brehon law but the Pale and towns abiding by the common law. Henry VIII envisaged a special legal code for areas which his administration aspired to reconcile to his rule in the early 1520s. By that time the Gaelic rulers themselves were moving towards the

European model of an increasingly centralised concept of public justice, with the brehons being employed in cases involving serious crimes and the punishment of perpetrators being undertaken by the lords. The brehons were as open to outside influences as their masters in the sixteenth century, some of the lords' hereditary judges becoming proficient in the common law as well as the canon law. They also adapted traditional Irish jurisprudence to the circumstances of the advance of the English common law institutions through Ireland from the middle decades of the century onwards. As a way of surviving an era of change this was necessary, as lords were becoming accustomed to appointing as jurists non-hereditary lawyers, even of English descent. The state administration continued to uphold aspects of Gaelic law involving, for example, Irish gavelkind and tanistry, and the brehons were subsumed into the English system of local arbitration in chancery pleadings.[23]

The rise of chancery jurisdiction in the Elizabethan period meant that Irish women had more opportunities for recourse to the courts for redress of injustices. The legal status of Gaelic women at the end of the middle ages was overshadowed by their inability to inherit land. While lands which were purchased during a marriage could be held and administered by a woman separately from her husband, the property which she brought to a marriage was all that she was entitled to redeem under Gaelic law on the death of her spouse or the dissolution of the marriage. Unlike the situation that obtained under English law in which a wife was entitled to at least a third share in her late husband's estate, the Gaelic woman had no entitlement to the property of her husband. Gráinne (Grace) O'Malley expressed the insecurity of a widow under Gaelic law when she stated that sureties were necessary for the repayment of a dowry from the husband's estate in the event of his dying in a state of indebtedness. By degrees a more secure form of guarantee of this minimal entitlement of women in Gaelic Ireland was developed with the mortgaging of lands (which could still be enjoyed by the man) in the wife's favour as a surety for the redemption of the dowry. Amounts of dowries could be substantial, with stock and household items forming the bulk of them, and a considerable amount of portable wealth being tied up in the dotal system at any given time. Some chieftains cessed their subjects with levies as contributions to the dowries for their daughters. Given the restrictiveness of the 'Irish gavelkind' mode of succession, property could not be transferred from the land of an agnatic clan to that of an intermarrying one, and the legal system upheld this position. When aggrieved heiresses and widows resorted to chancery proceedings in the later part of the century, the court took a sympathetic view of their position, notwithstanding the usually liberal attitude to the brehon law.[24]

Another factor leading to the distress of Gaelic women was the frequency of divorces or rejections by spouses. Gráinne O'Malley also mentioned the putting 'from him' by a husband of his wife, 'without any lawful or due proceeding', as sometimes leading to women's impoverishment. The case of Margaret Tobin whose husband repudiated her after four years of marriage, 'without divorce, aid or consent of holy church', to marry another is only one of several illustrative of the vulnerability of wives in Gaelic and gaelicised society. Her father was forced to sue for the return of a substantial dowry of livestock and domestic items. Secular or 'clandestine' marriages involving the consent of both partners, although not blessed by the church, were valid and binding down to the sixteenth century, and Gaelic law sanctioned other marital practices which were uncanonical. Trial marriages and concubinage were common, and the ban on unions between those related by blood or affinity was little heeded. Many men and women among the aristocracy had a succession of spouses, leading to the proliferation of some of the major families. The example of Richard Burke of Clanricard, who died in 1582 leaving behind five of the six wives he had married, is notable but not unusual. There had been in the medieval period a court of appeals for wives too lightly divorced by their husbands under the secular customs of brehon law, and the frequency of requests by Gaelic Irish suitors to Rome in the fifteenth century for papal dispensations to allow marriage within the forbidden degrees perhaps reflects changing social attitudes. But it was not until the flourishing of the mission of the Observant friars and later the Reformation and Counter-Reformation that the dismantling of the old system of endogamous secular marriages was to begin in earnest.[25]

Notwithstanding the social and economic disabilities associated with the marriage and succession laws, women played an important political role within the Gaelic system. Among the most famous were Gráinne O'Malley, Lady Agnes Campbell and Finola MacDonnell ('Iníon Dubh'), whose marriages to Irish chieftains brought dowries of ships or mercenary soldiers, and who took an active part in military and political events. Catherine MacLean, the Dowager Countess of Argyll, who married Calvagh O'Donnell, was 'a good French scholar with a knowledge of Latin and a smattering of Italian' at a time when the standard of Gaelic Irish women's education languished behind that of men's. Of more far-reaching significance, however, in the earlier sixteenth century was the function of women in the promotion of personal relations, not just between local alliances, but also within and between the great inter-ethnic factional networks. The marriages of Eleanor Fitzgerald, daughter of the eighth Earl of Kildare, firstly to MacCarthy Reagh and secondly, as a widow, to Manus O'Donnell helped to consolidate the great Geraldine faction in the western half of the country. By contrast, her sister Margaret's marriage to Piers Roe Butler failed in the longer term to cement relations between the Fitzgeralds and the other great faction, that of Ormond. The diplomatic influence of such women, and others from many lesser families, accounts for the high standing which they enjoyed among their kinsfolk. This was symbolised by the prime place occupied by the woman at the great set-piece of Gaelic celebration, the ceremonial banquet.[26]

Women may have been severely restricted under Gaelic law in their inheritance rights, but they had a special power to influence the way in which property was transmitted to the males. This lay in the practice of their 'naming' of children as sons to men with whom they had had liaisons. The offspring of casual relationships and temporary marriages who were affiliated to fathers by sworn declaration of the mothers were accorded the same status as the children born within the recognisedly permanent marriage. All the sons of a father, whether born inside or outside of valid wedlock, were entitled to share in the paternal estate. The most famous case of affiliation in the sixteenth century was that of Matthew O'Neill, the son of a Dundalk blacksmith's wife. She claimed, when Matthew was in his mid-teens, that he was born of a brief affair with Conn O'Neill, the first Earl of Tyrone, who accepted his own paternity of the boy, with momentous consequences for his clan. While the custom of 'naming' of sons may have contributed to instability within families, that of fosterage had a confirming effect. The practice of sending children at a very early age to be brought up in the household of another, thereby establishing close bonds between natural and foster family, was extremely common. Foster-children developed an intense loyalty to their fosterers, as in the case of Shane O'Neill, for example, who had that relationship with the O'Donnellys. Not only did fosterage cement alliances among Gaelic clans, but it also helped to transcend divisions between them and families of English origin, advancing the pan-insular networking of inter-ethnic factions. For example, Garret Mór Fitzgerald's son, Henry, was fostered by the O'Donnells of Tyrconnell, while the Butlers of Ormond entered into fosterage relations with the O'Mulryans. So much sought after for fostering were the children of the aristocracy that families would give five hundred cows and more for the honour.[27]

Noble families throughout Ireland enhanced their prestige by patronising the church and learning, and all classes in Gaelic society displayed great respect towards clerics and scholarly practitioners. Indeed, many learned families were of ecclesiastical origin, and they shared with the clergy their exemption from military service and chiefly exactions in return for carrying on their professions. Most distinguished of all the priestly recipients of lay beneficence were the Observant friars, many houses of whom were founded in the predominantly Gaelic provinces of Tuam and Armagh. The princely patrons of the new friaries were motivated by spiritual zeal for their own salvation, perhaps hoping to take the habit in their declining years and be buried in the community's cemetery. The fine buildings containing the patronal family tombs also bore testimony to the status and achievement of the benefactor within the community at large. Sponsorship of the learned professionals yielded similar benefits. The lord of a territory conferred upon the officially recognised head of the hereditary learned family the title of *ollamh* or master of the scholarly discipline which he professed, such as law, history, medicine, music, smithcraft or poetry. The poets were very important in Gaelic society, being perceived as having quasi-sacerdotal powers which they could use to visit harm on their enemies by cursing them in verse. More positively, the poets eulogised their patrons, commemorating in their productions the personal qualities and attainments of the chieftains. Drawing upon a large stock of motifs expressed in highly stylised forms, the 'rhymers', as they were called in English (bards being lesser poets), celebrated the victories of *Gaeil* and *Gaill* (foreigners) alike, sometimes providing a roll of battles and genealogical information about their patrons.[28]

The poets had a crucial role to play in forging the identity of the ruling clan with which they were associated. The hereditary historians and genealogists also compiled records to boost the standing of their patrons. Pedigrees of sixteenth-century chieftains were drawn up by the professional genealogists to endow their rulers with as ancient and hallowed an ancestry as possible, and similarly the historians were eager to recount the glories of the leading families, frequently exaggerating or changing the facts to achieve their purpose. Professional musicians added lustre to the ceremonial occasions presided over by the chieftains, especially their feasts. The Gaelic Irish physicians were also hereditary, practising their medicine on the basis of their study of contemporary European texts. As with the brehons or professional lawyers, the families of the medical and literary *ollaimh* kept schools for novices, and they themselves were wont to travel for study purposes throughout the Gaelic Irish and Scottish cultural zone. The literati may have derived from their wider contacts and mobility a fairly sophisticated sense of ethnic identity which transcended the local and regional loyalties informing their usual practice. There is little evidence, however, of a national consciousness in their work before the later sixteenth century, if even then. References to the 'unity of Banbha' (or Ireland) in the poetry were not apparently charged with any added significance because of the course of events at the time, the concept being of ancient origin and relating to cultural rather than political integrity.[29]

The professional learned classes underpinned Gaelic social and political institutions in a number of ways. Through their affirmation of the power of the successful ruling chiefs, the drive towards lordship and overlordship was given respectability. The system of heredity and succession in operation among the clans of learned professionals mirrored that of Gaelic society at large and gave acknowledgment to its norms. The overlapping of ecclesiastical and lay scholarly families and personnel added stability to the conduct of relations between church and secular administration, and the powers of the 'holy church and rhymers' were often conjointly invoked against the violators of treaties. Not surprisingly, the poets were the targets of Tudor reformers' censure in the mid- to later century as efforts were made to proscribe them along with other groups of 'idle' persons. Much of this contempt for the Gaelic professional learned groups was governed by the humanists' scorn for the deliberate mystification of learning and the qualification by heredity. But more significant was the role of the professionals in reinforcing bonds among the great pan-insular dynastic networks, working as they did for Gaelic and Anglo-Norman families without distinction of race. In this way their contribution was complementary to the ties of marriage, fosterage and trade which bound the major families together. In the early sixteenth century the Geraldine faction was forging a tenuous political unity throughout Ireland, and it is to the circumstances of this phenomenon that we now turn.

The Kildares and their Critics, 1500–20

A T the aptly named Knockdoe (literally, 'hill of the axes'), eight miles north-east of Galway city, opposing alliances fought a battle on 19 August 1504. The forces of the king's Lord Deputy, Garret Mór Fitzgerald, eighth Earl of Kildare, met and defeated those led by Ulick Finn, lord of the Burkes of Clanricard, in the heartland of the latter's south Connacht territory. Both sides, comprising 'the greatest power of Irishmen that had been seen together since the [Norman] conquest', and commanded by men descended from Anglo-Norman families (though Burke's had long become gaelicised), contained Gaelic warriors. At the core of the two fighting machines were several battalions of galloglas, participating in the largest set-piece battle fought by these professional axemen down to that date. The hostilities raged on the elevated and fertile land above the meandering Clare river, with Kildare's archers and billmen fending off a fierce onslaught by Burke's galloglas. The Knockdoe affray (which incidentally introduced the handgun to the Irish battlefield) attests the growing militarisation and bellicosity of Irish life in the early sixteenth century, if not a concomitant sophistication and modernity in martial affairs. Kildare's victory on the field of Knockdoe represented the success of his system of collective security throughout the island and also the triumph of his network of dynastic alliances over that of a major challenger. To the citizens of Galway, which welcomed the Lord Deputy's celebrating troops within its walls after the battle, Burke's defeat helped to preserve their newly won and fragile chartered liberties in the face of local magnate aggression. And King Henry VII, Kildare's royal master, acknowledged the battle as a routing of the crown's enemies by investing Garret Mór Fitzgerald as Knight of the Garter in 1505.[1]

Later accounts of the battle of Knockdoe by sixteenth-century Gaelic and Old English writers differ greatly in their emphases, reflecting the divergent political perspectives of their two communities. The Gaelic annalists were impressed enough to describe the confrontation as unparalleled in 'latter times' for the numbers killed, both of *Gaeil* and *Gaill* (i.e. English of Ireland), but they did not regard the conflict as more than another episode in the dynastic struggles of the Burkes and their allies and enemies, despite the range of the participants. The Old English chronicler in the Book of Howth, on the other hand, tended to stress the role of those of English origin on the side of the Earl of Kildare at the expense of their fellow-fighters from the Gaelic lordships. Thus the exploits of Viscount Gormanston, the barons of Delvin, Killeen, Trimlestown, Slane, Howth, Dunsany and Navan, and Darcy, the giant lord of Platten, are magnified, while those of the galloglas and Gaels are diminished. The overall perspective, crystallised at the time of the chronicle's composition in the later sixteenth century under the patronage of the St Lawrence family of Howth and the Plunkets of Dunsoghly, County Dublin, is of the victory of the English of Ireland over the Irish natives.[2]

Certainly the number of Irish lords involved on both sides raised the battle above the level of a routine regional or local skirmish. The pattern of rivalry in the west of Ireland was familiar enough in 1504: Ulick Burke of Clanricard's ambitions threatened the expansion of the O'Kellys of Hy Many (Uí Maine), and when Burke demolished three of his castles in 1504, Melaghlin O'Kelly appealed to the Earl of Kildare for assistance. O'Kelly was allied to the Burkes of Mayo (known as the MacWilliams of Lower (i.e. north) Connacht and the inveterate enemies of their Clanricard namesakes). Ulick Burke's close ally was Turlough O'Brien, lord of Thomond, who rallied to the Clanricard lord's side with his own client, MacNamara of Clancullen. Complementing the Connacht participation at Knockdoe were the lords MacDermott of Moylurg and O'Connor Roe, both at odds with the Clanricard Burkes at this time. The spreading of the war outside the west was due to the Kildare nexus on the one hand, and long-standing Gaelic connections on the other. Hugh Roe O'Donnell, lord of Tyrconnell, fought alongside his Connacht allies, O'Connor Roe and the Lower MacWilliams, but he was also linked to Kildare as foster-father of Garret's son, Henry. The presence of the lords of the O'Kennedys of Ormond and the O'Carrolls of Ely among the ranks of Ulick Burke's army is explained by their being old companions in arms of Turlough O'Brien and Clanricard in a dispute in north Munster. Deployed on the Earl of Kildare's side were the lords of Ulster and the midlands who rendered him allegiance: members of the O'Neill clan of Tyrone, and also of the O'Reillys of east Breifne, the MacMahons of Oriel, the O'Hanlons of south Armagh, the Magennises of Iveagh, the O'Farrells of Annaly and the O'Connors of Offaly.[3]

In the Fitzgerald annals as in later histories, Garret Mór's victory at Knockdoe in 1504 is seen as marking the apogee of his political career, but recent accounts have played down the notion that the earl's triumph displayed his quasi-kingship of Ireland. As a way of governing Ireland, the delegation of full royal power to the aristocratic Kildare house was tested for an unbroken quarter of a century down to 1519, and an analysis of the nature of the Geraldine regime and the contemporary reactions to it form the essence of this chapter. An examination of the Earl of Kildare's position, straddling as it did the cultural and political divisions in Ireland, and drawing support from Old English and Gaelic Irish while maintaining the English king's trust, may show to what extent it was adaptable, modernising and durable. For Garret Mór and his son, who was, at sixteen, blooded at Knockdoe, the formula of consolidating gubernatorial prestige through diplomacy and good lordship, underpinned by military force, was to be relatively successful down to 1520. While the English monarchy showed but fitful signs of innovative thinking towards the Irish lordship, the Old English gentry and mercantile elites, fully represented at the battle in Clanricard's country, were to be among the most articulate proponents of political and social reform. Their later antipathy to Gaelic lords was not so evident in the opening years of the century, as they evolved their political ideology of Englishness in an Irish setting. The involvement of contingents of townsmen from Dublin and Drogheda is a reminder that the earl's campaign of 1504 was largely devoted to the liberation of Galway and nearby Athenry from the threat of magnate oppression, and municipal aspirations were certainly well reflected in the political debates of the ensuing period. While most of the Gaelic Irish participants on both sides were impelled by the traditional dynastic responses so well established in previous decades and even centuries, Knockdoe demonstrates that ethnic divisions were not ingrained, and that co-operation with political factions was a matter of expediency based on local and regional considerations. Military developments among them may have made their society less stable than that of the Old English, but there was no Gaelic ideological barrier to political coexistence under a Geraldine awning. Against the backdrop of factionalism and reform movements in England and on the continent in the second and third decades of the century, this system of political interrelationships was to be severely challenged, and the resultant new configuration brought about a radically changed polity by the later 1530s.[4]

The basis of Kildare family power

Henry VII restored Garret Mór Fitzgerald to the deputyship of Ireland in 1496. The king's 'assured hope and affiance' in the earl was based on an astute assessment of the benefits and risks involved in reverting to indirect rule of Ireland through Kildare. At the very least, as a competent administrator and well-connected local nobleman, the earl could govern the Irish colony at no expense to the English crown. Moreover, the brief experiment of direct rule through Englishmen in the mid-1490s, while proving costly, had established a framework within which Kildare's regime could be constrained. Under the terms of Poynings' Law (1494), Kildare as Lord Deputy could not call parliament or place bills before it without prior authority from Henry. Administrative and fiscal reforms had attempted to impose more control from England over official appointments and also over revenue sources and collection. And Henry had acquired valuable information about the balance of political forces in various parts of Ireland, especially in the Pale, Ulster and the south, and was to maintain direct contacts with some of the principal lords and cities. Reassured by the recognition of his own dynastic legitimacy throughout his realms, including Ireland, Henry could afford to be liberal in his commission to Garret: the deputyship was conferred for ten years initially and thereafter 'during pleasure'; all leading offices of state, except the chancellorship, could be filled by Kildare nominees; king's lands recovered from the Irish could be retained by Kildare in tail male; and all the revenues of Ireland were to be assigned and spent by him without account. In return, the earl was to defend the island against outside invasion and preserve it from rebellious activity within, especially on the part of the Earl of Desmond in Munster.[5]

There was a new bond of mutual esteem between Henry VII and Garret Mór. The peaceful conduct of Anglo-Irish diplomacy down to 1509 was founded on the warm and harmonious relationship between monarch and deputy, and cemented by the marital ties between the Kildare house and English connections of the Tudors. As part of the earl's restoration in 1496, he agreed to marry Elizabeth St John, Henry's first cousin. Garret's heir, Garret Óg, who remained at court in London until 1503, was wedded to Elizabeth Zouche, a more distant relative of the king. The latter marriage was sealed on the occasion of the earl's three-month visit to court in 1503 on foot of a summons from Henry VII. Kildare's cordial reception was facilitated by the regular gifts of goshawks and horses which he had been sending to the king since his restoration as Lord Deputy. Henry continued to reciprocate with royal grants: in 1505 Garret Óg was made Treasurer of Ireland, and in the following year his father the earl received the manors of Carlingford, Greencastle and Mourne, a combined lordship worth £150 per annum which consolidated a tenuous Geraldine holding in Ulster.[6]

There is no doubt about the impact of the charismatic personality of Garret Mór Fitzgerald on his English and Irish contemporaries. Reaching towards the height of his powers as he returned to Ireland in 1496 at forty years of age, he brought to bear upon his official duties his considerable qualities of charm and energy as well as his vast experience of the country. Described as 'open and plain' in his dealings and as possessing the Geraldine irascibility and unpredictability, the eighth earl had nevertheless mellowed by the second phase of his deputyship. Certainly he had the shrewdness to conciliate the leading member of the Butler family in Ireland, Piers Roe, to keep the Earl of Desmond quiet, and to exploit the extreme particularism of the English and Gaelic polities within the island. He was astute enough to temper 'simplicity in peace' with 'valour and policy in war', deploying the full gamut of his aristocratic resources, with the English kings' benediction of his rule. Essentially his was the mode of action of the martial nobleman who regularly mounted punitive expeditions against defiant lords. In the seventeen years of his second spell as deputy down to 1513 he marched his hostings into each of the provinces, going on personal campaigns at least fifteen times. On many occasions the destruction or capture of castles of recalcitrant leaders was the result. Yet Garret Mór was posthumously eulogised as a builder also by his chronicler, Philip Flattisbury: he had caused castles, fortifications, towns and bridges to be raised in many parts, especially on the borders of the Pale.

The 'Great Earl's' complexity of traits as a man of war and peace, of artlessness and guile, and a destroyer and builder, bulked large in contemporary accounts, and the influence of his personality in the forging of a powerful Geraldine ascendancy in early sixteenth-century Ireland cannot be exaggerated.[7]

That Henry VII chose not to 'frown a little with his countenance' when told of the Earl of Kildare's victory at Knockdoe in 1504, but rather to see it as an advancement of the royal interest in Ireland, is significant. Garret Mór's ceremonial installation in the elite Order of the Garter *in absentia* in May 1505 was the seal of the king's approval on his deputy's actions. Having committed himself to devolving full powers to Kildare to defend and expand the English colony in 1496, Henry was prepared to let the Irishman be the best judge of the appropriate methods to be used to gain those ends. In late 1506 he toyed with the idea of 'a voyage personal for the repress of the wild Irish and the reduction of all the land' and asked the advice of his council. The logistical problems and projected expense of bringing the recommended force of 6,000 men, the household, labourers, seamen, artillery and supplies dissuaded the king from such an intervention, and besides, English foreign policy was fully occupied at the time with delicate Burgundian negotiations. While not regarding the Kildare house as indispensable for the governing of his Irish lordship, Henry VII had rejected the alternative of direct rule on the pragmatic grounds of there being 'little advantage or profit' therein and never wavered after 1496 from his strategy of trusting the earl to uphold public order in Ireland. It was because of the all-embracing nature of the Geraldine ascendancy there that Henry VII was prepared to countenance Garret Mór's wide franchise in his approach to the deputyship.[8]

Convergent interests of Tudors and Fitzgeralds in turn gave the Irish dynasty access to a reservoir of patronage, wealth, military force and prestige with which they, with individualistic flair, consolidated their existing power-base. Set at the core of a system of manors in many shires was the county of Kildare, strategically significant as part of the southern Pale. The expansion of the county heartland under Garret Mór and his father benefited both Fitzgeralds and English crown. From being in a vulnerable position in the mid-fifteenth century, the Kildare manors, centred on Maynooth and Leixlip (secured by grant in 1484), had by the early sixteenth been encompassed by an expanding circuit of stoutly fortified acquisitions.

Garret Mór's first marriage to Alice FitzEustace brought a secure jointure of estates in the county on the eastern borders with the Gaelic clan of O'Toole, and expansion in the south-east marches of the Pale was attested by Garret's recovery of Castlekevin and Fassaroe and the building of Powerscourt castle by 1500. Fitzgerald influence advanced southwards into the key artery of the Barrow valley in Carlow. To safeguard his hold over newly recovered Carlow territory, Garret Mór had had all the lands of absentees between Calverstown and Leighlin Bridge vested in him in 1483 as repossessed land of Irish rebels. To the west of the county of Kildare the stronghold of Rathangan had been won back from the O'Connors of Offaly, as well as Moret and Lea (in modern County Laois) castles and manors, while to the north the Berminghams ceded charge of Carbury to the Kildare family, and Portlester in Meath was part of the FitzEustace inheritance. From the coherent system of estates thus created, stretching out from the Maynooth nerve-centre and encompassing many manors and castles, came the bulk of the earldom's landed income of close to £1,000 per annum.[9]

The heads of the house exercised jurisdiction as fully as their counterpart earls in Ireland did as lords of the soil, dispensers of justice, economic arbiters and military leaders, their power in Kildare being buttressed by their liberty jurisdiction which was revived between 1509 and 1514. As king's deputies for the decades spanning the turn of the century, however, the earls had an added incentive for maximising the resources of their patrimony. Thus profits from rents, judicial proceedings and trade flowed into the family treasury, and a vast range of dues in kind or service was exploited. Landholding for the gentlemen of the shire, the tenants-in-chief of the earls, was burdensome owing to their lord's exactions as well as colonial taxes and the duty of rising-out regularly in military array. While agriculture was apparently improved, at least by the ninth earl, and demesne farming carried on, economic advancement was geared not just to Geraldine domestic consumption but also to their national interests. The Kildares' love of hunting is shown by their fostering of horsebreeding on a large scale and also by the breeding of dogs and birds of prey. The failure of the Kildare towns to prosper, despite the reopening of trade routes in the pacified shire and its environs, may have been due to the restrictive force of the county magnate family and the failure of agricultural surpluses for the markets. Some saving to residents of the shire may have accrued from the re-establishment of liberty courts and the general fortifying of the borders, but the main advantages were to the Geraldine family. While the Renaissance artistic style may not have been imported into Kildare until after 1503 with Garret Óg's return from the English court, their households had long borne the hallmarks of substantial wealth. The valuable collection of gold and silver plate, held at Maynooth, Kildare and Portlester castles, had been built up over the generations, and the 'great and rich' furnishings, hangings and utensils at Maynooth, 'one of the richest earl's houses under the crown of England', made handsome plunder for the successful besiegers of 1535.[10]

The impressive military force which the eighth and ninth earls deployed so consistently throughout their careers, for the most part with the English kings' approval, rested on the resources of their earldom as well as of their deputyship. Garret Mór's army in 1504 was made up of private retinues raised by himself and his allies, professional soldiers in his own and others' employ, and the militias of the English shires and the towns, raised in hostings. His own Kildare band would have comprised his household followers and the tenants-in-chief on his manors with their retainers, bound to the earl by military tenure. He had at his disposal at least 120 galloglas and 120 kerne who were maintained by coign and livery principally on Counties Kildare and Carlow, despite the parliamentary ban of 1494. They were billeted on local households which had to feed them, their horses and attendants. From the loyal shires of the Pale and the municipalities of Dublin and Drogheda were recruited temporary militias of billmen and bowmen, mustered under the Lord Deputy's authority and paid for by the community through taxation. A standing army for the colony, set up in the 1470s and 1480s by the seventh and eighth earls, may have lapsed by the early 1500s. The Brotherhood of Arms, also known as the Guild of St George, had consisted of 120 archers, forty spearmen and forty pages under the captaincy of the Lord Deputy. An elite corps of thirteen gentlemen officers was constituted as a military order to conduct the affairs of the Brotherhood. Its establishment attested the chivalric ideals of the Geraldines and their far-reaching powers of patronage and martial control, as all members of the elite corps were close connections of the family. The power of the Kildare deputies as military commanders of the colonial administration was aided by their near-monopoly of artillery in the country which enabled them to take and retain castles at will, and it was effectively symbolised by the sentries guarding Garret Mór's Dublin residence at Thomas Court toting state-of-the-art German muskets.[11]

As with other contemporary aristocratic families, the Fitzgeralds contracted propitious marriage alliances to further their dynastic interests. Whereas the alliances with eminent English families helped to forge the bond of trust between the Tudors and the restored earls after 1496, unions of Geraldine men and women with members of the Anglo-Irish and Gaelic nobilities strengthened considerably the diplomatic nexus which underpinned the Kildare ascendancy in Ireland. Matrimonial links with the leading nobility of the Pale, such as the FitzEustaces of Portlester, the Flemings of Slane, the Plunkets of Dunsany and the Darcys of Platten, were reinforced within the Geraldine system of patronage. Roland FitzEustace, for example, was appointed Treasurer of Ireland and first captain of the Brotherhood of Arms by his father-in-law, the seventh earl, and Sir William Darcy played a large part in two of the eighth earl's most stirring adventures: the coronation of Lambert Simnel and the battle of Knockdoe. Marriage too facilitated one of Garret Mór's greatest diplomatic triumphs: his reconciliation of Kildare Fitzgerald and Butler interests was assisted by the nuptials of Margaret, Garret's daughter, and Piers Roe, the head of the Polestown branch of the Butlers. Plans for another marriage between members of the two great earldoms of Ormond and Kildare—George St Leger and Eleanor Fitzgerald—came to nothing. While the Desmond earls were amenable to Kildare's regime, the only alliance involving their dynastic connection was the one between Sir James Fitzgerald and the daughter of the White Knight, a collateral of the southern Geraldines. The marriage between Ulick Finn Burke of Clanricard and Eustacia Fitzgerald, Garret's daughter, did not prevent the great conflict between Ulick and his father-in-law in 1504. Martial prowess was the key to Kildare success in the complex Gaelic political world, but the pattern of relationships was set by the Geraldine weddings to principal lords. Both the Great Earl's sister and daughter were married to leading members of the Dungannon O'Neills, a factor which had a huge bearing on succession in that lordship in the sixteenth century. The close links established with the Tyrconnell O'Donnells through the fosterage of Henry, Garret Mór's son, by Hugh Roe were further forged by the marriage of Eleanor to Manus O'Donnell as her second husband: she had wedded firstly MacCarthy Reagh, thereby securing for the family an ally in the south. And in the unsettled central region ties with O'Carroll and O'Connor chieftains were designed to confirm the defensive system around the earls' patrimony.[12]

The Earls of Kildare and Gaelic Ireland

The economic, political and military bases of the Fitzgeralds' authority as Lords Deputy were fused in another set of compacts, enveloping twenty-four Gaelic lords of greater and lesser status in a wide arc about the Pale and farther afield. In return for the earls' protection against their rivals, these leaders paid tributes in money or in kind to Kildare. In the north of Connacht and Leinster, MacDermott, O'Rourke and MacRennall, and O'Farrell, MacMahon and O'Reilly were subscribers to the *slánuigheacht* or 'slantyaght' system (see p. 52); in the midlands, MacGeoghegan, O'Connor and O'More; in southern Leinster, O'Toole, O'Byrne and MacMurrough; and in north Munster, O'Dwyer of Kilnamanagh. The latter, for instance, had to supply a nest of goshawks yearly at Lammas, while Brian O'Farrell of Annaly paid a yearly rent, was to support a battalion of Kildare's galloglas for a quarter of a year, and was to attend military hostings at the earl's request. The contributions involved ranged from sums of 4d for every cow and 1s for every quarter of land possessed to twenty cows per annum. Other forms of service were, most importantly, the billeting of battalions of the earls' galloglas and the supplying of set numbers of kerne when needed. Fines were imposed on those who broke the Geraldine protection, ranging from sixty to seventy cows to forfeiture of all of one's land. The ultimate sanction was the punitive raid by the impressive forces of the Kildares. The earls were intricately engaged with the Gaelic political system, becoming involved not only in providing slantyaghts but also intervening in succession disputes, arbitrating in legal quarrels and seizing opportunities for buying up lands held in pledge. Accordingly, they could hope to impose some order on the Gaelic polity in furtherance of their royal commission while advancing their own family interests.[13]

For their part, the Gaelic rulers from the rank of provincial king down were willing to acknowledge the Earl of Kildare's protective role because of their perception of him as overlord. The payment of annual tribute and the billeting of the earl's soldiers were part of a system of 'black rents' in reverse, the consequences of failure to participate being very clearly understood by the chieftains. In decisive ways the Anglo-Norman system of military protection was similar to the increasingly martial administrations of the Gaelic lords, particularly those who had provincial paramountcy. The degenerate vassalage relationships of the Anglo-Norman earls, and particularly the Kildares, summed up in the phrase 'bastard feudalism', depended less on the traditional bond of homage between landlord and tenant, and more on a network of retainers, household functionaries and indentured gentry being sustained by offices, pensions and individual service agreements. Similarly by the early sixteenth century the major Gaelic lords had come to assert rights over vassal kings in an innovative and forceful way. They relied more heavily on professional administrators in their households than on hereditary official families. They exploited the system of primogeniture quite successfully in their direct lineage's favour, had been centralising the judicial legal system of brehon law in their courts, and had effected political lordship outside their hereditary territories, bringing under their submission many of the rank of lesser king.[14]

The acceptability of Garret Mór as overlord was vividly manifested in the submission of the principal Gaelic chiefs of Ulster, Leinster and elsewhere on his return as Lord Deputy in 1496, and in his prestige as warlord demonstrated at the Knockdoe hosting in 1504. His status as king's representative in Ireland enhanced the allure of his dominion in a milieu of interlocking Gaelic and English lordships. The resources of the deputyship stiffened the spine of the Leinster Geraldine military clientèle, centred on the earldom and maintained in part by the Gaelic billeting system. The marital network enmeshing major Gaelic lordships reinforced the practical political considerations of chieftains within the direct range of the Earl of Kildare's influence in the midlands and south Ulster. His slantyaght was a *sine qua non* of security, as many in defiance of it found to their cost, such as Morirte and Melaghlin MacGeoghegan, who forfeited half a ploughland to Garret Óg for inflicting injury on Kildare's vassal, Fergal MacQuin. The Kildares were perceived to be fully participant in the Gaelic legal and social system. In fostering Garret Mór's son, Henry, Hugh Roe O'Donnell was according the Fitzgeralds equal aristocratic standing with his own

Tyrconnell clan. The earls intervened in succession disputes in Gaelic lordships in the manner of Gaelic paramount chiefs: Garret Mór's influence over Ulster politics was considerable through the marriage alliances between his house and that of the Dungannon O'Neills, and he disposed of this power in backing the election of his kinsmen, Donnell (1498–1509) and Art Óg O'Neill (1513–19), as O'Neill. The brehon law system was used as appropriate throughout the Geraldine sphere of influence; Garret Mór bought up Gaelic lands held in pledge in the midlands; and he was called upon to arbitrate in disputes between opposing Gaelic lords such as O'Neill and O'Donnell.[15]

Was there more to the Gaelic acceptance of the ascendant Fitzgeralds as overlords than mere recognition of political realities? It used to be held that the Kildare family had achieved quasi-regal status in view of their widespread authority over much of the island. Indeed, one of the eulogies composed by a Gaelic bard on the death of Garret Mór referred to the deceased earl as 'a knight famous in deeds of arms, royal and just in word and judgment'. More recent accounts have stressed that Geraldine power was deployed in the royal interest. Certainly there is little evidence that the eighth earl, for example, aspired to the high kingship of Ireland; the indications are that he saw his role instead as that of aristocratic agent of royal governance. In Gaelic eyes, the position may have been different. The Fitzgeralds had all the trappings of royalty within the Gaelic sphere. They had at their disposal great martial resources of a multi-racial character. Their residences had the éclat of monarchical power, with magnificent furnishings and the symbols of potency. At their courts they fostered members of the Gaelic *aos dana*: bardic poets, historians, annalists, musicians, physicians, genealogists and brehons. In the Annals of Ulster Garret Mór was praised as 'the unique foreigner who was the best and was of most power and fame and estimation'. The stylised nature of the encomia on Garret's death and his being called 'Gearóid Mór' or the 'Great Earl' reflect his status as a major lord of the front rank, but there is no indication that localised and regional concerns in the Irish polity were being set aside in an embracing of Geraldine sovereignty. And yet *de facto*, as Dr Katharine Simms has recently pointed out, the period of Fitzgerald supremacy in the early decades of the sixteenth century sees the culmination of a process of centralisation in Irish politics which 'was aborted before unity was achieved' after 1534.[16]

A striking example of the centrifugal force of local dynastic politics among the Gaelic clans is provided by the O'Brien lords of Thomond (modern County Clare). Their struggle to assert their power in north Munster reached a climax in the confrontation between Turlough Donn O'Brien and Garret Mór in 1510. During the previous fifty years ambitious leaders had, from their geographically and politically secure Thomond base, thrust their overlordship on lesser clans to the east of the Shannon in the borders between Tipperary and Limerick and exacted an annual 'black rent' from the county and city of Limerick. In petitioning for extra troops from England to counter the challenge from O'Brien, Garret Mór described the newly elected Turlough Donn as 'a mortal enemy to all Englishmen and the most maliciously disposed of any that I heard spoke of'. Although the request for soldiers was unsuccessful, O'Brien was defeated at Knockdoe in 1504 in the general routing of the forces of his ally, Ulick Burke of Clanricard. Despite this setback, Turlough Donn raised a monument to his ambition with the building of O'Brien's Bridge over the River Shannon at Portcrusha, north of Limerick city, about 1506. Rightly seeing this as a major threat to his power, lands and influence in the south, the Lord Deputy appealed once again for assistance to Henry VII, who, as has been seen, briefly considered personal intervention. When Garret Mór, with a hosting from the Pale and assistance from Desmond and Hugh Óg O'Donnell of Tyrconnell, came face to face with his rival, Turlough Donn, and his allies outside Limerick in 1510, the result was a significant rebuff for the earl. The decline of the deputy's powers, perhaps already setting in, is usually seen to have been hastened by this defeat at the hands of a doughty regional lord, and the signs of an era ending are magnified by the new style of monarchy then beginning in England.[17]

Kildare's apogee and the rise of Old English reformers

The deaths of both partners to the reconciliation of 1496 within four years of each other, in 1509 and 1513, left their heirs to find a *modus vivendi*. Henry VIII was content to retain Garret Mór as Lord Deputy, accepting the earl's apologies for not obeying a summons to the court and renewing his patent of office. When Garret died aged about fifty-seven while characteristically prosecuting a

military campaign—this one in the midlands in the late summer of
1513—his son, Garret Óg, took his place as governor with the minimum of upheaval. From then until 1519, with a short break of four
months in 1515, the ninth earl held his position with as much
authority as his father had exercised. In fact after that brief hiatus,
coinciding with a questioning of Garret's conduct in office, the rapprochement effected boosted the deputy's position to a new fulness
of delegated power. Garret Óg's new commission entitled him to
appoint to the thitherto reserved offices of Chancellor and Chief
Justice. In 1512–13 Henry VIII appointed the Englishmen John
Kite, William Rokeby, Hugh Inge and John Rawson to important
secular and ecclesiastical posts and membership of the Irish council,
but there was no departure from established traditions. Continuity
was the keynote of the approach of Henry and his chief minister,
Cardinal Thomas Wolsey, to the lordship of Ireland during these
years. The king was prepared to trust his childhood acquaintance,
Garret Óg, to maintain order and to prosecute his enemies with the
same methods as had been applied in the time of both their fathers.[18]

The twenty-six-year-old Kildare was already experienced as
courtier, administrator and soldier by the time of his appointment
to the deputyship in 1513. Described as 'wise, deep, far-reaching
and well spoken', the new earl was better versed in the social graces
and cultural fashions of the time than was his father. His ten-year
sojourn at the early Tudor Renaissance court had ensured that his
aristocratic influence would be channelled more fully into his
service to the state. In his domestic life he was a devoted husband
successively to Elizabeth Zouche and Elizabeth Grey, a concerned
father, a connoisseur of valuable objects, a patron of sculpture, an
exemplary pious layman, a generous host and a bibliophile. During
his earldom the Kildare estates were augmented and well managed,
agricultural improvements being attributed to his interest. From his
appointment as Treasurer of Ireland by Henry VII in 1504 onwards,
Garret Óg showed himself to be efficient in his administration, and
in his policy towards the policital communities in Ireland he was
diplomatically able and 'politic without treachery'. In spite of his
successful governance and impressive aristocratic influence, Garret's
career, when examined from the perspective of the disaster which
befell his house after 1534, has been seen as having had a quality of
incipient decline, even from its early stages. The chronicler who
posited the 'Great Earl's' apogee as 'corsy [prelusive] to the adverse

part' of the family history was the originator of that view of inevitable fall. Yet although Garret Óg did make errors of judgment and manifested inflexibility in the face of political change, the later vulnerability of his position was due not so much to personal defects as to the combination of growing factionalism and an articulate reform movement in both England and Ireland.[19]

The earl's trip to England in 1515 to discuss questions relating to his father's estate proved to be an occasion for the public airing of complaints about his management of the affairs of the Irish lordship. Spearheaded by Sir William Darcy, the analysis of the political ills of Ireland before the English Privy Council in 1515 gave a fillip to the phenomenon of reform-mindedness among Old English gentry and patricians. Darcy, who had been replaced as Under-Treasurer the previous year by the Lord Deputy and dismissed from Kildare's private council, was apparently joined by some of the other members of the Irish council who travelled to England in that year. The substance of Sir William's memorandum on the 'decay of Ireland' was that a combination of magnate aggrandisement and royal neglect had led to a major diminution of the colonial area of the lordship, and that the remaining four loyal shires of the Pale would be lost to English control unless reform were undertaken. As current upholder of the Kildare tradition of governing in the king's name, Garret Óg was the object of severe censure in Darcy's critique. Not only was he implicated in assuming full fiscal, military and judicial powers from the crown within his own earldom (as were the rulers of the Ormond and Desmond earldoms in theirs), but he was also seen as threatening to absorb the Pale shires within his Geraldine liberty. Kildare's main faults in this respect lay in his militarising of the area and its boundaries through imposing coign and livery, his deciding to make war without the Irish council's consent, and his countenancing of a tendency towards gaelicisation on the part of the colonial lords and gentry.[20]

Sir William Darcy, the 'father of the movement for political reformation in Ireland', was one of a number of commentators of similar background who attempted to diagnose the country's ills and suggest remedies in the decades down to the mid-century. Of gentry or urban patrician rank, and usually with legal and official experience, the reformers from the Pale and other English areas of Ireland wished above all for social and economic security in their own environments. Conditions for prosperous agriculture and commerce were being hampered by the pursuit of dynastic ambitions by the great aristocrats. There was a long history of gravamina from the prosperous freeholders and town corporations directed to the English court in the later medieval period, but the corpus of petitionary material of the early sixteenth century was more thoughtful, better ordered and more exactly directed towards a receptive audience in London. There was also a convenient whipping-boy: the Geraldine deputyship. The favoured framework within which the arresting of decline would take place was the colonial zone affirmed a century and a half previously by the Statutes of Kilkenny. The equilibrium thereby established had allowed colonial identity to mature, and crown relationships with the Gaelic Irish lordships to be regulated. In the intervening time, however, the feudal magnates had upset the balance by building up their own armed retinues and overlording the Irish chiefs through the use of Gaelic practices such as coign and livery and the exaction of slantyaghts. As a consequence, tenants on baronial estates were levied arbitrarily to the detriment of agricultural production and the normal marketing of towns. Merchants were also forced by the magnates to pay heavy tolls on trade in their jurisdictions. The adoption or condoning of Gaelic succession, inheritance and legal customs by the Anglo-Norman lords, as well as linguistic and cultural modes, was insidiously undermining English civility, even in the heartland of the old colonial area, and compounding the problems caused by socioeconomic malaise.[21]

Prescriptions for remedying of ills initially fell short of advocacy of a full conquest of the island, though the account by Giraldus Cambrensis of the subjection of Ireland in the later twelfth century enjoyed currency among the Old English in the sixteenth. In concentrating their attention on the anglicised regions, the reformers could draw considerable comfort from the revival of English administration throughout the colonial zone in the half-century since 1470. Under the auspices of the Kildares as governors, the physical borders of the colony had been extended, and the judicial and fiscal regimes of the Dublin government were to a greater or lesser degree effective even in parts of the remoter colonial territories such as Kerry and in the outlying cities of Galway and Limerick. Also gentry and urban communities in Desmond, Ormond and Ulster, not to mention the Pale, were available as supporters of civil and ecclesiastical order in the counties, given conditions of stability.

The centralising of government and the assertion of crown control could only continue, however, through the curtailing of magnates' power in their liberties, and especially the phasing out of armed retinues. Normal patterns of communal defence based on feudal hostings would lead to a demilitarisation of colonial society and make way for social and economic reforms. The desiderata of royal constables in border castles and more chartered boroughs would foster settled agriculture and trade in a reciprocating economy of manor and town. And an acknowledgment of the rights of tenure of the Gaelic lords in the 'natural frontiers' of the colony—south Leinster and the midlands—would be a prelude to their conversion into civil landlords holding their lands and titles as an English feudal nobility.[22]

Through their links with the English universities at Oxford and Cambridge and the Inns of Court in London, it is likely that members of the gentry in the Pale came into contact with Christian humanism. This was the fusion of the new learning of the Italian Renaissance and the scriptural and patristic studies of northern European centres. The central concern of the northern scholars such as Erasmus was the reform of the church and the body politic through the application of models drawn from pristine Christianity. In their writings the Christian humanists exhorted clerical and lay leaders to advance the religious, political and social state of their subjects by fostering education, pursuing peaceful rather than bellicose policies, extirpating social injustices, and facilitating a revival of true piety. The Old English reformers came to embrace most of this agenda in their treatises down to the 1540s. Erasmian humanism would certainly have stimulated the commonwealth thinking which gave a new dimension to the reform literature. Infusing their tracts with a moral force, the gentry and merchants of English Ireland opened out their thinking to embrace the reform of the whole of the island's population. The entire system of military oppression which underpinned the wielding of political power among both Gaelic and Anglo-Norman lords weighed down upon the 'poor commons' of the country, causing them social and economic distress. From their developing perspective, the reformers advanced the notion of a general reformation of the island's polities, based on the abolition of private military levies and the evolution of a tenurial and political system which would accommodate the Gaelic lords within the constitution.[23]

On this early occasion of the voicing of criticisms, most of the arguments missed their target. Not only did Henry VIII by his actions in 1515–16 underwrite Garret Óg's deputyship, but he also enhanced the Kildare family lordship. As governor, Kildare's new commission was as large as Sir Edward Poynings's was in 1494, and the licence to hold parliament was based on the acceptability of the measures proposed by Garret Óg. Among those which duly went through in 1516 was the confirmation of the liberty jurisdiction in the home county of Kildare. The earl received royal grants and charters, and also a licence to found a collegiate church at his principal base of Maynooth. There is accordingly no evidence of any diminution of confidence in the earl on the part of the English king and his chief minister, Cardinal Wolsey, and yet within four years the foundations of his ascendancy began to become a little shaky. Before examining the reasons for this, and in the light of the perspectives of Gaelic and Anglo-Irish political leaders, it may be helpful to assess the image of aristocratic power which the Kildare family were creating in order to see to what extent the Leinster Geraldines were adaptable and open to modern influences, or to what extent they were bound by the dynastic traditions of their house and resistant to change.[24]

Reference has been made to aspects of the portrait of Garret Óg presented by the chronicler Richard Stanihurst, who wrote forty years after the earl's death. Chief among the qualities celebrated were his statecraft, piety, resourcefulness, husbandly devotion and hospitality. Composed at a time of nostalgia among the Old English for the era of aristocratic devolution of power from London, Stanihurst's character-sketch no doubt magnified the traits in Garret Óg which fitted him for the highest standing among his fellows. The construction of a vibrant image of noble honour, underpinning the right to rule, was well under way, however, by the end of Kildare's career. Philip Flattisbury of Johnstown, Naas, in County Kildare, the ninth earl's chronicler, compiled a history of the family at his request and was also associated with the conservation of Geraldine records such as the Red Book of Kildare and the earl's rental of 1518. Both Stanihurst and his mentor, Edmund Campion, drew on Flattisbury's annals for their histories. Perhaps Flattisbury was also involved in the correspondence initiated under the eighth earl with the Gherardini family in Florence. Addressed by Garret Mór in his letter to them as 'our beloved brethren', he received in return their fraternal greetings, to which he responded with a résumé of the achievements of the 'many branches' of the Geraldines in Ireland, including the Desmond family. Summing up their success, Garret Mór asserted that 'our house has increased beyond measure, in a multitude of barons, knights and noble persons, holding many possessions, and having under their command many persons'. He asked for details of the origin and spread of the Gherardini on the continent. There is evident in the patronage of Flattisbury the preservation of family lore and the quest for roots motivated by that historical self-consciousness which marked the development of Renaissance culture in Europe in the fifteenth and sixteenth centuries.[25]

Kildare dynastic éclat which facilitated the accumulation of substantial power was deliberately cultivated by the Fitzgeralds, father and son. In attempting to expand the Brotherhood of Arms into a military order for the rewarding of loyal followers, Garret Mór was applying chivalric martial traditions to the advancement of his house, in a way that was similar to the practice of the contemporary Burgundian and Spanish rulers. Garret Óg's foundation of the collegiate church at Maynooth in 1516, while part of a pattern of Geraldine ecclesiastical patronage, may be seen as preliminary to the establishment of a university institution under Fitzgerald auspices, in the manner of some of the German princes. While the college seemed to have been organised along the lines of a traditional chantry in its twenty years of existence, there can be little doubt about the ninth earl's pretensions to learning and control over the church within his jurisdiction. The six resident clergy of St Mary's, Maynooth, were called fellows of the college, and the master had quasi-academic authority. The younger Fitzgerald added many printed volumes to the library of Maynooth castle which reveal an interest in the work of Italian scholars such as Lorenzo Valla and in the early stages of the Reformation controversies in England. Garret Óg had witnessed court ceremonial in England, at the funeral of Prince Arthur, for example, and had acquired highly fashionable and gorgeous clothes in London. No doubt the rituals of aristocratic pomp were transposed to the Kildare residences and state offices on his return to Ireland. If indeed he did attend at the Field of the Cloth of Gold in France in 1521, then Garret was present at one of the most extravagant pageants of the century and was presumably appropriately apparelled. The highly ornate council board which is inscribed with his name and the date, 1533, gives a hint of the artistic style which was favoured in the period. And there was at least one portrait of the earl in existence after his death—the one which his widow, Elizabeth Grey, was accustomed to kissing every night before sleeping.[26]

Behind the cult of aristocracy thus strengthened, however, there are signs of a real consciousness on the part of the Geraldines of the realities of contemporary political and economic trends, and of a capacity for change. Garret Óg recognised explicitly in 1525 that all of his power rested on the favour of the English monarch: if he did other than serve the king 'before all the princes in the world', 'it should be the destruction of me and my sequel for ever'. That there was an option to royal service had been acknowledged forty years previously by his father when Garret Mór threatened that he and his clientèle 'would become Irish every of them' if they were forced to submit to a repugnant bond. Clearly, then, the line of demarcation between 'becoming Irish' and relating very closely to the Gaelic world while at the same time serving as king's deputy was one with which the Kildares were comfortable. Within that broad scope of activity which they had allotted themselves, the heads of the family could effect innovations. The consolidation of a baronial council, attested by the references to the dismissals of Sir William Darcy and Robert Cowley in 1515, mirrors the growth of state conciliar power in England and Ireland. However noisome the impact of the earls' billeting policy was on their subjects, the deployment of a professional army, in the king's name, added greatly to their hegemony. His own patrimony provided Garret Óg with a profitable base, aided by the efficient style of estate management, as evidenced in the 1518 rental, and the improvement of agriculture and demesne farming on the estates. Borough development was fostered with the charters for Athy and Kildare and the walling of towns in Kildare and elsewhere, and the ninth earl manifested his interest in the commercial activity of the Ulster ports over which he was granted rights. Control over the episcopacy of Kildare may have eluded him in the 1520s and 1530s, but Garret Óg exercised influence over many ecclesiastical benefices within the diocese through advowsons and rights of appointment. And there is testimony to the earl's respect for, and according of equality to, his wife, Elizabeth, whom, for example, when he bought a suit of apparel for himself, he would suit with the 'same stuff'.[27]

While the efforts of the Old English reformers to interest Henry VIII in overhauling his Irish administration proved unavailing down to 1519, the king's attention was drawn to the dispute concerning the title to the earldom of Ormond around this time. The growth of factionalism between the great magnate families and their followers in Ireland, and among their respective English courtly backers, which accompanied this legal wrangling, served to destabilise the politics of the lordship which had been held in equilibrium under the Kildare ascendancy since 1496. And although at no time before 1534 was there a serious doubt about the continuing power of the Geraldine party, its nemesis emerged in the form of the rival dynastic force of the Butlers led by Sir Piers of Polestown. On the death of Thomas, the English-based seventh earl of Ormond, in 1515, succession to his title and Irish possessions was claimed by Sir Piers, his deputy in Ireland. The latter asserted that he was the heir male by descent from the brother of the fourth earl, whose male line had become extinct. The English claimants to the earldom who were backed by Henry VIII were two heiresses, Margaret Boleyn and Anne St Leger, daughters of the seventh earl. When Garret Óg supported the claim of Sir Piers to the title of Earl of Ormond and to the Irish estates of the earldom, he was ordered by the king to have the case heard before the Irish council. The matter was suspended until a resolution occurred in 1526, with Piers retaining the possessions in Ireland and calling himself Earl of Ormond. Despite the Earl of Kildare's upholding of Sir Piers's case and his fostering of amity between Butlers and Fitzgeralds through the marriage of his sister, Margaret, to Sir Piers, the 'old grudge' between the families was revived and the two men became enemies. Butler became a focus for anti-Kildare feeling for a decade and a half, and a conduit for complaints about Garret's conduct to the English court.[28]

When in January 1519 Henry VIII once again summoned the Earl of Kildare to London to discuss aspects of his administration of Ireland, the king was entering a phase of active rule on many fronts, at home and abroad. He had already evinced a personal interest in the well-being of the southern towns of Cork and Waterford, and in the Earl of Shrewsbury's liberty of Wexford. Now he requested the Lord Deputy's presence in order that he answer complaints, probably about his failure to stop the Earl of Desmond's negotiations with England's continental rivals. Henry posited the overall aim in consultation with his council 'to devise how Ireland may be reduced and restored to good order and obedience'. Whether this meant removing Kildare from office in the medium to longer term is doubtful, but certainly Garret Óg had to relinquish his commission (albeit to his uncle, Maurice Fitzgerald — as vice-deputy) before his departure for England in September 1519. Either because of the damaging rift between the earl and Cardinal Wolsey (who was said to have 'hated Kildare's blood'), or because of the general tenor of the complaints against his regime, Henry decided to remove the deputyship from a Kildare for the first time in over twenty years and confer it on a leading English nobleman and experienced soldier, Thomas Howard, Earl of Surrey, and later Duke of Norfolk.[29]

Kildare Power and Tudor
Intervention, 1520–35

WHEN the king's new Irish governor, Thomas Howard, Earl of Surrey, rode through the gates of Dublin at the head of his retinue towards the castle on 23 May 1520, the citizens must have gasped at the sight. Accustomed as they were to displays of Geraldine pomp, they could not but have been impressed by Surrey's force of several hundred soldiers, including 220 newly liveried guardsmen drawn from Henry's household. In an age when the image of princely power was being cultivated by European rulers, here was proof of the Tudor monarch's authority being displayed ceremonially at the heart of his Irish lordship. The governor to replace the Earl of Kildare had been carefully chosen by Henry himself, who admired the young nobleman's martial talents and statecraft. To add prestige to his tenure, Surrey was dignified with the most honorific title of Lord Lieutenant (usually applied to an honorary office-holder of royal birth) rather than that of Lord Deputy. Henry VIII was determined that through his agency Ireland would be 'reduced and restored to good order and obedience'. Surrey's own impressions on that day, by contrast, would have been disheartening. The castle into which he rode was so dilapidated that he was forced to base himself elsewhere. The city of Dublin and its hinterland were being ravaged by plague. And, worst of all, his new Under-Treasurer and fellow-Englishman, Sir John Stile, was soon reporting that the revenues of the lordship had been completely appropriated by Kildare.[1]

Even in his absence the Geraldine spectre haunted the councils of the newcomers and the territories of the natives, whether supporters or opponents. So why did King Henry VIII risk jeopardising the patchwork of stability which his astute father had allowed the eighth Earl of Kildare to fabricate in Ireland, and which he himself had presided over for ten years? No doubt the gravamina of the Anglo-Irish population concerning Garret Óg's abuses of power weighed with a king who was beginning to assert his own ruling personality, and some of these at least were presented in the form of schemes for reform of the existing colony and the extension of jurisdiction beyond it. Compounding this agenda of accusation may have been the Butler party's grievances, which would have centred on the threat from the Earl of Desmond's intrigues with continental powers. In his domestic and foreign policies, Henry was, in consultation with Wolsey, giving expression to reforming zeal, perhaps under the influence of Christian humanists at his court. He planned that the Old English should reaffirm their allegiance, that the king's peace and taxes should be restored over the island, and that the church should be unified and anglicised under Wolsey's legatine authority. By dispatching the Earl of Surrey to Ireland in 1520, moreover, the king was hoping to cut a dash as a ruler, and to emulate his princely rivals, Charles V and Francis I. Although conquests, let alone mere intervention, in Ireland were not likely to rate as particularly glorious, there was always the possibility that a successful expedition would result in more revenues for more prestigious deeds elsewhere, as well as in the acquisition of a secure western bailiwick.[2]

That the attempt in this chapter to chart a pattern in the events from 1520 to 1535 is fraught with difficulty attests the breakdown of the stability in gubernatorial office-holding which had held for almost a quarter of a century. In contrast to the virtual Kildare monopoly of office down to 1519, there were to be a dozen changes in the governorship down to 1535. Even when out of office, however, the Kildare family continued to dominate through their clientèle and allies, and there was nothing inevitable about their total demise as a political force by the end of the period under review. Although the Surrey expedition may have laid down a marker for future English policy in Ireland, the gulf revealed between aspiration and achievement left the government in a weakened position, and local and dynastic rivalries in all parts of the island were unaffected by the brief experiment. Factional dispute between the Fitzgeralds and Butlers did intensify during the 1520s, however, compounded by the latter family's festering grievance over their claim to the Ormond inheritance. This, as well as Desmond quixotism, tended to influence the politics of the Old English gentry and the Gaelic Irish lords and was reflected to some extent at the English court of Henry VIII. Thus was guaranteed a supervisory approach to the Irish lordship on the part of the king and his minister, Wolsey, even if the contending aristocrats there were kept mainly on a loose rein down to 1530. With the growing isolation of England after the royal divorce and the break with Rome, a reassertion of control at least over the Irish church was envisaged, and this coincided with the raising of general reform thinking to a new plane, and with the formulation of more pointed Anglo-Irish projects and a clear-sighted minister, Thomas Cromwell, in a position to absorb them after 1532. Pressure came on both the Kildares and the Butlers to separate out their private magnate interests from their official state responsibilities within an increasingly bureaucratic framework of government staffed by royal functionaries. Unlike their great rivals to the south, the Kildare Geraldines resisted vigorously, and with the revolt of Thomas, Lord Offaly, in 1534–5, the royal fire was turned relentlessly on the Kildares, shattering their nationwide system of hegemony, with major reverberations for Irish and English alike.

The Surrey expedition and its significance

During the summer and autumn of 1520 the Earl of Surrey's military campaigns to the north, midlands and south were quite successful. Conn Bacach O'Neill made a treaty with the Lord Lieutenant, as did the Tyrconnell chief, Manus O'Donnell. The O'Mores were pacified, albeit only temporarily, while in Munster the Earl of Desmond showed an interest in coming to terms with the crown and his Butler neighbours, and Cormac Óg MacCarthy of Muskerry and Donal MacCarthy Reagh both submitted readily. It was quickly evident, however, that the English yeomen of the guard were unsuited to fighting in Irish conditions, and Surrey was forced to replace most of them with fresh troops from England and locally recruited cavalry and kerne. His army of some 550 proved to be much more costly for the crown to maintain than had been envisaged. Henry VIII was requested to send an additional £4,000 to pay the wages of officials and soldiers. Logistical problems in marshalling and remunerating forces, the apparent economic weakness of the Pale heartland, the unreliability of sources of revenue, and the limited gains to be made by diplomacy—all served to underscore the difficulty which Surrey faced in bringing efficient royal government to Ireland. Despite his use of Kildare's tactics of inter-spersing force with negotiation, the personal presence of Garret Óg himself was missed by Geraldine supporters such as O'Carroll and O'Connor, who were suspected of subverting the lieutenant's efforts to procure peace in Leinster, apparently with Kildare's encouragement from London. Backing for Surrey's activities, however, was forthcoming from the leading resident magnate, Sir Piers Roe Butler, Earl of Ormond, and official gentry such as Sir William Darcy, Sir Patrick Finglas (newly appointed Baron of the Exchequer) and Sir Patrick Bermingham (long-time Chief Justice of the King's Bench). With the aid of this supportive coterie, the councillors of English birth in Dublin, and his army, Surrey may have felt after four months in Ireland that, the defects in the state apparatus notwithstanding, he had the basis for the successful attainment of Henry VIII's objectives for his Irish lordship.[3]

Although he expressed his appreciation of this early progress in a famous letter to his Lord Lieutenant in late 1520, the king revealed therein his larger thoughts about the ultimate aim of royal policy. Judging the submissions of the Gaelic chiefs obtained to that point to be mere show, achieving the 'appearance only of obeisance', Henry outlined a grandiose plan for the extension of his jurisdiction over the whole island by treating the Gaelic people as full subjects within the lordship, rather than associating them with it externally through temporary treaties. In creating a new paradigm based on the recalling of rebels to allegiance rather than on the vanquishing of enemies, the king was hoping not only to cut expenditure but also to establish 'peace, amity and concord' through conciliation. To achieve this, he suggested that the lieutenant use 'sober ways, politic drifts and amiable persuasions, founded in law and reason, [rather] than rigorous dealing, comminations or any other enforcement by strength or violence'. While reserving his 'absolute power' as 'their sovereign lord and prince' who was 'above the laws', he was prepared to make strategic compromises in two key areas to gain the Gaelic lords' 'congruence': their observance of the law, and their holding of lands recovered from the Anglo-Norman conquerors. As long as they were prepared to recognise 'some reasonable law', Henry would countenance a mixture of approved Gaelic and modified English laws. In regard to lands, the king was willing to relinquish all territories possessed by the Gaelic lords except those to which the crown had title by escheat or forfeiture. The ideal of constitutional consensus aspiring to the concept of a unitary state and an end to conquest by force in

Ireland became official policy after 1541, but in 1520 Henry VIII paid little attention to the practical problems of meshing the English and Gaelic legal and landholding systems, or to the longer-term implications of his shadowy blueprint for a unified common-wealth.[4]

Having been encouraged by the king to order these matters on the basis of his experience of the country, Surrey gave vent to his growing disillusionment in December 1520 by writing that 'this land will never be brought to due obeisance, but only with compulsion and conquest'. Six months later he gave his professional assessment of what was needed for a subjugation of the island. While not overtly opposed to the policy of the recognition of the crown's sovereignty throughout the island, the Lord Lieutenant disagreed with the proposed means of conciliation followed by assimilation. Instead he suggested a forceful conquest, either with 2,500 men for a piecemeal progress through the Gaelic territories or with 6,000 for a more speedy result. Even with the larger number, Surrey estimated that the subjection of the entire land would take at least ten years and probably much longer. To consolidate the territorial gains, a network of castles and towns would have to be established. Thereafter he envisaged a scheme of widespread colonisation of the conquered areas with English settlers because, unlike his royal master, he believed the natives to be irremediably lacking in civility and because of the low population density. Already on record as doubting the usefulness of his mission, Surrey probably hoped that the projected costs of his plans would lead to their outright rejection and to his own recall to England. It was clear to him that Henry was backing away from his own elaborate design, unwilling to commit himself in the early part of 1521 to 'the great puissance of men, the great cost of money and the long continuance of time' which would be involved in its fulfilment.[5]

Why, given the high hopes for its success in May 1520, did Surrey's lieutenancy lead to his disenchantment and official discharge within a year and a half? Certainly the inauspicious physical conditions which he met with on arrival affected his family and retainers, some deaths occurring among his household and he himself complaining of being a victim of the 'disease of the country' by Christmas 1520. While bad socio-economic conditions may not have dented his martial resolution, the implications for his administration were serious. Henry VIII expected Surrey's governance of the lordship to become completely financed from Irish revenues after the initial outlay of £10,000 from England in 1520. The Under-Treasurer, Sir John Stile, however, found that, even with the most stringent retrenchment, only about £750 Irish could be raised from Irish exchequer receipts. Disappointingly for Surrey, the Old English community, which welcomed royal intervention in principle, proved unwilling through its parliamentary representatives to fund the lieutenant's amplified military establishment. At the assembly convened in June 1521 its M.P.s refused to grant a subsidy and rejected two money bills designed to increase revenue. Frustrated in his efforts to obtain support for an independent standing army, Surrey was forced to fall back on the coign and livery system in the Pale shires. His initial gains as soldier and diplomat were eroded in a welter of intrigues and inter-family factionalism, which even led him to petition for the return of the Earl of Kildare. Added urgency was lent to this plea when it became apparent in early 1521 that a Scottish invasion under the Earl of Argyll to join with dissident Irish nobles was likely. To answer his request for 800 extra troops to defend the island, Henry VIII sent a diplomat, Sir John Peachey, whose visit in the spring of 1521, while overtly to convey an emollient message, tacitly signified the shelving of Henry's far-reaching proposals of the previous year. Surrey was asked to consider alternatives to further funding from England, was told to concentrate on defending the Pale, and was informed that the king's priorities were the pursuit of honour in continental diplomacy, the defence of the northern English borders against the Scots, and the aiding of his lieutenant in Ireland, in that order.[6]

About to play a notable role as military commander in other 'higher enterprises', particularly in an invasion of France in 1522, the Earl of Surrey got his longed-for recall from Ireland, first for consultations in January of that year, and finally, after a brief sojourn in Dublin to wind up his administration, in the following March. The delay in his departure was to prevent the disheartening of Surrey's local gentry supporters, who believed that in his eighteen months of office he had laid a solid base for political and social reform. His removal confirmed, these Pale officials were nevertheless inspirited by the evidence of the king's interest in his Irish lordship, and were given the confidence to continue their representations on the subject of reform to the English court, where Surrey (from 1524 the Duke of Norfolk) became an influential adviser on Irish matters. In fact the main achievements of Surrey's mission were the acquisition of more detailed knowledge of the island's vexed politics, the deployment of English soldiers in many parts thitherto untraversed by such bands, and a first-hand awareness of the socio-political decay of much of the old colony. It was possibly as a response to the latter problem that the lieutenant had steered through parliament an act to prevent the export of wool and flocks in an effort to stimulate native industry. And more generally, while a full-blown project for the extension of royal sovereignty throughout the island by the enfranchisement of the Gaelic Irish was not to be attempted for another twenty years, there had appeared no insuper-able barrier to the forging of new relations with them and the repairing of old ones with the feudal magnates.[7]

The rotating governorship in the 1520s: Fitzgerald and Butler in balance

The fairly intensive debate over who should succeed Surrey as chief governor was informed by the new awareness at King Henry's court of the practical realities of the lordship's politics. The main difficulty faced by Surrey was his lack of the means and the skill to wield the local and regional polities into a national equilibrium. He himself had realised how pivotal a role the Earl of Kildare played in this process and had requested Garret Óg's dispatch to Ireland in late 1520. The king refused to countenance such a course of action in 1521 or 1522, even after Kildare had been restored to favour at court, chiefly by means of his marriage to Elizabeth Grey, which cemented his connection to the prestigious faction led by the Marquis of Dorset. Counterbalancing the attractions of a financially self-sufficient, revived Geraldine governorship were Henry's regal pride in his original judgment when replacing Kildare, his perception of Garret Óg as being himself a cause of factional dispute with the Butlers, and his commitments given to various individuals in Ireland that Kildare would not be restored. And yet it was inevitable that Kildare would have to be involved in some way. Although not immediately interested in an activist Irish policy after 1522, the king was concerned enough now to exercise close supervision of his Irish administrators in the decade to the early 1530s, starving them of resources yet demanding results in the light of his fresh information. Rather than be seen to be backtracking, Henry opted to appoint as Lord Deputy Sir Piers Roe Butler, unrecognised by him as Earl of Ormond, who had been acting as deputy lieutenant to Surrey since late December 1521.[8]

Ormond's swearing-in on 26 March 1522 inaugurated another of the brief governorships which marked this period. The king tried to curb the deputy's patronage rights by reserving to himself the appointment of the eight principal state officials, while not restricting unduly the new governor's functions, especially his peace-keeping role in a post which the Kildares as fellow resident magnates had made their own before 1519. While comparisons with the Leinster Geraldines were bound to be made, Piers Roe had his own impressive credentials for office-holding at the highest level. As a very substantial landowner, principally in Counties Kilkenny and Tipperary, with his seat at Kilkenny castle, he rivalled Garret Óg in his ability to deploy vast human and material assets in the exercise of his jurisdiction. And Henry VIII threw Piers back on his resources as magnate by not granting him any funds over and above the meagre Irish revenues. Piers's own achievement in welding together the Butler estates and pacifying the various branches of his family was imposing. A shrewd practitioner of Gaelic Irish and Anglo-Norman politics in Munster and elsewhere, a sophisticated courtier and a patron of economic, social and cultural advancement in his lands, Piers won the respect and admiration of many in England and Ireland, including the king and the Earl of Surrey. Grooming James, his apt son and heir, for lordship, he almost achieved a major coup when a marriage was proposed between the younger Butler and a daughter of Sir Thomas Boleyn, fellow-claimant to the Ormond inheritance. This plan would have consolidated Piers as holder of the earldom, the key to his security, especially *vis-à-vis* Kildare. For his power base, while conferring great advantages, had significant handicaps. In a report to Surrey in 1522 he confirmed the fears of many regarding an Ormond deputyship. Because his presence was sorely needed in his own southerly territories, Butler admitted that he was unable to defend the Pale, particularly from attacks by the Gaelic Irish whom Kildare had formerly constrained successfully.[9]

On 1 January 1523 Garret Óg, the Earl of Kildare, accompanied by his new wife, arrived back in Ireland after an absence of almost three and a half years. Restored to royal favour, he was now looked to by Wolsey and Henry to pacify his own bailiwick of Kildare and, in concert with Ormond, to defend the interests of the colonists. The unresolved feud between the two noblemen was stoked, however, by Ormond's assumption of the position which Kildare had come to regard as a family perquisite and by Kildare's refusal to back Butler's claim to the Ormond title. Quarrelling between the earls and their allies gave rise to complaint and counter-complaint to the English court from mid-1523, with the countesses, Lady Ormond and Lady Kildare, as partisans on their husbands' behalfs. Kildare, acting as if he himself were deputy, led an army of his retainers into Ulster without consulting Ormond. There he attacked the O'Neills of Clandeboye, some Scots and also Carrickfergus, ostensibly in defence of his lands in the old earldom of Ulster. In turn, Ormond, it was alleged, had seized some castles within Kildare's sphere of influence. In an effort to settle 'all grudges, strifes, demands and debates' between the two which threatened to destabilise the whole lordship, an arbitration council concluded an agreement whereby Kildare would be paid £100 per annum as captain of the Pale shires, the Earl of Ormond would be entitled to take official coign and livery rights within the liberty of Kildare, while Kildare himself could exact unofficial dues from his tenants, and each surrendered to the other enemies to be judged by them. This settlement soon collapsed, however, when Robert Talbot, sheriff of County Dublin and avowed antagonist of the Geraldines, was murdered by Kildare's brother, James, as he travelled on the road to Kilkenny to spend Christmas of 1523 with Ormond.[10]

The malevolence of the vendetta prompted action from the English court in early 1524. Both factions had their champions before Wolsey and Henry VIII: James Butler forcefully pleaded his father's case, while the Marquis of Dorset, who was extremely 'wrought' on his son-in-law's behalf, had as an ally the Earl of Surrey, a convert to the Geraldine cause. To Cardinal Wolsey in particular, faced with unrest in various parts of the Tudor dominions at that time, the proper response seemed to be the assertion of firmer control over the remoter regions. Accordingly, he sent three leading commissioners from England—Dr James Denton, Dean of Lichfield, Sir Ralph Egerton, a knight of Cheshire, and Sir Anthony Fitzherbert, a justice of the common pleas—to arbitrate in the earls' dispute, to reform the government in the Pale, and to arrange a transfer of power from Ormond to Kildare if it were justified. On arrival, they quickly won pledges from forty leading landlords of the Pale and its marches not to maintain more men as retainers than were permitted by the deputy, and then only for the times and rates laid down, to aid the king's officials and to keep the king's law. The differences between Kildare and Ormond were to be resolved by an elaborate composition, regulating their retaining of no more soldiers than were necessary for the defence of the country. After the reconciliation Kildare was declared Lord Deputy on 4 August 1524, with Ormond to serve as Treasurer. The commissioners departed in September, bringing with them James Fitzgerald, who was paraded in London with a noose around his neck before being pardoned.[11]

After almost five years Garret Óg was back in the office to which he felt he had a quasi-proprietorial claim. The indenture of his appointment addressed the key issue of limiting his rights to levy dues within the Pale for his armies, and it also bound him to rule with his council's advice, to allow crown officials and courts to operate independently, and to end his bickering with Ormond, Sir William Darcy, Lord Delvin and others. While the nomination of the Geraldine sympathiser John Barnewall, Lord Trimblestown, as Under-Treasurer in September 1524 may have jarred with Lord Treasurer Ormond and his supporters, Garret Óg appears to have worked amicably enough with the English and native-born members of the Irish council for some time. The office-holding gentry would have been grateful at least for the strong presence at hand of the Earl of Kildare to curtail raids on the Pale shires, thus allowing the functions of the administration to be carried on routinely. It was in this capacity of controller of the political and military responses of a large number of Gaelic lords in the midlands and elsewhere that Kildare's principal asset as deputy was seen to lie. No clearer symbol of his status in the Gaelic polity could be adduced than Conn Bacach O'Neill's bearing of the sword of state before Garret Óg as he left Christ Church in Dublin after his restoration as governor. And Kildare associated both O'Neill and Manus O'Donnell with his regime by summoning them to afforced council meetings in Dublin. When agreements broke down with other chiefs, Kildare resumed the customary tactic of leading military forays, marching into Munster in 1524, for example, and into Connacht in 1526. A relatively new element in his relations with the Gaelic lords was his orchestration of attacks on his rival, the Earl of Ormond, and his enduring of reciprocal Ormond-inspired onslaughts, once the feud was rekindled in 1525.[12]

In contrast with the hegemony which he exercised in Ireland down to 1519, Garret Óg now found that his position there was increasingly superintended from England as relations between the three resident earls became more vexed. As planned in August 1524, Piers Roe had consolidated his Kilkenny county base, but hopes that he could police the actions of James Fitzgerald, Earl of Desmond, proved to be ill-founded. In concert with the O'Briens of Thomond, Desmond raided the Tipperary estates of Ormond and exploited disaffection among the junior branches of the Butlers. In turn, Ormond allied with a Desmond dissident, Sir John Fitzgerald, uncle of the earl, as well as Cormac Óg MacCarthy, lord of Muskerry, but he was under severe pressure from Geraldine alliances on two fronts, owing to Kildare's insistent raiding to the north. As part of his contribution to the 'informations of new treasons, passing to and fro' Kilkenny, Kildare and London, Ormond linked the two Geraldine earls in a serious conspiracy. Desmond's intrigues with the French king, Francis I, at the height of Anglo-French hostilities had resulted in a treaty signed on 20 June 1523 at Askeaton castle, County Limerick, whereby the earl, acting as a sovereign prince, agreed to support the French candidate for the English throne, the Yorkist Richard de la Pole. Although the plot finally collapsed with de la Pole's death in the French defeat at Pavia in Italy in 1525, Desmond was to continue his continental intrigues, and Ormond accused Kildare of deliberately failing to arrest him. Garret Óg vigorously denied the charge, but it is not surprising that he may have been reluctant to campaign against his Munster ally. In August 1526 Henry VIII decided to summon Ormond and Kildare to London in an attempt to get them to work together to forestall Desmond's plotting. Ormond complied first, departing in September 1526, secure in the knowledge that his son, James, was ensconced as acting lord of Ormond, while Kildare travelled from Ireland three months later, having left his brother, Sir Thomas of Leixlip, as his vice-deputy.[13]

The removal of the Earl of Kildare's physical presence from Ireland for another three and a half years down to 1530, coupled with Piers Roe's absence for part of that time, led to intensified disorder in the Pale and its marches, in Ormond and in many other lordships. Sir Thomas Fitzgerald attempted to deploy the resources of the Kildare earldom to defend the loyal shires in 1526–7 in his brother's name, but he was replaced as vice-deputy in September

1527 by Richard Nugent, the Baron of Delvin in the west of Meath, a member of the Butler faction. As no supplies of money or troops were sent from England to support his government and the Irish revenues were insignificant, Delvin was forced to supplement his own small retinue from the Pale borders by imposing or attempting to impose heavy military dues on the Pale counties and the Ormond territories for the purpose of maintaining order. Lacking the requisite status beyond his native Meath gentry for effective ruling, Delvin was unable to keep O'Neill and O'Connor Faly pacified. Spurred on by Garret Óg's partisans, including Sir Thomas of Leixlip, and apparently through the intrigue of the earl's daughter, Alice, Brian O'Connor of Offaly, Kildare's son-in-law, kidnapped Lord Delvin at a castle belonging to Sir William Darcy on 12 May 1528 and demanded his unpaid 'black rent' and the return of Kildare to Ireland. The administration, thrown into disarray by the abduction of the vice-deputy, succumbed to Geraldine pressure, at least to the extent of appointing Sir Thomas Fitzgerald 'general captain for these parts', the Pale being 'destitute of good captains'. While the return of Piers Roe Butler with his new title of Earl of Ossory to take over as Lord Deputy in August 1528 helped to restore a modicum of stability at least in the southern half of the country, Delvin languished in captivity for some months, pending the negotiation of an agreement concerning O'Connor's 'black rent'.[14]

As his great adversary earl showed his wonted gift for timely compromise to retain royal favour, what of Kildare at court in the months and years after December 1526? Certainly there is no evidence of flexibility in the account of his confrontation with Cardinal Wolsey which Geraldine sources preserved for later circulation. The debate as conveyed therein reveals the earl's perception of his role in Irish affairs and the view which the king's chief minister was purported to have of it in the later 1520s. The nub of the case against Kildare on his summons to London was the 'wilful hoodwink' alleged to have been perpetrated by him in not apprehending his 'lewd kinsman', the Earl of Desmond, on foot of his treasonable dealings. The cardinal, in a style reminiscent of an accuser at Henry VII's court in 1496, used the occasion sardonically to refer to the earl as 'the king of Kildare' at whose 'courtesy' were the 'hearts and hands, lives and lands' of all in Ireland. Self-depreciatingly proclaiming his lack of 'schooltricks' in debate, the earl nevertheless proceeded skilfully to deride the charges on the basis of lack of evidence, before answering the broader complaint:

> Little know you, my lord, how necessary it is, not only for the governor, but also for every noble man in Ireland to hamper his uncivil neighbours at discretion, wherein if they waited for process of law, and had not those lives and lands you speak of within their reach, they might hap to lose their own lives and lands without law.

Contrasting Wolsey's comfortable exercise of power in England with his own disturbed jurisdiction in Ireland, Garret Óg chillingly declared that, while the cardinal was 'begraced and belorded, and crouched and kneeled unto', he found 'small grace with our Irish borderers, except I cut them off by the knees'.[15]

In this revealing apologia for the pursuit of private justice within particularist polities Kildare firstly assumed his family's indispensability in the governing of the lordship, a point of view which no doubt justified the stirring up of trouble for administrations which attempted to operate independently of the Geraldines. Secondly, in defending the use of extra-judicial methods to quell disorder, he was answering the critics of the efficacy of dynastic and local politics. The only alternative to a 'new conquest' was to permit the Irish aristocracy, with Kildare at its head, to have a free hand in keeping peace and pursuing malefactors. The arrest of Desmond or the cutting down of Gaelic clansmen were not necessary if the system of private jurisdiction were operating fully, with Kildare's own personal power at its nucleus.[16]

Thus the earl could point to the extremely turbulent state of many parts of Ireland, particularly the Pale marches, during his absence as testimony to the necessity for Geraldine oligarchy to govern Ireland in the name of the crown. There may have been external climatic and epidemic causes of social unrest in the period: a drought in the summer of 1525 followed by a very wet autumn had resulted in a disastrous harvest. Yet the principal source of disorder seems to have been politico-military. The two main communities contributing to the armies of the governors—the Pale shires and the Ormond counties—were inured to yielding substantial aids, dues and services for their local defence, but in times of weak government such as 1527–8 the burdens become intolerable when

s with insufficient private resources ruled. The taxpayers
lony in town and county seemed agreeable to paying
only to a Geraldine administration throughout the period
down to 1536, and despite the clarion-calls for political and social
change from many Old English politicians, there was communal
antipathy to innovative methods of funding reforms. The threat to
the borders from disaffected Gaelic and gaelicised raiders could be
dealt with most effectively by Kildare's policy of 'knee-cutting':
those who broke his 'slantyaght' or bond of security were prosecuted
relentlessly by the Geraldine bands. Complaints from the towns,
excluding the major port cities, centred not so much on magnate
control as on disorder in the hinterlands which endangered merchants going about their business: banditry, extortion, weiring of
rivers and forestalling of markets were features of life in the vicinities
of towns in the southern and midland parts of the country, associated with restless junior branches of major families. The overriding
impression one gets is that in the later 1520s the various social
groups had, by and large, accustomed themselves to the aristocratic
system of rule, preferably with a Geraldine headship, and the introduction of any alternative mode would be fraught with extreme
dangers.[17]

While Kildare was detained in London in the Duke of Norfolk's
custody, Piers Butler was appointed Lord Deputy in his stead on 4
August 1528. A reluctant nominee, he was in part being rewarded
for his acquiescence in the settlement of the long-running dispute
with the heirs general over the Ormond inheritance. Earlier that
year the king had granted Sir Thomas Boleyn, who with his
daughters, Mary and Anne, was high in Henry's favour, the title of
Earl of Ormond and had settled upon him the earldom's lands in
Ireland to the east of the River Barrow. Piers accepted the title of
Earl of Ossory and a thirty-year lease of the residual properties.
His losses in terms of land and prestige were balanced by the
security of a settled lordship, a regulation of the friction with his
Leinster arch-rival, and the testimony of the king's gratitude in the
form of the Irish deputyship. Courtiers had canvassed options such
as the appointment of James Butler, Piers's son, as Lord Justice to
an absentee Lord Deputy Kildare or, alternatively, the return of
Garret himself. But Henry VIII refused to be bullied into a position
in which it would seem that 'his grace could not be served there,
but only by him'. Ossory spent some time in his Munster lordship,

which was disturbed by the vigorous attacks of the Earl of Desmond, and eventually came to Dublin to be sworn in on 4 October, leaving James to battle against Desmond and his supporters. As predicted, the new deputy found it very difficult to defend the Pale shires, resorting to bribery to gain support from some Gaelic chiefs in the midlands and only managing to secure Lord Delvin's release after five months of negotiation. By the spring of 1529 Ossory was anxious to return to the south to consolidate his lands, complaining of the pro-Geraldine complexion of the Irish council and appealing for resources from England to establish order in the Pale marches. Eventually he was released from the deputyship in June, and the opportunity presented itself for a new experiment in Irish government.[18]

A pressing reason for Ossory's wanting to depart southwards was the threatening posture of the Earl of Desmond. Not only had he enlisted the support of disaffected Butlers such as the lord of Dunboyne, but he had also engaged the interest of the Holy Roman Emperor, Charles V, in the possibility of a pact against the English crown. So persuasive did Demond's attractions as potential ally seem that Charles dispatched an envoy, his chaplain, Gonzalo Fernandez, in February 1529 to reconnoitre the Desmond region. Even without the death of the earl on 18 June 1529, his audacious plans would have cautioned the Habsburg envoy against taking the nobleman seriously. In regional politics, the removal of the eleventh earl paved the way for the conciliatory Thomas, the deceased earl's uncle, to take over, and he was already on friendly terms with the leading Butlers. While the crisis in Desmond country thus resolved itself, the danger to which Henry VIII was alerted in July 1529 moved him to send his Master of the Ordnance, Sir William Skeffington, to report on the military situation in the country. At the same time Henry appointed his natural son, the Duke of Richmond, to be Lord Lieutenant, and the governorship was held by a bureaucratic commission of three: the newly arrived Chancellor and Archbishop-elect of Dublin, John Alen, a trusted servant of Wolsey, Lord Treasurer John Rawson and Chief Justice Patrick Bermingham. This Wolseian scheme was in line with what the cardinal had attempted in the north of England and Wales in the mid-1520s, but the members of this 'secret council' did not get more than a paltry sum of money to fund their administrative and defensive duties. Ossory was deputed to rule the Ormond territories, including

Counties Kilkenny and Tipperary, in the king's name; the new Earl
of Desmond co-operated; and Skeffington assessed the defences of
the Pale before departing to report to the king in March 1530. The
working of the bureaucratic triumvirate or 'secret council' was further
impaired by the disgrace by association of Archbishop Alen with
Cardinal Wolsey, who fell from power in the summer of 1529.[19]

At Henry's court in June 1530 the most influential advisers were
the Duke of Norfolk and the Earl of Wiltshire (as Thomas Boleyn
had become), along with the Grey family, and they counselled the
king to appoint Skeffington as Lord Deputy in Ireland and to send
the Earl of Kildare with him as mainstay. The first English com-
moner to hold office since the mid-1490s, Skeffington, who was
provided with 300 soldiers and heavy siege-guns, was funded initially
from England, pending an Irish parliamentary grant. He was instructed to foster amity between the three earls, enlisting their help in
defending colonial areas against the Gaelic clans. Kildare was to
have a key role in pacifying the border chiefs, being permitted to
use the deputy's troops when Skeffington was unavailable. There
was an auspicious start to the partnership in August when on arrival
the deputy and earl were accompanied by the mayor and citizens of
Dublin in solemn procession into the city, 'cheerful countenances'
registering delight at Kildare's return. The practical results were
seen in the first year of Skeffington's tenure. As the arrangements
previously made with Ossory and Desmond held, Skeffington and
Kildare, campaigning jointly and separately, overcame opposition
in the south, west and north of the Pale, subduing the O'Tooles and
O'Mores and gaining the submission of O'Donnell and O'Neill,
though continuing payment of O'Connor's 'black rent'.[20]

Plans began to go awry by the summer of 1531, however.
Skeffington had to cut back his army owing to the heavy costs of
£5,000, in circumstances where billeting caused a 'great fray' between
citizens and soldiers in Dublin. The Lord Deputy, known in
Ireland as 'the gunner' because of his former office, fell out with
Garret Óg, whose supporters used the term disparagingly because
of Skeffington's 'mean birth'. Although Ossory claimed that
Skeffington favoured Kildare, the Irish council believed the opposite
to be the case. It seems that the deputy was rekindling the Butler–
Fitzgerald feud in order to secure his own freedom of action, and
he may have encouraged some of Kildare's kinsmen and erstwhile
Gaelic allies to oppose him. In the parliament of late 1531

Skeffington failed to win support for a bill for reviving the subsidy. An act which was passed revoked the right of the Earls of Kildare to lands of absentees in Kildare, Carlow and west Wicklow. This was to benefit the Earl of Ossory and the Archbishop of Dublin, John Alen, both of whom were hoping to re-establish former settlements in the region, to the detriment of the Earl of Kildare. The kidnapping of M.P.s from the Kilkenny area while on the road between Dublin and the Butler territories attests at least the unsafe conditions for travelling southwards, if not the vengeance of the Kildare party in face of this challenge. By early 1532 it appeared that Skeffington's viceroyalty was terminally marred, with complaints about his stewardship from all sides in Ireland reaching London, and in April Kildare, James Butler, Lord Treasurer Rawson and Patrick Bermingham were summoned there for consultation on the Lord Deputy's governance.[21]

As a result of their evidence presented to the English council, and on the advice of the Dukes of Norfolk and Wiltshire, Henry dismissed Skeffington and reappointed Garret Óg as governor on 5 July 1532, 'thinking it expedient in so fickle a world to have a sure post in Ireland'. Ostensibly it did seem to be a return to the position in 1524. Enjoying majority support on the Irish council, which included the new Chancellor, Archbishop George Cromer of Armagh, a Kildare supporter, Garret Óg had unrestricted use of the Irish revenues and patronage rights over many offices in the administration. His hold over Kildare county, while not quite as secure as formerly, gave him a bastion within the Pale from which he managed his network of relations with the bordering Gaelic and gaelicised clans, and his military capacity was unimpaired. Yet the 'fickle world' of the early 1530s had smoothed the path to statemanship of Thomas Cromwell, chief minister to Henry VIII by January 1533, whose determined actions helped to precipitate the ill-fated revolt of Thomas Fitzgerald. It was his spearheading of the programme for the annulment of Henry VIII's union with Katharine of Aragon and marriage to Anne Boleyn, coupled with the rejection of papal jurisdiction in England, that had brought him to prominence after the failure of Wolsey and Thomas More. By later 1532 he was extremely well briefed on the problems of the Irish lordship and the other regions of Henry's dominions. The Old English critics of magnate rule in Ireland found a ready auditor in Cromwell, and he was to begin a systematic assault on the basis of Geraldine power in

1533. Thus, against a backdrop of far-reaching ecclesiastical and political changes in England, and concerted anti-English diplomacy on the continent, centring on the rejected queen's nephew, Charles V, Garret resumed his wonted supremacy at a time when plans were afoot for its diminution.[22]

Causes and course of the Kildare rebellion

Scores were settled in the first few months of the deputyship. Skeffington, who had been seen to favour Kildare's rivals, was publicly humiliated by the Lord Deputy while taking a muster of the troops and forced to 'dance attendance' on him in his city residence. When he returned to England in late 1532, Skeffington assisted those who were working there and in Ireland for the bridling of Kildare's power. The feud with the Butlers was further intensified, reaching a pitch of malignancy when Piers's son, Thomas, was killed by Geraldine supporters before the end of 1532. Ossory had already begun to address complaints about Garret Óg's behaviour to a receptive Thomas Cromwell, who in the earlier part of 1533 organised his own intelligence network. Two of his chaplains were dispatched to Ireland at that time; Irish merchants trading with Flanders were questioned about Geraldine commercial links with Habsburg regions; and John Alen, cousin of his namesake, the Archbishop of Dublin, travelled to England to report on Irish matters. He was promoted to the office of Master of the Rolls, as well as Clerk of the Council in July 1533. As the Irish council was then regarded as 'partly corrupted with affection' towards Kildare, and 'partly in such dread of him that they will not or dare not do anything that should be unpleasant to him', Cromwell was determined to appoint to the great offices of state independent politicians who had evinced an interest in reforming the Irish polity. One such figure was Patrick Finglas, a pioneering reformer, whom Cromwell wished to appoint as Chief Justice of the King's Bench in the later summer of 1533 in succession to the deceased Bartholomew Dillon. Christopher Delahide, a Butler supporter, was advanced as a judge in the same court. Kildare wrote to Wiltshire at court, urging him to delay any suit for the office of Chief Justice pending the advice of the Irish council and to forestall the appointment of Finglas or Delahide, both 'assured unto the Earl of Ossory'. This and other changes, including minor appointments for Thomas Cusack and Thomas Finglas, were stayed for many months because of Kildare's obstinacy, which in the short term merited a royal reprimand in August 1533. As a response Garret Óg began to transfer the king's ordnance to his own strongholds, ostensibly to defend the borders of the Pale, but really to cause trouble in the event of his being replaced as Lord Deputy.[23]

In September 1533 Henry VIII summoned Garret as well as Piers Butler and others to court, in circumstances in which the Irish council was recommending the selection of an English-born governor. Kildare sent his wife, Elizabeth, instead to plead indisposition on his part. Certainly the very serious thigh wound which the earl sustained from a gunshot in later 1533 while campaigning at Birr castle on behalf of his son-in-law, Fearganainm O'Carroll, greatly debilitated him. When the king rejected the excuse of illness, Kildare continued to delay until early 1534. By then his dismissal had been agreed in England, with Cromwell informing some Gaelic chieftains of the change in personnel in the administration. A proposal to send the Lord Lieutenant, the Duke of Richmond, in person was vetoed by Henry, and the choice fell instead on Sir William Skeffington, who was bound to be unacceptable to Kildare. In contrast with the schemes for government put in place under Skeffington from 1529 to 1532, however, Cromwell's plans in 1534 envisaged the resolute enforcement on the Earls of Ossory and Kildare of the arrangements in mutual harmony and in co-operation with the reshuffled administration. Perhaps the first application of printed instructions to the Irish lordship in the form of the *Ordinances for the government of Ireland* symbolised more clearly than anything Cromwell's determination. Ossory proved to be amenable to the political and ecclesiastical functions proposed, though there was no threat to his own liberty jurisdiction in County Tipperary. By contrast, the Earl of Kildare's 'pretended' liberty in his home county was to be abolished. It was the assurance that he could depute his son, Thomas, in his stead while absent that persuaded the ailing earl, in spite of the evidence of a planned transfer of power, to travel to court some time in the early spring of 1534. The twenty-one-year-old Lord Offaly, installed as vice-deputy in February, was publicly commended to the wisdom of the Irish council by his father, but was to be privately advised by a Geraldine family council during the difficult months that lay ahead.[24]

Kildare's feeble physical condition on arrival for his examination at the English court in early March 1534 convinced observers there that he had not long to live. Among the interested commentators was Eustace Chapuys, the Emperor Charles V's ambassador in London, who was briefing his master on the worsening relations between the Geraldines and Henry VIII with a view to possible future joint actions on the part of enemies of the schismatic king. Although 'manifold enormities' were proven against the earl, he was not imprisoned in the Tower while alternative arrangements for the government of Ireland were being considered, and before his son, Thomas, was safely in London. The evidence of that spring-time of negotiations suggests that Thomas Cromwell was not singling out the power of the aristocratic Kildares for exemplary truncation (except in the matter of their liberty), but that he was instead proposing the reduction of both the Butlers and Fitzgeralds within a more independent government. While Ossory was prepared to accept the conditions in May 1534, Kildare held out against them. Once his supersession was confirmed with the provisional appointment of Skeffington as Lord Deputy at the head of 150 troops, coupled with a summons to London for Lord Thomas, Garret prepared for the defence of the Kildare hegemony in the by now traditional manner. He dispatched several members of his family and retinue back to Ireland to stand by Thomas, and sent a message to his son instructing him to 'play the best or gentlest part' and warning him against trusting the Irish council and against obeying a summons to London. The receipt of that summons from the hands of the Cromwellian agents, Thomas Cusack and Thomas Finglas, in early June, combined with a report from Thomas Cannon, Skeffington's secretary, about the imminent demise of the Geraldine dynasty, convinced Lord Thomas and his advisers, such as James Delahide, that the earl had been defeated politically in London and that the time for action had arrived.[25]

On the fateful day, 11 June 1534, Lord Thomas led a party of 140 silk-jacketed horsemen through Dame's Gate to St Mary's abbey, beside Dublin, where a meeting of the council had been summoned. There, denouncing the king, he yielded up the governor's sword of office to Lord Chancellor Cromer. He then withdrew to the rest of his army at Oxmantown to begin organising 'the knot of all the forces of Ireland' which were 'twisted under his girdle' in protest against the displacement of his kin. Well-prepared for this crisis, Thomas was not the immature and headstrong fop of legend: the 'silken' epithet was a piece of bardic whimsy; his twenty-one years made him older in 1534 than Charles V was, for example, when assuming the ruling of an empire; and he had already had martial experience, albeit less than distinguished, in one of his father's sorties. Under sage Geraldine counsel, Lord Thomas had in the weeks before 11 June solicited support from traditional or sometime Kildare allies, Conor O'Brien of Thomond and the Earl of Desmond in Munster, Conn Bacach O'Neill in Ulster and O'Connor Faly in Leinster, as well as senior members of his own family. Initially at least he deployed his formidable forces with skill if in a dilatory way, aiming to paralyse the apparatus of the lordship, pending a full restoration of the family to power. He received strong backing from government officials in Dublin, both among the minor Geraldine appointees and also among the major reserved office-holders. The Vice-Treasurer, Chancellor and Chief Justice were supporters from the beginning, and even Cromwellian replacements of the latter two were implicated. But how did a 'public relations exercise' orchestrated by the Geraldines grow into full-scale rebellion, posing a serious challenge to the authority of Henry VIII?[26]

In committing Garret Óg Fitzgerald to the Tower on 30 June, the king was raising the stakes, but he was to leave the way open for diplomacy as he monitored the confused reports from his Irish lordship during the summer of 1534. It was obvious, however, that, in the context of England's isolation in European politics in the wake of the divorce and subsequent schism, an armed uprising within the king's dominions was charged with extra significance. Already an agent of Charles V was visiting Dingle in late June to make contact, it was feared, with the Geraldines and the O'Briens as a prelude to an imperial invasion of Ireland. In London Eustace Chapuys continued to canvass the usefulness of Irish disaffection as part of a widespread campaign of defiance of Henry's religious policies to the advantage of the emperor. Reports reaching Spain, France and Rome during the summer of 1534 presented the upheaval in Ireland as a crusade against an excommunicated ruler. Certainly some of Thomas's actions soon after his demonstration suggested a conjunction of political and religious grievances: a proclamation ordered English-born persons out of Ireland, the king was declared a heretic, and oaths of allegiance to Thomas himself, the pope and the emperor were to be demanded. Lord Thomas and his supporters were said to be boasting that they were 'of the pope's sect and band, and him will they serve against the king and all his partakers', and furthermore that they would have the aid of 12,000 Spanish troops. Among the prominent supporters of Lord Thomas from the start were many priests, who seized the opportunity of rebellion to protest against Henry VIII's ecclesiastical policies.[27]

It was hard to square the assassination of the fleeing Archbishop Alen by Thomas's partisans near Artane, County Dublin, on 28 July with a religious cause: the former Chancellor had, however, antagonised not only the Kildares but also many leading Pale gentlemen, including Sir John Burnell for example, by his single-minded attack on lay appropriators of ecclesiastical properties. Although compelled to continue his conciliatory overtures to Lord Thomas for want of resources in the lordship, Henry VIII was convinced after Alen's murder that an aggressive response was needed, and belatedly plans for dispatching Skeffington with a large army were put in train. During August 1534, meanwhile, Lord Thomas and his followers gained control of most of the old colonial zone from Louth to Wexford, and in south Munster, except for Ormond country. He copperfastened Geraldine alliances with many of the most prominent Gaelic Irish chiefs, most notably Conn O'Neill, with whom he parleyed at the head of an army of 2,500. Using intimidatory tactics against his foes, such as burning and seizure of properties, hostage-taking and even sea raids, Thomas arrogated the administration of the Pale from the enfeebled royal officialdom through forfeitures, oath-taking of the gentry and demands for revenues and military service. Efforts at placating the Earl of Ossory and his son having been rebuffed, Thomas was compelled to campaign in Butler territory in company of Gaelic clans, and after capturing Tullow castle and success at Thomastown, he deployed a defensive shield of Gaelic allies, including O'Connors, O'Mores, MacMurroughs and O'Byrnes, to cover the southern approaches to the earldom.[28]

Having become the tenth Earl of Kildare on the death of his father on 2 September 1534, Thomas was now concentrating on the capture of Dublin Castle, the symbol of power over the country. Some of the top anti-Geraldine officials, such as Sir John Alen, Master of the Rolls, had sought refuge there, appealing for aid for city and castle, the loss of which 'were a plain subversion of the whole land'. Dublin, along with its counterpart boroughs of Waterford and Kilkenny, had held out against Fitzgerald's army, but in the wake of the loss of eighty citizens in a skirmish with Burnell and the O'Tooles at Salcock's Wood, near Kilmainham, the city fathers were forced to allow a Geraldine band to besiege the castle (but not before provisioning the garrison with ample food supplies). On being reassured of the king's succour 'with all speed', however, the city authorities revoked their agreement and ejected the besiegers. Kildare now increased the pressure on the city, cutting off water supplies and burning the southern and western suburbs. A foray of some 400 citizens at Newgate avenged the deaths at Salcock's Wood by the killing of 100 Geraldine galloglas and the near-capture of Earl Thomas. In ensuing negotiations with the corporation, Fitzgerald revealed the extent of his demands: as well as practical aids such as money, supplies and armaments from the citizens, he asked for their support at court for his pardoning and for his tenure of the chief governorship of the lordship for life. After several weeks of siege down to mid-October, however, the delaying tactics of the Dubliners were about to pay off, as a large English fleet was observed off the north Dublin coast. Kildare withdrew to check the defences of Maynooth castle and then doubled back eastwards to fortify the coastline of Dublin Bay. The soldiers of Earl Thomas failed to prevent the landing of Sir William Skeffington's 2,300-strong army at Dublin and his triumphant reception by the citizens on 24 October.[29]

Skeffington's assumption of command transformed the military situation in Ireland. It was absolutely clear that the king had decided to regard Earl Thomas not just as a disgruntled demonstrator but as a rebel. To that end, the new Lord Deputy lost no time in having Thomas Fitzgerald proclaimed a traitor at the market cross of Drogheda. Those members of the Pale gentry who had been wavering in their support for the crown were now confirmed as loyalists, though doubts persisted about Henry's ultimate intentions regarding the Kildare house. The deployment of such a large force in the lordship persuaded Thomas himself that a change of tactics was necessary. Pending the arrival of Spanish Habsburg troops, he prepared to make his stand in Kildare and the Pale marches rather than face the English army in the open fields of Fingal. After inflicting significant losses on the Geraldine army in taking Trim castle in mid-November, Skeffington returned to Dublin and wintered there for twelve weeks in very poor health and conscious of serious problems among his forces. Morale and discipline began to disintegrate, and there were accusations of corruption in the expending of funds. Earl Thomas, while making some raids into the inner Pale, was bent on a defensive strategy and lost the opportunity to capitalise on English disorder. On the contrary, Skeffington's cautious policy had attritional results: Thomas's uncles, Richard and James, defected to the deputy's side; key personnel were captured, including Dame Genet Eustace, the earl's foster-mother; and his sea-captains, William Brody and Edward Rookes, and his two lieutenants, John Teeling and Nicholas Wafer, were stricken with grave diseases. By the time full campaigning resumed in the spring of 1535 the earl had lost the initiative and was to face a challenge to his earldom. Using heavy artillery, Skeffington's army invested Maynooth castle, which was defended by a garrison of 100, mostly gunners.[30]

The fall of Maynooth castle on 23 March 1535 proved to be of decisive, psychological significance. Although the fortress was taken after a six-day siege by the treachery of the constable, Skeffington claimed full credit in his self-congratulatory letter to Henry VIII. The forty defenders who survived were executed *in terrorem*, and the deputy proceeded to occupy the castle himself. The way into the heart of the Leinster Geraldines' fastnesses lay open as Thomas fell back to the woods and bogs in the west of his territory. Still hoping for continental assistance, he sent two close aides to Spain to plead again for military aid. But Charles V, having become preoccupied with the security of his Mediterranean dominions, was preparing for his expedition to north Africa in 1535 and had lost interest in the Irish rebellion. Nevertheless, his flirtation with the situation had been important: it had increased Henry's determination to quell the revolt and perhaps caused Thomas to prolong his campaign into the late summer of 1535. By that time, his home county desolate and unsafe for him, the Earl of Ossory stirring up unrest among his Gaelic allies and many of them having submitted to Skeffington, Thomas had taken refuge in the woods and bogs of Allen with his brother-in-law, Brian O'Connor. When the deputy was threatening to pursue them with a force of 1,000 kerne, Thomas Fitzgerald and O'Connor surrendered on 24 August 1535.[31]

The circumstances of Thomas's submission to his uncle-in-law, Lord Leonard Grey, newly arrived in Ireland as marshal of the army, are controversial. In return for surrendering, it was reported, Thomas had been promised that his life would be spared. Henry VIII, while gratified at the apprehension of the ringleader of the rebellion, was unhappy at the conditions. With the advice of his leading courtiers, he determined on the course of exterminating the male members of the Fitzgerald family of Kildare after a suitable interval. Thus when Thomas was ensconced at court in October 1535, he was arrested and imprisoned in the cell in the Tower where his father had died. Subsequently his five uncles, including the two who had assisted Skeffington and another who had been inactive during the revolt, were transferred to England. All six, along with Sir John Burnell, were executed on 3 February 1537 at Tyburn in London. The seventy-five leading figures who were executed included the bulk of the sixty-six who were attainted. Among the Geraldines who survived were several of the women who had helped to foster the Kildare ascendancy, notably Eleanor MacCarthy Reagh, who shielded the nine-year-old half-brother of Thomas, Gerald, from the authorities prior to his being spirited away to the continent. For the large number of gentry of the Pale shires who were implicated in the revolt, however tangentially, pardons were freely available on payment of fines. As King Henry needed the support of their representatives for the passage of his important programme of legislation through the Irish parliament, they were conciliated, but the threat of the restoration of a Kildare ascendancy (with the consequent possibility of reprisals against their foes) was held in reserve until it was deemed appropriate to remove it by the Tyburn executions.[32]

With the destruction of the hegemony of the house of Kildare, whether willed or not, the English monarchy was forced to confront a totally new set of circumstances in its approach to ruling its lordship of Ireland. Whereas the Fitzgeralds had hitherto been an ever-present consideration in the political balance within the island even when removed from gubernatorial office, now their demise left a huge vacuum, in geographical, political and social terms. The collapse of the Kildare earldom and the reversion of its lands to the crown left an avenue of opportunity into the Gaelic midlands; it also was potentially a roadway of ruinous raids from the erstwhile Gaelic clients of the Geraldines. Moreover, Henry had now to countenance the retention of an English garrison in Ireland to replace the shattered retinues of the Kildare earls. The expense involved on a continuing basis, not to speak of the costs of defeating the rebellion, were to cause a radical rethinking of policy. There was to hand, admittedly, a broad new reservoir of confiscated lands, soon to be swollen with monastic and absentees' holdings, but how best to exploit this resource was extremely problematic. Some of the Irish councillors were now arguing for a policy of limited conquest of the Gaelic regions of Leinster, coupled with a resettlement of newly conquered areas, and with this Thomas Cromwell tended to concur. But Henry was veering towards retrenchment in Ireland, based on a vastly reduced army. Aristocratic delegation was out of favour as a mode of governing the lordship, and English-born viceroys were seen as the most acceptable heads of the Dublin administration, within the framework of more bureaucratic, London-controlled rule within a unitary state. But a solid following would be necessary to keep such a system functioning satisfactorily, and the risks of the alienation of the Old English community, especially in the Pale, were real in the aftermath of the traumatic events of 1534–5. The delicate matter of royal ecclesiastical authority had to be broached also. With the death of Skeffington on the last day of his year of triumph, 1535, the task of managing the post-Kildare Irish lordship fell to Lord Leonard Grey, appointed chief governor on 1 January 1536.[33]

Religion and Reformation, 1500–40

FATHER James Humphrey, parish priest of St Audoen's church in the heart of Dublin, was celebrating high mass there on the first Sunday of May 1538. After the gospel, when the time came for the recently approved bidding prayers, Humphrey refused to read them. Included in the new 'form of the beads' was a prayer for King Henry VIII as supreme head of the Irish church. The curate, dutiful to an oath of the king's supremacy rather than to his parson, hurried up into the pulpit and began the prayers. Before he had got very far, however, Humphrey started on the next stage of the liturgy and signalled to the choir to sing, drowning out the curate's words. Some members of the congregation later reported the incident to Archbishop George Browne of Dublin, whose task it was to enforce the king's ecclesiastical authority. As a canon of St Patrick's Cathedral, Humphrey, already noted for his dissidence, was a prominent priest of the diocese. Accordingly, Browne decided to have him arrested and held until the king's will was known, both for his earlier refusal to swear to Henry's headship of the church and because of his public defiance of the archbishop's formula. Instead of becoming a martyr, however, Humphrey was released within a fortnight on the orders of Lord Deputy Leonard Grey, and Browne was left ruefully complaining that 'the simplest holy-water clerk is better esteemed than I am'.[1]

This episode, which took place exactly two years after parliament met to legislate for the royal supremacy in Ireland, sums up effectively the ecclesiastical position during the early decades of the Reformation. The key issue was jurisdiction over the church and not doctrinal innovation. Apart from a period in King Edward VI's brief reign (1547–53), religious belief and practice remained substantially unchanged until 1560. James Humphrey's defiance of the Act of Supremacy of 1536 typified clerical opposition to the abolition of the pope's headship in the dioceses where the measure was promulgated within the English sphere of influence, much of the country remaining unaffected. The parishioners of St Audoen's included some of the wealthiest patrician families in the city, to one of which Humphrey himself belonged. Divided opinions reflected among the clergy at that mass in 1538 were also a feature of the lay worshippers' response to the change in headship, as only 'certain of the parish' presented the matter to Browne. The archbishop's predicament in having his authority overridden accorded with the experience of many of his episcopal contemporaries and successors in the Church of Ireland. While the reforming aims of secular and spiritual leaders might be appointed by royal dictum, disagreement over objectives and methods of fulfilling them militated against the efforts of conscientious administrators. Thus, while it may be seen that reactions to the earlier phase of the royal Reformation among clergy and laity were mixed, there were no martyrs among the dissidents.[2]

With the introduction of the Reformation through the mediacy of the English monarchy in the 1530s Ireland was brought into the mainstream of European events. Though motivated principally by his matrimonial needs, Henry VIII's assertion of control over the church in his dominions was part of a pattern of secular rulers wresting ecclesiastical authority as part of their drive towards the wielding of greater and more unitary powers. In Ireland the substitution of royal for papal ecclesiastical supremacy in 1536 had been signalled for some time, and it was enacted in the context of Henry VIII's assumption of greater political authority over the administration of the Irish lordship in the aftermath of the eclipse of Geraldine power. Indeed, the full realisation of his ecclesiastical claims in the island rested on the advancement of English jurisdiction outside its confines of the mid-1530s. Although there was no coherent religious reform movement in pre-Reformation Ireland, the vigorous native drive for the reanimation of Irish polity and society, touched as it may have been by Christian humanism, certainly encompassed the revival of aspects of religious life. Accordingly, a strong royal unifying force within Irish Christianity would not have been unwelcome to influential members of the political elite of the old colony.[3]

In order firstly to comprehend the nature of the church in Ireland in the early sixteenth century and to assess the need (perceived or otherwise) for its improvement, it is necessary in this chapter to sketch in the background of religion among clergy and laity on the eve of the Reformation. In doing so we have to take into account the socio-political contours of the country which bulked large in the first two chapters of this book and which also helped to shape the ecclesiastical pattern. In detailing secondly the measures taken under Henry VIII to direct Irish ecclesiastical matters from 1536, it should be possible to appraise royal policies in relation to the state of the church as described and to evaluate responses on the part of clergy and laity to the implementation of the early Reformation in the light of our understanding of the realities of church structures and devout practices among Gaelic Irish and Old English communities.[4]

The pre-Reformation church among the English of Ireland

The framework within which pre-Reformation church life in Ireland is normally considered is a divaricate one. The legal separation of the church into English (*inter Anglicos*) and Irish (*inter Hibernicos*) sectors in the fourteenth century was originally for reasons of political control, but by the late fifteenth century the fluid boundaries between Gaelic and English jurisdictions reflected the cultural and social realities on the ground. Ethnic strains showed up occasionally among both secular and regular clergy, as in the case, for example, of the antipathy between Archbishop Richard O'Hedian of Cashel and Bishop John Geese of Lismore and Waterford in the early fifteenth century. But a policy of consensus had evolved, based on patterns of patronage and language in diocese and parish: by and large, English churchmen did not seek access to zones of Gaelic interest and influence, and vice versa. Ten dioceses, mostly in the richer ecclesiastical provinces of Dublin and Cashel, usually had bishops of English background; Gaelic bishops invariably held thirteen sees, mostly in the poorer provinces of Tuam and Ulster; and there were nine other bishoprics which fell to candidates of either race, depending on the powers prevailing locally. In Rome the papal curia, well informed on the state of the Irish church, was sensitive to jurisdictional and pastoral conditions and did not force candidates for benefices of one tradition and speech on areas inhabited by those of the other. A *modus vivendi* developed in many places, particularly in the archdiocese of Armagh, where the archbishop, always an Englishman but respected across the cultural divide as the successor ('coarb') of St Patrick, ruled over the Pale region from his County Louth base, while the deans of Gaelic origin

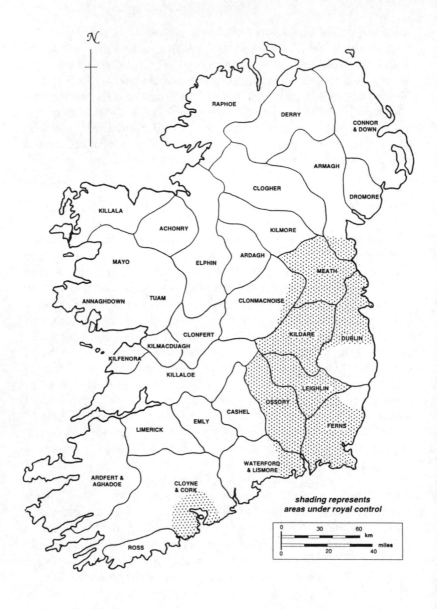

Sixteenth-century Irish dioceses

administered the northerly part *inter Hibernicos* from Armagh. Among the ranks of the clergy a palliation of inter-cultural friction may have been effected through the common assumptions derived from a broad legal training and, for graduates of universities overseas, through the shared experience of being part of an Irish *natio,* a term implying not only common statehood but also the Gaelic notion of *muintearthas.*[5]

In the dioceses in anglicised Ireland the episcopacy failed collectively to provide a dynamic, reforming leadership in the early sixteenth century. Nevertheless, certain individual Irish bishops did attempt the improvement of religious observance among their flocks. The nomination of bishops within the old colonial zone was in the gift of the king, though local preferences were canvassed and the form of election by cathedral chapter was maintained where possible. Those favoured for sees in Anglo-Ireland were usually well-trained English-born canon lawyers and servitors who were expected to double as secular administrators. Thus, for example, six of the eight Lord Chancellors who held office between 1500 and 1536 were bishops either of Meath, Armagh or Dublin. Despite their official state responsibilities and in the face of cultural divisions, the Archbishops of Armagh had a good record as diligent pastors and spiritual supervisors. In the Armagh registers the activities of successive incumbents in the century or so before the Reformation are recorded, and these testify to a regular round of metropolitan and ordinary visitations, even of regions *inter Hibernicos,* and the convening of provincial and diocesan synods prescribing reforms. In early sixteenth-century Kildare the appointment successively of two dedicated bishops, Edmund Lane and Walter Wellesley, helped greatly in the reorganisation of the church there. Lane in particular was noted for his programme of building, his revamping of the chapter of the diocese, and his presiding over the foundation of St Mary's collegiate church at Maynooth in 1518. Wellesley, the prior of the Augustinian friary of Greatconnell, who had gained a reputation as an outstanding theologian, a rare enough accolade among bishops of that era, overcame Geraldine opposition to his preferment to the see of Kildare in 1529 and won approval for his diocesan management.[6]

As elsewhere, the institutional church was closely interlocked with the secular establishment. Families of the socio-political elite from the Kildares down endowed the ecclesiastical sphere and enjoyed a proportion of the profits and patronage arising from its temporal possessions. The crown administration also looked to the church as a source of patronage for clients, a body of expert officials and some financial gain. But down to the late 1520s there was no coherent attempt on the part of church or state to centralise ecclesiastical jurisdiction, revenues and patronage, with consequent loss of privileges and rights. With the appointment of John Alen, commissary-general of Cardinal Wolsey's legatine court, to the archbishopric of Dublin in 1529, however, there began a short-lived attempt to unify church authority within the lordship under his metropolitan see. Although his cardinal-patron fell from power within six months of Alen's arrival in Ireland in February 1529, the new archbishop pressed ahead singlemindedly and brusquely with a programme of reform, using his expert knowledge of common and canon law and mastery of administrative minutiae. Its objectives were to recover and augment sources of diocesan revenue which had been appropriated by lay people over the previous century.[7]

It seems that there was a change in the ultimate aim of Archbishop Alen's programme after Wolsey's dismissal. Instead of asserting the legatine jurisdiction in Ireland, the archbishop's new goal was leadership of the church within the colonial area through the establishment of Dublin as the primatial see, with the *ecclesia inter Hibernicos* being let go its own way under the Archbishop of Armagh. In no sense an early Reformation enshrining royal supremacy, Alen's scheme was in fact undermined by Henry VIII when he fined the archbishop £1,466 13s 4d in 1531 for his attachment to the late cardinal's prelacy. Thus weakened, Archbishop Alen had to face a range of bitter foes in Ireland. These included Archbishop George Cromer of Armagh, appointed Lord Chancellor in 1532 in succession to Alen, the Earl of Kildare, whose rights to several ecclesiastical properties had been called into question and who saw Alen as a political opponent, and many members of the local lay and clerical elites whose privileges the archbishop had undermined. Small wonder, then, that he was a marked man at the outbreak of the Kildare revolt in July 1534, and he paid the price with his life. Even though not an agent of the Reformation, Alen during his brief episcopacy had none the less raised questions about the nature of the church in Ireland and the extension of royal ecclesiastical control within the island which his successor in the see of Dublin had to face head on.[8]

Efforts to recover advowsons (rights to nominate clergy) and endow vicarages in the 1530s were closely linked to the provision of a 'sufficient' ministry in the parishes. Episcopal control over clerical appointments was essential for the maintenance of high standards of pastoral service, yet even in the most anglicised bishoprics the advowsons of more than half of the benefices were in the hands of monastic houses, cathedral chapters and lay individuals and corporations. Rectors, vicars, chaplains and prebendaries might very well be presented on the basis of their spiritual suitability, but inevitably local factors such as family ties arose in most cases. The lack of a university in Ireland for most of the century seriously affected the supply of a highly trained clergy. Although some religious orders ran their own programmes of study for their novices, those aspiring to successful careers in the diocesan church had to go abroad to the English universities, especially Oxford, or to continental academies such as Paris and Louvain. Most of the promising graduates of these colleges gained posts in diocesan administration and would at best provide, as absentee rectors, vicars in their cures to minister to their parishioners. It is not surprising that in many parishes a poorly trained and badly paid lower clergy failed to provide more than a rudimentary administration of the sacraments. Research has shown that up to two-thirds of benefices in the old colonial areas yielded no more than subsistence incomes of £7 10s per annum to clergy, and many even less. Reports of simony (the commercialising of holy offices and services) and pluralism (the holding of two or more benefices) are credible enough in the circumstances. And a poverty-stricken ministry may have attracted few recruits in the early sixteenth century from Old English families, with the possible result that Bishop Edward Staples of Meath, for one, was nominating Gaelic Irish priests to Pale benefices in 1531, in contravention of statutes. None the less, lay testators of all ranks continued to vote confidence in the local clergy by invariably donating great and small sums of money for the edification or repair of their parish churches.[9]

Many of the parishioners in the Pale in the late fifteenth century also left bequests to 'the four orders of the friars' in Dublin, Drogheda and elsewhere. Among the religious orders, in English Ireland no less than in Gaelic Ireland, the mendicants at that time represented the most fragrant bloom among fetid vegetation. In particular the Observant movement among the friars, a return to the pristine values of the orders' founders, was reinvigorating the Franciscans,

Augustinians and Dominicans, and to a lesser extent the Carmelites. While comparatively few of the ninety new houses of friars founded in the country during the previous century were in dioceses of the Englishry, nevertheless several of the long-established communities in the towns became Observant, especially the Franciscans. As a result, these houses, some of which had a mixture of Old English and Gaelic Irish members, formed congregations which were virtually independent of the English provinces of their orders. Besides routine testamentary bequests, Old English respect for the friars was marked by more substantial endowments, such as that for Thomas de Bermingham's chantry chapel in the Dominican church in Athenry about 1502, and by requests for burial in cemeteries of friaries, as, for example, when Richard Boys, an English merchant living in Dublin, asked to be buried with the Friars Preachers there in the early 1470s. That the preaching of the friars was attuned to the needs of urban congregations is shown by the large number of works on practical piety listed in the library catalogue of the Youghal Franciscans in 1523, and the brethren were in contact with rural-dwellers through their questing visits, or alms-seeking missions.[10]

Much less zealous as missionaries or inspiring as Christian exemplars were the longer-established orders of monks and nuns. Nevertheless, the decline in charitable services and in the observance of rules among the monastic communities of Anglo-Ireland was not general. On the eve of the suppression of the monasteries in 1539 the Irish council recommended that six houses should be continued as religious communities because of their educational and social value at least. These were St Mary's and Christ Church in Dublin city, Grace Dieu, a convent girls' school in the north county, Greatconnell in County Kildare, and Kells and Jerpoint in County Kilkenny. In the absence of a full programme of visitations of monasteries prior to dissolution as was carried out in England, the evidence for conventual life is sketchy. Commissioners' findings of monastic abuses in County Tipperary have to be tempered by doubts about the impartiality of jurors, while the absence of serious charges beyond some concubinage and neglect of divine office points up the possibility of exaggerating spiritual malaise. And impressive building works on older monastic sites and new constructions of friaries in the boroughs in the later fifteenth century certainly betokened optimism for the future in the form of continuing endowment of religious institutions.[11]

Such investment in buildings on the eve of the Reformation can be seen, on the other hand, as testimony to the fundamental malaise of the late medieval monastic order: creeping secularisation. Just as the upper orders in lay society maximised coign, or arbitrary taking, including building charges for masons and carpenters, the heads of monastic communities benefited by the system of exactions for access to relatively cheap construction, particularly of defensive buildings. Monastic and secular worlds were very closely meshed, as, especially in the remoter colonial areas, local families supplied the leading members of houses. The property-rich monasteries, described as 'joint-stock enterprises' for lay and ecclesiastical figures, were heavily involved in leaseholding and landlording. Almost one-fifth of the land of County Dublin was owned by religious houses at the dissolution in 1539–40, and many holdings there and elsewhere were leased for long periods at very favourable rents, often to kinsfolk of the superiors. Besides their engagement with the orders through landholding and office-holding, the lay gentry in the Pale and outside were commonly retained by them as stewards and legal agents. Lack of central supervision within dioceses and congregations meant that local monastic houses were free to pursue commercial ends in tandem with magnate families, sometimes with resultant alienation of properties. But while headships of monastic communities were sought after by local nobility and gentry, the evidence suggests that there was a falling-off in new entrants to novitiates. For example, All Hallows monastery in Dublin, a large premises, had five pensionable members at its dissolution, and St Katharine's in Waterford and Athassel, County Tipperary, had four each. Whatever the size of memberships, however, monasteries controlled the patronage to over half of the benefices within the dioceses coterminous with the old colonial areas, and therefore had great control over clerical and material resources.[12]

The entwining of sacred and secular spheres throws into relief the force of lay involvement in the pre-Reformation church. Lay enjoyment of ecclesiastical property and patronage reciprocated spiritually motivated religious endowment. For the laity such benefaction of the church brought profits and prestige, but the edification of self, one's kinsfolk and one's community was a desirable concomitant. Archbishop Alen contended with vested lay interests when seeking to recover Dublin diocesan possessions which had been granted to local gentry for reduced rents by his predecessors.

Alen also attempted through litigation to force gentlemen such as Sir John Burnell and the Baron of Delvin to disgorge advowsons of rectories. Down to the eve of their suppression, monastic communities gave very attractive leases to lay people such as Nicholas Benet, a merchant, who in 1538 got a forty-year lease of the rectory of Palmerstown from St John's priory at Newgate in Dublin. The families of heads of monastic houses may have benefited unconscionably: for instance, Abbot Alexander Devereux of Dunbrody, County Wexford, leased to Stephen Devereux a townland for sixty-one years at a bargain rent of £1 6s 8d in 1522. Gentlemen lawyers of the Pale, such as Sir Patrick Barnewall and Thomas St Lawrence, served as stewards of monastic properties, and many members of the legal profession were on retainers from the religious houses to defend their interests as suppression loomed in the late 1530s. In the south-east in 1540 members of local magnate families held about half of the monastic superiorships, and, while the pattern was less pronounced in the Pale, some religious houses there such as Lismullin nunnery in Meath, and Mellifont and Ardee in Louth were headed by members of local gentry families—the Cusacks, Contons and Dowdalls respectively in those cases. Such quasi-proprietorial ties were almost impossible to break at the time of Reformation without the risk of resentment on the part of the leaders of lay society.[13]

Lay endowment of institutions, diocesan and regular, accustomed men and women to exercising these hereditary rights in relation to the church. In the century before the Reformation the gentry and merchant patriciates of the Pale had been active sponsors of new church-building and the restoration and ornamentation of existing structures. In County Meath, for example, the Plunketts of Dunsany and Killeen in County Meath patronised the building of churches on the two manors close to their castles. In his will of 1463 Sir Christopher Plunkett, the principal benefactor, conferred many valuables, including a chaplet of pearls, on the statue of the Blessed Virgin in the new Dunsany church. His son, Edward, inherited the manor and also the advowson of the rectory of Rathmore, to which he presented two clerics, one of whom was to serve as chantry priest at the altar of the Blessed Virgin. Aristocratic families erected colleges for small groups of priests who served nearby parish churches and chantries. At Howth, for example, the St Lawrence family provided housing for four priests attached to their chantry in St Mary's about 1500; the Fleming and Verdon families built colleges at Slane in 1512 and Ardee before 1487 respectively; and most notably of all, the Fitzgeralds erected the collegiate chapel at Maynooth in 1518. Inside the parish churches impressive funerary monuments enhanced the buildings. Many churches were endowed with chantry chapels, specially funded establishments to support a priest or priests to chant or say mass for the souls of benefactors and their relatives. Among the more important were the Portlester chapel of the Eustace family in St Audoen's parish church, Dublin. In addition, numerous bequests from men and women to their parishes included money and materials for the repair and maintenance of churches, donations for the purchase of sacred objects such as chalices, gifts of jewellery to bedeck favoured shrines, and offerings for the keeping of perpetual lights before hallowed statues.[14]

As well as adding to the beauty of their churches, lay people of all ranks were patrons of priests, supernumerary to diocesan clergy, who were guaranteed an income and sometimes lodgings in return for the saying or chanting of masses for their benefactors. For the wealthy the erection of manorial churches, colleges of secular priests and chantries conferred the privilege of appointing chaplains of their choosing who were independent of diocesan supervision. In County Louth a system of interdependent manors and benefices became institutionalised, as lords of the manor presented vicars and chaplains to chantries, while each new heir to the manor had to receive a renewal of the original grant of feudal possession from the clerical incumbents who were the trustees. For the less affluent there were opportunities for the selection of clergy through the religious and trade guilds. The former were established by royal charter in many Irish towns and some rural areas in the hundred years or so before the Reformation for the spiritual benefit of members and their families. Most were open to the less privileged social orders, although some, such as the Guild of St Anne in St Audoen's parish, Dublin, were patronised by wealthy merchants or gentry. St Anne's, founded in 1430, supported six chaplains to offer masses for deceased benefactors and members from the permitted income of 100 marks per annum (or £66 13s 4d). Each of the chaplains, appointed by the members, served at one of the six side-altars in St Audoen's and they resided in a large residence adjacent to the church. In Naas the Guild of the Blessed Virgin, the Blessed Trinity and St Katharine in St David's church had its priests appointed by the provost and burgesses of the town. Members of the trade and craft guilds in towns such as Dublin and Drogheda also supported priests to serve the chapels. The Trinity Guild of merchants in Dublin, for instance, had its chapel in the cathedral of Holy Trinity to which it nominated its own chaplains to provide spiritual benefits for members and their families.[15]

Besides the endowment of diocesan and regular institutions, and the employment of an independent clerical corps, lay people in Anglo-Ireland cultivated their own pieties, virtually unbridled by official church supervision. Devotion to particular saints was incorporated in the iconography of shrines and tombs with the frequent depiction of family patron saints, such as St Lawrence in the case of the Plunketts of Dunsany. Patronal dedications of chantry chapels and religious guilds were reflected in the celebration of the feast-days with solemn processions, liturgies and banquets. Special festivals such as Corpus Christi, St George's Day and St Stephen's Day were marked by the staging of sequences of mystery or miracle plays in towns such as Kilkenny, dramatising events from the Bible or the lives of the saints. Most famous of all was the Dublin Corpus Christi cycle, organised by the guild of that dedication, in which all of the trade guilds enacted scenes from the scriptures with appropriate casting, such as the fishermen in the guise of the apostles and the butchers as the tormenters of Jesus. Wayside crosses such as those of the Dowdall family in County Louth of the late fifteenth century were extra-church landmarks, as were holy wells such as St Doulagh's, County Dublin, and shrines of popular resort such as that of St Mary at Trim, County Meath. While the gentry and merchant elites may have had prayer-books and other works of holiness, religious shows and rituals, as well as illustrations in churches, conveyed the truths of religion to a predominantly non-literate populace for whom the sacred was comfortably encompassed by the temporal world.[16]

Religion in Gaelic Ireland in the late middle ages

The contours of the political and social world of the Gaelic lordships snugly accommodated the church, making the disentangling of the two spheres almost an impossibility. Certainly the papacy did not try, even though it had much to do with the personnel of the Gaelic church. In fact down to the later sixteenth century the curia, the papal administration at Rome, far from initiating reform, tolerated and even encouraged deviations from the norms of canon law among Irish clergy. During the fifteenth century the curia received an increasingly large number of petitions from Irish churchmen, many of them in person, seeking provision to benefices ranging in importance from bishoprics to vicarages. Because of the slender hold of the English monarchs over much of the country, the limitations which operated in the anglised dioceses in the matter of papal appointments to benefices did not apply. Thus the well-informed curial officials decided on cases brought by 'Rome-runners', not from any profit motive (as Irish benefices were mostly poor) but in pursuit of extending papal power and diplomacy. In general, they were careful to accept the political status quo, occasionally making allowances for shifts in the power balance between the cultural groups, but underpinning this exercise of jurisdiction was an acknowledgment of the position of the King of England as Lord of Ireland. Indeed, the acceptance by the Vatican of the authority of the English cardinal protectors in relation to presentments to Irish episcopal sees in a formal way after 1514 seemed to prefigure an era of closer Anglo-papal co-operation in the reforming of religion in Ireland. The hopes for the systematising of appointments were shattered with the sundering of those relations in the 1530s.[17]

Judged by the standards of episcopates elsewhere in the era before the great reforms, the Gaelic Irish bishops, no less than their Anglo-Irish counterparts, had comparable strengths and weaknesses. They present themselves to us as a corps of men of the world for the most part, caught up in the political and economic strivings of their contemporaries. Some undoubtedly were well fitted to the spiritual guidance of their flocks. Bishop Thomas MacBrady of Kilmore, who died in 1511, was described as 'a luminous lamp that enlightened the laity and clergy by instruction and preaching', and Bishop Nicholas Maguire of Leighlin, who died about 1512, had studied at Oxford, was a noted scholar and preached with 'great learning'. Other Oxford graduates among the episcopate were John O'Hedian and Maurice O'Fihely, while friar-bishops such as the Franciscan Bishop of Derry, Donal O'Fallon, another 'famous preacher', were products of the *studia particularia*, or schools privately run by the orders. In order to function effectively—or indeed to function at all—bishops needed to be accepted by the local secular authority. Some bishops such as William O'Farrell of Ardagh and Richard Barrett of Killala were themselves chiefs of their name and were accordingly involved in dynastic contention in their lordships. Many others belonged to powerful clerical families such as the ecclesiastical branches of the Maguires, O'Gradys and O'Kellys. Reflections of civil strife between kin-groups are seen in the ecclesiastical sphere, as for example in the schismatic rivalry of two men claiming to be Bishop of Kilmore, Thomas MacBrady, already mentioned, and Cormac Magauran, both of whom signed diocesan decrees in the 1490s.[18]

Two aspects of episcopal heredity are revealed in the affinities of these rival Bishops of Kilmore at the turn of the century. Cormac Magauran, son of Bishop Cormac of Ardagh, was born when his father was already a priest. Bishop MacBrady's daughter, Siobhán, married Thomas, son of Cathal Óg MacManus Maguire, Dean of Lough Erne and canon of Armagh and Clogher, who had at least twelve more children. The dean was celebrated as 'a gem of purity and a turtle-dove of chastity' in the Annals of Ulster, which he helped to compile. Before the twelfth-century reform of the church by St Malachy had brought the enforcement of clerical celibacy, hereditary succession to ecclesiastical offices and clerical marriage had been extremely common in Gaelic Ireland. Their flourishing in the late medieval period owed much to the curia's practice of freely granting dispensations to sons of clergy to hold church offices from which they were technically debarred if born after their fathers' entry into major orders. The papacy's policy seems to have been acceptance of clerical marriage, though forbidden by canon law, and the continued predominance of ecclesiastical dynasties upon which they were based. That the practice was culturally acceptable for all levels of Gaelic Irish secular clergy, including that of bishop is attested by the example of Bishop Matthew O'Brien of Kilmacduagh (1503–33), son of Bishop Turlough of Killaloe, who married Ranelt, daughter of Turlough O'Brien, lord of Thomond. Their union produced another Turlough, who later became Bishop of Killaloe in 1554. Among the ecclesiastical families themselves, the forging of mutual alliances mirrored the secular system of shoring up status and power through marriage, with the added attraction that the thriving of traditional interests at local level was a barrier to the intrusion of outsiders who might threaten the status quo. This may have seen as lending stability to the church at diocesan and local level, and also as an acknowledgment of the norms of heredity and succession among the Gaelic clans.[19]

The church with which religious reformers came into contact in Gaelic dioceses in the later sixteenth century was thus distinctive in crucial ways from its Anglo-Irish counterpart. The ecclesiastical organisation of the provinces of Tuam and Armagh centred very much on the coarbs and erenaghs, traditional office-holders in the Gaelic church. These individuals, elected in the normal way to the headship of the clans in which the offices were vested, were a vital link between the hereditary clerical families and the laity who worshipped in the parish churches. In fact they successfully straddled both orders of laity and clergy. Although by 1500 the standing, privileges and duties of the coarbs and erenaghs showed marked regional variations, and though the differences between the functions of the two offices were becoming blurred, each had essential characteristics which conferred coherence and identity on the institution *inter Hibernicos*. The coarbs (*comharba*) as successors of the saintly founders of early medieval monasteries had the greater prestige and learning, although their responsibilities in the sixteenth century lay in the occupying and administering of diocesan and not monastic property. By contrast, the erenaghs, while also farming ecclesiastical lands, were of slightly humbler status, having descended from the *airchinneach*, the superior or administrator of monastic lands, with more emphasis on the stewardship of the properties. Some coarbs and erenaghs proceeded to ordination in major orders, such as, for example, many members of the O'Grady coarb family of Tuamgraney, County Clare, but by the late medieval period it was accepted that even minor orders were not a prerequisite, and certainly marriage was an integral part of their drive to succession within their clans. Being episcopally confirmed as well as hereditary occupiers of diocesan lands, the coarbs and erenaghs had clearly defined duties towards their local bishops. As well as paying taxes and dues to him annually, they were responsible for providing board and lodging for the bishop and his party when he came on his official visitation. Also within the remit of coarbs and erenaghs was the responsibility for maintaining local churches in good repair, and, in some cases, the keeping of houses of hospitality for travellers and pilgrims.[20]

The pastoral care of parishioners in Gaelic Irish areas was rendered extremely difficult because of the disorganisation and poverty of the ecclesiastical infrastructure. Whereas in the east and south of the country the successfully colonised regions evolved a system of small, compact and comparatively well-endowed parishes corresponding to manorial units of settlement, the parishes in the west and north were large and sometimes inchoate. Large expanses of territory in rural parishes might contain several chapels of ease without resident chaplains. Where parochial boundaries were super-imposed upon the older rectorial and vicarial divisions, confusion arose in relation to the appropriation of the tithes. Again there was a contrast with the tithing system *inter Anglicos*, where there was a clear division of the income from the benefice in the proportion of two to one between the rector and the vicar; in the benefices *inter Hibernicos* a three- or four-part division of the tithes was common, with the bishop and possibly the cathedral chapter of the diocese claiming a share. The great rural rectories might encompass many parishes, the incumbents being drawn traditionally from the ecclesiastical families. The norm in a Gaelic benefice was for the rectory to be a sinecure, held by a scholar perhaps, while the cure of souls was carried out by a poorly paid vicar.[21]

Unfavourable views of the pre-Reformation church among the Gaelic Irish, and indeed other communities, have been due chiefly to the shortcomings of the lower clergy, who were the familiar representatives of the church for the bulk of the faithful. In Ireland the problem of poorly trained priests was compounded by the lack of a native university. Those clerical students who travelled abroad for an academic training were usually motivated by ambition for administrative careers rather than zeal for pastoral work in poor parishes. Another feature which was detrimental was the overriding of local bishops' jurisdiction by papal provisions. In their efforts to secure their desired offices, Irish plaintiffs at the Roman curia vigor-ously denounced their rivals, the existing incumbents, presumably painting as damning a picture as possible. One of the recurring charges was that benefice-holders, many of them vicars, had failed to seek ordination to the priesthood, and thus the parishioners were bereft of a pastor to administer the sacraments. Besides the host of dispensations in the papal registers for sons of clerics to hold benefices, many of them in direct succession to their fathers, examples of permissions being granted for the holding of two or more benefices on the part of upwardly mobile young careerists are legion. Where living conditions were very straitened, with sometimes subsistence wage levels or below for the less ambitious or well-connected, the temptation was to seek solace in matrimony. Impoverished clergy found it very difficult to keep their churches in repair and would have alienated parcels of church land to boost their incomes. Some, indeed, were forced to supplement their stipends by engaging in commerce or the professions: Eugene Ó Faoláin, a cleric of Cloyne, was in 1484 trading in salt, iron and other merchandise, as well as teaching in schools of civil law, while Matthew Mulryan, the abbot of Holy Cross, was accused in 1490 of, among other things, engaging in the wine trade, he being one of his own best customers.[22]

The spiritual dynamism of the older religious orders in the Gaelic church had long ago been eroded by the secular trends at work among the diocesan clergy. Many Cistercian houses, for example, suffered the decay of their sheep-raising enterprises in the fourteenth century, as well as the loss of communal spiritual fervour. Although some religious houses in Ulster and Connacht, such as those of Newry and Boyle, for example, retained manorial interests in arable lands, mills and market tolls, by the end of the fifteenth century most were poorer than their counterparts in English districts. Socio-political changes had resulted in debilitating divisions within the Cistercian order, to the extent that in 1498 Abbot Troy of Mellifont asked to be excused from visitation of Irish houses as many of the abbeys were garrisoned by their non-Cistercian and, in some cases, non-priestly heads. Troy also testified to the decline of religious observance: in no houses outside the Pale was the habit of the order worn, and there was a general swing to control by great lay families of the monasteries and their properties. Marriage among the monks led to the abandonment of communal living, with the dispersal of families throughout the hinterlands of houses. Hereditary patterns of abbatial appointments are evident among families such as the MacDavids, who produced heads of Boyle and Mellifont abbeys in the fifteenth century. There was generally a mercenary quality evident in the dealings of lay and clerical families towards the abbeys, with incidences of pluralism, as in the case of Prior Glaisne Magennis in Iveagh, who held three separate priorships in the 1520s, and simoniacal deals such as the transfer by Abbot William O'Dwyer of his abbey of Holy Cross to a layman in 1534. Despite the exemplary asceticism of some anchorites and the splendour of building or reconstruction works, the strong impression one gets of the monastic establishment on the eve of the Reformation is that there was not much left to reform.[23]

Of all the clerical groups among the Gaelic Irish, the mendicant orders encapsulated the spirit of late medieval Christianity and served as a conduit for the expression of popular piety. The status and influence of the friars were commented upon favourably by sixteenth-century observers, their diligence in preaching being especially noted. The emphasis in their activities seems to have been on pastoral work, though they contributed much to the flourishing of literary and artistic fashions in devotional art in the late middle ages. One outstanding feature of that period was the large number of new foundations of friaries, ninety in all between 1400 and 1508, of which sixty-eight were in the provinces of Tuam and Armagh. The friars in these regions were predominantly rural-based, in contrast to their forerunners, who had located themselves principally in towns. While the setting up of networks *inter Hibernicos* offered the benefit of congregations independent of English provincials, the main attraction of the remoter regions for the new and reforming older mendicant communities was the challenge of living out their ideal form of Christianity from modestly endowed houses and relying on alms. This is particularly evident in the appeal of the west and north for new Observant foundations, though the move-ment made rapid headway through converting older communities, especially Franciscan, in the colonial zone down to the 1530s. Through their reforming energy and leadership, the mendicant orders absorbed some of the old ecclesiastical families within their communities, showing thereby their compatibility with the struc-tures of Gaelic society, and they also straddled the politico-cultural divide, accommodating brethren of Old English and Gaelic origin in the many mixed communities in the towns, such as Dublin, Drogheda, Waterford and Trim.[24]

Without the lavish patronage of the Gaelic lords of Ulster and Connacht, it is difficult to envisage such a renaissance of mendican-tism in the country. In 1433 MacCon MacNamara sponsored the first foundation of a Franciscan Observant house at Quin, County Clare, for example, and the famous friary in Donegal town was built in 1474 with the support of Hugh O'Donnell, lord of Tyrconnell, and his wife, Finola O'Brien. These chieftains wished to further their own prestige while winning spiritual benefits for themselves and their families. Hugh and Finola were buried in the cemetery of the friary, as were many of their descendants. One of these, Manus, later chieftain himself, gave expression to the general respect on the part of the Gaelic aristocracy for the friars' teaching when explaining that his rivalry with his father was due to their censures of O'Donnell senior's lifestyle. In patronising the building of friaries, the chieftains of the west and north helped to foster a beautiful architectural style, the 'Irish Gothic', of which Quin is a fine example, as are the friaries of Moyne, County Mayo, and Sligo. Some at least of these newly founded mendicant houses became centres of learning for clerical students. Lectors in theology were to be found in Moyne and Ennis Francisan friaries, and the Dominican order had two important *studia*, or schools of the humanities and arts, at Athenry and Dublin. In the absence of a university in Ireland, such academies fulfilled a valuable function, particularly in the training of canon lawyers. Again it is significant that members of the great hereditary families of learning, some already connected to the church as erenaghs, were members of the mendicant orders, contributing to the great efflorescence of devotional literature in the pre-Reformation Gaelic church. The poet Pilib Bocht Ó hUiginn, who was an Observant friar, was adjudged 'the best and greatest religious poet in these latter times' according to the Annals of Ulster.[25]

It was in the communication of religious faith through a variety of literary genres that the vital interplay between friars and populace took place. The library of the Observant Franciscan friary of Youghal has been mentioned as a repository of works which were primarily practical in their application in pulpit and confessional. Many of the works of piety and edification to be found therein were available elsewhere in translation from Latin into Irish, obviously to meet a demand. The more literary works of religious poetry and prose in the original may have been written essentially for an elite audience or readership, but these could also be adapted for popular sermons. Part of the Bible was translated into Irish in the fifteenth century by Urard Ó Maolchonaire. The influence of the mendicants on the laity may have been felt not only through preaching but also through their questing visits within the territorial limits of their houses. More than just alms-gathering excursions, these had a social and spiritual dimension and would have kept the ideals of the friars before the country folk. And in the phenomenon of the Franciscan Third Order Regular, which spread through the founding of forty houses in the fifteenth century, mostly in Ulster and Connacht, there was a conduit for lay piety among the Gaelic Irish, perhaps similar to the *devotio moderna* of the Brethren of the Common Life in the Netherlands and northern Germany. There did seem to be an educational dimension to this tertiary movement, which attracted some of the diocesan clergy to its foundations.[26]

To judge by the character of the most commonly translated works of devotion in the pre-Reformation period, Gaelic congregations had a taste for emotionally charged hellfire sermons and stirring accounts of the lives of Christ and the saints. In this they were not dissimilar to their European contemporaries, though instead of dramatic renditions of sacred events in the form of mystery plays, oral stories may have had to suffice in areas remote from towns. Nevertheless, some Irish-language folk-prayers, such as the 'Lament of the Three Marys', may have been adapted from the Easter vigil drama of the empty sepulchre enacted in church. The pious exercises of preparation for the sacraments such as penance and extreme unction were served by confessional manuals and similar texts. Popular religious exercises such as pilgrimages, patronal festivals or 'patterns' and endowment of extra-ecclesial shrines characterise late medieval Irish Christianity, though it has been suggested that lay religious fraternities may not have taken root in Gaelic society because the natural strength of kinship ties pre-empted the creation of artificial ones. Lough Derg had a European-wide reputation, as we have seen, but the bulk of the pilgrims to the famous cave must have been Irish. The pilgrims' ways to shrines overseas were well worn, particularly to Santiago de Compostella in northern Spain and to Rome. Holy wells and other places associated with local saints were much frequented throughout the sixteenth century, pre-Christian folk traditions being carried on in some rituals. Lay patronage of religious art was not confined to the churches. Crosses and crucifixes of stone, timber or metal were erected in public roads and private houses, while the iconography of the surrounds of monumental tombs of wealthy families attest their devotion to particular saints.[27]

As elsewhere in pre-Reformation Europe, popular religious practice could easily topple over into excess. Among the most disturbing aspect for later reformers was the cult of the dead, with its stress on non-parochial burials and excessive waking of the deceased. Indeed, the phrase 'to weep Irish' was supposed to have originated in the immoderate lamentations and emotionalism of Irish funerals.

Fasting was a popular form of penitence, and valid when used to mortify one's flesh, but not when used as a form of sanction to punish or to visit harm on one's enemy. In 1530 some clergy of Armagh fasted against Niall Conallach O'Neill, who appealed to the archbishop for the sanction to be lifted, but even a predecessor primate of the fourteenth century had licensed an erenagh family 'by the authority of the bell' to fast against anyone who molested his tenants. Relics and sacramentals were also used as talismans or even shields in battle, as in the case of the *Cathach* of St Colmcille. While the strident millenarianism of communities in other parts of Europe may have been absent, violent undercurrents mixing religion and vengeance surfaced frequently enough in Gaelic Christianity; but such episodes merely serve to underscore the seamlessness of the sacred and secular spheres.[28]

The myriad forms of devotion throughout Ireland bear testimony to the vitality of religious life at all levels of society before the Reformation. Commentators noted that the 'Irish are very attentive to religious matters', and there was little or no sign of anticlericalism in the early decades of the sixteenth century. Many aspects of popular practice may have been in need of direction towards religious truths, but there is no doubt that reform was not needed to foster spirituality among the Irish. A failure of leadership—from the Vatican and London, and at episcopal level within the two ecclesiastical jurisdictions—led to misdirection of devotion. Only the friars were providing inspiration, and they were to be the clerical spearhead of the Counter-Reformation. Certainly civil unrest did not help Christian practice, and the source of socio-political ills was being explored by the native reformers, at least some of whom incorporated the advancement of religion among their aims. Some bishops may have been attempting the reform of their dioceses, but they were impeded by institutional weaknesses. Of all the efforts to improve ecclesiastical administration before the Reformation, Archbishop Alen's were the most determined if not the most diplomatic. Before the schism of the 1530s Henry VIII and Wolsey may very well have been working towards a concordat with the Vatican for the control of the church in England and Ireland. For while the papacy's influence on Irish church matters before 1541 was negative, there was at least a recognition that the Lord of Ireland, by appointment of an earlier pope, was in the best position to institute reforms. The divorce controversy in England

and the Kildare rebellion in Ireland ensured that the path of reform which was actually taken after 1536 was very different to that being charted, however tentatively, before the murder of Archbishop Alen. With the determined imposition of royal supremacy, couched in assertive Anglican terms, the way was open for later doctrinal changes. The quintessential features of late medieval Christianity were not so compatible with either radical evangelical or Tridentine reforms.[29]

The early Reformation under Henry VIII

Although already signalled in instructions issued to Lord Deputy Skeffington in 1534 and in actions by him and the Earl of Ossory in 1535, the supplanting of papal by royal authority over the Irish church did not receive formal public expression until the parliament of 1536–7. In this important assembly the ecclesiastical measures were subsumed within the overall purpose of centring all power in church and state on London. A church of Ireland within the overall Anglican communion of Henry VIII emerged, offering its royal head the challenge of reforming institutions and practice, at least within the areas where his authority was acknowledged. What was the legislative basis for his new role? Although not passed until the final session of parliament in 1537, the 'act against the authority of the Bishop of Rome' affirmed all ecclesiastical laws passed in the previous months by imposing a credenda in the form of a detailed oath for clerical and lay officials, renouncing the pope's authority and accepting the king's. The latter was firmly based on the Act of Supremacy of 1536, which decreed that Henry and his heirs and successors were to be the only supreme heads of the church of the whole of Ireland, *Hibernica ecclesia*. That heritage was appointed by Acts of Succession: the validity of the rights of the children of Henry's marriage to Anne Boleyn was asserted by the first (1536), under pain of treason penalties for opposition, while the second, over a year later, settled the succession on the issue of the most recent royal marriage to Jane Seymour. By the Act of Slander of 1536 a range of penalties, including those for high treason, was laid down for those who spoke publicly against Henry's supremacy or his remarriage after divorcing Katharine of Aragon. Three major acts implemented practically the transfer of power from the papal curia to the royal administration: an Act of Appeals (1536) made the Court of Chancery in Ireland the final ecclesiastical court of appeal instead of the Roman one; an Act of First Fruits (1536) required clergy to pay the first year's income from their benefices to the crown instead of the papacy; and an Act of Faculties (1537) dictated that ecclesiastical dispensations and licences should be issued to clergy by the Primate of Ireland rather than the curia.[30]

A brief résumé of the laws passed in 1536–7 shows the framework within which the Irish church was to operate, but it does not reveal the delays and official frustrations which marked the parliamentary proceedings. In order to understand the community's response to state-sponsored religious changes, we may begin by focusing on the reactions of the representatives to the ecclesiastical bills. The first set of measures, including the Acts of Supremacy, Succession and Slander, passed in the May 1536 session without significant opposition except from the clerical proctors, representatives of the lower diocesan clergy who sat as a separate house. Their recalcitrance led to their permanent expulsion from parliament by an act of a later session, held under the jurisdiction of royal commissioners. The spiritual peers, comprising bishops and abbots in the House of Lords, mounted their own campaign in these later stages against the changed constitutional role of the proctors, who may have been voicing their superiors' objections to the abrogation of papal supremacy.[31]

The commission, headed by Sir Anthony St Leger, had been dispatched by Henry on 31 July 1537 because of resistance on the part of the Lords and Commons to certain government proposals. Among the most contentious was that for the dissolution of eight Irish monasteries, which was fiercely opposed by M.P.s in the House of Commons, led by Sir Patrick Barnewall of Turvey, County Dublin. Arguing that the king's supremacy gave him the power to exercise spiritual jurisdiction over religious houses, the skilful lawyer rejected his authority over the church's temporalities, including monastic property. The atmosphere in the second parliamentary session had been soured not only by the delay in offering a general pardon for complicity in the Kildare rebellion, but also by the proposals for a general tax of a twentieth on income and for resumption by the crown of customs revenues of port towns. Therefore the monasteries bill was taken by the gentry and merchant M.P.s as predatory in intent. Furthermore, many of them held leases of monastic properties, as well as standing retainers for professional services to the monks. The fear was that these perquisites would be lost if a general suppression of the religious houses were to follow the selective closures proposed. Also in doubt was the disposition of the properties on dissolution: many newly arrived Cromwellian favourites seemed well placed to benefit at the expense of long-time residents of the Pale and colony. Therefore economic and political reasons can be adduced for the lay opposition to the monasteries bill. Once the issues were clarified after a delegation headed by Barnewall visited Henry VIII at court in early 1537, the Commons dropped their opposition, and thirteen monasteries were marked down for closure by a bill passed that October. As a *quid pro quo*, the one-twentieth income tax was to apply only to the clergy's income, and the customs proposal was dropped. The commissioners presided over the last session, demanding the co-operation of all members, in the absence of which, Henry had threatened, 'we shall look so upon [the recalcitrant one] with our princely eye as his ingratitude therein shall be little to his comfort'.[32]

The campaign for promoting Henry's headship of the church, as well as the validity of his latest marriage, was slow to begin. This was partly due to the disputes which had delayed the passage of key bills through parliament, and partly to the lack of unity of purpose among state and church officials. Also important was the tendency towards ecclesial inertia brought about by there being no dramatic changes on view at Sunday worship, as 'the ceremonies and decent order used in the church' were not to be affected by the new laws. The new Lord Deputy, Lord Leonard Grey, exacted the Oath of Supremacy from ecclesiastical and civic officials in Limerick and Galway during his military progresses in the south and west, but his overall approach to the Reformation was haphazard, more concerned as he was with peace-keeping than enforcing potentially unpopular changes. Of the native magnates, Lord James Butler, heir to the Earl of Ossory, was committed to extirpating the 'detestable abusions of the papistical sect' in his native Ormond. The two bishops who bore the brunt of popularising the new religious regime in the heart of the Pale, Edward Staples of Meath and George Browne of Dublin, differed fundamentally over the best methods to use. Staples, who, of the two Englishmen, was the more experienced in Irish conditions, favoured reasoning the king's supremacy 'by learning' rather than its maintenance 'only by power'. To that end he proposed that disputation conferences of Irish clergy should be held at Dundalk and Kilkenny. Staples quarrelled publicly with Browne over the latter's evangelical style of preaching, his heavy-handed approach towards the clergy, as seen in the James Humphrey affair for example, and his theological position on salvation, possibly influenced by Lutheranism.[33]

George Browne's appointment to the see of Dublin in 1536 was a reward for his strong support for King Henry's break with Rome and his marriage to Anne Boleyn. The Augustinian friar's rise to become visitor-general of the mendicant orders in England was under Thomas Cromwell's patronage, and as Archbishop of Dublin he was expected to be the principal agent of advancing the Reformation in Ireland. The rigorous means which he adopted to achieve this, while perhaps suitable for England where the secular arm was effective, were inappropriate for the Irish church. Having been rebuked by the king for delaying his work for a full year after his arrival in July 1536, Browne was stung into action. He exacted the Oath of Supremacy from his own diocesan clergy, imposed the new ecclesiastical taxes, and was a member of an expedition of councillors to Ormond at Christmas 1538 to follow up James Butler's efforts to enforce 'good and obedient conformity' there. In his sermons he raised questions of scripture, encouraging the people to read the Bible. In early 1538 the archbishop issued 'the form of the beads', instructions to congregations on what to pray for at Sunday mass, containing both a clear statement of the changed authority within the church of England and Ireland, and a definition of justification which, though rejecting indulgences, was unexceptionable in Catholic terms. Later that year Browne promulgated a version of the 'New Injunctions' which had been recently issued in England. These required the parish clergy to preach the gospel quarterly and discouraged 'superstitious' practices such as pilgrimages and veneration of saints' shrines and relics. Although an English Bible in every parish church was not required as in England, Browne caused English versions of the common prayers such as the Lord's Prayer and Hail Mary to circulate. The 'Injunctions' prepared the way for the campaign against images and shrines in the winter of 1538–9 in which Archbishop Browne was to the fore as a commissioner for suppression. In all, up to fifty shrines were visited in Ormond and the Pale, especially in Dublin and Meath, leading to the closure of some of the most famous, including Our Lady of

Trim, the Baculum Jesu, or staff of St Patrick, in Christ Church, and the Holy Cross of Ballyboggan, County Meath.[34]

Among the resident clergy there were instances of enthusiasm and dissent, but the general reaction of bishops and priests within the Pale, Ormond and the towns where the initial phase of the Henrician Reformation was implemented was nominally conformist to the king's title. Two archbishops and eight bishops took the Oath of Supremacy during the councillors' visit to Munster at the turn of the year 1538, and these, together with the other conforming bishops of the Pale and elsewhere, formed a majority of the episcopacy. While the Primate, Archbishop Cromer, was inactive owing to illness during the early Reformation years, George Browne acquired an episcopal ally in the person of Richard Nangle. Appointed by the king as Bishop of Clonfert and described by Browne as his suffragan, Nangle had the great merit of being able to preach in the Irish language. As might be expected from the stance of their proctors in parliament, the lower clergy were less than supportive of the changes, if not non-compliant with the oath. Some of the most avid Irish clerical supporters of the papacy after the schism between king and pope in England had been attracted to the banner of Lord Thomas Fitzgerald in 1534 and had suffered at least deprivation of their benefices. By early 1538 Archbishop Browne was lamenting that his diocesan clergy were silent in the king's cause, but 'in the corners and such company as them liketh, hinder and pluck back amongst the people the labour that I do take in that behalf'. Thus the archbishop's frustration at James Humphrey's defiance in May 1538 is understandable, especially as the St Audoen's priest seems to have been favoured by Browne's rival, Bishop Staples of Meath. In retaliation for Staples's support for Humphrey, Browne may have caused the Bishop of Meath's suffragan to be arrested. The most concerted resistance on the part of clergy to the Henrician programme, however, was among the Observant friars. Far from acting as propagandists for the royal supremacy as Browne hoped they would, the Observant Franciscans in particular, 'esteemed as young gods' among their flock, led a pro-papal campaign. Because of the number of Observant houses in Ireland, even in the Pale, Browne was unable to 'name them conventuals' as would have happened in England, and in 1538 he began a series of visits on his own authority to friaries to oversee reforms. By the end of that year, however, news had arrived of the total suppression of the mendicants in England, and both officials and friars began to face the prospect of such a campaign in Ireland.[35]

In general, there was no great objection on the part of the laity to the imposition of the king's supremacy. Taking their lead from the parliamentary members, lay people may have been content to obey the legislation through habitual loyalty, though few, except the most affluent or influential, could hope to gain materially from the new order. Public compliance with the terms of the act against the Bishop of Rome's authority is manifest in the oaths taken by the mayor and corporation of Limerick in the summer of 1537 before Lord Deputy Grey, while there were at least some conformists in St Audoen's parish, Dublin, to present the prebend for his defiance of the 'form of the beads' in May 1538. Little devotional change was effected, at least in the short term, to judge, for example, by the large crowds which coverged on Kilmainham on Palm Sunday 1538 to participate in the annual station and pattern at the holy well there: Archbishop Browne was particularly upset by the promulgation of a papal indulgence for those who assisted at the rituals. The fate of the mystery plays performed in some towns is not known, but there is a reference to the performance of the Corpus Christi dramas in Dublin as late as 1553, while the text of the Kilkenny plays was recopied in 1637 because it was so worn from use. Although the principles underpinning the 'New Injunctions' of late 1538 seemed to be inimical to belief in purgatory, devotions attached to chantry and fraternity membership were not formally quashed. The endowment of obits continued through the decades of the mid-century, but changing fashions in piety in Ireland as in England may have led to a decline therein. It is likely that minor local shrines and cults were shielded by the intervention of patronal gentry families who may have reappropriated donations of jewellery and precious objects. Circumspect official policies probably obviated conflict, and the thrust of royal ecclesiastical reform harmonised with the prevailing movement for renewal of the common weal.[36]

The suppressing of some derelict monasteries in the Pale borders had also been suggested as part of a programme of reform of the colony by native political leaders such as Sir Patrick Finglas in the early 1530s. In fact most of the religious houses which were closed before the full dissolution campaign of 1539–40 were selected because demographic decline or abandonment by their communities made the sites indefensible. Thus the buildings and properties of the first group of dissolved religious houses were to be secularised, essentially in order to strengthen the Pale's defences (a trend which ran counter to Archbishop Alen's plans for redeploying these monastic resources within the ecclesiastical sphere). Yet these measures for the amelioration of the commonwealth fell foul of the powerful gentry element in the Irish House of Commons in 1536 who wished to guard their own vested interests as leaseholders, stewards and legal administrators of monastic estates. They were, moreover, antipathetic to the political and social aggrandisement of a coterie comprising the Butlers and their adherents, as well as newly arrived Englishmen, all linked to Thomas Cromwell at court. Representations there by Barnewall concerning the disposition of the lands were successful, the king agreeing that the Old English would benefit proportionately, and the act for the suppression of a total of thirteen Irish monasteries was passed in parliament in October 1537. There ensued the suppression of these houses, including the Cistercian abbeys at Bective, County Meath, Baltinglass on the Kildare border, Tintern and Dunbrody, County Wexford, and Duiske in County Kilkenny, as well as the Irish properties of absentee English monasteries, such as the County Meath manors of the Welsh house of Llanthony (appropriated for the crown under the 1536 Act of Absentees). The pattern of surrenders of heads of houses to royal commissioners in return for pensions for themselves and their fellows, and the granting of the lands to lay people (in these early cases mostly English officials such as John Alen at St Wolstan's and Lord Grey at Ballyboggan), was established in the years down to 1539.[37]

The full-scale campaign of dissolution of the religious orders in the areas under crown control took place in the year or so from the summer of 1539. Those who hoped for profit were active in the twelve previous months, jockeying for position, and those who were threatened with redundancy tried to provide for the future. The keynote now was the exploitation of monastic resources for public or private gain, with little or no advertance to the religious dimension. Leading English officials such as Vice-Treasurer William Brabazon pressed for the diverting of some monastic income towards the state treasury, straitened after the years of local wars. The municipality of Dublin petitioned for a grant of either All Hallows or St John's, Newgate, to compensate for losses in the Fitzgerald revolt. Already individual suitors such as John Alen and Thomas Agard had been accommodated in the first phase of dissolution down to 1538. But now as the full suppression of the monastic institution proceeded in England the stakes were raised, and preparations were being made for a similar programme in Ireland. Information on the houses and lands of the monasteries in the Pale and Ormond was collected during 1538. Special pleas were entered on behalf of certain communities in anticipation of their suppression. Bishop Wellesley, formerly prior of Greatconnell in County Kildare, made a powerful though ultimately unsuccessful case for its preservation. The Irish council identified six monasteries in the Pale which it considered worthy of being spared because of their facilities for hospitality, if not their spiritual dynamism. And the Dublin citizenry successfully appealed for the conserving of the cathedral church of Holy Trinity, the religious community being changed into a secular chapter. Most religious heads, however, sought assurance by renting out properties at low rents for long terms to favoured local lay people. Close links between religious and gentry in the localities in terms of personnel and property were consolidated by the transactions on the eve of the dissolution. Members of orders provided for their futures through leasing lands in trust for themselves through relatives or other associates. In early 1539 the signs of a comprehensive campaign were evident in the activities of the commissioners for closing shrines. Meanwhile Dublin corporation acquired the house of Augustinian canons, All Hallows outside the Walls, on the surrender of the five-member community.[38]

In the spring of 1539 commissions for the dissolving and leasing of monastic houses within the crown's jurisdiction in Ireland were issued. The leading commissioners were Lord Chancellor John Alen and Vice-Treasurer William Brabazon from the Irish executive, the Master of the Rolls, Robert Cowley, Archbishop Browne of Dublin, the leading churchman, and a number of local politicians including Sir Thomas Cusack and Sir Patrick Barnewall. Their campaign of closure of religious houses began in mid-July with the surrender of several monasteries and nunneries in Counties Meath and Louth, most notably perhaps Mellifont, the sometime Cistercian flagship, and Lismullin convent, headed by Cusack's sister, Mary. Despite the military operations to counter the threat from the 'Geraldine League' (a confederation of Irish lords who banded together to protect the young Geraldine heir, Gerald Fitzgerald), the suppressions continued into the autumn with the closure of St Mary's abbey in Dublin city and the nunnery of Grace Dieu, north of Swords in the county. In November 1539 Sir Thomas Cusack took the initiative in the marchlands north-west of the Pale by winding up several houses of orders, including Augustinian canons as well as some mendicants, in the Longford and Westmeath areas. As elsewhere, the heads and members were awarded pensions, but the intricate interplay of religious and secular control within prominent Anglo-Norman and Gaelic families in the region determined a policy of patronage of local interests in the disposition of leases at very low rents. The sweep of the commissioners was southwards in the spring of 1540, with the closing of houses in the Ormond counties of Tipperary, Kilkenny and Waterford, the most notable cases being Jerpoint and Kells, County Kilkenny, and Kilcooly, County Tipperary. By the late summer of that year forty-two houses had surrendered to the commissioners, and the properties were ripe for redistribution to secular interests.[39]

The dissolution of the friaries in the eastern half of Ireland also took place in the period 1539–40. Most of the mendicant houses there were in the towns and were meagrely endowed by comparison with the monasteries. When the communities of friars had dispersed, the buildings were frequently converted to new uses. In Dublin, for example, the Dominican priory was turned into an inn of court for the residence of members of the legal profession; the Franciscan house in Waterford became a hospital; and other premises were taken over by the municipalities. Where local patrons of the friaries were influential, especially in the centres which were remoter from crown control such as Limerick and Galway, some communities survived intact, having transferred their properties to their lay benefactors on a temporary basis. During the closing years of Henry VIII's reign, from 1541 to 1547, the suppression of religious houses was carried out under the aegis of Lord Deputy St Leger's policy of conciliating local interests. Thus the extension of the campaign into areas outside the government's effective jurisdiction relied on the consent of the lords of the districts and regions of the west and the north. By the end of the Henrician period just over half of the monasteries and just under half of the friaries in Ireland had been dissolved. The ending of the era of the religious orders, at least in the older colonial zone, was seemingly received with equanimity by the population there. Many of the traditional social functions of the religious orders such as education, health care and poor relief were being taken on by public and private agents, and the duty of hospitality was neglected by most houses. While the economic services generated by religious communities were lost, those native gentlemen and merchants who benefited substantially by the redistribution of monastic properties were able to stimulate economic activity by their investments in town and countryside. The acquiescence of these elites in the early phase of the Reformation was crucial to its success.[40]

Political and Religious Reform and Reaction, 1536–56

D UBLIN was *en fête* during the session of parliament held in late June 1541. To mark the passage of an act declaring Henry VIII to be King of Ireland, great festivities were laid on by the Irish councillors who stage-managed the proceedings. Popular acclaim for the measure was enlisted in the inner Pale as residents were given the bonus of an extra public holiday, and a general pardon was extended to all but the most iniquitous criminals. Bonfires blazed in the streets, casks of free wine were broached, and cannonades boomed out to salute the new kingly title. The occasion had an all-Ireland dimension. Among the splendidly attired dignitaries of church and state who went in solemn procession to St Patrick's Cathedral to hear the act formally promulgated at high mass were some Gaelic Irish lords. For their benefit the Earl of Ormond had translated into Irish the oration of the Speaker, Thomas Cusack, in the House of Lords. This was symbolic of the fact that the constitution of Ireland as a sovereign kingdom was designed to accommodate all of the island's inhabitants. In contrast with these celebratory scenes, the enhancement of the royal title was not marked by special ceremonial at Henry VIII's court.[1]

Despite the monarch's reservations, his Irish-based administrators had come to see the act of kingly title as pivotal for the policies which they were formulating for the government of Ireland. In this chapter the constitutional changes will be set against the background of a range of options for reform being canvassed from 1536 to 1540. Concurrently the frenetic activity of Lord Deputy Grey indicated future goals while showing how not to go about achieving them. By the time his successor, Sir Anthony St Leger, was established in office, the ascendant group within the crown administration was pressing for the assimilation of regional and local lords in Ireland within a united polity by conciliation. With St Leger as its linch-pin for most of the succeeding sixteen years, the policy of extending English law and culture throughout the island by incorporating Gaelic and alienated Anglo-Norman inhabitants as subjects within the newly constituted kingdom became fundamental to the Tudor approach towards Ireland. Even when St Leger was replaced briefly for two spells by more militaristic deputies, the basic objectives of inter-ethnic peace and mutual allegiance to a common sovereign were pursued, albeit by different strategies. And St Leger himself was prepared to exercise flexibility and patience when defects in his initial arrangements showed up clearly by the early 1550s, modifying them substantially if necessary. Moreover, the popular political response elicited by the governor from most sections of the communities in Ireland down to 1556 may have calmed any turbulence caused at parish level in some areas by the introduction of radical religious changes in the mid-century years.[2]

Options for reform: the failure of Lord Deputy Grey

As his sister, Elizabeth, the bereft Countess of Kildare, and her younger son sought refuge with relatives in England, Lord Leonard Grey succeeded a fellow-Englishman, Skeffington, as viceroy on 1 January 1536. Thomas Fitzgerald and all the other leading Kildare Geraldines, with the exception of Gerald, the elder son of Garret Óg's and Elizabeth's marriage (and embarrassingly still at large), were sent to the Tower of London to await Henry VIII's verdict. The administration headed by Lord Grey realised that great opportunities for English advancement in Ireland had opened out. While awaiting firm instructions from Thomas Cromwell in London, Grey and the Irish councillors assessed optimistically the implications of the huge vacuum left in Irish life after the political demise of the Kildare family. With the principle of an English-born governor gaining acceptance, the executive members advised that the fear and insecurity caused among the Gaelic and Anglo-Norman Geraldine sympathisers by Skeffington's vigorous campaigns be capitalised upon for a general subjugation. Already the late Lord Deputy, using the substantial resources afforded him from England, had pacified the Pale's western and southern borders by his prosecution of a campaign of force mixed with diplomacy. Ireland was now 'in like case [as] at the first conquest, being at your grace's pleasure'; Irishmen were 'never in such fear as they be at this instant time'; the gentlemen of County Kildare were the 'most sorriest men in the world', and the Pale gentry viewed anxiously the toll of seventy-five executions and sixty-six attainders in the wake of the revolt. At a minimum, the coalition of English-born and native councillors believed that the chronically unstable Gaelic districts of south Leinster should be conquered and brought within the jurisdiction of the English lordship. While there was disagreement as to whether the defeated Gaelic natives should be assimilated or expropriated, the vast majority subscribed to the notion of a radical reform, even if geographically limited.[3]

Thomas Cromwell's own programme of reform for Ireland which had been broached initially in 1533 and 1534 was suspended for the duration of the rebellion. Cromwell now pressed ahead with realising in Ireland his concept of the state as applied in all of his royal master's dominions. Of course he tailored his designs to the financial constraints imposed as a result of crown expenditure of £46,000 in the years of the rebellion, and supported Henry's demand that the Irish lordship should be run out of internally generated revenues. The framework was to be constructed of direct rule from London, with a local executive headed by an Englishman, a permanent though reduced garrison of English troops, and a socially established bureaucracy containing a significant English-born element. Cromwell's abiding statist principle was the unifying of the king's outlying territories of Wales, the Calais Pale and the lordship of Ireland with the English realm, where the monarch had plenary civil and ecclesiastical powers unrivalled by competitors. In this context, the Irish executive was degraded to the status of a provincial council, along the lines of the Council of the North in England, the personnel being carefully chosen officials whose administrative competence and loyalty to Cromwell were usually unquestioned. The overhaul of the central administration which had been set in train in the early 1530s continued apace, with, for example, efforts being made to reform the treasury and exchequer. Local government was also to be transformed mainly through the dismantling of magnates' liberties and immunities, the extirpating of all forms of bastard feudalism, and the opening up of the Anglo-Norman lordships to the institutions and agents of the central administration. In sum, what Cromwell pushed throughout the

period until his downfall in June 1540 was the revival of the government of the English parts of Ireland, the Gaelic lords being treated
as alien to the jurisdiction, though open to contractual, temporary
agreements to keep peace with the lordship.[4]

Arrangements for a parliament to win assent from the loyal community for key points of the Cromwellian programme had been
put back on a few occasions before the actual assembly met on 1 May
1536 at Dublin. As well as the ecclesiastical legislation, of pressing
importance were measures to boost the crown's revenue in Ireland
by absorbing confiscatable lands, arranging for their strategic
leasing and imposing various forms of taxation. While Cromwell's
wish to have consultation in parliament with the political community
of Ireland was to be expressed in the passing of forty-two acts before
the assembly was finally dissolved in late December 1537, he and
his fellow English councillors limited the power of the Irish executive to initiate legislation by the device of suspending Poynings'
Law, passed as an act in the first session in May 1536. The requirement that proposed bills be certified first by the Irish council could
now be ignored, thus undermining a crucial executive function of
the Dublin administration and passing the initiative to Cromwell
and the English council in London. A pliant Commons was largely
assured by keeping the members dangling in respect of pardons for
implication in the recent rebellion, and opposition did not feature
in the proceedings until the second and subsequent sessions.
Accordingly, the major Reformation measures passed through the
Commons without demur, though later resistance to the subjection
of the church in Ireland to Canterbury led to successful calls for an
Irish-based commission for faculties to be included in the commission to administer the system. Three substantial pieces of legislation
which were to give a firm base to the Cromwellian revival of crown
government within the framework of a unitary commonwealth
were the act of attainder of the Earl of Kildare and his accomplices,
involving the forfeiture of their extensive lands, the act of absentees,
which resumed the lands of non-resident proprietors, and the act of
subsidy, which provided a ten-year tax to the crown from lands in
the loyal shires.[5]

Additional revenue-generating measures were presented to the
September session of parliament, which took place after a major
summer expedition by Lord Deputy Grey to the south of Ireland.
These included bills for the recovery of customs from municipal

control, the payment of a twentieth tax on all land, and the dissolution of eight monasteries on the borders of the Pale whose sites were desolate. All three bills were defeated in the Commons, and opposition in the House of Commons also caused the later rejection of proposals to align Irish money with sterling and to impose efficiency qualifications on officials (probably because these measures would limit the independence of the lordship's fiscal and patronage regimes). The final session of parliament in late 1537 was supervised by the four royal commissioners led by Sir Anthony St Leger, who had been dispatched to Ireland by the king to inquire into government, prepare for maximising revenues and investigate abuses and peculation. While their commission operated from September 1537 to April 1538 the powers of the Lord Deputy and Irish council were effectively superseded. The commissioners presided over the restating of laws forbidding residents of the colonial zone to marry Gaelic people, to speak Irish or to sport Irish-style garb or glibs and moustaches, thus attempting to conjoin economic security and social reform within a garrisoned Pale. As well as providing for an increase in revenues, the augmented crown lands in the borders and remoter colonial areas made available estates for the support of a garrison, the establishment of a new official landholding class and the consolidation of existing magnates. Among those who benefited in the initial disposition of the newly acquired estates were top English-born officials such as Lord Deputy Grey, who leased Grane and Ballyboggan in the Kildare and Meath borders, William Brabazon, who was granted the former lands of Llanthony priory, and John Alen, who got St Wolstan's; others who profited were military captains such as William St Loe, who received lands in Wexford, and loyal border magnates such as Eustace of Kilcullen.[6]

For a man of action, more comfortable in the saddle than at the council board, Grey would have chafed at any curtailment of his expeditionary plans. Indeed, despite the reduction by half in the 700-man garrison and niggardly subsidies from England, the Lord Deputy managed an almost ubiquitous presence in his defending of the colony and his pursuit of treaties with the external or estranged lords of the four provinces. Politically his policy was a link between the Kildare-centred nexus of alliances before 1534 and the comprehensive system of crown-sponsored compacts of the 1540s. While it is hard to divine an overall strategy in the pattern of raids undertaken from 1536 to 1540, Grey's tactics of cutting passes through forests and bogs to facilitate the movement of wheeled artillery carts and using fascines at rivers to storm castles or bridges proved successful in the short term and were a pointer to future advances into the interior. In the summer of 1536 Grey led a foray of English, Pale and Gaelic troops southwards to the Shannon, targeting Carrigogunnell castle and O'Brien's Bridge, symbols of Desmond and O'Brien defiance, for recapture and destruction. Grey's leadership inspired feats of gallantry in the taking of bridge and castle, and the royal flag was shown for the first time in living memory on the fringes of Desmond and Thomond. The spring, summer and winter of 1537 saw sorties led by Grey to western and southern Leinster against the principal O'Connor, O'Carroll and Kavanagh chiefs, the two latter, Fearganainm and Cahir MacArt, submitting, and the capture and destruction of Brackland and Daingean castles dealing a blow to the still-elusive Brian O'Connor. In the course of the marchland campaigns in 1538 Grey's army of Irish and English forced O'Connor's submission in Offaly and MacMahon's in Farney and reinforced that of the Kavanaghs in Carlow and Wexford. Most notable of all was a thirty-eight-day circuit, with Geraldine counsellors in tow, through Ely, Tipperary, Thomond, Clanricard and back across the Shannon at Banagher. As well as coming to terms with several leading Gaelic and Anglo-Norman magnates, including Conor O'Brien and Ulick Burke, Grey strengthened the municipalities of Limerick and Galway. If his progress was reminiscent of Garret Mór's in his heyday, the list of almost thirty arrangements with the heads of the main lordships resembles nothing so much as the rental of the Earls of Kildare at the height of their power.[7]

Grey's attempt to forge an alliance among the Gaelic lords who had traditionally adhered to the Kildare family was a pragmatic response to the problem of the power vacuum on the borders of the Pale. It was a dangerous gambit, however, given the Lord Deputy's affinity to the Geraldines through his sister's marriage, as well as his failure to apprehend his nephew, Gerald Fitzgerald. Not surprisingly, the Butler faction, headed by Earl Piers of Ossory (restored to the earldom of Ormond in 1538) and his son James, was virulently critical of such an appeasement policy, the latter calling Grey 'the Earl of Kildare newly born again' and accusations flying of the deputy's 'playing bo-peep' in allowing young Gerald to escape to the continent. Efforts by the Irish council to mediate these differences in 1538 were unavailing. In any case, personality clashes between Grey and principal councillors such as Vice-Treasurer Brabazon and Lord Chancellor John Alen were exacerbated by the unpredictability of his actions, and, especially for Archbishop Browne, by the taint of papistry in his pieties. The Lord Deputy may have placated urban communities in the west, but in the Pale there was bitter resentment of the burden of billeting and supplying the English garrison, which was, moreover, proving increasingly unable to prevent Gaelic raids on the heart of the colony. Even hopes for party support for Grey's aspirations to reconstruct a Geraldine alliance proved to be ill-founded. He suffered a loss of credibility in failing to prevent the execution of Thomas Fitzgerald and his uncles in February 1537, and his campaigns exacted too heavy a price in terms of services demanded in the indentures with the lords. The edifice of conditional agreements made between the chiefs and the English king proved to be insubstantial, as the more diplomatic Commissioner St Leger pointed out: 'The country is much easier won than kept; for whenso-ever the king's pleasure be to win the same again, it will be done without great difficulty, but the keeping thereof will be both charge-able and difficult.'[8]

Unwittingly Grey did help to bring about a pan-insular confed-eracy which has became known as the Geraldine League, but its very existence as a hostile force marked the Lord Deputy's failure, and its tenacity led to his downfall. Certainly the cult of the Fitzgeralds was as strong as ever amongst sometime allies, as Lady Eleanor, widow of MacCarthy Reagh of Muskerry, found when forming a protective network in the midlands, south, west and north for her young nephew, Gerald Fitzgerald. The central figure in the bur-geoning coalition was the suitor and later husband of Eleanor, Manus O'Donnell, who seized the opportunity offered by the cause of the young Kildare heir to ally with such traditional rivals as O'Neill of Tyrone and O'Connor Sligo. Contrasting with the campaign of Silken Thomas in 1534–6 in its transcending of the Geraldine factional nexus and in its Gaelic leadership, the Geraldine League encompassed regional objectives which outlasted the flight of Gerald to France in early 1540. A more menacing context was created by the preaching of friars in Gaelic areas against the king's ecclesiastical supremacy and the putting out of feelers to the Scottish king for his acceptance of sovereignty over the leaguers. The immediate cause of the military operations of 1539–40, however, was the perception on the part of the Irish lords of a threat of conquest in the punitive raids by Grey and the unduly harsh terms exacted by him in the sub-missions to the crown. Having failed to show up with Gerald for a meeting with Grey near Dundalk in the spring of 1539, O'Donnell and Conn O'Neill resisted responding to the Lord Deputy's provoc-ative sortie into south Ulster until August, when they mounted a major invasion of the Pale. The provincial chiefs, along with their satellite kings, plundered and burnt the towns of Navan and Ardee and penetrated as far as Tara for a symbolic muster on the hill. Grey acted immediately to summon a hosting of the Pale shires and towns to complement 140 of his own soldiers and pursued the marauders to the Meath–Monaghan border. A skirmish at the ford of Bellahoe ended in the routing of the Gaelic forces and the recapture of their booty.[9]

The governor's exploits in his final eight months in Ireland did not help to restore his plummeting reputation. Grey invaded Munster again in November 1539 with 800 men to receive submissions from chiefs in the Ormond baronies in the company of Earl James, newly succeeded to his late father, and to bolster the court-appointed Earl James FitzMaurice of Desmond. In the Cork region Gaelic and gaelicised chiefs came to terms with the Lord Deputy, but the rival Earl of Desmond, James FitzJohn, remained defiant. Early in the next year Grey marched northwards once more to try to apprehend the Kildare heir, and in frustration at the elusiveness of his quarry and of his protector Conn O'Neill, he preyed upon the countryside about Dungannon. It was on this northern foray that he was sup-posed to have desecrated the cathedral at Downpatrick. That such an apparently false and damaging report should have been chronicled by near-contemporaries attests the sulphurous atmosphere sur-rounding Grey's relations with his fellow-administrators and political enemies. His recall to London in April 1540 was followed by his arrest and trial on a long list of treason charges, including alleged collusion in the smuggling of his nephew, Gerald Fitzgerald, to France. Lord Leonard Grey's fate was sealed by the disgrace and death of his patron, Thomas Cromwell, in June 1540; bereft of friends in the newly ascendant court faction, he too was convicted of treachery and beheaded a year later. The linking of their final misfortunes was almost inexorable, given the fatal flaws in the Cromwellian policy which Grey was charged with implementing. The ambitious scheme for reform of the Irish lordship under direct rule from England had been starved of the requisite resources from that country. While the efficacy of the executive branch during Grey's tenure was diluted by the powers of the special commissioners from England and the curtailing of parliamentary initiative, the deputy's all-action military style was cramped by reduced troop numbers and paltry army pay. Above all, Cromwell's failure to initiate policies directed at securing a comprehensive settlement of the problem of Gaelic relations with the lordship meant that Grey's immense efforts at compact-making lacked a constitutional focus, and his own ruthless martiality compounded the resulting confusion and resentment.[10]

Accommodation and assimilation: St Leger's initial success

Sir Anthony St Leger's arrival as Lord Deputy in early August 1540 marked the beginning of his extended period of governorship, but he was not a novice in Irish politics. His seven-month tour of duty as royal commissioner in 1537–8, when he rapidly covered the old colonial zone, had won St Leger high commendation for his 'discretion and indifference' towards all with whom he came into contact. Confident in his own understanding of the mentality of the communities in Ireland and assured of the support at court of the now dominant Duke of Norfolk, himself an old Irish hand, St Leger sought appointment in 1540 driven by ideals of public service admixed with an aspiration to self-enrichment. A background of humanist training, coupled with practical experience of administration in his native Kent and on royal embassies in Calais, Flanders and Ireland had forged the former spirit, while the latter opportunism was fostered by the consolidation of family fortunes in south-eastern England and at Henry VIII's court. Combining 'gravity' and 'pleasantness' with 'exceeding good grace' in his personality, St Leger possessed political qualities of tact, rationality and statesmanship, as contemporaries and later historians have stressed. But he could exhibit toughness as well as tolerance when occasion demanded it, and, while highly principled in his policy-making, was prone to pragmatism and flexibility. He was apparently the ideal agent of a process of conciliation within a new constitutional framework.[11]

It soon became clear that the Lord Deputy's previous experience of Ireland was shaping his policy in two significant ways. Firstly, he was developing a sound understanding of the regionality of Irish politics, as witnessed, for example, by his decisive strikes against the attackers of the Pale. The autumn months after St Leger's arrival were marked by his resolute campaigns in the southern and midland parts of Leinster to pacify the clans of Kavanaghs, O'Tooles and O'Connors. These, and his later actions in relation to Munster, Connacht and Ulster, as well as to the urban communities, were to show that, while he saw the preservation of the Pale region as crucial, it could not be accomplished merely by erratic and arbitrary punitive raids but instead by strategic diplomatic embassies, backed up by the threat of force. Secondly, St Leger offered to Gaelic and Anglo-Norman leaders what he hoped would be permanent contracts with the crown based on mutual trust. The leaders of the Leinster clans, for example Cahir MacArt Kavanagh, Turlough O'Toole and Brian O'Connor, having submitted, entered into the by now conventional agreements to co-operate with the English administration. But more formal indentures were to follow. On the king's side, there was the decision, adumbrated by Henry twenty years earlier though now resisted by him, to relinquish his right to the territories which, though occupied by the Gaelic Irish and others, had been granted by his predecessors to their vassals. On the Irish lords' side, there would be acceptance of the king's sovereignty in all its forms, political, military, judicial and ecclesiastical, as flowing through the lordships which they had theretofore ruled with varying degrees of autonomy. Mediating this gradual process of assimilation by consent of the former enemies of the colony was the emollient yet tenacious St Leger.[12]

Unlike his predecessor as Lord Deputy, St Leger was careful to forge a broad coalition of English and native interests as a basis for the change in strategy as it was emerging at Christmas 1540. Secure for the time being in his backing at Henry VIII's court, the new governor was reasonably successful in winning over leading English Cromwellian appointees in Ireland such as Sir William Brabazon and Thomas Agard. A longer-serving incumbent, Edward Staples, Bishop of Meath, who was at odds with Archbishop Browne's castigatory approach to the implementation of the ecclesiastical changes, was influential in the new regime as the person who first advocated gradualism in policies within a freshly established kingdom of Ireland. St Leger's own entourage included men such as John Parker, his private secretary, and John Goldsmith, the clerk of the Irish council, who diligently advised him and acted as propitiators of would-be critics. A small number of the latter came from the community of the Pale gentry and patriciates but, for the most part, St Leger drew strong support from the leading lawyers such as Thomas Luttrell and Gerald Aylmer who had thitherto commended reform of the lordship by various means. Particularly significant was Sir Thomas Cusack of County Meath, who from the mid-1530s had shown a commitment to conciliating the Gaelic Irish lords and later to granting them constitutional equality within the commonwealth. Cusack was also a conduit for St Leger to the directionless Geraldine faction, the restoration of the heads of which, James FitzJohn as Earl of Desmond in later 1540 and Gerald as Earl of Kildare in 1554, brought about some stability. Nor did St Leger fail to attempt to placate the other main factional leader, James Butler, Earl of Ormond, though in this he was less successful. Also of concern to the Lord Deputy was the social stratum of lesser gentry and borough-dwellers in the outer region of the lordship whose bitter complaints against magnate oppression he had registered as commissioner on circuit in 1537–8.[13]

The keystone of the archway through which Irish people were to progress to a stable order and polity along English lines was the act of kingly title of 1541. This was to provide for political unity of all the island's inhabitants in a single community of subjects under the unilateral jurisdiction of the crown. The preamble to the act explained the problem to be solved:

> Lack of naming the king's majesty and his noble progenitors kings of Ireland . . . hath been great occasion that the Irishmen and inhabitants within this realm of Ireland have not been so obedient to the king's highness and his most noble progenitors, and to their laws, as they of right and according to their allegiance and bounden duties ought to have been.

Thus the framers of the act were linking the measure with the proposed system of agreements whereby the Gaelic and Anglo-Norman lords would recognise the sovereignty of the king in return for the extension to them of the full rights and protection enjoyed by existing subjects in Ireland and other realms. Instead of remaining outside the jurisdiction of the constitution of lordship as it evolved down to the mid-fourteenth century, the Gaelic Irish were to be accommodated within a new constitution of kingdom embracing the entire population. Of some minor significance to the council, if not to Henry VIII, was the consideration that the king's sovereignty needed to be positively asserted in the aftermath of the breach with Rome. With the abolition of the pope's jurisdiction, putative papal claims to temporal authority in Ireland had to be elided in order to discourage any external political relations. Meanwhile the enlisting of such a broad range of inter-ethnic support for the act's passage in June 1541 reflects a practical commitment to the use of parliament as a forum for consensus within the new constitutional framework.[14]

Within that framework, the dozens of agreements with the Irish lords could be worked out by St Leger, as in most cases aliens were transformed into vassals with the full rights and duties of subjects. The first of these were with the Leinster chiefs who had been the object of his vigorous campaign in the autumn of 1540. The opening phase of negotiations in the three following years with clans such as the O'Tooles, O'Byrnes, Kavanaghs, O'Mores and O'Connors ended with their leaders' acceptance of the king's political and ecclesiastical sovereignty and of their duty to attend parliament. They further assented to apply for a royal pardon, and to accept the crown's jurisdiction within their territories and the formal restoration of their patrimonies with a royal title. Thus the way was paved for agreements which have been called 'surrender and regrant' by modern historians. The O'Toole indenture has been taken as a prototype of this scheme. In 1540 Turlough O'Toole, the chieftain of the Imaal clan in north Wicklow and erstwhile raider of the Pale, submitted to Henry, who granted him the Powerscourt district of Fercullen which had been taken over by the Earl of Kildare. In return, Turlough was to hold his lordship by knight service in the feudal way and pay five marks in annual rent. The Lord Deputy and council recommended that the other leading men of the clan should be accommodated also, 'lest that the whole being granted to the brothers [Turlough and Art Óg], the others having nothing should be driven to be as those men have been'. Travelling in clothes which were bought at St Leger's expense, Turlough paid a visit to Henry's court, and the bargain was sealed, though it did not result in the granting of a title. Although Turlough was killed in 1542 by a rival, his cousin and namesake, the continuity of his line was hoped for by St Leger and his advisers, who, following the rule of primogeniture, backed the dead chief's son, Brian, in his struggle with the other Turlough who was the *tánaiste*, or choice for successor, of the clan.[15]

Most of these terms were replicated during the next few years in negotiations with the other Leinster chieftains. While the pro-administration chiefs of the O'Dempseys, created Viscounts Clanmalier, and the O'Byrnes of Gabhail Raghnaill, Rathdrum, County Wicklow, received grants of the entire clan lands, most of the others were treated similarly to the O'Tooles. In the cases of the other O'Byrnes, the O'Connors, O'Mores and O'Dunnes, for example, while the chiefs' lordship was restored by Henry VIII, the rights of the remaining septs of the clans were respected. MacGillapatrick was ennobled as Baron of Upper Ossory even before parliament first met in June 1541, and he sat as of right in the House of Lords. As the only Leinster lord to complete the course of negotiations with the government leading to full patentee status under the crown, MacGillapatrick was no doubt anxious in 1544 to submit disputes he had with O'Carroll of Ely to the arbitration of the amplified great council, now comprising administrators as well as lords of both races in the realm. With an eye to their strategic regional position straddling the vital Barrow artery, St Leger took special pains over surrender negotiations with the Kavanaghs. Bereft of their Kildare patrons after 1535–6, the leaders of the principal Kavanagh septs submitted to successive deputies, temporarily to Grey in 1536, and more permanently to St Leger in 1540, before final agreement in late 1543. Although more favour was shown to the junior branch chief, Cahir MacArt, than to the *taoiseach*, Cahir MacInnyCross, the territory was settled in such a way as to provide for internal clan stability within the Wexford and Carlow lands. Within their territories the agreement was to lead to subinfeudation of tenants-in-chief, the banishment of idle swordsmen, the rendering of knight's service and rent, the abolition of the 'black rent' extorted from County Wexford, and the inculcation of arable farming methods with the aid of loans for seeds and equipment from state funds. Although primogeniture was ordained for succession to patrimonies at all levels, the maintenance of peace in Kavanagh country in the following two decades dictated a flexible approach to tanistry, rotation of the chieftaincy among the rival septs being acceptable to the government.[16]

St Leger's appeasing of the lords of Munster and south Connacht to which he devoted much attention in the early part of his vice-royalty began at Christmas 1540. Journeying through the snowy terrain from Carlow to east Munster, the Lord Deputy made contact with James FitzJohn Fitzgerald of Desmond, who eventually assented to a formal reconciliation. A great pageant of propitiation was staged at Sir Thomas Butler's castle at Cahir in January 1541, attended by dignitaries of state and church, including the Archbishops of Dublin and Cashel and also two hundred 'Irish gentlemen'. Kneeling before St Leger, James was accepted as Earl of Desmond, and he agreed to renounce the apparatus of bastard feudalism in the same way as Piers Butler, Earl of Ossory, had done in 1534. The secular and religious jurisdiction of the king would be mediated by him throughout his earldom; his attendance at parliament would be resumed (being facilitated by the grant of a residence at Dublin), and his heir would be educated at the English court. Regional and provincial relations would be conducted not as thitherto on the basis of the traditional factional nexus, but rather within the framework of the crown's reviving arbitrational institutions of council, parliament and judicial commissions. Once reconciled with the crown and Ormond, Desmond was to play a full part, along with his fellow-earl, in the stabilising of Anglo-Norman and Gaelic lordships in the south of Ireland. Illustrations of Desmond and Ormond in this role may be adduced from events in 1542. In the early spring, when parliament held a session at Limerick, the Earl of Ormond was present to assess crown rents on the chiefs of north Munster, and in the autumn the Earl of Desmond accompanied St Leger on a circuit of the Cork region, the purpose of which was to bind the Anglo-Norman and Gaelic lords there to submit to royal justice and religious supremacy.[17]

St Leger's dealings in the southern half of the country down to 1545 further attest his concern for the hard-pressed lesser gentry and townsfolk of the remoter zones of the old colony. His agreement with Desmond asserted the freedom from magnate control of these Old English inhabitants, and his visits to the boroughs of Kilmallock, Cork, Galway and Limerick (to which he brought parliament on his second visit in 1542) inspirited the demoralised citizens. The latter city was also the venue in 1541 for the commencement of negotiations through Desmond's mediacy with the lords of Thomond and Clanricard, Murrough O'Brien and Ulick Burke. Both had been lured to view the Desmond spectacular at Cahir and now were ready to make their own submissions, their urban visit in itself being a novelty. O'Brien's surrender as Gaelic chief was the prelude to a complete restoration of lordship under the style 'Earl of

Thomond' by royal patent. Having agreed to waive primogenital succession rights by acknowledging Donough, his nephew and *tánaiste*, as next-in-line to the earldom, he also gave up his lordship rights over the MacBriens on the left bank of the Shannon, and those formerly exerted over his *uirrithe*, the MacNamaras. By the time of his trip to court in MacNamara's company in the summer of 1543 O'Brien had become an enthusiastic supporter of the preaching of Henry's religious supremacy. Also in that last party received by Henry in 1543 was O'Brien's old ally, Ulick MacWilliam Burke, now dubbed 'Earl of Clanricard' and agreeing to revert to feudal tenure of his lands rather than Gaelic. He was also accompanied by a principal *uirrí*, O'Shaughnessy, who was knighted and restored to his patrimony to hold directly of the king. As did his fellow-earls, Burke subjected himself to arbitration under the auspices of the great or afforced council to settle the succession to the earldom.[18]

Ulster, with its north Connacht periphery, was tackled by St Leger from the summer of 1541 onwards, the main objective being the netting of Conn O'Neill, the central figure, for the policy of *détente*. Knowing that the regional aspirations of the great Ulster lords spilled over southwards, the Lord Deputy, in accommodating Manus O'Donnell to the crown in August 1541, for example, brokered not only the usual subjection to Henry VIII's secular and religious jurisdiction but also agreement between the Tyrconnell chief and the Lower MacWilliam Burke (whose area of overlordship in Mayo was afforded little attention otherwise). St Leger's strategic diplomacy encompassed the MacMahons of Oriel, as well as the Magennises, O'Hanlons, Maguires, Savages, and even lesser O'Neills of Tyrone, some of whom desired to be released from the overlordship of the Tyrone chieftain, Conn Bacach. The latter was forced to come to terms after a series of campaigns by St Leger in alliance with the newly reconciled lords of the region in later 1541, culminating in a punishing December raid on his cattle and sheep herds.[19]

Once started, the talks on a full surrender and regrant of O'Neill's lordship proceeded to the point of fulness with the conferring of the earldom of Tyrone, and the king's wish for 'reconciliation by good and gentle means' was demonstrated in person to Conn on his epoch-making visit to London in September 1542. While admitting the sovereignty of the king to his Tyrone patrimony, O'Neill's internal position as great landholder there under Henry was secured by the binding to him of his internal rivals as vassals. And his rights to clientship over *uirrithe* such as O'Cahan were left open to later controversy owing to the incompleteness of the programme of sub-infeudation. O'Neill, O'Donnell and other chiefs submitted to the crown's legal arbitration apparatus: at the Trim session of parliament in 1542 disputes between O'Neills were settled; a commission in 1543 arbitrated on contention between MacQuillans and O'Cahans over the lucrative Bann fisheries; and the Dublin council sat in judgment on differences between the two great regional lords in July of that year. While ominously for the future Conn was allowed to nominate his son, Matthew, the newly created Baron of Dungannon, as his heir, to the exclusion of Shane, the clan's choice as *tánaiste*, St Leger's success in winning O'Neill's assent to the process of pacification assuaged Henry's concern over waiving of royal rights, including economic rents. Reluctantly in the spring of 1542 he had given his consent to the arrangements made in his name.[20]

Two phenomena in the period down to the mid-1540s in Ireland have been taken as attesting the immediate success of St Leger's policies in fostering an atmosphere of general goodwill. Firstly, when England became committed to a two-fronted war in France and the Scottish borders, there were none of the previous diplomatic overtures from Irish magnates to enemy rulers. Indeed, by contrast, the Earls of Desmond and Tyrone were among several lords who helped to organise levies of Irish troops to fight under English commanders in the two campaigns. The Lord Deputy himself had suggested the employment of Irish footsoldiers not only for their martial skills but also because they could be very well spared in the now pacified lordships. Thus was conceived the Tudor scheme for dealing with Irish swordsmen, who were to be rendered redundant by the surrender and regrant and composition policies, especially in the late years of the century. A force of 1,000 kerne, pages and boys, mostly Gaelic Irish and under their own captains, was recruited in the spring of 1544, and of these, 400 were deployed along the Scottish border while the rest joined the huge army of 42,000 bound for France. According to contemporary reports, the Irish acquitted themselves well in the fighting, proving to be adept at foraging and gaining a reputation for ruthlessness. Against the Scots the Irish soldiers, many of whom having been trained in the use of firearms, were engaged in raids in which significant losses may have been sustained. Late the following year a company of about 2,000 galloglas and kerne sailed from Skerries under the command of the Earl of Ormond in a flotilla of twenty-eight ships to aid the Earl of Lennox in his conflict with the mutual enemies of himself and Henry VIII. Despite the failure of this expedition, however, there could be no doubting the attitude of co-operation which marked relations between the Irish administration and the principal nobles.[21]

Religious jurisdiction was the second area of potential conflict which was defused by the emollient St Leger. Before 1540 attempts to assert royal power over bishoprics had culminated in Archbishop Browne's nomination of rivals to locally backed papal appointees. By contrast, the preliminary agreements with the Irish lords in the early 1540s (which incorporated recognition of the king's supremacy) acknowledged local rights to church patronage and local preferences in episcopal selection. Thus, with Bishop Staples as his chief ecclesiastical lieutenant, the Lord Deputy ensured that the surrendering Gaelic lords could expect royal ratification of their favoured episcopal candidates. The suit of Manus O'Donnell's chaplain for a bishopric, for example, was supported enthusiastically by St Leger in 1543, as was the advancement to the primatial see of George Dowdall, who accompanied Conn O'Neill to court the previous year. A policy of concession and compromise, paralleling that in the secular sphere, was also successful in outflanking a series of counter-reform measures undertaken by the papacy in relation to Ireland. Beginning in the late 1530s, Pope Paul III made a series of provisions to dioceses in all four provinces in which the incumbents were conformable to royal supremacy. The most important challenge was to the position of Archbishop Cromer of Armagh, who was faced with a rival administrator, Robert Wauchop. Under St Leger in the early 1540s an ecclesiastical version of the surrender and regrant policy saw some papal nominees submitting their bulls of appointment for ratification by the crown. Others were agreeable to accept suffragan or assistant status to royal appointees. Above all, Archbishop Dowdall's success in winning respect from the Gaelic and English parts of his diocese overarched harmonious church–state relations of the 1540s.[22]

The campaign for the suppression of the religious houses in the Pale, Ormond and the remoter colonial areas from 1539 onwards yielded a vast bank of properties for the crown which St Leger used to fuel his drive towards political consensus. Central to this concordance was the coterie of recently arrived officials whose permanant presence in Ireland was deemed to be a prerequisite for the reform of government within the new kingdom. The St Leger regime retained the support of most of the leading Englishmen in Ireland throughout its span because it fostered their ambitions for fortune-building. Sir William Brabazon, the Vice-Treasurer, was not only at the heart of the system of leasing, selling and accounting for newly acquired crown properties, but also benefited handsomely himself. Among the valuable abbey estates he took over were the Dublin site of St Thomas's abbey and lands of Mellifont abbey. Thomas Agard, Brabazon's chief clerk and the link between Vice-Treasurer and Lord Deputy, laid the basis of a rich patrimony with the Meath monastic lands of Bective and St Mary's, Trim. St Leger's secretary, John Parker, enriched himself considerably with former religious lands. The Lord Deputy too profited from the buoyant property market: his possessions included Louth friary, Ballyboggan, County Meath, and Graney nunnery, County Kildare. While these prominent administrators had the choice of premium properties, lesser civil and especially military servitors obtained more desolate lands in the Pale marches, where, it was hoped, well-defended settlements would develop into springboards for advance into Gaelic areas and nuclei of revived English communities. A web of conspiracy based on fraudulent dealings, including undervaluing of leases and purchases and negligent accounting procedures, radiated out from Brabazon's office, under the complaisant St Leger's protection. Arrears of £18,640 in rents were allowed to accumulate from 1540 to 1547, much of the sum due from instalments of crown leases to favoured clients, including the Lord Deputy. One leading English official, John Alen, the Lord Chancellor, was not mollified by the gains he made, mostly under the previous regime, and he was a participant in an Ormond-led coup against St Leger in 1546. Otherwise this generation of New English backed St Leger's policies and also became integrated through marriage, trade and politics with the Old English of the Pale.[23]

Among the latter community the popularity of the conciliatory policy and the concomitant granting of titles and lands persisted throughout the 1540s. Lesser Old English aristocrats such as Thomas Eustace, first Viscount Baltinglass, and Oliver Plunket, Lord Louth, shared in the dispensing of peerages in the early 1540s. While the obvious local beneficiaries of crown largesse were well-placed state officials such as Thomas Cusack, James Bathe and Nicholas

Stanihurst, and serviceable entrepreneurs such as Walter Peppard, a busy market in preferential leases operated at a lower level throughout the Pale as gentlemen and merchants invested in monastic properties, many of which conferred rights of advowson, or priestly appointment. Local officials and lawyers through their spokesmen voiced their support for the peaceful assimilation of the Gaelic Irish by which, Thomas Cusack wrote in 1546, 'those which would not be brought under subjection with 10,000 men come to Dublin with a letter'. The Old English were content to participate in this with St Leger, before whose time reform could have been advanced 'if such truth and gentleness had been showed to them [the Gaelic lords] by the governors and rulers'. Material interests were conjoined with political liberalism: the formal compacts signed with the Leinster chieftains gave some guarantee of secure landholding within the Pale, and although later Old English commentators traced the origins of 'noisome' taxes for the supply of the governor's household to St Leger's deputyship, there is no evidence that resentment was aroused at the time. On the positive side, St Leger's parliament tried to deal with serious obstacles to trade caused by the activities of 'grey merchants' in 1542. Moreover, aspects of Tudor urban policy were applied in Ireland: provision was made for the construction of walls around the decaying borough of Navan; city houses and sites of religious orders were conferred on civic councils; and in 1548 the Dublin municipality was raised to the status of county borough, resulting in enhanced economic and corporate privileges.[24]

The power of the Anglo-Norman magnates still stalked the urban populations of the south and west, despite St Leger's flag-flying visits. Yet the co-operative spirit elicited by the reconciliations of the great and lesser feudal lords in the remoter colony seemed to promise a more fruitful era of socio-economic progress. The luring of rare attenders in the upper house, such as Lords Barry and Roche from Cork, Bermingham from Galway and Fitzmaurice from Kerry, to parliament in 1541 was part of the regeneration of this old colonial aristocracy. In addition to the restoration of their constitutional and landholding rights, the leading lords were granted monastic land. That the Earls of Ormond, Desmond and Clanricard supported the new administrative arrangements is attested by their participation in and submission to the decision-making of great councils and their acting as commissioners for the surrender of the religious houses and levying of soldiers for service overseas. Furthermore, the enthusiasm of Desmond and Ormond for the dispatch of kerne from their earldoms in 1544–5 indicates their willingness to curtail their costly retinues. But despite the apparent factional rapproche-ment between the Butlers and Fitzgeralds in the 1540s, the Earl of Ormond emerged in 1546 as a critic of St Leger's actions. Abetted by Sir John Alen and Walter and Robert Cowley, Butler, posing as a 'zealous defender of his country', presented at court a number of charges against the Lord Deputy, including the levying of 'certain new and extraordinary impositions on the subjects'. The English Privy Council found for St Leger, who also attended, buttressed by glowing testimonials from Irish dignitaries. While Alen and Walter Cowley were discharged from their posts and imprisoned, Earl James was reconciled with St Leger. The earl never returned home, however: along with seventeen of his servants, he died of poisoning at his London residence in late October 1546 in circumstances which were never fully investigated.[25]

Among the tributes paid to the Lord Deputy's record in Ireland down to 1546 were some from Gaelic lords such as Conn O'Neill, who 'had wept and lamented the departure of so just a governor' when St Leger travelled to court. As in the case of the other groups, the principal Gaelic lords who had submitted, such as O'Brien, Earl of Thomond, received monastic leases where the commissions for suppression were allowed to operate. And, as with civil taxes on the newly reconciled territories, there was no question of insisting on full rents for former religious properties. Moreover, in some areas of Connacht and Ulster St Leger was sensitive to local interests by not pressing monastic closures. Ominously for the longer-term prospects for peace in Gaelic regions, however, Sir William Brabazon, who had been appointed Lord Justice during St Leger's absence in mid-1546, was campaigning against O'Connor in Offaly, where he refortified Daingean castle. In midland and south Leinster the arrangements forged in the early 1540s were unravelling as local political realities obtruded. Among the O'Tooles, the first clan to come to terms with St Leger, the murder of Turlough in 1542 initiated a struggle for headship between Brian, Turlough's son, favoured by the English administration, and Turlough MacShane, the *tánaiste* and ringleader of the opposition. Contention between the government-favoured Cahir MacArt Kavanagh and the rival sept broke out at Hacketstown in the mid-1540s, though by and large the lordship was quiet until Cahir revolted in 1548. To the west the renewed raiding of the Pale by the O'Connors and O'Mores was countered by the punitive expeditions of Brabazon, a major grantee of land in the midlands. Thus, although the conciliatory policy fostered much goodwill on the part of individual Gaelic lords, the strains of enforcing compacts in the regions and localities, especially in the Pale marches, cast doubt over its continuation in its pristine form.[26]

Despite his displeasure at the mounting deficit in the Irish revenues, averaging £5,850 per annum since 1540, Henry VIII persevered with the governorship of St Leger down to his death in January 1547. With the accession of Henry's son as King Edward VI, the faction which had backed the Lord Deputy at court was ousted by the successive ascendancies of the parties of Protectors Somerset and Northumberland, and at each courtly upheaval St Leger was recalled to England for two-year intervals. Yet although he was in office for only about a quarter of the period to late 1553, St Leger's was the controlling influence behind the policies followed by his replacements, Sir Edward Bellingham and Sir James Croft. This was because, while both were primarily military leaders at the head of substantial armies in Ireland, the force they deployed was essentially in support of the local and regional arrangements entered into in the earlier 1540s. Rather than curbing expenditure, these militaristic deputies of the mid-century spent vast sums on campaigns, garrisons and settlements, culminating in a deficit of £52,000 Irish for 1552. Incorporated within the administrative briefs of Bellingham, St Leger and Croft were instructions for implementing the progressively more radical elements of the religious reform in England. Mainly because of the balancing presence of St Leger at critical times, the impact of Protestantism was cushioned, so that it did not become a source of contention. Notwithstanding the alienation of certain Gaelic lords whose menacing of the Pale led to their being targets for aggression, the bulk of the local political leadership, especially the Old English of the Pale, were brought along in amity during this phase of highly assertive government activity.[27]

Militarism and modification of policy in the mid-century years

Sir Edward Bellingham, who had first come to Ireland in June 1547 as captain-general, took over as Lord Deputy in May of the following year with ample supplies of troops and money. An experienced military commander, he devoted most of his eighteen months in office to overcoming hostile forces in the Pale marches and to providing for the longer-term security of that increasingly extensive region. Bellingham campaigned to the point of exhaustion and placed much responsibility on martial rather than civil followers. The northern approaches to the Pale from Ulster were to be controlled by the setting up of Nicholas Bagenal as lord of Newry and Andrew Brereton in Lecale. To defend the southern Leinster corridor, Bellingham divided the area corresponding to the lordships of the Kavanaghs, O'Byrnes and O'Tooles into three administrative districts under English captains as seneschals with bands of soldiers. Plans for the reconstruction of an existing ward, at Leighlin, and the foundation of a new one, at Shillelagh, key ingresses to Kavanagh and O'Byrne countries, were crucial to the role of these politico-military functionaries as peacekeepers and local arbiters. Using a combination of Gaelic, common and martial law, the seneschals were to ensure stability within septs by the listing or 'booking' of all inhabitants under principal landowners and extirpating those who were 'masterless'. As a further contribution to stability, the levies exacted by the Gaelic lords were to become rents payable to the seneschals for their domestic and public uses. Thus was introduced a class of soldier-settlers who, although envisaged as temporary agents in the transition of Gaelic areas to English civility, themselves became major players in Irish regional and local politics.

Bellingham's immediate concern on arrival in the summer of 1548 was the prosecution of a war of attrition against the rebellious MacGillapatrick O'More and Brian O'Connor and their followers in Leix and Offaly. The two clans had been provoked into making common cause by Brabazon's punishing expedition in 1546, and Bellingham already had experience of defending the south-western Pale against their attacks. Now he led a hosting into O'More's country, where Fort Protector (matching the already founded Fort Governor at Daingean in Offaly) was established with a garrison of soldiers under the command of Sir William St Loe. Cahir, brother of Brian O'Connor, broke out in rebellion shortly afterwards, and the continuous fighting in later 1548 ranged from Kildare through Leix and Offaly to the Shannon, and to the environs of Nenagh and Athlone. By the spring of 1549, the O'Mores and O'Connors having submitted and Cahir having been executed for treason,

Bellingham prepared to organise the midland region radiating out from the two forts in Leix and Offaly, linking them with a system of lesser forts to Nenagh and Athlone. After initial supplying from the established Englishry, the garrisons of Fort Governor and Fort Protector were to become self-financing with the provision of land in their vicinities for farms for the soldiers. Confiscation of O'Connor and O'More land in Offaly and Leix was a prelude to the tentative settling of new military proprietors in the frontier region, and to the full-scale civil plantation of the area planned in the mid-1550s. Thus by late 1549 Sir Edward Bellingham had laid the basis of a fortified ring around an enlarged Pale.[28]

As well as pursuing the military and political objectives of Protector Somerset's regime in Ireland, the Lord Deputy was commissioned in late 1548 to supervise the introduction of ecclesiastical changes there. Since Edward VI's accession a series of innovations in religious practice had brought the church in England towards the Zwinglian form of Protestantism. As well as the sacrificial nature of the eucharist, this confession rejected stone altars, shrines and other objects of piety in church buildings, sacramentals such as prayer-beads and holy water, the invocation of saints, and institutions such as chantries. The initiatives of reformers in England were canalised in the First Book of Common Prayer, introduced in mid-1549. The incoherent pattern of reform in the English church maximised the difficulty for the eager Bellingham at the remove of Ireland. The 'Injunctions' against Catholic rituals and the institution of the new order of communion were put into practice in the Pale in the autumn of 1548 without a parliament being held to gain the assent of Lords and Commons. A 'Book of Reformation' which preceded that of Common Prayer was issued to Archbishop Browne for the instruction of his suffragan bishops. Simultaneously, preaching in the new evangelical mode to the laity and worship in the English vernacular were tentatively begun by Browne and Bishop Staples of Meath. No measure for the suppression of the religious guilds and chantries in Ireland was undertaken for fear of jeopardising local goodwill, and thus was left in place the system of obituarial prayer sustained by belief in purgatory (which was anathema to advanced reformers).[29]

Already in late 1547 Archbishop Browne had called for the foundation of a university and grammar schools in his diocese for the instruction of the youth in the religious beliefs then being adopted in England. As a disseminator of the reformed tenets, Browne himself was uninspiring and lacklustre, being outshone by a Scottish preacher in Dublin, Walter Palatyne. Bishop Staples followed the new line with much more conviction at Christmas 1548. In doing so, however, he antagonised the gentry in his Meath diocese, who were aghast at his denial of the sacrificial mass and the efficacy of the cult of saints, to the point where they were prepared to have him burnt for heresy. A more notable reverse for the Protestant cause was the point-blank refusal of Primate George Dowdall to countenance any change in doctrine. With few exceptions, diocesan lower clergy appear to have been ill-informed and unenthusiastic and may have carried on as before with the minimum of change. Thus congregations were spared the full impact of liturgical innovation, at least in the first phase of the Protestantising of the Irish church. While there were some dedicated reformers among the communities of natives and English-born civil and military servitors, no doctrinal ferment or disputation had marked the Irish scene down to 1548. Moreover, the government's failure to dissolve the chantries and religious guilds removed from its disposal a further incentive for attracting conformity. Lacking the inducement of more secularised ecclesiastical largesse, and eschewing the instruments of coercion, the administration headed by Bellingham had little progress to report in the matter of imposing the state-sponsored religious reform down to December 1549.[30]

Following the eclipse of his patron, Protector Somerset, Sir Edward Bellingham departed for England in December 1549, where he died within a short time. His garrisoning and settlement of the marchlands of Leinster had achieved a securer Pale in the short term, but after nine months of the successive justiceships of Sir Francis Bryan and Sir William Brabazon the return of Sir Anthony St Leger as Lord Deputy was decided upon to placate those in Ireland who been alienated by forceful political and religious actions. The stability of Munster had been threatened by the restiveness of the Earls of Desmond and Thomond, while in Ulster the main chieftains had come under the influence of Franco-Scottish enemies of England. The reason for their antagonism, as expressed by their ambassador to the court of Henry II of France, George Paris, was their fear that they would be 'driven out of their ancient possessions, one after the other, in such sort as had lately been served to O'More and O'Connor'. Ominously, the papally appointed Primate of Armagh, Robert Wauchop, had landed in the north, albeit without gaining support from ecclesiastical or civil powers there, including Archbishop Dowdall. St Leger, using his wonted 'gentleness' and 'humanity', lost little time in regaining the confidence of the unsettled rulers. In east Ulster, for example, he supervised the removal from Lecale of Andrew Brereton, an English settler who had gravely offended Conn O'Neill, remarking that 'such handling of wild men had done much harm in Ireland'. But although he did send encouraging letters and gifts to Desmond, Thomond, Clanricard, the O'Donnells, O'Reillys and others, he upheld the defensive system set up by Bellingham and endeavoured to make arrangements for the plantation of Leix and Offaly by tenants of English stock.[31]

The Lord Deputy also tried to fulfil his ecclesiastical remit during this eight-month tenure of office. He feared a conjunction of political and religious disaffection in the event of war breaking out, with the possibility of the French winning 'more friendship among this nation than for their own sakes', and therefore his approach continued to be lenitive. Public conformity to the practice of the reformed faith was ordered on 6 February 1551, and was to be assured through the dissemination of the First Book of Common Prayer in English areas of the east, as well as in Galway and Limerick. A printing-press was established in Dublin in 1551 for the purpose of producing texts, though a Gaelic version of the Prayer Book was not proceeded with at this time: instead the deputy had authority to experiment with a Latin translation of the book where circumstances made it advisable. St Leger also continued to appoint natives to senior positions in the Irish church wherever possible in order to procure local political support for the regime rather than advance the Reformation radically. For example, the aged Bishop of Limerick, John Quin, who was reluctant to acquiesce in the new order, was persuaded to resign in favour of William Casey, a Desmond protégé. With George Dowdall, Archbishop of Armagh, however, the diplomacy of St Leger proved unavailing. Having failed to carry his arguments at a conference of the clergy with the Lord Deputy in Dublin, Archbishop Dowdall retired to his northern diocese and refused to change from the older order of liturgical practice. St Leger was forced to hand over the leading reforming role in the Irish church to Archbishop Browne of Dublin, with whom he was out of sympathy, at the very least temperamentally if not doctrinally.[32]

As in the period before his replacement by Bellingham, St Leger's authority in the spring of 1551 was diluted by the arrival of another military figure and later successor, Sir James Croft. The brief of the latter, at the head of over 2,000 troops, was to secure the southern Irish ports against a rumoured French invasion and to negate the threat from their Scottish allies in the north. To Croft also, as Lord Deputy from May 1551, fell the tasks of pressing on with the colonisation of Leix and Offaly and pushing the advanced Protestantism of the new regime of Protector Northumberland in the smaller island. Having been briefed by the departing St Leger, the new Lord Deputy successfully carried out his instructions regarding the coastline from Waterford through Dungarvan, Youghal, Cork and Kinsale to Berehaven and Baltimore in west County Cork, for which he proposed an English settlement. The stability of the Munster hinterlands was to be ensured through the confirmation of the Earl of Desmond's superintendence of the south-west and the reconciliation of MacCarthy More to royal civil and ecclesiastical power. Turning his attention to Ulster in the autumn of 1551, Croft ordered a thirty-one-day hosting into the heart of Antrim to flush out the MacDonnells who dominated that area north of Belfast Lough. No contact having been made with the Scottish defenders, Croft ordered an expedition to raid Rathlin Island, the base of operations of James MacDonnell. This ended in disaster when one of the boats foundered and its crew were either killed or held for ransom. The emboldened Scots consolidated their hold on the north-east, as far south as Strangford Lough. West of the River Bann, however, the lords of Ulster from O'Neill of Tyrone and O'Donnell down submitted to Croft at Carrickfergus. Garrisons were left there and at Armagh, where Sir Nicolas Bagenal and Matthew O'Neill, the Baron of Dungannon, were charged with restoring internal order in Tyrone. The rivalry between Matthew and Earl Conn O'Neill's eldest son, Shane, was only temporarily shelved, with repercussions in the later 1550s.[33]

Sir James Croft was credited by near-contemporaries with the official initiation of plantation policy in Ireland, specifically in Leix and Offaly, but little actual progress was made during his tenure. The *ad hoc* arrangements which emerged out of the military operations of the late 1540s included the leasing of some estates of former rebels' lands to Old English and New English tenants, as well as the provision of farmlands for the soldier-settlers at Fort

Protector and Fort Governor. The entire area having been surveyed by Walter Cowley in 1550, schemes were put forward in the next year by a consortium of native gentry and English officials for planting Leix, and by St Leger, while Lord Deputy, for settling both Leix and Offaly. These did not find favour in London, and Croft attempted to resolve the ongoing debate by expanding the area under consideration to include all of the confiscated territories of O'Connor and O'More. Projecting its shiring into two units for administrative purposes, Croft planned to have substantial free-holdings for newcomers, rather than small estates leased for short terms. While accepting the former proposal in principle, the London government favoured a large number of small short-term leaseholds, and the planning was further deferred beyond Croft's departure in December 1552. While the comprehensive plantation schemes failed to advance beyond the drawing-board, and the garrisons in Leix and Offaly continued to be a drain on central and local resources alike, costing 7,000 marks a year to keep, Croft was more successful in arranging for the victualling of Carlow and Leighlin garrisons and in maintaining peace among the Kavanaghs and O'Byrnes.[34]

Like Bellingham in 1548–9, Croft attempted to incorporate religious changes within his assertion of royal authority. He recognised that without reform at episcopal level, the popularisation of the new creed among the lower clergy and the laity was unlikely to occur. A major blow in this respect was the implacable opposition of the Primate, Archbishop Dowdall, leading eventually to his defection to Rome in the summer of 1551 after his vigorous but fruitless defence of the mass in disputation with Protestant divines. Croft looked to England for suitable candidates for the vacant bishoprics of Armagh, Cashel and Ossory, or at least for a competent adviser in ecclesiastical matters. The poverty of most Irish sees made postings there unattractive to Englishmen, but eventually in 1552 Hugh Goodacre and John Bale were found agreeable to taking up the dioceses of Armagh and Ossory respectively. Croft was not in Ireland to witness the consecration of these two zealous nominees whom his persistence had induced to come to Ireland. One of them, Goodacre, died in May 1553 before taking possession of his see of Armagh, while Bale was pastor for six turbulent months in Kilkenny before being forced to withdraw in the following September when Roman Catholicism was restored under Queen Mary. The keynote of both episcopacies was struck by Bale's insistence on being ordained according to the pared-down rites of the new English ordinal, and on preaching in Ossory according to the radical Second Book of Common Prayer, introduced in England in 1552 but barely known about in Ireland. John Bale's campaign of iconoclasm and evangelism, while gaining some support in Kilkenny and environs from a younger age group, was bitterly resented by the majority ('helpers found I none among my prebendaries and clergy,' he wrote), who lost no time in reverting to traditional rituals and liturgies, 'with smilings and laughings most dissolutely', once Edward VI's death was announced in July 1553.[35]

Sir James Croft's force of up to 2,500 was sufficient to buttress the fortifications of the extended Pale and old colonial zone, but little more. In the spring of 1552 he expected to have effective control over the entire south of the country and the area from the Shannon and Lough Erne as far as Carrickfergus. A second foray to the northeast failed in the summer of that year, and although an expedition into Connacht to stabilise relations among the Burkes of Clanricard was moderately successful, a pacification of the western province was not attempted. Instead Croft hoped that the fort at Athlone which effectively dominated the Westmeath area would exercise martial jurisdiction. It was left to Sir Thomas Cusack, the Lord Chancellor, to report progress in the coming to fruition of the conciliatory policy which he had so enthusiastically supported in the 1540s. Undertaking a circuit of the west and north, Cusack commented favourably on the development of tillage farming in Clanricard, where ploughs had increased fivefold. Passing eastwards, he found the chieftains of the drumlin belt—O'Farrell of Annaly, O'Reilly of Breifne, MacMahon of Uriel, O'Hanlon of Armagh and Magennis of Iveagh—were in varying degrees well disposed towards the Dublin government. Ominously, those farther north, among them the MacDonnells, O'Neills of Clandeboye and the Shane-led O'Neills of Tyrone, were not amenable to his suasions, and he could only express his hope for the appointment of a resident governor for the region.[36]

While the policy of military containment of internal and external enemies may have achieved some success, the cost of the English establishment in Ireland had increased substantially since the beginning of King Edward's reign. The activist policies pursued down to 1556 drained the English exchequer of an average £24,000 per annum, the deficit reaching £52,000 Irish at the height of Croft's regime in 1552. The returns from the Irish revenues continued to be most disappointing in spite of the acquisition by the crown of a vast store of property. As a method of defraying the expenses accruing to the English exchequer, the government of Edward VI stepped up the practice of issuing debased coins for circulation in Ireland. Whereas these 'harps' of inferior quality to English coins in terms of silver weight had been manufactured for Ireland in London and Bristol down to 1548, between then and 1552 a mint was set up in Dublin, producing money which was up to three times less valuable in silver content than the English equivalent. As well as the offloading in the country of a large number of debased pennies from York, this minting policy led to a slump in business confidence, the hoarding of coins in the hope of the base money being decried, and actual financial hardship to merchants, farmers, rentiers and stipendiaries. Inflation affected city and countryside, and Croft requested a return to nummary fiduciality to prevent a collapse of the fabric of administrative and economic life. Stability of the currency was not restored for several years, and the chaos of the mid-1550s caused increasing scrutiny to be focused from London on the conduct of Irish government.[37]

Among the most importunate plaintiffs to Croft for the establishment of monetary parity between the kingdoms were the merchants of the port towns. Previously, during Bellingham's deputyship, the civic communities of the south coast had complained of the lack of faith of their neighbours, both Gaelic Irish and Anglo-Norman, in the new money. This, combined with the activities of pirates along the coasts, had served to handicap them in their commercial activities. By 1552 the situation had worsened considerably, with credit slumping and great confusion being caused, so that merchants were forced into being farmers, and farmers merchants. Croft's expedition to the south in that year at least showed the flag against pirates. Another real factor influencing financial and general economic welfare in both town and country was the burden of supporting the augmented military and political establishments in their outreaching activities. St Leger had initiated changes in the early 1540s whereby the purveyance and hosting duties of the loyal community were commuted into cash payments and assessed as positive taxes. For his sorties in 1548–9, Bellingham had placed purveyance on a more regular footing, 10,720 pecks of wheat and malt and 2,120 cattle being requisitioned in 1549 alone. Although he had paid at rates which compared favourably with market ones, there was resistance from the mayors of Dublin and Drogheda to the cessing of supplies and carts on their municipalities in lieu of hostings. Croft followed Bellingham in cessing for military forays into the midlands, but the policy was not pushed too far. In any case, the urban communities were compensated for the monetary and purveyance burdens by having their chartered liberties enlarged.[38]

Croft had feared that, but for the army's unprecedented size, the country was 'never liker to have turned to a revolt by means of the money, and decay of the cities and towns'. On his recall to England at the end of 1552, a caretaker administration headed by Sir Thomas Cusack and Sir Gerald Aylmer as Lords Justices was installed as the Privy Council considered how to cut costs and pacify the Gaelic chiefs. The inevitable decision reached, before the death of King Edward in July 1553, was to restore St Leger to the deputyship. His return in November under Queen Mary was popular, and he set about repairing relations and facilitating the reversion to the old religious rites. The latter task was rendered all the easier as the liturgical innovations had not struck deep roots. The fate of Bishop John Bale reflects the triumphalism of some of the conservative clergy and laity, who harried him to the point of fleeing Kilkenny for England and thence the continent. George Dowdall was restored to the archbishopric of Armagh. Among the bishops deprived for having married were Browne of Dublin, Staples of Meath and Lancaster of Kildare, who were replaced by Hugh Curwin, William Walsh and Thomas Leverous respectively. While religious equilibrium was easily re-established, it was much harder for St Leger to strike a political balance. The restoration of the exile Gerald Fitzgerald to the earldom of Kildare and the return of Thomas Butler, the young Earl of Ormond, from court were designed to secure relations in Leinster and east Munster, but problems arose in Thomond and Tyrone over disputed successions to political lordship. Despite St Leger's progress in forming his own broadly based party in Ireland, the old factional networks of Butlers and Fitzgeralds were still in being, with the leading opponents also taking sides in the struggles of rival O'Briens and O'Neills.[39]

Even before he was replaced as Lord Deputy by Thomas Radcliffe, Lord Fitzwalter (later the Earl of Sussex), as a result of a court coup in 1556, Sir Anthony St Leger faced political and financial difficulties in his government of Ireland. Although he displayed a flexible approach in his revision of the terms of the surrender and regrant agreements in relation to the O'Tooles, Kavanaghs and O'Neills, for example, it was clear that many of the lordships throughout the country were disordered. The failure to preserve the Pale from raids by its disgruntled neighbours, the continuing rebellion in the midlands fuelled by the Earl of Kildare's assertion of his position as regional magnate, and the rivalry between the two Anglo-Norman earls of Munster and within the Thomond and Tyrone ruling families, all combined to call into question the successful implementation of the policies of St Leger's earliest deputyship. And while the Lord Deputy had fairly widespread backing among the political groups in the country on account of his magnanimity and patronage, he was at odds once more with an Earl of Ormond — Thomas, son of James. The political disillusionment at St Leger's failure to prevent the spread of pan-provincial faction-alism was compounded for English observers by the continuing high costs of administration and the disappointing revenue returns for Ireland in spite of much-augmented royal properties. St Leger's tenure of office became especially frail when the spotlight was turned on his financial management in 1554.[40]

The principal agent of London's scrutiny of the accounts of the St Leger regime was Sir William Fitzwilliam, who was to be for almost forty years a key figure in Irish affairs. This was the first thoroughgoing, independent auditing of the Irish finances since the late Sir William Brabazon had become Vice-Treasurer and Treasurer of Wars in Ireland in 1534. Brabazon had been succeeded in office by his son-in-law, Sir Andrew Wise, unusually (for an incumbent at that level) a native of the country. There may have been personal animus between Wise and Fitzwilliam, and certainly the latter was of an opposing faction to St Leger at the English court. The exami-nation of the books duly uncovered the tracks of Brabazon's short-changing of the crown: the undervaluing of leases and purchases of state property, the mounting up of substantial arrears of rents payable from favoured lessees and the endowing of the clientèle of Lord Deputy and Vice-Treasurer with bounteous grants. A total of £2,100, for example, was being lost annually owing to undervaluing of leases. The Lord Deputy himself owed the crown almost £5,000 Irish on his Irish estates. Of course, St Leger could argue, as he had done on the previous occasion of his being called to book in 1546, that such a system of alleged graft and corruption was perfectly justified in view of his need to win friends for his conciliatory policies from a broad cross-section of the population of Ireland.[41]

The deterioration in the viceroy's political and financial credibility was a prelude to a drive against him at court in 1556. William Fitzwilliam became a stalking-horse in Ireland for his brother-in-law, Lord Fitzwalter, who replaced the veteran deputy in the later spring of 1556. The way had been paved by the removal of some key members of St Leger's civil and military entourage, leaving him exposed to his political foes. Fitzwilliam himself took over from Sir Thomas Cusack as Keeper of the Great Seal in 1555, and John Parker, the Master of the Rolls, and Gerald Aylmer also lost office in the shake-up which presaged St Leger's departure. The Irish factional network headed by the Earl of Ormond meshed with that of the Howard faction at the English court to outflank St Leger, whose own political backers were in eclipse at that time. Fitzwalter was appointed governor of Ireland in May 1556, having sought the office on a promise of outperforming St Leger. Instead of lethargy and laxity he guaranteed action, instead of peculation he gave assurance of probity, and instead of long-term, uncertainly costed reform schemes he pledged a short-term, precisely budgeted programme. Having laid the basis of the policy to be followed by his successors, Sir Anthony St Leger was recalled to England in April 1556 without, at least in his own view, having been given the time necessary for its fulfilment.[42]

Elizabethan Ireland

The Pale and Greater Leinster, 1556–88

ON 25 August 1580 several thousand, mostly inexperienced, troops under the command of the new viceroy, Arthur, Lord Grey de Wilton, stumbled down the steep slopes of the south Wicklow mountains into the rocky defile of Glenmalure. The English-led army was on the march to engage and destroy the rebel band of James Eustace, Viscount Baltinglass, and his Gaelic ally, Feagh MacHugh O'Byrne. Against the better judgment of some older hands such as Sir Francis Cosby and Jacques Wingfield, Grey had determined to confront his enemies in the heart of their rugged fastness. The brightly clad soldiers with their scarlet and blue doublets and white hose were easy targets for the allied fighters, waiting behind their natural shelter of trees and boulders with their guns, bows and axes. As feared by the veteran English officers, the venture into the glen had disastrous results for the disoriented pikemen, who were led to attempt to escape the ambush by scrambling up the side opposite their descent, the bodies of the slain rolling down into the craggy, red-stained river-bed below. Sir William Stanley, among whose rearguard company there were several casualties, wrote a graphic description of the action in that glen 'full of slippery rocks, stones, bogs and wood' and commented that 'it was the hottest piece of service for the time that ever I saw in any place'.[1]

Expeditions into the Gaelic zones of Leinster by prominent Englishmen, from King Richard II in 1399 to the Earl of Essex two hundred years later, came to grief in the face of guerrilla-type tactics of chieftains operating within protecting landscapes. Lord Grey de Wilton's discomfiture in 1580, all the more embarrassing for its happening less than thirty miles from Dublin, serves to show that extreme political disaffection in inhospitable terrain was a recurring problem for the central administration. Despite the continuities fostered by polity and place, however, there can be no doubt that by the late 1550s Leinster, of all the provinces, was the one most dramatically affected by political and social changes since the early 1530s, its pacification and defence being a key element in all of the policy designs forthcoming in that span. Extreme dislocation had been caused by the defeat and fall of the Kildare Geraldines in the mid-1530s, not just in the south-western Pale but all through the Gaelic and gaelicised midlands to southern Ulster. It was only after the eleventh earl's restoration in 1553 that renewed equilibrium became possible. Successive English governors from Lord Leonard Grey onwards had tackled the political problem of Gaelic Leinster partly by onslaughts on the physical environment. Grey's own forays into Offaly in the late 1530s resulted in the cutting of wide border passes; St Leger's grants to favoured supporters envisaged settlements on crown lands in the border territories; and Bellingham's fortresses at Daingean and Ballyadams in Offaly and Leix were consolidated by Croft. For the Palespeople and the Gaelic Irish of the midlands and south, the policy of outreach in Leinster was presenting acute challenges of accommodation not just with physical changes but also with social, economic and political developments.[2]

In this chapter the pace of change in Leinster will be gauged by reference to the policies of the English administration, the aspirations of the extended Pale community in town and county, the extremes of reaction of Gaelic clans from acquiescence to war, and the character of the New English settlement. The objectives of the province-minded Elizabethan regimes in relation to Leinster bear scrutiny, particularly in view of the opportunities presented by the accessibility of most of the population. In view of the political and religious divisions which opened up in the later years of the century, the question of the Palespeople's role in facilitating or frustrating the government's designs assumes major significance, especially given the costs to them of the government's ambitious schemes for the rest of Ireland. Within this context may be seen the impact of state concerns on the urban communities, including Dublin, and on the Anglo-Norman aristocrats. For the Gaelic population of the midlands, confronted with full-scale colonisation, rebellion may have seemed the only option, but varieties of response are evident on the part of clan chieftains and sept leaders, while for the non-planted Gaelic parts of southern Leinster the presence of military governors brought acceptance, compromise or rejection. The socio-economic and cultural influence of the comparatively dense New English settlement is worthy of study in a final conjunction of elements which may lead to a fuller understanding of the crisis in Leinster in the early to mid-1580s, as crystallised in the Glenmalure episode.

Ambitious lord deputyships and Leinster, 1556–79

With the arrival of Thomas Radcliffe (later Earl of Sussex) in Ireland in the late spring of 1556 a pattern of pan-insular, programmatic government was established which lasted until the late Elizabethan period. In contrast to the gradualism of the St Leger years of the mid-century, the mode of administration adopted by Sussex and by his successors as viceroy, Sir Henry Sidney and Sir John Perrot, was characterised by determined, carefully costed action based on preselected objectives to be attained within short spells. Although the overall aim of reforming the communities in Ireland through the systematic extension of English law remained constant, the inflexible commitment to planned targets marked these governors' strategy apart from their predecessor's. They promised the queen speedy results, founding their governance on factional backing at court and independence of the networks of affinity within Ireland. A key factor in their schematised approach to solving the country's problems was the provincial perspective, Munster, Connacht and ultimately Ulster to be ruled by presidency councils, and Leinster, with its contrasting regions, to be the mainstay of English civility. A *sine qua non* of successful viceroyalty was the protection of the Pale bastion against raids from restless neighbours. Thus the defensive features of previous regimes, including the rebuilding of wards, the appointment of seneschals, the settlement of derelict outposts with martial residents and the furthering of plantation in Leix and Offaly, all had to be retained. Colonial enterprise was to be prioritised, not just as a shield for the Pale shires but also for its exemplary force in the thrusting new programmes for Ireland, even if detrimental to the surrender and regrant agreements still in being with most Gaelic lords. While native reformers were not cultivated as warmly as before, the maintaining of the well-being of the indigenous communities continued to be important for the governors after 1556. In spite of proposed measures for easing commercial and social problems, however, there is no doubt that military concerns, mostly in other provinces, contributed much to the disaffection of Palespeople, faced with increased demands for purveyance and billeting. Moreover, care had to be taken that the reinstated Earl of Kildare did not become a focus for dissidents of English and Gaelic origin in all parts of the province who were growing resentful of the administration's tactics.[3]

From the start Sussex promised to satisfy his court backers by restoring crown prestige in Ireland and by governing honestly through his chosen officials. The former aim was to be fulfilled by the strict upholding of the surrender and regrant agreements, especially in Tyrone and Thomond, the expulsion of the Scots from the north-east of the country, and the establishment of the plant-ation in Leix and Offaly. The latter aim was to be attained through judicious appointments, such as those of his brother, Sir Henry Radcliffe, his brothers-in-law, Sir Henry Sidney and Sir William Fitzwilliam, and Sir George Stanley, Sir Jacques Wingfield and Captain Nicholas Heron, all of whom were to be agents of reform of the civil and military administrations. The new Lord Deputy envisaged savings to the English treasury in martial expenditure not just by operating with a smaller garrison but also by demanding an increase in purveyance and other contributions from the Pale com-munity. A man whose style and rhetoric raised artificial expectations of what he could achieve, Sussex boldly applied himself to test cases in Irish government, the first of which he identified in 1556–7 as the settlement of a proper colony in Leix and Offaly. For the rest of Gaelic Leinster he was happy to allow the existing arrangements made under St Leger to stand, with his own chosen seneschals and constables exercising a military and civil jurisdiction compounded of Irish and English law.[4]

At his parliament of 1557–8 Sussex pressed on with giving legal effect to the midland plantation. The languishing of the original arrangements under Edward VI was a source of grave embarrassment to royal authority. Now with the creation of two new shires, Queen's County (Leix) and King's County (Offaly), the hope was that the system of self-financing centres of English civility could be set up, securing the Pale frontier to the Shannon and controlling the indigenous population. The plans for those remaining Gaelic Irish inhabitants were for their integration into the new core society of ordered villages and a stable economy, rather than for their extirpa-tion or enslavement. In characteristically optimistic fashion, Sussex expected that within a year of the settlement being established English law and civility would be embraced by the Gaelic Irish. But already by the summer of 1557 this flagship settlement, crucial for

Sussex's grand national design as well as for regional stability, was running into great difficulties. The O'Mores and O'Connors had submitted to the Lord Deputy on his progresses through the two counties, but broke their pledges almost immediately. While the captured Conal O'More was executed at Leighlin Bridge, Donough O'Connor seized Meelick castle on the Shannon, which Sussex and his army had to relieve in the summer of 1558. The countryside in the east of the counties remained most disturbed, with Philipstown (Fort Governor) being burnt and Maryborough (Fort Protector) besieged, and the garrisons being maintained at great cost to the inhabitants. By the end of Sussex's tenure in 1564 Henry, his brother, as governor of the region, far from supervising any significant settlement there, had barely managed to hold the forts.[5]

Besides damaging his reputation, Sussex's failure in one of his national aims in relation to Leix and Offaly had serious implications for policy in Leinster. Not only did the security of the Pale suffer because of continuing Gaelic revolt in the midlands and raids by the defiant Shane O'Neill in the northern borders, but also the incessant martial activity against avowed enemies resulted in a huge burden of taxation falling on the loyal community there. Sussex lost no time in levying the shires of the Pale for the supply of the forts in Leix and Offaly, and also in extracting large supplies of food in lieu of general hostings. As the numbers in his army increased to well over 2,000 by 1560, costs of victualling and maintenance rocketed to an average of over £30,000 per annum, a sum which was irregularly recouped from London. Therefore the country paid dearly in terms of feeding the household and garrison at fixed state rates which fell well below the market prices, as well as in commuted hostings and carting fees and the billeting of troops in the border zones. All of these elements were subsumed within the pejoratively termed 'cess' form of taxation. Sussex responded sharply to mounting criticism of the cess by native establishment figures such as Archbishop Dowdall and the Anglo-Norman magnates by claiming that the protests were self-interested and shortsighted, and in particular citing the allegedly disgruntled Earl of Kildare as a prime conspirator against him. Having surmounted one concerted challenge to his regime in 1558, and having refloated his government with the more prestigious title of Lord Lieutenant, conferred on him in 1560, Sussex was later challenged by student lawyers and gentlemen of the Pale in 1562 who questioned the application of the cess before

Elizabeth at court. At that time Sussex's factional backing there was losing out to the group led by Lord Robert Dudley, and he found himself increasingly vulnerable to charges of fiscal mismanagement and misappropriation. His programme in ruins, Sussex had no option ultimately but to seek a recall in 1563.[6]

The principal investigator of embezzlement in the army, alleged by Pale critics of Sussex, was Sir Nicholas Arnold, who came to succeed him in the governorship on his departure in May 1564. Although resented by the senior military for his tactics of listening to complaints of the rank and file, Lord Justice Arnold, a veteran client of the Northumberland–Dudley faction, gained popularity with the community of the Pale for his smaller army, his break with Sussex personnel, and his consultation of local political interests. Symbolic of this bond of trust was the revival of Sir Thomas Cusack's career and the prestigious upgrading of the Earl of Kildare's position in the midlands command. But if Arnold hoped to revive the politics of goodwill of the later St Leger years, his optimism was ill-founded, as bitter factionalism erupted in Munster between Ormond and Desmond, the dynastic struggle festered in Thomond, and the inveterate Shane O'Neill reneged on a treaty engineered by Cusack and other intermediaries. Worse still, O'Neill and the O'Mores and O'Connors attacked the Leix and Offaly settlements and renewed the invasion of the Pale, now more vulnerable because of a reduced garrison. Arnold was recalled, and replaced in October 1565 by Sir Henry Sidney, who, though an earlier confidant of Sussex, had become Leicester's protégé. A man experienced in Irish affairs through his terms as Vice-Treasurer and Lord Justice there down to 1559, he had added lustre to his high aristocratic ranking through his successful presidency of Wales in the early 1560s. As had his predecessor, Sidney offered the queen an economically costed package of specific reforms to be achieved within a short time-span through the agency of a competent and personally dedicated following. While his programme was not strikingly different from Sussex's, there was much more stress on provincial government through presidency councils as experienced by him in Wales, and individual colonial schemes were furthered with greater determination, perhaps in the light of his familiarity with Spanish colonial thought.[7]

At first the new Lord Deputy aspired to the cordiality of relations within Leinster which Sir Anthony St Leger had enjoyed down to the mid-1550s. As an earnest of such amity, the Earl of

Kildare was given high military responsibility in the Pale borders, and St Leger's son, Warham, came in Sidney's entourage as adviser and President-designate of Munster. By securing guarantees of regular pay from England for his garrison of 1,500, 'Sir Harry', as he was affectionately known among the Palespeople, hoped to prevent further impoverishment of the eastern counties. Moreover, his anticipated establishment of presidency councils in Munster and Connacht would, it was believed, lead to the incorporation of hundreds of thousands of acres of territory within the crown's jurisdiction, from which substantial subsidy payments would be forthcoming to increase revenues. The money thus raised would go towards the campaign for the eventual pacification of Ulster. But Sidney's priorities were changed in early 1566 owing to internal factionalism in Ireland, particularly in Munster, and also court pressure to do what Sussex had failed to do: overthrow Shane O'Neill. The combination of augmented military resources bearing down heavily on the loyal community of the Pale, as well as the unveiling of plans for nucleated English settlements by private individuals after Shane's death in June 1567, served to embitter the Lord Deputy's dealings with the political elites of the Leinster region after a promising start, and at the crucial juncture of the meeting of parliament in January 1569.[8]

That much-delayed assembly was intended by Sidney as the occasion for legislative action on three fronts which would, he thought, ultimately benefit the Pale and its environs: firstly, the reclaiming of Ulster for the crown in pursuance of an internal provincial settlement would secure its borders with Leinster; secondly, the banning of levies by the feudal lords for private armies would aid the process of demilitarisation of the lordships within and without the Pale; and finally, a variety of economic and educational measures would foster prosperity and culture. In principle, the policies of colonialism and garrisoning to be embarked upon after the destruction of Shane, at Newry, for example, and in Antrim, were similar to those already in train in Leinster. The very slow evolution of the military-style plantation in Leix and Offaly into a civil, fully anglicised community was encouraged by Sidney, with the incorporation of Maryborough and Philipstown as boroughs in 1569 and a network of estates and farms radiating out from them. In practice, the settlements remained under siege from some of the displaced natives, but a population of at least 500

English came into the area. For the Gaelic inhabitants of the central and southern parts of Ulster, the Lord Deputy had in mind arrangements very similar to those which he so actively made in Gaelic Leinster within months of his appointment. He had inspected and reformed the seneschal scheme, looking forward to the payment by the native chiefs of rent to the crown instead of military exactions to an overlord or English captain. To this end, he was less insistent on rigid adherence to primogeniture on the part of clan leaders, but was prepared to negotiate indentures with elected *tánaistí*.[9]

What caused destabilisation in Leinster was Sidney's allowing of the claims of Sir Peter Carew from Devon to the barony of Idrone in Carlow, occupied by the Kavanaghs under Butler overlordship, and the manor of Maston in Meath, where Sir Christopher Cheevers resided. Carew's research and legal proceedings were aided by the Lord Deputy as part of the overall drive to settle Englishmen on confiscated lands in Ulster, Munster and now Leinster. These successful land claims overshadowed much of the proceedings of the parliament of 1569–71. Mistrust of Sidney on the part of the members led to constitutional clashes over the rights of certain M.P.s to sit in the Commons. The dramatic withdrawal of Sir Edmund Butler, one of the leading opposition figures, to head a revolt in the Barrow region jeopardised the bill for outlawing coign and livery. Even the well-intentioned proposals for the reform of trading and manufacture were treated with suspicion by the merchants and gentry in the Commons, though fiscal measures for a subsidy and a duty on wine imports eventually passed into law. Sidney later claimed that popish reaction was behind the recalcitrance of the parliamentarians. More likely as a contributory factor was the resurfacing of entrenched resistance to cessing and billeting of an augmented army deployed to deal not just with the Leinster revolts but with four near-contemporaneous uprisings in Munster and Connacht. These were also occasioned by insensitive intrusions of adventurers sponsored by Sir Henry Sidney into areas in the possession of leading Anglo-Norman families.[10]

Sir William Fitzwilliam, who served as Lord Justice after Sidney's recall in the spring of 1571, was appointed Lord Deputy in the following December and remained in office until the autumn of 1575. Already very experienced through his decade and more as Vice-Treasurer in Ireland, Fitzwilliam's modest ambition on assuming the viceroyalty was to gain remission of a huge debt with which he was charged on his service. His low-key, unpretentious approach to the job initially recommended itself to Queen Elizabeth, who was exasperated by the prodigality of Sidney's programme. After the failure of the presidency councils in Munster and Connacht to foster socio-political reform, and the antagonising of loyal populations there and in Leinster by colonial ventures, a time of minimal activity with a reduced garrison seemed to be called for. Thus Fitzwilliam, with a force of 1,300 at his disposal, presided over a system of virtually autonomous provincial regimes, with Sir John Perrot ruling in Munster, Sir Edward Fitton in Connacht, and the Earl of Essex briefly becoming governor of Ulster. His own preference for involving the more tractable and loyal elements in the administration meant that the period of the early 1570s in Leinster was one of relative calm. Because there was little or no attempt on the deputy's part to integrate the aspects of government, the Pale community was relieved of having to bear the burden of an elaborate pan-insular policy. Meanwhile he maintained the scheme of seneschals, relying on these English captains to control and police the Gaelic regions of south Ulster, the midlands and south Leinster, where the reverberations of the Carew land claim in Idrone continued to be felt. The Earl of Kildare was given command of the southern and western borders of the Pale at the head of an army of 400, but in 1574 he was arrested on suspicion of colluding with Gaelic rebels, including Rory O'More. The weakening of Fitzwilliam's position was mainly due, however, to the escalating costs of policies outside Leinster over which he had little control and of which he disapproved.[11]

As Fitzwilliam's administration tottered, Sir Henry Sidney offered to serve again as Lord Deputy and was appointed in August 1575. Having seen his earlier presidency schemes fail through the mishandling of the provincial magnates, Sidney now believed that he knew how to deal with their objections to the spreading of English law and administration. This is why he confidently contracted to make Ireland financially self-sufficient within three years at a cost of £60,000 to the crown and the deployment of an army of 1,100. The new scheme incorporated analysis by his erstwhile private secretary, Edmund Tremayne, and the actual experience of Sir Edward Fitton as President of Connacht in the early 1570s. President Fitton had been forced to demand a fixed tax of a mark on every ploughland in the south of the province to feed and supply the army needed to put down rebellions against his authority.

Honing Fitton's and Tremayne's ideas, Sidney planned to replace the coign and livery system of arbitrary exactions for war purposes by the lords for a tax or rent to the crown, according to the value of such services to the lord. The immediate advantage for the overlords in the provinces, besides relief from foraging for their 'cuttings', was that they could be guaranteed military support by the new 'overlord', the provincial president and his army. For the lesser lords, too, the advantages of this system of support for a provincial army were marked. For the payment of a 'composition' rent to the crown they were freed from the intolerable incubus of coign and livery, and thus their independence of the superior was adumbrated (though a separate, compensatory rent was still payable to the traditional overlord). For the state administration the attractions were financial and socio-political. Sidney's dream of extending crown jurisdiction to the provinces seemed to offer sufficient enrichment to relieve the drain on the English treasury. And he was also confident that the reordering of financial, military and political relations within this new scheme for national composition would be an engine of social reform, with the emergence of a shired, freeholding society modelled upon that of England.[12]

It was upon the Pale that Sidney centred his attention in his anxiety to get his plan for national composition off the ground in the autumn of 1575. By commuting the government's own military charges on the loyal territories into a fixed annual tax, not only would a headline be set for the other provinces, but a valuable resource would be tapped for the ambitious countrywide scheme. Immediately on his arrival, therefore, the Lord Deputy ordered the provision by the landholders of the eastern counties of a substantial amount of food for the garrison, or, if they preferred, the payment of a low monetary tax, at a rate of £2 13s 4d per ploughland. This alternative, which Sidney presented as a bargain, was to subsume all the existing exactions, such as cesses, billeting, hosting and cartage, and was to be distributed equitably as exemptions for larger landowners were phased out. In the wake of two consecutive poor harvests and a severe outbreak of plague, however, the lords of the Pale reacted negatively to Sidney's proposals. Thus, as regional councils and composition schemes were set in place in both Munster and Connacht, Sidney faced mounting opposition in Leinster. Countering the objection of the Pale community that his new composition tax was being imposed illegally without reference to parliament, Sidney argued that the revenue was incident to the crown by virtue of its prerogative and accordingly was not negotiable. A massive campaign of resistance to cess demands in the shires, organised by lords such as Gormanston, Howth and Baltinglass, culminated in a petition of three lawyers, Barnaby Scurlock, Richard Netterville and Henry Burnell, to the Privy Council in early 1577. After terms of imprisonment in the Tower of London for the delegates and in Dublin Castle of some leading gentlemen, Sidney's position was gravely weakened by the countenancing of the petition at court, where Kildare and Ormond gave support. While the principle of the queen's prerogative was not conceded, a compromise was sought on the basis of alleviation of the cess bill. Once again disillusioned by the failure of her Irish deputies' promises to govern economically, maintain the friendship of loyal locals and defend the Pale, Elizabeth was preparing for Sidney's final recall from the country in September 1578. As he left, the Gaelic region of south Leinster was in uproar owing to the raids and burnings of Rory O'More, Feagh MacHugh O'Byrne and Conor MacCormac O'Connor, and the massacre of O'Connor and O'More clansmen at Mullaghmast, County Kildare, in late 1577.[13]

Coexistence and conflict among Old English, Gaelic Irish and New English

Sir Henry Sidney's elaborate national programme had effectively been destroyed by the opposition of the leading politicians in the Pale. By 1578 their disenchantment with English government policy had intensified to the point where the members of the social elite of the eastern region comprised an opposition to the administration, rather than a participant element therein. A consensus was being forged despite the regional, political and socio-economic differences at work among the group. Undoubtedly it was the collection of exactions, known pejoratively as the cess, which had crystallised for them the issues at stake. Innocuous enough in times of benign governance down to 1556, the government's systematised taking had become increasingly burdensome under the ambitious deputyships of Sussex and Sidney. Concurrently, as the garrison was consolidated and then increased in numbers, power which the local loyal community may have hoped to wield through the Dublin executive was diluted by the centring of policy-making in defence and other matters on the London court. Worse still, the state militancy of the 1560s and 1570s, directed against troublesome elements in the other provinces, proved to be unsuccessful at the point of deployment, and also in securing the Pale shires and its extended hinterland from attack. So the community leaders railed incessantly, in an increasingly organised way, against the depredations of the English troops and the exactions of the governors. In doing so they were voicing their concern at the diminution of traditional privileges of representation and consultation which were vested in their ancient commonwealth.[14]

Essentially conservative in their harking back to an idealised past, the core group of activists who spearheaded the anti-cess campaign were skilled in the ways of constitutional manoeuvring. Such litigious representation underlay the development of a set of more sharply defined principles, social, economic and religious, forming the sum of hallowed rights to be preserved in the face of mounting challenge from rivals. The key question as it presented itself to governor and community defenders alike in the mid-1570s was the balance between royal prerogative and the subjects' rights and duties. For Lord Deputy Sidney the principle was simply stated: 'Examine not [the prince's] authority, neither decipher his power. Compare not your principles with his authority, neither dispute your liberties with his prerogative.' The queen's loyal Irish subjects, on the other hand, insisted that the governor was innovating by raising occasional feudal levies to the status of permanent positive taxes, to be levied without parliamentary approval of their representatives. To press their case, the Palespeople deployed a variety of defences, including parliamentary remonstration (focused on opposition to the suspension of Poynings' Law and the representation of newcomers), civil disobedience and subverting the governors by presenting suits at the London court. In the consequent imbroglio, Sidney's elaborated view of the constitutional position conflicted with some key points of political belief of the older colonists, among them their right to be consulted about plans for the island's future and their role in the expansion of English power therein. To accompany their growing sense of frustration, the Pale leaders slowly separated themselves out in name as in constitutional aspiration, not just from the Gaelic inhabitants of the region and outside, but also from the newcomers from England who were increasingly agents of the discriminatory policy embodied in Sidney's provincial designs. Thus from the later 1560s they self-consciously referred to themselves as 'Her Majesty's old faithful English subjects of Ireland' and by the end of the century had abbreviated this simply to 'Old English'.[15]

It is certain that the issues arising out of the cess controversy impelled the process of alienation of the Old English and their forming of themselves into a separate elite by the later Elizabethan period. But in Leinster there were varying levels of economic and political aspiration and experience among the old colonials which conditioned their reactions to government policy, thus ensuring a differing rate of disenchantment among specific groups. These, taken in combination with other factors at work among the loyalist population, make it necessary to examine in greater detail economic and social developments among the rural and urban members of the Old English community. Although the cess was universally hated, its burdensomeness varied from place to place within the counties, and as between the city and country areas. Moreover, while it was fashionable to complain about the depredations of the soldiery, the grounds for valid grievances shifted. Along with these aspects, and the politico-constitutional ones already adverted to, may be studied the cultural forces at work among the community members as they came to terms with newcomers as well as Gaelic Irish among their neighbours. In this connection, the importance of religion in their mentality may be discussed.[16]

The economic pressure on the inhabitants of the less settled shires of Leinster was intense. In the lordships of Kildare and Ormond's Kilkenny the earls' coign and livery demands were compounded by the raiding of the O'Mores, O'Connors, Kavanaghs and even Butler and Geraldine rebels. Losses amounting to £50,000 were sustained, for example, by the natives of Kilkenny during the 1569 campaign of the insurgent Butler brothers and their Fitzgerald allies, and the gentlemen of Kildare had to bear the costs of their earl's campaigns in the midlands. The aristocratic families of Westmeath and south Kildare, the Nugents and Eustaces, also maintained their vulnerable positions through coign and livery, which burden, as well as that of other rents and dues on the tenantry of the estates, depressed the economy and meant that there remained little or no agricultural surpluses. Yet the gentry of English descent in these outer counties — Kildare, Kilkenny and Westmeath — as well as in north Louth and Wexford were nothing if not adaptable, and they clung to their leases of monastic land gained in the great bonanza of the mid-century to sustain their economic positions. Evidence suggests that despite the exactions of their lords and the depredations of troops, English-style tenure was maintained, certainly in Kildare and Kilkenny, and much agrarian activity was carried on into the later century. Trading difficulties persisted as in the 1530s, with recurring complaints about 'grey merchants' and disruption of riverine and road routes. It is not surprising that, with the exception of Kilkenny, Ormond's premier city, most of the inland towns of Leinster, such as Naas, Kildare, Athy and Mullingar, continued to languish.[17]

By contrast, the residents of the inner Pale—in County Dublin and east Meath—enjoyed favourable economic conditions in the mid-Elizabethan years, the complaints of the leaders of the anti-cess campaign notwithstanding. Although bad harvests occasionally constricted supplies, as in 1575 and 1576 for example, the commercial success of the ports of Dublin and Drogheda in the export of raw materials suggests that there was a fairly prosperous hinterland between the Liffey and Boyne valleys. Opportunities for investment in land and property in the sheltered inner Pale facilitated the gentrification of urban patricians who had already benefited by crown leases. Efficient managers of county estates could make profits through the supplying of the increased garrison from the later 1560s onwards. Close ties between the mercantile and gentry sectors led to the effective exploitation of food supplies and other products such as sheepskins, flax and wool for domestic and foreign markets. There may have been a dearth of enclosures in the Pale by comparison with England, but the population of Fingal was 'addicted to all points of husbandry', and the impression is given of a mixed farming economy, profitable in most years, though vulnerable to the demands of cessors and garrison commanders. It is not surprising that the opposition to the cess should have been greatest among the county gentry, who had most to lose. And Sir Henry Sidney's efforts to close loopholes for those who evaded the cess evoked much resentment from those who saw their lucrative exemptions in jeopardy.[18]

While the M.P.s of the port towns of Leinster may have supported their gentry counterparts in opposition in the House of Commons in 1569–71, the regime continued to view the municipalities benignly down to the 1580s. The chartered privileges of the corporations and merchant guilds ensured that economic prosperity underpinned political loyalty in the critical years of Elizabeth's reign. The enforced supplying by the Dublin merchants of the garrison did cause resentment to flare sporadically, as in 1569 for example, and the onus of billeting troops fell with increasing insistence upon the civic households of those below patrician status. But the commitment of the administration, particularly Sidney's, to the commercial and industrial welfare of the port towns was evident in the package of mercantilist measures presented to parliament in 1569. Designed to direct the flow of trade through recognised head ports, to foster manufacture by preventing the export of certain raw materials such as wool and flax and to regularise the customs regime, the bills were changed, mostly to take account of mercantile fears of losses of privileges, with only the impost on wines having medium- to long-term benefits for the government's revenues. For the rest, the towns managed to win even greater control over customs revenues for their treasuries, the restrictions on exports were evaded, and certain duties such as that on sheepskins were exploited for great profit by the Dublin merchant guild. As with their counterpart leadership at colonial level, the civic authorities operated a most effective lobbying system with conduits to the royal court, and thus any attempts by officious state servants to interfere with commerce in Dublin were easily outmanoeuvred by the urban elite.[19]

The patricians from the major towns had attained substantial political influence under the auspices of the Tudors, and this was reflected in their social ascendancy within and without the walls of the boroughs. Aided by their acquisitions of monastic leases, the most prosperous patricians gradually became integrated into county society through propitious marriage alliances and ties of wardship. The construction of country seats by gentrified patricians bore testimony to this trend, and from the urban–gentry matrimonial nexus in the east of the Pale region there radiated out systems of affinity which incorporated the higher aristocratic families of the peripheries. Added social coherence was achieved through the trading contacts of city merchants with rural suppliers in the Pale interior, the agents of the townsmen operating with magnate approval. Yet uniformity in English social mores was not evident, particularly to newcomers in the early Elizabethan period, one of whom wrote: 'All the English and the most part with delight, yea even in Dublin, speak Irish and are greatly spotted in manners, habit and conditions with Irish stains.' Adverse comment also came from New English officials on matters such as the oppressive authority of landowners over their tenants, increasingly of Gaelic origin, the exaction of coign and livery, failure to maintain institutions of local adminstration such as courts, and the inefficiency and partiality of native lawyers and agents of government. Most of these criticisms applied to the outer fringes of the Pale because, while the speaking of Irish had permeated the eastern towns and their hinterlands, the system of landholding there was differentiated more along English shire lines and the framework of local government was intact.[20]

As social cynosures in the Elizabethan period, the two provincial earls proved to be disappointing. The eleventh Earl of Kildare, with his scientific and Neoplatonist interests, was a man of the late Renaissance, and his castles were foci of his social ascendancy and power within the earldom. Yet the weight of expectation upon him as exemplar and ally coming both from the government side and from the natives of English and Gaelic background proved to be too crushing for him, and Earl Gerald ended his days in prison away from Kildare, mistrusted by all. The Earl of Ormond's construction of his mansion at Carrick-on-Suir, unfortified as an earnest of his trust in a peaceful future, was accompanied by his settling of his Kilkenny county estates after his success as general in the Desmond wars down to 1583. Kilkenny city under Earl Thomas advanced in architectural sophistication with the erection of merchant housing, though it was only later that the building of castellated dwellings, in Counties Louth and Wexford for instance, could be abandoned in favour of conventional manor-houses. But Ormond too fell victim to New English suspicion and jealousy. The Kildare and Ormond social systems deviated from the English norm in continuing to maintain retinues within the principal castles. Despite the efforts of the government to dissolve the private armies, circumstances in the outer regions of Leinster were not appropriate for the relinquishing by the lords of their defence corps. In the inner Pale, house styles were comparable to those of the English shires, with the cage-work houses of leading merchants dominating the streetscapes of Elizabethan Dublin and Drogheda. Here dress too was in accordance with English norms, if a little behind metropolitan fashions. But even in the old colonial heartland the dialect of the inhabitants, especially the rural-dwellers, was anachronistic by the standards of their contemporaries across the water, with 'the dregs of the old ancient Chaucer English' being retained, most notably in Wexford.[21]

There is a consensus among modern writers that their strong commitment to Catholicism by the end of the Tudor period was a result of and not a cause of the alienation of the older colonials from the state. Certainly the ideas of the European Counter-Reformation came to be central to the mature constitutional stance of the Old English in the early seventeenth century, counterbalancing the Protestant colonial mentality of the New English. The parents of the Pale who sent their offspring to the continent could not have been unaware of the curricular implications of choosing the academies at Louvain and Douai. The easy-going church-papistry of the 1560s and early 1570s in the Pale allowed a predisposition to religious conservatism to blossom into recusancy by the 1580s. In the absence of a thorough programme of evangelisation on behalf of the state religion, devotional and institutional continuities with the pre-Reformation era were maintained. With no further material incentive to change, the majority of the gentry and merchant groups, as well as the clergy of the province, remained rooted in the old ways. The native intelligentsia, small though it was, still fostered the humanistic ideal of reform of the island's Gaelic population through education and persuasion, and a scheme for a university college which would harness Erasmian principles to state educational policy about 1570 came to nothing. Attachment to the Catholic reform movement did not efface cultural antipathy of Old English to Gaelic Irish, and indeed the norms propounded by the Council of Trent served to intensify the zeal of the former for the social regeneration of their fellow-islanders. But for a small number of younger members of the Pale community, trained in the law and highly politicised during the cess controversy, Catholic conviction merged with intense opposition to the regime in the 1570s to foster radical religious dissent.[22]

It seemed in 1578–9 as if the Pale community had gained a lasting victory with the recall of Sir Henry Sidney and the installation of a lower-profile lord justiceship, first under Sir William Drury until September 1579 and then under Sir William Pelham. But events in that year outside the province in Munster, where the Geraldines revolted at the instigation of James FitzMaurice Fitzgerald, created insecurity and tension. While in the more settled areas of Leinster the gentry and merchants watched events with embarrassment, the radical analysis of the politico-religious situation propounded by the disaffected young lawyers found favour with the more gaelicised elite families in the outskirts of the Pale. The Geraldine dynastic nexus, deployed in sympathy with the Desmond rebels, brought some of the leading old colonials, including Fitzgerald collaterals, the Eustaces and Nugents and their supporters, into a confederation of extreme antagonism to the government. The Earl of Kildare was under pressure from English and Irish factions to lead a rebellion, but fought shy of active involvement. Among the Eustace family at least the force of the Counter-Reformation crusade was felt in resonance with FitzMaurice, as was apparent when James Eustace, Viscount Baltinglass, who had spent some years at Rome in the 1570s, gave clear evidence that he was susceptible to Catholic priestly influence at home. Linked as many of them were to their Gaelic neighbours through marriage and trade, and participant in their cultural milieu of bardic literature and Irish-speaking, these Old English families were also sensitive to spasms of anger among the clans at New English encroachment. Thus, with the eyes of Lord Justice Pelham fixed firmly on the Munster conflagration, the Dublin government was caught off-guard when Baltinglass rose in revolt in the south-western Pale, with the backing of Feagh MacHugh O'Byrne of Gabhal Raghnaill.[23]

That Feagh became a focus for extreme reaction to the trend of government policy in south Leinster among older English as well as Gaelic inhabitants points up the interlocking nature of the two societies. The fusion of concerns was quickened in a milieu of intensive interaction between central and local power in extra-Pale Leinster since the 1530s. The violent outbreak of some leaders down to and beyond the mid-Elizabethan period was not the exclusive or characteristic mode of Gaelic magnate dealings with the crown. A variety of responses from full assimilation of reform to outright rejection thereof marked the demeanour of individual clanspeople, many of whom veered from one option to another within their own career spans. Full and consistent political loyalty was forthcoming from clans such as the O'Dempseys; socio-economic changes were absorbed, as among some north Wicklow O'Tooles and O'Byrnes to an extent; and cultural transformation was embraced by the resort of the children of chiefs such as Brian MacCahir Kavanagh and Rory Caoch O'Connor to schools in the Pale and universities in England. The crisis of the early 1580s, however, denotes a fairly pervasive failure to effect peaceful conciliation of the key Gaelic clansmen as envisaged by the surrender and regrant policy pioneered by St Leger in the 1540s. The initial arrangements between the crown and the Gaelic lords were not sufficiently cognisant of the complexities of the Gaelic socio-political system, especially its power structures, succession pattern, militarism and inter-sept rivalries. Modifications of the agreements in the wake of initial breakdowns in Leinster took the form of the garrisoning, warding and policing strategies of the mid-century period. Under their auspices came the new English servitors who became military-style settlers in the region, acting with or without official sanction to consolidate a niche for themselves. The viceroys after 1556 were preoccupied with programmed pan-insular administration which sometimes allowed newcomers too free a hand in Leinster or sometimes itself bore too heavily on the existing fabric of habitation, as in the midland zone of Leix and Offaly.[24]

Inter-sept strife among the Kavanaghs, O'Tooles, O'Connors and O'Mores in the 1540s and early 1550s prevented the evolution of ordered society in Gaelic southern Leinster. The English captains introduced by Bellingham, St Leger and Croft in the mid-century years were to keep the peace from warded positions such as Ferns, Leighlin Bridge, Carlow and Newcastle. Cahir MacArt Kavanagh, the head of his clan, displayed his restiveness with this constricting of his Carlow and north Wexford lordship with raids on Kilkenny in the late 1540s, but down to 1556 the role of the captains such as Francis Agard was defensive. Under Sussex, however, their supervisory and policing functions became more pronounced in the effort to secure the Leinster chain, and after 1565 Sidney further refined the position of the seneschals (now officially so termed) by adding judicial powers to those of commuting the Gaelic lords' military exactions, booking or registering their armed retainers and extracting rents. Concurrently with their increasingly self-interested and autonomous military operations, the seneschals were competing for land titles with the native residents. Thus, for example, Captain Nicholas Heron and Captain Thomas Masterson, consecutively constables of Leighlin, antagonised the Kavanaghs in the 1560s and 1570s by their dogged pursuit of titles to crown lands at Ferns. Accordingly, Brian MacCahir and Donal Spainneach Kavanagh, successively leaders of their clan, were heavily attracted to campaigns by other discomfited lords in the region, such as Rory Óg O'More, Feagh MacHugh O'Byrne and the MacCormac O'Connors, in their resistance to encroachment by newcomers. Most unsettling of all was the irruption of the would-be seneschal, Sir Peter Carew of

Devon, into the barony of Idrone in Carlow, where some Kavanagh septs lived. Brian MacCahir joined in the widespread revolt led by Sir Edmund Butler in June 1569 in defence of native English and Irish lands against outsiders.[25]

Among the principal targets of the 1569 insurgents were military posts in the midlands plantation. Since the concerted effort at settlement of the two new shires in 1563–4, the rurally based military colony had been subjected to much harassment from displaced and unaccommodated former residents. Almost a third of the grantees of estates in the plantation, however, were Gaelic Irish, some of them members of O'More and O'Connor septs, and others being former *uirrithe* of the ruling lords such as Owen MacHugh O'Dempsey of Clanmalier in Offaly. These Gaelic grantees faced great difficulties in fulfilling the conditions of their leases owing to the frequent pressures upon them from rebellious fellow-clansmen or overlords, and indeed a large proportion, especially in Leix, lost their holdings in the four decades of constant strife down to 1603. Owen O'Dempsey's experiences in the 1560s and 1570s reflect the conflicting forces acting on a native grantee. Awarded over 3,000 acres in Offaly, Leix and Kildare for his good service to the government, he was favoured in successive deputyships while subjected to great intimidation by the rebellious O'Connors and a rival proprietorial claimant in Offaly, namely the Earl of Kildare. Although successful in outmanoeuvring those local forces with government patronage, rising from vassal to major landowner, O'Dempsey paid with his life for his ambitions in 1578 when killed by a follower of Rory Óg O'More, the most inveterate opponent of the regime at that time. His patrimony and position were asserted posthumously, however, through the successful career of his nephew, Sir Terence O'Dempsey. The efforts of dispossessed members of the O'More and O'Connor clans to gain access to the plantation establishment through a variety of stratagems, including recourse to the common law, show that Owen O'Dempsey's stake was widely aspired to among the native community.[26]

Even the most hostile Gaelic clansmen such as Rory Óg O'More and Conor MacCormac O'Connor aimed at the status of full participants in the new order in the midlands. But such attempts at co-operation were bedevilled by reciprocally exacerbating state intransigence, inter-sept and inter-planter rivalry, and factional struggles. Despite the clarity of purpose with which the dispossessed among the O'Mores and the O'Connors sought redress, they found

themselves re
lion from 156
O'Connors c
and were suc
were the attri
army and alli
Based in his
ostensibly see
Sir Henry Sid
in the plantati
and Ormond.
Sidney tacitly
to act with du
an inflationar
Mullaghmast
agents of Rob
sequent break
on Naas, Athy
1578 at the ha
of Upper Oss
the wave of Ir
was deployed
massacres by s
assassinated) I
by the mid-15
ished by the d
the death betw
Conor MacC
watching cour

[handwritten annotation: Massacre of Mulleghmast In Kildare]

[handwritten annotation: Barbaric device of Gladichorial Combat]

pel-
nac
60s
ble
ong
ors.
and
by
ake
are
and
ins
on
at
of
ib-
ids
in
on
of
rce
and
ter
ace
in-
to
and
the

The varying degrees of adaptability of Gaelic Irish leaders in the face of state-sponsored political change were not so marked in the areas of economic and social reform. The absence of settled conditions in much of Gaelic Leinster during the early Elizabethan decades meant that the hoped-for demilitarisation of society did not take place. Instead coign and livery persisted as much as ever throughout the lordships to the detriment of economic activity, and the predatory rebels raided the settled shires of the Pale as well as the new plantation estates. Despite the upheavals, some limited progress was made in turning the Gaelic participants in the colony into profitable farmers, and among the non-dispossessed clans some residual economic incentives of the surrender and regrant scheme were evident, particularly in the agrarian advancement of the north Wicklow area. Overall, however, the fostering of tillage among the clans does not seem to have borne fruit at this time to any great extent. Nor did the induction of more and more of the Gaelic Irish population of Leinster into a closer relationship with the state regime lead to a noticeable improvement in trade or the development of a monetary economy. The seneschals tended to perpetuate the old system of cessing in kind for the forts and their own establishments, and apart from the newly incorporated boroughs of Philipstown and Maryborough, there was no emergence of a strong network of towns as an engine of commercial growth. Naturally there were business connections between Gaelic areas and old and new English ones, especially in the hides and timber trades, but the impression one gets is of the failure of newcomers, either seneschals or planters, to promote economic reform among the Gaels and to prevent the ever-increasing amount of Gaelic indebtedness to mortgagers.[28] Even less manifest in the intact lordships was progress towards the desired subinfeudation of the clanspeople. Some of the original agreements of the 1540s sought to set up embryonic freeholding systems by incorporating sept leaders and *uirrithe* as participants, but these quickly broke down.[29]

The overall thrust of government policy during these decades of programmatic rule was still predominantly conciliatory, aiming at the demilitarisation and, increasingly, the social and legal assimilation of the Gaelic clans. The agreement of 1571 between Sidney and Brian MacCahir Kavanagh, for instance, rehearsed the main points of the 1543 surrender and regrant agreement with the clan, but the emphasis now was more on the individual landholders of the sept. Sidney also brought the O'Farrells of Longford to terms in 1575, shiring their territory of Annaly and partitioning the lands among the main sept leaders, now set up as freeholders. This was to be a prelude to the bringing in of sheriffs, justices and other organs of county administration to the area. Even Rory Óg O'More was taken into formal submission and pardon by Sidney in 1575, preparatory, it was hoped, to his being given land in the Leix plantation. That the brehons of some of the Leinster chiefs most directly engaged with government reform schemes were legitimising the legal innovations by selectively interpreting and rendering Gaelic law tracts is attested by the scholarly work of the O'Doran legal family of the north Wexford and Leix areas in the later 1570s. Yet despite such political success and mediatory approaches, the fact of intensive warfare in the region from that time onwards points up the basic failure of the state's reform schemes for the Leinster Irish. Two reasons for this may be adduced from the above: firstly, the sanctioning of extreme degrees of brutality by the military in response to Gaelic recalcitrance, including treachery, massacres, and mass executions at dubious legal sessions or by martial law; and secondly, the pursuit of land claims to territory over which the sitting Gaelic clans had rights by newcomers such as Jasper Bosher, Peter Carew and Thomas Masterson.[30]

Aggressive and acquisitive settlers may have provoked angry Gaelic reaction in the region, but there are many instances of co-operation between natives and newcomers. Many hundreds of English people came and settled in the urban and rural areas of Leinster from the earlier decades of the century onwards, drawn by opportunities for advancement in business, career or social status. At first a small coterie of officials who gained handsomely in the redistribution of Henrician confiscations, this New English community swelled after the mid-century with the expansion of governmental activity into the midland and southern marches. Although the core of the group was military, the nature of the members' engagement with the native populations developed to encompass landholding, trade and marital relations. Influenced by as well as influencing the course of events throughout the early decades of their involvement in the province, they varied greatly in their perception of the older inhabitants. Certainly a vocal element among them, conditioned not just by the circumstances of rebellion and resistance on the ground but also perhaps by ideas drawn from colonial experiences elsewhere as well as radical theological trends in England, came to articulate the attitudes of the *conquistador* in their relations with the Gaelic Irish. Others saw members of the Irish community as suitable tenants, political allies, business partners or even spouses.[31]

Among the community of *arrivistes* the new politico-military agents of stability and security, the seneschals, had the highest profile of all, certainly in the Gaelic areas of Leinster. Originally deployed under Sir Edward Bellingham's garrison policy of the late 1540s, the seneschals had their functions refined in the successive deputyships of Sussex and Sidney. By the latter phase they had acquired, in addition to the roles of military supervisors and rent-gatherers, judicial responsibilities, operating a blend of common and martial law. As well as playing to the full their parts as soldiers and carrying out other duties as constables of castles throughout southern Leinster and lieutenants of the new forts in Leix and Offaly, the seneschals became part of the community of settlers in the region. But seneschals such as Sir Francis Agard, Sir Henry Harrington, Sir Nicholas Heron and Robert Pipho were essentially men of action who had little interest in high politics or religious reform, forging marital alliances with the families of fellow-seneschals and government officials. In engaging with their Gaelic charges in Carlow, Wicklow, Wexford and elsewhere, they exploited native practices such as coign and livery and brehon law to dominate the zones allotted to them. Drawn into the complex political world of the clans, they could use violence or conciliation in an arbitrary fashion to carve their own niches. Agard and Harrington successively fostered alliances with Hugh O'Byrne and his son, Feagh; Cosby's protection of Rory Óg O'More gave rise to great controversy; and the initially hated Sir Peter Carew became a good lord to the Kavanaghs once he had become established as seneschal of Leighlin. Conversely, the Kavanaghs were bitterly antagonised by the greedy land claims of Thomas Masterson, seneschal of Wexford, and Robert Hartpole, constable of Carlow. The seneschals were left to their own devices by the administration in the interests of the maintenance of some semblance of order in the frontier.[32]

Although charged with bringing English social and economic practices to the confiscated areas of the Gaelic midlands, the settlers there had to be more concerned with martial matters in order to survive. Indeed, most of the English planters of Offaly and Leix were soldiers, and they never lost their military preoccupations. Once the land was secured, their purpose then was to bring agricultural innovation and nucleated settlement to the former O'Connor and O'More territories, thereby providing an exemplary impulse for the clanspeople who were accommodated within the plantation. As it turned out, however, there was little agrarian reform, though Rowland White, an Old English mechant and commentator, reported that planters were turning their lands to profit by 1571. Very little manufacture seems to have been possible in the unsettled conditions of the mid-Elizabethan period, and the trade of the two new boroughs, Philipstown and Maryborough, was stunted. In fact the evidence of the failure on the part of settlers to pay rent or military levies indicates that indebtedness due to warfare was a severe problem. Strategies for endurance of the harshness of life in the midland plantation included exploitation and assimilation of Gaelic people and practices. The early Elizabethan lieutenant of the forts in Leix and Offaly, Sir Henry Radcliffe, was known to have encouraged the rebellious O'Connor and O'More leaders in their resistance to government plans for plantation in order to bolster the case for the retention of army strength. Sir Edward Moore fomented the disturbances in the planted shires in the 1570s as a way of damaging his rival for the lieutenancy, Sir Barnaby Fitzpatrick. Gaelic kerne were used by these and other planters 'of evil respect and winkers at rebellion' in their own local aggrandisement. Perhaps the most notable example of a planter family fostering a Gaelic individual was that of the Hovendons of Leix bringing up the young Hugh O'Neill, later Earl of Tyrone.[33]

In the settled areas of the Pale and the towns of the east coast the integration of newcomers was smoothed by economic and social intercourse with the established residents. The Alens, who settled at St Wolstan's (renamed Alenscourt) in County Kildare in the 1530s, consolidated their holding in the second generation through marriage alliances with the gentry of the surrounding counties. The traffic of English and Welsh merchants with the eastern seaboard of Ireland was long established, and the later sixteenth century afforded opportunities for many to put down more permanent roots. When commercial activity was closed by charter to all but the members of the merchant guilds of the cities, principally Dublin, cross-channel merchants wishing to gain a stake in the trade of the Pale had to enter the circle of privilege either through apprenticeship or marriage into patrician society. That several were thus acceptable is attested by the fact that almost a fifth of the families which achieved aldermanic status in Dublin in the seventy years after 1550 were of English origin, mostly from the north-west or the London area. While the majority of these English families who achieved high social standing in the Elizabethan period intermarried with Protestants of English or Irish origin, once absorbed within the municipality they became staunch champions of civic and guild liberties. Those officials who remained aloof from the local nexus by choice or as a result of discrimination, however, were vociferous in their criticism of the system of civic privileges and exemptions which appeared to obstruct the course of financial and political reform.[34]

Public complaints by some English-born servitors about those of older English descent in the towns and the countryside were a fairly new feature of political discourse in the late 1570s. Previously the two groups had been working, at least overtly, in tandem to reform the society and polity of the Gaelic Irish throughout the island. There had been misgivings voiced by English officials about the commitment of the Old English to religious reform and the partiality of their judges in the conduct of law cases. After the failure of Sidney's regime, however, there remained in office a number of disillusioned clients of his who laid the blame for their patron's discredit on the community of the Pale. New English critics began openly to question the loyalty of the older colonial community to the state, linking their allegedly dubious allegiance to their retention of Catholic practices. Such nonconformity was all the more dangerous, it was argued, at a time of mounting inter-national tension fuelled by religious divisions. The more implacable newcomers were anxious to stress their reliability by eschewing marital ties with Catholic members of the local community and instead married into the small group of Protestant Old English families or the English planter class. As a way of countering the lack of trustworthiness of the Old English, their opponents advocated the appointment of only English-born Protestants to positions within the civil and military establishment in Ireland. Events within the Pale and its marches after 1579 served to confirm the opinions of those who claimed that political dissidence and attachment to the unreformed religion were concomitant among sections of the older colonial community.[35]

Crisis in the Pale, 1580–86

It was the revolt of James Eustace, Viscount Baltinglass, and its aftermath which helped to clarify the political and religious issues for the Old English as well as the New English of Leinster. In mid-July 1580 Baltinglass came out in armed opposition to Queen Elizabeth as a heretic who had moreover oppressed the 'poor subjects' of her land of Ireland. A long-established aristocratic family of English origin, the Eustaces had played an important part in the affairs of the colony and their locality of south-east Kildare. James, the third Viscount Baltinglass, had trained as a lawyer in

London and had spent some time in Rome at the court of Pope Gregory XIII before entering into his inheritance in 1579. Already imbued with the idealism of the Counter-Reformation and susceptible to the influence of leading Catholic missioners operating in Leinster, Eustace was inspirited by the short-lived crusade launched by James FitzMaurice in Munster. Determined to rise in sympathy in Leinster, Eustace, with the help of militant priests such as the Jesuit Robert Rochford, canvassed the support of leading nobles and gentlemen in Kildare and Westmeath. Most of these, including the Earl of Kildare and the Baron of Delvin, paid lip-service to the ideals of Eustace but were reluctant to participate in rebellion. Eustace, the son of a champion of the anti-cess campaign, did attract active support from some marcher lords who feared the implications of the Pale composition scheme, and also from a group of fellow-lawyers who had been to the fore in the constitutional struggles of the previous decade. Many of these had come to espouse fervent Catholicism. While the vast majority of the residents of the inner Pale remained aloof from the conspiracy, two leading merchant patricians in Dublin, William Fitzsimon and Alderman Walter Sedgrave, supplied the viscount with weapons and powder. With alliances among disaffected Gaelic clans, including the O'Byrnes, Kavanaghs, O'Mores and O'Connors in southern and mid-Leinster, Baltinglass began his campaign to spread the holy war into the heart of the Pale.[36]

The victory of the army of Baltinglass and Feagh MacHugh O'Byrne at Glenmalure in August 1580 proved to be the highest point of achievement of the rebels. Thereafter their activities were mostly confined to raids on towns in the outskirts of the Pale and on settlements in the midlands. Baltinglass and John Fitzgerald, brother of the Earl of Desmond and the effective leader of the rising in Munster after the death of James FitzMaurice, crossed briefly into each other's zones of insurgence in generous but ineffective gestures of mutual solidarity. Increasingly, however, the newly installed Lord Deputy, Arthur, Baron Grey de Wilton, deployed contingents of his 6,500-strong army about the southern Pale and its marches to good effect in the autumn and winter of 1580. By Christmas the menace to the state from the Leinster uprising was abating and Grey had imprisoned the Earl of Kildare and the Baron of Delvin in Dublin Castle on suspicion of having abetted Baltinglass. Another conspiracy ensued, centred on William Nugent, who aimed at securing the release of his captive brother, Delvin. Dozens of gentlemen, mostly in Meath and Westmeath, were drawn in on oath by Nugent and his agents, although few were contemplating protesting in arms. Well represented among the Nugent conspirators in 1581 were younger sons of gentry families whose access to state appointments was uncertain, and also Catholic zealots such as George Netterville. William Nugent secured the assistance of Brian MacGeoghegan and Brian O'Rourke among the Gaelic leaders of the northern midlands, but by late 1581 the government had unravelled the strands of the conspiracy and many of its leading figures were under arrest.[37]

With the separate flights of Viscount Baltinglass and William Nugent to the continent in November 1581 and January 1582, Grey's administration could concentrate fully on the task of wreaking vengeance on their followers and compensating English servitors in Leinster. A radical Protestant, Grey himself was stern and unbending in his approach to the defeated rebels. Under his aegis civil and ecclesiastical officials conducted a full-scale investigation into the extent of the involvement of a substantial number of prominent Palespeople. Scores were arrested and questioned in the years between 1581 and 1584. About twenty gentlemen were tried, convicted and executed for their parts in the Baltinglass revolt or the Nugent conspiracy, including members of families of leading opponents of the regime in the 1570s. Some of these died in the manner of Catholic martyrs, proclaiming that they were suffering for their religious beliefs. The most prominent casualty was Nicholas Nugent, Chief Justice of the Common Pleas and leading commonwealth spokesman, whose links to the conspiracy were tenuous but who fell victim to a private vendetta conducted by the loyalist Sir Robert Dillon. In addition, an unspecified number of men of 'mean calling' were executed by martial law. Simultaneously the monetary worth of the rebels was calculated and the distribution of their properties was begun. The main beneficiaries of the confiscated lands were Grey's officers, much to the chagrin of non-favoured officials in Dublin, who complained to Queen Elizabeth. In 1582 the Privy Council in London ordered Grey to end the rewarding of his close associates, to discharge hundreds of soldiers, and to extend a general pardon to the rebels. Subsequently dozens of Pale gentlemen received their pardons on payment of fines of up to £100, and most of those who had been attainted ultimately had their lands restored to them.[38]

In the summer of 1582 Lord Grey was recalled to England and was replaced by two Lords Justices, Archbishop Adam Loftus and Henry Wallop, the Vice-Treasurer. Although the total number of leading Old English who had paid with their lives in the aftermath of the events of 1580–81 was comparatively small, the overall effects of the follow-up operations on their community were traumatic. In that tightly-knit, endogamous society, the executions had an impact on the dead ones' ramified kin-groups in town and countryside. Despite the foolhardiness of Baltinglass's actions, his version of the oppressive nature of the regime was shown to have been validated by the ruthlessness of government reaction to the revolt. The bravery with which the young Catholic conspirators went to their deaths for the sake of their religious beliefs had a galvanising effect on many of their fellow Old English who had up to then been ambiguous in their confessional stances. From the mid-1580s open recusancy marked the demeanour of the majority of the Old English and the aspiration to liberty of conscience became firmly fixed on their political agenda. For its part, the government helped in the coalescing of the political and religious issues by its prosecution of the Catholic Archbishop of Cashel, Dermot O'Hurley. Although interrogation under torture yielded no evidence of links with the Desmond and Baltinglass conspirators on the continent, the Lords Justices proceeded against O'Hurley by martial law and had him hanged outside Dublin in June 1584. The early 1580s had witnessed unrelenting state repression, and the leaders of the commonwealth were frustrated at the lack of any constitutional outlet for their grievances. With the arrival of Sir John Perrot as Lord Deputy in mid-1584, however, a political focus for their representations was to hand once more.[39]

Perrot may have lacked the social standing of Sussex and Sidney, but he did have experience of Ireland, having served as Lord President of Munster in the early 1570s. Despite the increasing absorption of English foreign policy with the Low Countries, the new viceroy did win scope for a programme of government which was as ambitious and pan-insular as those of his two illustrious predecessors. Perrot wished to secure a permanent settlement of surrender and regrant by means of a general composition. This scheme was to include the Pale and would operate on the basis of a uniform unit of assessment. Another major aim was the enforcement of religious conformity by applying to Ireland anti-Catholic legislation already passed for England. To launch this national plan, Perrot proposed to hold a parliament. Before that assembly convened, however, the Lord Deputy antagonised key New English officials such as Vice-Treasurer Wallop and Lord Chancellor Loftus by his arrogance in council. The latter became locked in a bitter dispute with Perrot over the governor's proposal to dissolve St Patrick's Cathedral in order to endow a university. Perrot came to depend upon the support of the surviving Old English members of his administration, including Luke and Robert Dillon and Sir Nicholas White. When he approached parliament for the ratification of aspects of his programme in 1585, the Old English majority in the Commons were resolute in their opposition, thereby bringing about the failure of Perrot's grandiose plans.[40]

Although the expansion of English influence in Ireland since the earlier Elizabethan parliaments was reflected in increased representation in the two houses, the New English membership remained proportionately small. Thus the Old English M.P.s from borough and shire had a dominant role in the proceedings of 1585–6. The government's nominee, Nicholas Walsh, was elected Speaker despite opposition, and the proposal was put to both houses for the suspension of Poynings' Law in order to give flexibility to the administration to order the business of parliament. The debate on the suspension measure offered the leaders of the Old English opposition a chance to argue cogently that Perrot was intent on abrogating constitutional liberties by imposing a permanent tax on the country in lieu of cess, and that he was also determined to suppress liberty of conscience. Evidently they had prepared well for the defence of their convergent rights in these areas, and the bill was heavily defeated in the Commons. The proroguing of parliament for a month to allow for pressure to be put on the recalcitrant members to support the reintroduced suspension bill was unavailing, and attempts to legislate for composition and for the introduction of anti-Catholic measures failed similarly. When parliament was reconvened for three weeks in April 1586, half of the bills were either defeated or heavily amended, leaving very little of Perrot's legislative programme intact except for the attainders of Baltinglass and the Earl of Desmond and his accomplices and the renewal of the custom on wine imports. Meanwhile Perrot compounded with the Pale community for the sum of £1,500 Irish in lieu of all cesses. Also a suit to the court from the Pale procured a directive restraining the

Lord Deputy from enforcing the Oath of Supremacy. In his closing address to parliament Speaker Walsh asserted the principles upon which the privileges of the queen's Irish subjects rested: constitutional government, the equality of all groups of subjects, and the political autonomy of the kingdom of Ireland.[41]

The victory of the Old English parliamentarians over the imperious Perrot helped to affirm their political and religious stance on behalf of the old colonial community. Their alienation from the governorship had emerged gradually in the 1560s and 1570s, culminating in the mid-1580s, while their success was attributable to the dual strategy of parliamentary opposition and representation of grievances at the English court. Thenceforward the Old English country population would proclaim their loyalty to their sovereign and eschew any dealings with Gaelic rebels, while becoming overtly recusant and more convinced in their Catholicism. For their part, New English commentators in the later 1580s pointed to this phenomenon as proof of the untrustworthiness and unfitness for office of the Old English. Particular concern was expressed at the migration of young members of the Old English community to continental colleges where they came into contact with the Counter-Reformation. Rather than being perceived as agents of reform throughout the country, the Old English were now seen by certain New English as targets for social, political and religious reform themselves. For both groups, the Gaelic Irish were seen as reformable, despite the chronic unrest among the Leinster clans in the early 1580s, but some New English were despairing of the conciliatory approach adopted in the mid-century decades. Instead they advocated more firmly the need for plantation schemes of new settlers who would take over proprietorship from the native lords and military men. Yet in the mid- to late 1580s the state continued to renew compacts with some clans, and the seneschals were heavily involved in the socio-political world of their Gaelic Irish neighbours.

Munster: Presidency and Plantation, 1565–95

AT Affane, County Waterford, in February 1565 the evenly matched forces of the two great earls of the province of Munster, Desmond and Ormond, came into armed conflict. The encounter, at a ford on a tributary of the Blackwater, near the foot-hills of the Knockmealdown Mountains, was in the borderland between the earldoms, on Ormond territory. Among Desmond's supporters were Geraldines such as the White Knight, the Knight of Kerry and the seneschal of Imokilly, John FitzEdmund, Desmond vassal lords including Lord Power, Gaelic allies from, for example, the O'Connor and O'Brien clans, and disaffected Butlers such as Sir Piers of Cahir. On the side of the Earl of Ormond were his three brothers, Edmund, James and Edward, and other Butler relatives, Ormond sub-lords of Anglo-Norman and Gaelic origin, and certain disaffected Geraldines, such as Sir Maurice Fitzgerald of the local Decies. Apparently lured into a carefully prepared trap, the Desmond army charged at the enemy, having displayed its banners. Among the casualties from that charge was the Earl of Desmond himself, who received a thigh wound from Sir Edmund Butler's pistol-shot. Many of the routed Geraldine soldiers who attempted to flee the battle by swimming the Blackwater were intercepted by armed boats. Desmond himself was carried as captive to Clonmel and thence to Waterford, where both he and the victorious Ormond were subjected to strict interrogation concerning their conduct. The angry Queen Elizabeth summoned the two earls to court, grievously affronted at the display of banners in a private war.[1]

The short-term cause of the friction between Thomas, tenth Earl of Ormond, and Gerald, fifteenth Earl of Desmond, was the latter's intrusion into the Decies forcibly to collect taxes and dues from Sir Maurice Fitzgerald. Ormond's complaint over Desmond's interfer-ence in the shire of Waterford was the latest in a series of disputes, the resolution of which was pending state adjudication. Conflicting claims to lands and to customs duties were compounded by the demands of the Earl of Ormond for the return of his mother's dowry from the Geraldines. The widowed Countess of Ormond had married the Earl of Desmond in the interests of inter-family reconciliation, but her death in 1564 led to increased bitterness. The old pattern of Desmond raids upon Butler tenants and retaliatory Ormond strikes was resumed, but the more isolated Geraldine leader was finding it difficult to prevent his own collaterals such as Sir Maurice of Decies seeking the protection of the better-connected Ormond. The affray at Affane brought into sharp focus not just the traditional provincial rivalry between the two great houses, however, but also their *lèse-majesté* and their pan-insular factionalism. Private armies of household retainers and swordsmen supported by coign and livery faced each other in a confrontation over matters which bore at least partially upon palatine jurisdictions and liberties. More generally, the rival earls were able to call upon extra-provincial allies within their national networks of support, demonstrating the indomitability and danger of the great polarity of Ormond and Geraldine parties. This pattern of alliance would be repicrocated at Affane and on many other occasions within Munster.[2]

The history of events in Munster in the thirty years after 1565 reveals an integrated attempt on the part of the administration to order the province along English lines and the responses thereto of the inhabitants. The overall aim of successive viceroys was, as elsewhere, for crown jurisdiction to flow throughout the lordships, great and small, with the elimination of the overlordship of major aristocrats over lesser gentlemen. Given their dominance, the prime targets in the southern province were the Anglo-Norman earldoms, encompassing two palatinates, Kerry in Desmond and Tipperary in Ormond, with the more powerful Gaelic lords of the south-west also being taken from under the earls' clientship. The basic tool, agreed upon before the mid-1560s and spearheaded most notably by Sir Henry Sidney during his deputyships, was the presidency with provincial council, coupled with colonial ventures in the southern coastal region and the cossetting of port towns, so vital for security as well as economic well-being. Initial responses varied from acceptance to the kind of outright rejection as manifested in the revolt of 1569–73. Another strategic weapon deployed, again mostly under Sidney's aegis, was the commutation of arbitrary taxes and levies into fixed rents for all social levels. Again reaction was not uniformly hostile, and there were some notable successes for the crown, but the press of circumstances within and without the province, embracing a complex mix of motives—political, social, economic and religious—led to a major insurrection in 1579 fronted eventually by the Earl of Desmond. He paid with his life, but there were few enough native winners in the aftermath of the attritional campaigns of the early 1580s. The intended final solution for Munster was plantation with entrepreneurial newcomers, and their progress in settling there in the first decade after the suppression of the insurrection merits attention in the concluding section of this chapter.

English activity and native reaction, 1565–73

With the subsiding of the perceived threat of a French invasion through the south, Munster became less of a priority of government in the early 1560s. In default of any attempt at enforcement of the crown's jurisdiction there, the great feudal lords were left to settle their own disputes through force, to the detriment of social and economic life in town and countryside. Already in 1562 the Earl of Desmond had been summoned to court to answer for his riotous behaviour towards Ormond, and had been kept there in easy confinement until 1564. The Earl of Sussex had proposed provincial presidencies for Munster, as well as Connacht and Ulster. Backed by small armies, the presidents would have had the primary purpose of providing courts for the arbitration of quarrels between provincial lords such as Ormond and Desmond in Munster. Despite the enthusiasm of Ormond and many Old English politicians for this scheme, it perished in the downfall of Sussex's regime. His successor, Sir Nicholas Arnold, allowed these local officials such as Sir Thomas Cusack to act as peacemakers between contending southern lords. The renewed phase of Butler–Fitzgerald feuding, culminating at Affane, ruined these hopes, however, and contributed to the breakdown of Arnold's government. After a lengthy examination before the Privy Council in London in the summer of 1565, Ormond and Desmond were released and bound over in £20,000 Irish each to keep the peace. As a sign of the government's intention of subverting overlordship, and Desmond's in particular, Donal MacCarthy More, chieftain of the mountainous south-west area of Cork and

Kerry, surrendered his lands to the queen in June 1565 and was regranted them with the title of Earl of Clancare.[3]

The new Lord Deputy, Sir Henry Sidney, appointed in October 1565, approved wholeheartedly of MacCarthy's being detached from Desmond's clientship, for he was committed to undermining the power bases of the feudal lords. The main agency in his programme for reform was the provincial presidency and council, based on his experience as President of the Council of the Welsh Marches. The council as envisaged for Munster would have an Englishman at its head as president, and its role was to be political and economic, as well as administrative. Politically it would preside over all of the lords, whether feudal magnates, lesser nobility or gentry, its judicial functions overriding any palatine liberties. An army of fifty troops would be at the disposal of the president to keep order, displacing private levies, and recourse to martial law was to be countenanced. Economically the presidency council was a vehicle for the establishment of fiscal self-sufficiency through the exaction of taxes for maintaining the president's force instead of the arbitrary taking of coign and livery, and the fixing of set rents from landowners to the presidency instead of to regional overlords. By these means, Sidney and his backers at court hoped, the social structure of the province would be transformed by the setting up of independent proprietors, subject only to the crown, having recourse to its courts, being protected by its army at conciliar level, and willing to serve in local offices such as shrievalties. Sidney's first step towards accomplishing a Munster presidency was symbolic and tactful, and received a positive reaction from the Earl of Desmond at least. Sir Warham St Leger, son of Sir Anthony, was chosen as president-designate and acted as special commissioner in Munster in 1566. His friendship and largesse, extended to the earl during his recent English custody at Leeds castle in Kent, were reciprocated by Desmond's lease to him of lands in the barony of Kerrycurrihy, south of Cork city.[4]

By contrast, however, the Earl of Ormond was implacably opposed to Sidney's plans for Munster, for reasons both of personality and principle. Sir Warham's appointment revived memories of the old Butler–St Leger antagonism over land titles and, more recently, in Sir Anthony's time, over the governor's pro-Geraldine sympathies. For Ormond, this posting seemed to confirm the administration's promotion of Fitzgerald factional interests throughout

Ireland at the expense of the Butlers'. Earl Thomas also objected strenuously to the proposed attack on his palatinate of Tipperary and resented Sidney's exemplary arrest of his brothers for imposing coign and livery. Deploying his personal influence with the queen at court, where Sidney's rivals were temporarily dominant, Ormond persuaded her in April 1566 to countermand the appointment of St Leger to the presidency of Munster and to order the Lord Deputy to favour Ormond in all of his suits 'as reason shall require'. For the Earl of Desmond, Queen Elizabeth's decision to readjust the factional balance in Butler's favour meant the loss of his genuine expectations for Geraldine ascendancy under the new regime. He soon felt the effects of Sidney's withdrawal of support: in 1567 the Lord Deputy adjudicated upon the Ormond–Desmond feud and found against Earl Gerald, who was ordered to forfeit the bond of £20,000 Irish which he had given in London as a surety for keeping the peace. Desmond was arrested by Sidney on a charge of plotting treason and by the end of 1567 had been sent to the Tower of London, there to remain for several years. The earl's capable brother, John Fitzgerald (John of Desmond), was knighted by the governor and appointed special commissioner for the peace in the Desmond lordship, pending the selection of a president. Meanwhile Sidney, despite the royal rebuffs, pressed on with laying the groundwork during his spring tour of Munster in 1567. He held sessions of assize in each county and recommended the release of Desmond's vassal lords, such as Viscount Barry, Lord Roche and Sir Dermot MacCarthy of Muskerry, from his clientship. Sidney was forced thereafter to attend to events elsewhere, and Munster suffered comparative neglect from the administration for a year and more. In 1568 the bungling by the Privy Council of the appointment of a president and Sir John of Desmond's arrest under pressure from Ormond left a dangerous political void within the earldom of Desmond and the province at large.[5]

One of Sir Henry Sidney's designs in setting up presidency councils was to identify lands which could be peopled by English-born settlers. Owing to the delay in appointing a president for Munster in the late 1560s, the colonising aspect of the programme came into sharper focus than was perhaps intended. Sidney's plan did not necessarily embrace straight confiscation, but rather envisaged searching out titles to monastic lands and forfeited estates. On these, nucleated settlements of newcomers would be encouraged to dwell in order to provide a model of civil living for the natives. Although Ulster was primarily targeted for this approach, Munster was not neglected in colonial venturing. Jacques Wingfield, a Leinster seneschal, had been authorised by the Lord Deputy to seek out crown titles to monastic estates in Munster, and the coastal reaches with which Spanish fishermen and traders trafficked were regarded as ripe for English resettlement. But it was upon Sir Warham St Leger, his president-designate, that Sidney pinned his highest hopes for successful colonisation in Munster. With his foothold in Kerrycurrihy secured, Sir Warham, with his nephew, Richard Grenville, aspired to expand his holdings. Thus a corporation of gentlemen from the English West Country, backed by London merchants, proposed an elaborate scheme for a colony in southwest Munster which would entice farmers and tradespeople to settle and would exploit the natural resources of timber and minerals. Besides profiting both the colonists and the government, the security of the coastline was to be assured. Little progress was made by the early 1570s, however, and the canvassing of such entrepreneurial schemes caused uneasiness and apprehension among both Gaelic and Anglo-Norman residents. The latter were especially vexed by the association with the projected Munster settlements of Sir Peter Carew, the opportunist land claimant in Leinster, whose irruption into Butler and Palesmen's lands led to armed revolt there in 1569.[6]

In June of the same year James FitzMaurice Fitzgerald, first cousin of the Earl of Desmond, sparked off a more serious revolt with a concerted attack on the Kerrycurrihy colony, Tracton and Carragaline castle in County Cork. Reflecting the fears of Munster aristocrats for the loss of lands and liberties, his leadership role paralleled that of the Butler brothers in Idrone. FitzMaurice's analysis of the trend of royal policy, however, was more radical than that of contemporary feudal rebels in Ireland and was based on a synthesis of personal, factional and credal concerns. Appointed captain-general of Desmond by Earl Gerald during his absence in England, James had proved to be an excellent defender of Geraldine interests. The archetypical landless swordsman, he had been ousted from his tenancy of Kerricurrihy by the St Leger lease. FitzMaurice provided a rallying-point for those nobles and gentry who rejected Sidney's reforms, and he had the martial qualities to force reluctant collateral Geraldines and vassal lords to follow his lead. From the start of his campaign, moreover, he adopted the rhetoric of the Counter-

Reformation and supported the embassy of Maurice MacGibbon, papal Archbishop of Cashel, to seek King Philip II of Spain's aid for Catholic opponents of Elizabeth. Present at the onslaught on the English settlers outside Cork city was Donal MacCarthy, Earl of Clancare, who renounced his English title in favour of that of the MacCarthy More, and several other Gaelic chiefs of the south-west who were threatened with expropriation joined the rising, including O'Sullivan More, O'Sullivan Beare and O'Keeffe. The siege of Cork, where English families had sought refuge, was the prelude to attempts on many Munster towns such as Kilmallock, Waterford, Youghal and Limerick. Also targeted were the lesser nobility of the province such as Lord Roche, Sir Dermot MacCarthy of Muskerry, and Viscounts Barry and Decies (formerly Sir Maurice Fitzgerald) who hoped to gain from a presidential regime. The seriousness of the rebellion for the entire southern half of the country was evidenced most clearly in the joint action of FitzMaurice, Clancare and the Butler brothers, with 4,500 men in laying siege to hub of Ormond's earldom, Kilkenny, in July 1569.[7]

Sir Henry Sidney responded by leaving Dublin for the south with an army of 600 late that month, by which time the threat to Kilkenny had diminished. The Earl of Ormond, sent back to Ireland in August by the queen to detach his brothers from the rebellion, blamed the disorders on Carew's land claims with Sidney's connivance. Faced with the prospect of being upstaged by Ormond as the principal peacemaker in Munster also, the Lord Deputy forged ahead with his campaign through Tipperary, Cork and Limerick, with the added fillip of a relief force of 400 sent by sea to Cork. During his expedition he recaptured some castles, including Mitchelstown, Carragaline and Castlemartyr, and accepted the surrender of lesser Geraldine and other rebels, but the principals, including the White Knight, the seneschal of Imokilly and FitzMaurice himself, remained elusive. After this initial sortie Sidney proceeded to appoint Humphrey Gilbert as colonel and governor of the province in September 1569. Although nominally assisted by a council comprising the mayors of the towns, Sir Richard Grenville and Sir Warham St Leger, his actions were unrestrained by bureaucracy. Empowered to govern by martial law and requisition troops and supplies at will, Gilbert carried out his task of quelling the revolt with ruthless efficiency. Within six weeks he had taken twenty-three castles and slaughtered all occupants, men, women and children.

His savage methods, such as the killing of non-belligerents and the grisly use of a corridor of severed heads to induce abject surrenders, won him notoriety and introduced a new dimension into Irish warfare. But Gilbert was successful in subduing the worst of the rebellion, and by the end of 1569 Clancare and most of the Geraldines had submitted, although FitzMaurice remained at large in the Glen of Aherlow in Tipperary.[8]

By early 1570 Sidney was so pleased with Gilbert's pacification of Munster that he claimed that 'the iron is now hot to receive what print shall be stricken on it'. Yet another year elapsed before an appointment to the presidency was made, and meanwhile Ormond was busy as general, successfully reining in the rebellious Earl of Thomond, who had leagued himself with FitzMaurice. At last Sir John Perrot, a distinguished knight of Haverfordwest, Pembrokeshire, received his commission for the presidency of Munster in late 1570, and he arrived in Ireland in the following February, just as Sir Henry Sidney, the great advocate of the office, was preparing to relinquish the deputyship. Perrot's terms of appointment envisaged civil and judicial normality, but in reality his brief at least initially was to mop up the revolt. Displaying great energy at the head of his army of 700, the President went on the offensive in pursuit of FitzMaurice, who had lately burned Kilmallock, making it 'an abode of wolves'. Using Gilbert's extreme methods of executing those captured in arms and spoiling the country of rebels, Perrot brought to his side at Cork most of the province's lords. While FitzMaurice roamed from Aherlow to south-west Cork with varying numbers of soldiers, the President's strategic objective was the fortress of Castlemaine, to which he laid siege unsuccessfully for five weeks during the summer of 1571. FitzMaurice hit back with an attack on some English sailors along the shore of Cork harbour. Perrot was driven to desperate measures by his fruitless hunt for the rebel ringleader: he challenged FitzMaurice to single combat which was refused, and he called for Sir John of Desmond's return from his English captivity to order the restless Geraldines.[9]

Nevertheless, in the spring of 1572 Perrot asserted that his presidency had laid the foundations of civil government in Munster. Before he came, according to him, no one could walk in safety a mile outside Cork, Limerick, Youghal, Kinsale, Kilmallock, Dingle or Cashel, but now the rebels had been reduced from 1,000 to 'fifty poor kerne and ten or twelve bad horsemen'. A decisive blow against them was the capture of Castlemaine after a three-month blockade, although FitzMaurice's forces repulsed an attack along the shores of the Shannon estuary. During the autumn and winter the Earl of Ormond's brothers again proved their conversion to good service for the government by mounting punishing raids on FitzMaurice's camp in Tipperary. Finally by early 1573 the rebel leader was ready to seek terms from Perrot, and in February he submitted in company with the seneschal of Imokilly at Kilmallock, scene of his former depredations. The President was then free to pursue the real reforming aims of his office as envisaged by Sidney. Already he had established the pattern by conducting common law sessions throughout the province at which hundreds were convicted of felonies and treasons and executed. Besides this innovative juridical regime, Perrot banned aspects of the Gaelic system, including brehon law, coign and livery, private maintenance of troops, bardic poetry and native dress. The key restriction was on 'masterless' men: all followers of lords were to be booked and accounted for, in default of which they faced death. In July 1573 Perrot further reported that 'the plough doth now laugh the unbridled kerne and rogue to scorn'. The decision to send the Earl of Desmond back to Ireland in early 1573 greatly displeased Perrot, and his forebodings seemed justified when, on the very day of the ex-President's departure from Munster in November following his resignation, the earl escaped from Dublin where he had been kept since the previous March.[10]

Desmond, the presidency and rebellion, 1573–83

Desmond's return after seven years of detention had had the desired effect of inducing James FitzMaurice's surrender, but the release was on carefully arranged conditions. The earl agreed to abolish coign and livery within his lordship for his 'greater quiet and greatest gain' and renounced overlordship of former vassals and other lords such as Barry, Courcy, Viscount Decies, the MacCarthys and O'Sullivans. Returned to Dublin for examination pending his reinstatement, Desmond found the prevailing atmosphere inimical. Lord Deputy Fitzwilliam, a client of the former Lord Lieutenant Sussex, was a friend to the Earl of Ormond, and Perrot, besides having his own ties to the Butlers, feared for the diminution of his newly won authority within Munster. Both officials attempted to impose tougher terms on Desmond for his restoration, determining to dismantle the palatinate of Kerry. Eventually, impatient after eight months of 'easy restraint', the earl broke away, and having arrived at Askeaton in November 1573, he threw off his English clothes and donned the dress of a Gaelic chieftain. Within days the fortresses of Castlemaine and Castlemartyr had been repossessed, and it seemed as if Perrot's work was being completely undone. But Desmond found that the south-western region had changed greatly in his absence. His own financial position, parlous enough before 1567, had deteriorated now to the point of crisis. Compounding that problem was the independent-mindedness of his vassal lords, who had, buoyed up by the President's reforms, cast off the earl's economic and political yoke. On the other hand, the radicalised Geraldines under the rampant FitzMaurice rejected the presidency as an alien, heretical influence, bent on the destruction of the old order. Somehow the earl was going to have to come to terms with the new, while trying to reassert his former mastery of the multifarious social elements.[11]

The sundering of his factional alliance with Sidney in 1566 had affected Desmond so deeply that, although at liberty, he maintained a defiant, anti-government posture well into 1574. Thereafter a new equilibrium was painfully established, with the gradual mollification of the earl at the queen's behest by diplomacy. Yet relations within the Geraldine sphere of influence were extremely difficult to reconstruct in the aftermath of such great political and military upheaval. Although Desmond's return galvanised the faltering militancy of his FitzMaurice-led collaterals, he had to regain the leadership which had passed to his abler cousin even while seeking political and social rehabilitation. The strident Counter-Reformation tone and Gaelic symbolism adopted by FitzMaurice's campaign were embarrassing encumbrances, while compromise with English law and social customs was anathema to the conservative Geraldine activists. The Earl of Desmond's vassals in the south-west, who had been quite prepared to accept key aspects of the presidency, and who had been pacified after the initial stages of the rebellion, were to feel once more in 1573–4 the pressure of overbearing lordship in the form of importunate demands for support for the earl's private army. The position of the Gaelic chiefs might have been particularly delicate, given the exploitation by insurgent Geraldines and their allies of the trappings of Gaeldom, including dress, appearance, regalia and titles. Yet Sir

Cormac MacTaidhg MacCarthy and Donough MacCarthy Reagh of Carbery were among those thanked by the queen for their services under Perrot in early 1572, and both they and the erstwhile rebels, the Earl of Clancare and the O'Sullivans, were ready to accept with alacrity the offer of direct dependence on the government within a broadened surrender and regrant context.[12]

Two other sectors stood to gain from the setting up in the province of firm structures and institutions representing central authority: the lesser aristocrats and gentry of Cork and Waterford, and the urban communities. Both groups had attempted repeatedly since the late middle ages to break the informal constraints under which they were held by the Geraldine lordship, but not until the direct intervention of the government in the mid-1560s had they had a chance of fully achieving this. Prominent among the lesser landlord class were James, Lord Barry, and David, Viscount Roche. They had been oppressed by Desmond during the early 1560s, but with the reversal of the earl's fortunes after 1566 had begun to extend their own influence in Munster at his expense. Despite intimidation at the hands of the FitzMaurice-led troops, both lords are mentioned in the list of those who attended Perrot at Cork in 1571 and of those thanked by Queen Elizabeth in the following year. The towns were particularly badly affected by the events of the rising from 1569 to 1573, but the establishment of the presidency promised to foster more favourable conditions for municipal and economic development. While not all had experienced the dire fate of Kilmallock, towns and cities such as Cork, Kinsale, Youghal, Waterford and Limerick which gave succour to enemies of the Geraldines were threatened at one time or another by sieges and starvation. During Gilbert's colonelship the mayors of towns served on an advisory council (which was largely ignored), and some magistrates suffered indignities and even death at the hands of the rebels. The legislation of the parliament of 1569–71 for the creation of head ports and the promotion of manufacture was seen as a boost. The return of Desmond in 1573 was a grave blow to the modest hopes of the urban communities for whom the new structures seemed to be potentially beneficial.[13]

Unlike the shaky position in which the Earl of Desmond found himself in 1573–4, the Earl of Ormond's was one of strength. He emerged from the turbulent years of the rebellion with his reputation enhanced and his earldom consolidated. From the time of his return to Ireland in 1569 to pacify his bellicose brothers and channel their energies into hunting FitzMaurice, Earl Thomas had shown considerable skill in mixing diplomacy and arms to placate trouble-makers and to deal with threats to the security of his own lordship. Approved of by Lord Deputy Fitzwilliam and Lord President Perrot, the earl was strong enough now to be able to fend off any potential intrusion on his liberty of Tipperary or other parts of his patrimony. His energetic presence managed to contain the centrifugal tendencies of his Butler collaterals such as Lords Dunboyne and Cahir, and would-be opponents of his clientage among the vassal lords such as MacGillapatrick (Fitzpatrick) of Upper Ossory or O'Carroll of Ely were vehemently opposed. The Gaelic lords within his Munster bailiwick, such as the O'Mearas and O'Kennedys, were chained closely to the Ormond system. The press of Butler influences on urban settlements within the earldom was not as oppressive as that of the Earls of Kildare or Desmond in theirs, allowing a modicum of municipal growth for towns like Carrick-on-Suir and Clonmel. Kilkenny was enhanced greatly in the 1570s and 1580s under Earl Thomas's patronage. In the mid-1570s, his credit high with the Dublin administration and his influence strong at court with his cousin, Queen Elizabeth, Ormond seemed to have outmanoeuvred handsomely the Earl of Desmond and set himself up for untrammelled lordship, no matter what plans the presidency of Munster might have.[14]

Those plans were revealed in 1575–6 with the return of Sir Henry Sidney as Lord Deputy and the appointment of Sir William Drury as President of Munster. Whereas his predecessor, Fitzwilliam, had little faith in the provincial presidencies as agencies of administration, Sidney was more convinced than ever that they could effect real political and social change. His new programme enshrined the concept of composition as articulated by his secretary, Edmund Tremayne, and others. A new presidency of Munster would be a particularly powerful instrument for initiating the system of substituting fixed money rents for military obligations such as the billeting and provisioning of troops. The rule of Gilbert and Perrot had shown, according to Sidney, that an alternative source of martial authority to that of the provincial lords could operate effectively. Now that a presidency was established, however tentatively, the incumbent could agree with the great and lesser lords to commute their martial dues to him to a money payment. Not only would the costs of the presidential army be defrayed by such levies, but also the retention of private armies, responsible for such chronic disorder and instability, would be redundant. From the nexus created by payment of fixed dues to the president, and in turn by underlords to their superiors in the ranking system, would, it was hoped, flow a model, rent-paying feudal hierarchy in which the energies of prominent individuals would be channelled into productive farming and commerce and office-holding. As a prelude to installing a president on these terms, Sidney undertook another provincial tour in the winter of 1575–6, and he met with general compliance.[15]

The keystone of this edifice of composition was the Earl of Desmond. Sidney, who met with the submissive Earl Gerald first at Dungarvan, gave him practical assurances of the crown's goodwill, and promises of future prosperity and peace if he would commute his martial dues. Ormond and his vassal lords on the other hand absented themselves from a general assembly of magnates at Cork, preferring to remain aloof from the jurisdiction of a President of Munster. All of the other lesser lords and gentry rallied round, however; some, such as Lords Power, Decies and Barry, were visited by the Lord Deputy, and these and the others attended Sidney at Cork for an impressive six-week convocation. Sidney also made a point of confirming the loyalty of hard-pressed townsfolk in the southern ports. At Cork he extracted guarantees from the Anglo-Norman and Gaelic lords of the south and south-west that they would disband the bulk of their 'idle' retinues and that they would pay rent to the crown instead of the military aids which they had provided theretofore. In particular the lesser lords were to pay an annual rent to the Earl of Desmond instead of the former coign and livery, and in return they would be promised freedom from intimidation and extortion from his agents. The guarantor of all of this was to be the Lord President with his army, supported in part at least by the local community. As an earnest of ordered familial bonds in the new society, the presence in Cork of so many lords' wives and widows was especially heartening for Sidney. He proceeded to give a foretaste of English-style justice by holding sessions to settle disputes between landlords, but his exemplary treatment of unlisted and therefore 'masterless' swordsmen was harsh: many executions of such men were carried out at the Cork sessions. By 1 July 1576 Sidney judged that Munster was ready for the entry of the new Lord President, Sir William Drury.[16]

Drury was to have a crowded four-year stint in Ireland until his death there late in 1579. As President of Munster down to mid-1578, his active pursuit of the goals laid down for him by Sidney brought much progress towards reform. He was determined to continue the undermining of the great lords by boosting the status of their underlings, to garner rents from all levels of landlords to defray expenses and promote demilitarisation, and to extirpate all landless soldiers. Included temporarily within the President's jurisdiction was Thomond, but exempted was the earldom of Ormond. Drury went about his work by stamping out coign and livery and negotiating with lords for rents in lieu of their military exactions to the new overlord, the presidency: for example, MacCarthy Reagh of Carbery compounded for £250 per annum, and Lord Barry for £150. These and other lords of their rank who were vassals of Desmond were to pay to him also a money rent, compounding the services which they owed to him. Desmond's acquiescence in the new scheme was hard-won, but Drury gradually managed to win the confidence of both the earl and Countess Eleanor. Already Desmond had been erratically disbanding his retinue of followers in response to coaxing from commissioners and deputy, and finally after a meeting with Drury at Kilkenny in early 1578 he agreed to a select household group of twenty horsemen, and to pay something towards the presidency's expenses. In return, Desmond was relieved of having to compel his vassals to pay him dues by force, receiving instead the compounded rents. Drury's neutralising of the private war machines continued on another front with his execution of 400 unregistered soldiers in less than two years. The projected income of £1,170 6s 6d from the lords of Munster was indicative of the drift of an intimidatory warrior class towards a rent-paying feudal hierarchy, although expenditure of £3,815 on the presidency far outstripped the annual rents. Drury could report considerable progress towards peaceful conditions when called upon to take up the lord justiceship in Dublin in April 1578 on Sidney's departure.[17]

Within eighteen months, however, another major insurrection had broken out in Munster, this one with the Earl of Desmond eventually at its head. Such an outcome seemed most unlikely, even as late as January 1579, as relations between Drury and Earl Gerald were further cemented by gestures of trust on both sides. The sudden crisis which occurred in the later part of the year had its origins in the hopes and fears raised as Desmond lost and gained official favour during the changeful period since 1565. Those lords such as Lords Barry and Decies who had become accustomed to being independent of Desmond during his eclipse found it galling to have to pay the commuted dues to a new overlord in the form of Lord President Drury. Compounding this irritant was the duty bounden on the legitimate vassals of the Earl of Desmond to pay him the former services due him in the form of composition rent, especially as Desmond himself was exempted from payment of rent to the presidency. Most disgruntled of all those expectant of government favour was Sir John of Desmond. Once feted by the government administrators such as Sidney and Perrot as the real Geraldine leader, Sir John now found himself impoverished in the later 1570s and spurned not only by the government but also by Desmond, the health of whose son and heir blocked John's avenue to the earldom. He was thus on a par with other Geraldine swordsmen for whom Desmond's rehabilitation had negated the effects of armed struggle against the new social and religious order. In fact there was literally no place at all for armed retainers with the ending of coign and livery and the disbanding by Desmond of his private army. For them the options were bleak: they could turn to the unaccustomed and despised activity of farming, or they could if lucky find employment in the small household band of the earl, or they could risk execution as 'masterless' men by living as outlaws.[18]

A small number of displaced swordsmen chose to emigrate in the company of James FitzMaurice Fitzgerald, who at the close of the 1570s was a focus for all disaffected elements in Munster (and beyond). His personal plight came about as a result of Desmond's repossession of some farms he had granted his cousin in 1574 in lieu of Kerrycurrihy. Landless and without a protector, FitzMaurice sailed for France in early 1575 with his wife and family, as well as the seneschal of Imokilly and Edmund Fitzgibbon, son of the late White Knight. Ostensibly a victim of Desmond's ungraciousness and a supplicant for Queen Elizabeth's pardon, James was soon in touch with the Catholic diplomatic nexus first at Paris, where he spent two years, and then at Rome. Although King Philip II of Spain was becoming more directly involved in northern European matters, he was reluctant to intervene in Ireland, and he failed to give a hearing to FitzMaurice's request for an expeditionary force. By contrast, Pope Gregory XIII seemed anxious to help launch a militant Counter-Reformation mission, but FitzMaurice's plans were cut across by the posturings of the English adventurer Thomas Stukeley. He was a former seneschal of Kavanagh country in the late 1560s who renounced his allegiance to affect the part of an exiled nobleman of Ireland at European courts. Stukeley was put at the head of 1,000 Italian swordsmen with the pope's blessing and FitzMaurice's approval in early 1578. Most of the force was commandeered at Lisbon by King Sebastian of Portugal, however, and ended up fighting against the Moorish ruler of Morocco at Alcazar, where Stukeley was killed. FitzMaurice managed to assemble another smaller force of many nationalities, including the remnants of Stukeley's soldiers, and in July 1579 his fleet sailed from Corunna with Dr Nicholas Sanders, an eminent English priest exile, on board as papal commissary.[19]

The landing of the squadron at Smerwick harbour near Dingle in County Kerry on 18 July was to galvanise the situation in the south-west of Ireland, but not immediately. Flanked by Sanders, a bishop, and several friars, and in the shadow of a papal banner, James FitzMaurice proclaimed the holy war sanctioned in letters from Pope Gregory. While the initial response from magnates in the region to this summons was disappointing, so too was the reaction to the Earl of Desmond's rallying of the Geraldines to arms in opposition to the invaders. The earl had assured Lord Justice Drury of his intention to cope with the challenge in his own way. The event which did electrify the Fitzgeralds and their allies in the succeeding fortnight was the assassination by Sir John of Desmond and his brother, Sir James, of the Englishmen Henry Davells and Arthur Carter in Tralee. Davells, then constable of Dungarvan, had befriended many of the lords of the south, including Sir John, during his long residence in Ireland, and he was thus considered suitable as a government envoy to inspect the entrenchment at Smerwick and to liaise with Desmond. While sleeping in a tavern in Tralee, Davells and Carter, the provost-marshal of Munster, were killed by the Fitzgerald brothers on 1 August 1579. The action catapulted Sir John into the leadership of a nakedly political revolt, and to his headquarters in the Kilmore woods flocked hundreds of swordsmen and galloglas from lordships in Kerry, Cork, Limerick and Tipperary. By contrast, the floundering Earl of Desmond, his authority being flouted on all sides, was left with only sixty men in his own household. Sir John and FitzMaurice attempted to make common cause, despite the differences in their objectives, but the latter then set out on a sortie to Connacht. While crossing the Shannon near Castleconnell on 18 August, his men seized some horses belonging to the Burkes of Clanwilliam, recent beneficiaries of the government's policy of favouring lesser landlords, and in the ensuing skirmish FitzMaurice was killed.[20]

In the face of the threat of the now undisputed leader, Sir John of Desmond, and his army of 3,000, the government's strategy was at first unco-ordinated. Frantic efforts were made to secure the coast of Munster from further invasion by the commissioning of Humphrey Gilbert to patrol the offshore waters with a fleet. Lord Justice Sir William Drury was in failing health as the rebellion gathered momentum, but he came to Limerick to take command with an army of 600 by September. Drury empowered Sir Nicholas Malby, the President of Connacht and the most experienced commander in the field in Ireland, to take over the governorship of Munster with his force of 1,100. As long as the hostilities were conducted in guerrilla fashion, however, the advantage was with the Geraldine army, and moreover Sir John dominated the key artery of west Munster from Cork to Limerick by his control of Liscarroll (seat of the Barrys), Kilmallock (through the Kilmore woods) and the Glen of Aherlow. An encounter at Springfield near Lough Gur in which disoriented English troops were scattered by the Geraldines proved the point. Malby (who assumed full control of the military campaign after Drury was borne away to die at Waterford) avenged this defeat when, at Monasternenagh on the Maigue river on 3 October, on open ground and with professionally deployed soldiers, he inflicted severe losses on Sir John's army. Now the Earl of Desmond was confronted with an ultimatum to surrender all authority, as the governor brought systematic destruction to life and property along the north Limerick way to Desmond's bailiwick at Askeaton. An attack on the castle was resisted, and within days, on Malby's advice, the newly arrived Lord Justice, Sir William Pelham, proclaimed the earl a rebel.[21]

Those compelled to justify the outlawing of the Earl of Desmond to an uneasy Queen Elizabeth claimed that he had foreknowledge of FitzMaurice's plans, condoned the murder of Davells and provided protection for the rebels, including Dr Sanders. His own apologia—that he had notified Drury of the invasion, aided in the capture of Bishop Patrick O'Healy of Mayo, victualled the Lord Deputy's men and yielded up his heir as hostage—counted for nothing. The vacillation of the previous months ended, Desmond could now supersede his brother as leader of unsettled Geraldines as well as retainers and clansmen of the Munster lords who were themselves procrastinating. Desmond's spectacular break-out was staged at Youghal on 13 November. Taking advantage of decrepit defences, the earl's followers sacked the town, abusing the women-folk and carrying away rich plunder. The ferocity of the government's reaction to the rebellion during the following months and years had many causes, but the devastation of Youghal certainly coloured the attitude of the Earl of Ormond, appointed general in Munster. Acting in concert with Lord Justice Pelham in the spring and summer of 1580, Ormond was party to the campaign of burning of lands and property which were of potential value to the insurgents and also the indiscriminate killing of non-belligerents. A staunch Protestant, Pelham was determined to deal with the revolt as a Spanish plot against the church and the monarchy, and hence his targeting of all areas which might give succour to rebels, native or foreign, and his relentless pursuit of Dr Sanders. Ormond and Pelham laid waste the Desmond lands of Limerick and the border-lands with Cork before bringing fire and sword into north Kerry. The capture of Carrigafoyle castle and the slaughter of its garrison led to the surrender of the strongholds of Askeaton and Ballilogher. By the summer of 1580 lords such as Decies, Roche, Barry and Sir Cormac MacTaidhg were responding with alacrity to Pelham's summons to Limerick, the Gaelic lords of Kerry had come in to Ormond, and the notable belligerents were offered pardons only if they gave up their superiors. To Desmond, now a fugitive in the Kerry mountains, unconditional surrender alone was offered. With the Munster revolt apparently fizzling out, the uprising of James Eustace, Viscount Baltinglass, in Leinster in July 1580 threw all into uncertainty once again.[22]

Although unco-ordinated with the Munster rebellion and many months too late for a united crusading venture, the viscount's insurrection inspirited the followers of Sir John of Desmond and Dr Nicholas Sanders. Together they travelled through Aherlow into Leinster to meet up with James Eustace in Leix, but the Earl of Desmond had no wish to leave the south. During the next two months a new front was opened up along the Barrow valley by the Leinster and Munster insurgents. When news of a landing of continental troops at Smerwick on 10 September reached them, Sir

John and Dr Sanders crossed over with Baltinglass into the south-west, rendezvousing with the Earl of Desmond near Tralee. The swift manoeuvres of Ormond and Lord Grey de Wilton, the Lord Deputy, prevented a joinder of anti-government forces from taking place, and the 600 expeditionary soldiers, mostly of Italian birth with some Spaniards who were dispatched by Pope Gregory, barricaded themselves in the fort of Dún an Óir, which had been used by FitzMaurice in 1579. While Ormond harried the Irish rebels through north Kerry, and Baltinglass departed for home by the end of October, Grey sat at Dingle with his army, awaiting the arrival of Admiral Sir William Winter with ships carrying heavy guns and provisions. By early November the scene was set for the bombardment of Dún an Óir. Battered by the English cannon, the outworks of the old fort proved inadequate, and within two days the commander, Bastiano di San Giuseppi, was ready to surrender. Grey accepted the submission of the defenders unconditionally and, having herded them back into the fort without their armour and weapons, as he chillingly reported, 'put I in certain bands, who straight fell to execution. There were 600 slain.' The massacre at Smerwick had national and international reverberations, although Queen Elizabeth did not disown her governor's actions. The Munster rebellion continued, but the morale of the leadership never recovered. In particular the hopes of the papal commissary, Nicholas Sanders, were blasted, and he died of dysentery about the beginning of April 1581, mentally and physically broken.[23]

Queen Elizabeth and her advisers in London were anxious to curtail the massive expenditure which fielding an army of over 6,400 had entailed. Accordingly, a general pardon was offered to all but a few named individuals in May 1581. Besides Desmond, Sir John and Baltinglass, Lord Grey excepted several others from pardon, including Countess Eleanor for her encouragement of rebels, and David Barry, to whom Lord Barrymore had conveyed all his lands. The issue of whether to pardon the rebels or to treat Munster as a *tabula rasa* for a complete new settlement, the option favoured by ambitious servitors, had been exercising English officials such as Sir Edward Waterhouse since the beginning of the revolt. In this connection, the Earl of Ormond as general of Munster was attacked by the New English, for example Captain Walter Raleigh, one of the Smerwick executioners, as being too partial to the families of the insurgents and too prone to offer them pardons. Thus the queen was persuaded to dismiss Ormond, officially in order to save money, at the same time as issuing the general pardon and ordering a substantial reduction in army numbers. The effect of these decisions on the ground in the five counties was to delay the final quelling of the revolt for another two years. With no coherent military strategy and restricted companies, individual captains operated independently, antagonising previously loyal landowners into joining the revolt, as for instance in the case of Baron Fitzmaurice of Lixnaw in April 1582. Countess Eleanor travelled to Dublin that summer to surrender to Grey, but the queen ordered her to go back to her husband, unless she could persuade him to surrender unconditionally. The earl ranged freely throughout the province, striking at his enemies, but the real leadership had been removed. Sir John of Desmond had been surprised by a party of soldiers north of Cork city in the early days of 1582 and had been killed, his head being sent to Grey as a 'new year gift'.[24]

Arthur, Baron Grey de Wilton, was himself removed from office as Lord Deputy in the summer of 1582. His reputation among his fellow New English for inefficacious severity was scarcely higher than it was among the local community which regarded him as a 'bloody man who regarded not the life of subjects more than dogs'. At the time of his departure alarming reports were reaching England of the devastating effects upon the Munster inhabitants of the policies with which Grey was most closely associated. The tactic of systematically 'burning their corn, spoiling their harvest and killing and driving their cattle' did not originate in Grey's regime but it reached its fullest expression therein. During his own period of governorship Grey's predecessor, Pelham, wrote that 'the poor people that live only upon labour and fed by their milch cows offer themselves with their wives and children to be slain by the army than to suffer the famine that now in extremity is beginning to pinch them'. By 1582 famine conditions were rife in many parts of the province, coupled with disease brought on by malnutrition. Not only were resources of corn and animals wantonly destroyed to prevent their providing sustenance to the rebels, but also large herds of cattle and sheep in Cork, Kerry and Limerick were preyed upon by the expanded soldiery and the insurgents. Within a six-month period down to mid-1582 at least 30,000 people were said to have died. Flight from the land to the towns was useless: Sir Warham St Leger claimed that in Cork city between twenty and seventy deaths were occurring daily from starvation, and the other towns were badly impoverished owing to the war. The poet Edmund Spenser, Grey's secretary, described the survivors as looking like 'anatomies of death', creeping forth from glens and woods upon their hands to feed on carrion or watercress or shamrocks. Such mortality led to depopulation on a large scale. Areas of Cork and Kerry seem to have suffered most in this respect: an extreme example is the estate of John FitzEdmond of Cloyne, a loyalist, which lost over ninety per cent of its inhabitants.[25]

The Earl of Ormond was reappointed as lord general of Munster at the start of 1583. Queen Elizabeth thereby gave her backing to the strategy of drawing away from the Earl of Desmond his principal supporters by a mixture of diplomacy and violence. Some of these, such as Lord Lixnaw and the White Knight, were thought to be still in rebellion through fear of Desmond's reprisals if he were to be restored to favour. Consequently it was made absolutely clear that there would be no pardon for the Geraldine magnate. Furnished with an army of 1,000, Ormond quickly got into his stride by attempting to localise the rebellion. This he succeeded in doing by closing off the Glen of Aherlow as a bolt-hole and confining Desmond and a small band to the mountains of Kerry and west Cork. Gradually, as the spring and early summer of 1583 wore on, the lure of pardons coupled with war-weariness proved too attractive for Lixnaw, the seneschal of Imokilly and the Countess Eleanor to resist, the latter surrendering unconditionally in June. The operation of the double-edged campaign of Ormond is attested in his claim before the end of May that 134 people had been slain and 247 protected. Pressure came on the lord general to make a 'quick end' to the war by trapping Desmond by fair means or foul. By now, however, the fugitive was in dire straits in the mountainous southwest, having an ever-dwindling band of followers. After a few narrow escapes Desmond was tracked to a cabin at Glanageenty, to the east of Tralee, by the O'Moriartys on 2 November 1583. His plea for mercy proved unavailing, and the injured Desmond was beheaded, the body being displayed at Cork and the head sent to Queen Elizabeth.[26]

The planning and practice of plantation

The province of Munster in early 1584, much of it depopulated and leaderless, lay open to a major scheme of resettlement by either natives or newcomers. Even before the inducting of a new Lord President, John Norris, and the formal assumption of power in Dublin by a new Lord Deputy, Sir John Perrot, in June, plans had been set in train for what would ultimately be the plantation of Munster. On the ground in the counties there was a firm expectation of land acquisitions on the part of those who had served the government against the Geraldines. Sir Walter Raleigh, for example, had received a custodiam of an area in the Lee estuary from Lord Grey and was no doubt hoping to apply his colonial theories as landowner in Munster. The Secretary of State, Geoffrey Fenton, another proponent of plantation, was also confident of attaining an estate—in north Kerry—before official decisions were made. Long before the Earl of Desmond's death the disposal of his vast territories and the dismantling of his Kerry palatinate had been the subject of intense interest on the part of New English administrators in Dublin. Before definite plans could be made, of course, the full extent of the land available had to be determined. While estimates of extent and value continued to be made before the formal survey of 1584, a range of suggestions emanated from sources in Ireland as to reordering of the Desmond estates. These included the sale of the lands to the highest bidders to defray the enormous costs of £300,000 Irish spent on quelling of revolt from 1579, the endowment of institutions such as the presidency or a new university with confiscated land, and the transplantion of troublesome Leinster clans such as the O'Connors and O'Mores to the south-west. In 1584, however, the consensus for colonisation emerging among Irish official circles found favour with the influential coterie of Privy Councillors in London, including Burghley and Walsingham.[27]

A preliminary step was the commissioning of an overall survey of the attainted lands to supplement the local inquisitions of the escheator. Sir Valentine Browne, who had wide experience of surveying in England and Ireland, was chosen for the task, along with Sir Henry Wallop, the Vice-Treasurer. Technical expertise was at hand also in the persons of Arthur Robbins, an estate surveyor, and Francis Jobson, a cartographer. The surveyors were instructed to discover the extent, value and occupiers of escheated lands in Munster, as well as to record details of topography and natural resources. Beginning on 1 September 1584 and travelling for thirteen hectic weeks, the commissioners gathered intelligence from juries of residents on the status of lands of Desmond and associated rebels. In Tipperary the work of assessing Desmond's estates there was hampered by the Earl of Ormond, who asserted his palatinate rights. Limerick was more thoroughly surveyed, the county being proclaimed 'most fertile', particularly in the eastern attainted lands, which were ninety per cent inhabited. Desmond's manors in Limerick and those of other rebellious families of Fitzgeralds as well as MacSheehys, and individuals such as the Knight of Glin, amounted to over 100,000 acres. The southern half of Kerry, populated mostly by Gaelic Irish clans was regarded as impenetrable by the commissioners, but they surveyed the northern zone, centring again on the Earl of Desmond's manors. The impression gained of the county was of severe depopulation, 'the people be dead, the inhabitants gone' being a comment of one of the party. For all of Cork, except for the west, there was much detail forthcoming of the lands of hundreds of rebels, the most notable being the late Sir John of Desmond, who had rich estates in the Awbeg valley in the north of the county. Waterford, surveyed last of all, had significant lands and rentals of Desmond and his collaterals to the west of the county. After almost a year the commissioners issued their report. It valued the attainted lands of Munster at £10,000, 70 per cent of which sum was accounted for by Desmond's lands, rents and charges; the commissioners calculated that there were 577,645 acres involved. They admitted that their estimates were rough and that they had not surveyed all of the lands. Later valuations found that low rates of value per ploughland were adopted and that the extent of the lands was exaggerated, as no more than 300,000 acres were later granted to settlers.[28]

Before a plantation could be implemented on the basis of the 1584 survey, attainder of the rebels had to be confirmed formally in parliament. The process took longer than anticipated in 1585 because of errors in the drafting of legislation and some opposition, notably from the supporters of Ormond, who claimed the lands of the Tipperary rebels as part of his palatinate. Eventually in 1586 the names of 136 were listed in the acts of attainder, three-quarters of whom were Old English and only nine of whom were still alive after the rebellion. Many of the larger Munster landowners who had been in revolt with Desmond, such as the seneschal of Imokilly, had been pardoned. Meanwhile the planning of the articles for a plantation was proceeding in London. The decision had been taken in principle by 1586 to settle people of English birth on the confiscated lands. This was regarded by the leading Privy Councillors as the best way not only to provide for a model of English civility in the south of Ireland but also to ensure the security of Munster in case of an attempted Spanish invasion. There was too the attraction of providing for restless and adventurous younger sons from families particularly in the west of England. More idealistic colonial thinkers were enthused by the prospect of applying classical practices of settlement on a sweeping scale so close to home. Informed by both theoretical and practical considerations as well as by the surveyors in late 1585, the extremely well-briefed Lord Burghley, together with Sir Francis Walsingham, Thomas Egerton, the Solicitor-General, and John Popham, the Attorney-General, honed the proposals for the Munster plantation which were finally proclaimed in London on 27 June 1586.[29]

The lands were divided into seignories of 12,000, 8,000, 6,000 and 4,000 acres, each to be granted to an undertaker, who could hold no more than 12,000 acres. The undertaker was to hold in common socage from the crown and not by knight's service as had been envisaged in the 1569 plantation scheme. Each seigneur undertook to bring ninety-one families from England to his estate: his own, six freeholders, six farmers, forty-two copyholders and thirty-six cottagers. The latter categories were to hold from 400 acres down to ten at the undertaker's discretion. Rents for 12,000-acre seignories, full payment of which was to be waived for a seven years' settlement phase, varied from £200 in the old Desmond heartland of Kerry to £66 13s 4d in Cork, Waterford and Tipperary, based on profitable acreage only. The equivalent of tax breaks, some for the probationary period and others in perpetuity, were offered to lure investors. Imports of supplies and exports of produce were to be exempted from customs levies. Obligations for defence were bounden on each seignorial corps after the probationary phase, fifteen horsemen and forty-eight footmen being the required force for each. The strict conditions regarding racial origins of original settlers—they had to be of English birth—did not apply at the level of tenants of and purchasers from settlers: there was scope for Old English participation in those cases, but the Gaelic Irish were ruled out absolutely as residents on the plantation estates. Nor was marriage of heiresses of settler families to be allowed other than to spouses of English parentage. The London government envisaged dealing with individual leading settlers rather than with companies or corporations whose ventures would be less amenable to supervision.[30]

Thirty-five undertakers were successful in taking out letters patent for their estates during the years from 1587 to 1595. Not only had they to be of substantial status and wealth to get court approval and afford the investment involved in their undertaking, but they also had to have stamina to survive the 'obstacle course' which officialdom placed in their paths. English country gentlemen made up the most numerous category. Men such as Sir William Courtenay of Devon and Edmund Mainwaring of Cheshire were canvassed through the network of local administration in the western counties of England. The sales drive was oversubscribed, with more than eighty applicants requesting over 800,000 Munster acres. Strong competition came from the group of military men in Ireland who claimed grants of land in lieu of arrears of salary; some of these, such as Sir George Bourchier and Edward Berkeley, were already custodians of confiscated territories. Favoured administration officials such as the Earl of Ormond and Sir Edmund Fitton were well placed to apply for prime estates, and closeness to the English court benefited Sir Walter Raleigh and Sir Christopher Hatton among others. Although the English county undertakers had agreed among themselves on a rough division of the lands according to shire groupings by mid-1586, the government modified the composition of the plantation by providing for the crown servitors, including army and official personnel. To deal with competing claims from English people in Ireland and England, the government set up another commission for surveying and measuring the lands. The work proved slow and inefficient and some undertakers pre-empted the findings, Sir William Herbert, for example, sending an advance party to sit on his Kerry estate. By 1587 the legal machinery was in place for the thirty-five undertakers to enter into possession of their allocations in the five counties, even though in some cases the boundaries of their estates were not clearly defined; all were in possession by the end of 1588.[31]

While the estates as envisaged on paper by the planners were models of symmetry and social organisation, the reality which met the undertakers on the ground in Munster was of disjointed holdings.

Within the boundaries of seignories there were dwelling independent freeholders on unconfiscated lands, aptly termed 'intermixers'. Some of these may have been refugees in 1584 at the time of the first survey and have returned to their residences thereafter. The inadequacies of that survey and the later one of 1586–7 for allocating the land not only hindered the initial progress of the plantation in 1587 but also contributed to the large number of legal claims concerning land in the following decades. By anticipating the slow work of the measurers and surveyors in 1586 and 1587, the undertakers speeded up the process of gaining certificates for their grants and entering into possession. But disputes flared between rival undertakers, such as Sir William Herbert and Denzil Holles in north Kerry, to whom had been given in their separate certificates the same allotment of Tarbert. Also common were disagreements between settlers over seignory boundaries and tenants, the practice of poaching peasant families from neighbouring estates occurring especially in more depopulated regions. By far the most numerous complaints to come before judicial tribunals in the years after 1587, however, were those of natives of the province who claimed on a variety of grounds that their lands should be exempt from the plantation. The volume of such claims was so great that the government established a special commission to settle all controversies in 1588, and, following that body's failure to do so, another for adjudicating on land titles and other matters in 1592.[32]

One of the most contentious causes of claims against the plantation was the matter of 'chargeable lands' occupied by those who, although having paid exactions such as coign and livery to the Earl of Desmond as overlord, nevertheless asserted that they were freeholders. These lands having been included by the 1584 surveyors in the forfeited estates, the undertakers argued that the inhabitants were tenants-at-will of the rebel earl and thus were without proprietory rights. Sir Warham St Leger with Sir Richard Grenville, for example, had acquired a seignory at Kerrycurrihy which incorporated the lands leased to him in 1568 by the Earl of Desmond. The inhabitants of these lands claimed to be freeholders, who had been subject to the earl's extortions, and not tenants as contended by St Leger and Grenville. After much bitter litigation the claims of the freeholders were upheld and St Leger lost possession of 6,000 acres. Among the major Gaelic claimants against the settlement of 1587 was Donal MacCarthy More, the Earl of Clancare, who successfully argued that all the lands confiscated from various MacCarthys and O'Donoghue More in south Kerry were within his lordship, and not therefore part of the seignory of Sir Valentine Browne. Another group of plaintiffs against the planters were those who claimed to hold mortgages on certain of the Desmond estates, obtaining possession of the lands thereby, in accordance with Irish custom. As redemption of mortgages had been uncommon, the mortgagor was in effect selling the property to the mortgagee. Accordingly, many an undertaker found that parts of his seignory were occupied by others who could not be removed until his predecessors' debts were paid off. In general, when cases came to be adjudicated upon by commissioners and others, mortgages tended to be upheld, and the rights of mortgagors to repay and re-enter their lands were allowed.[33]

The government approach to the plantation in the first decade as formulated essentially by the Privy Council in London and operated by the presidency and commissions in Munster was lacking in consistency. Principles of Gaelic law of succession and landholding, for instance, could be adduced or rejected to suit the government's case. Bureaucratic delays hampered the undertakers in the early years, and the native claimants were antagonised by the blanket rejection of their cases. The climax of the latter process was the outcome of the 1588 commission. Set up to deal with all disputes relating to landownership in Munster and comprising leading jurists from England and Ireland, the commission examined almost eighty petitions in a brief session at Cork. All except one were dismissed, mostly on the grounds of lack of any documentary proof of ownership. It seems clear that the commissioners were most anxious to uphold the crown's title to the escheated lands at all costs, irrespective of whether the undertakers had taken possession or not. By 1592 the policy had changed: the commission of that year, manned solely by serving Irish officials with experience of Munster, heard 119 suits, the vast majority being of Old English or Gaelic natives against the undertakers. Almost half of those which were resolved were won by the plaintiffs, in stark contrast to the outcome in 1588, and many were referred to other courts. For its part, the government had learned to take cases on their merits, but the overgenerous indulgence of native claims, as they saw it, was lamented by those 'daunted [and] dismayed' New English who feared the undermining of the plantation. Settlers adopted a variety of stratagems to consolidate their holdings in these circumstances, some resorting to Irish mortgage arrangements to acquire property, some, such as the Browne family, intermarrying with the native aristocracy of both races (in their case the O'Sullivan Beare family), and some acting as guardians to wards to advance their positions.[34]

The seven-year probationary period ordained for the undertakers to accomplish the settlement of families on their estates ended at Michaelmas 1594. By that time, if each of the twenty-five full seigniories in Munster had its designated complement of ninety-one households, including that of the undertaker, the total settler population should have been about 11,300, allowing for five per household. A study of reports compiled in the early 1590s, however, has revealed that the English population may only have reached a third of that projected figure. Some undertakers such as Sir Henry Oughtred in Limerick resided fairly continuously on their estates and arranged for the travel of dozens of followers from England to Munster. Others had overriding interests elsewhere and, having established households on their estates in the late 1580s, spent little time there afterwards. As well as residence, real commitment to the plantation entailed a major investment in transport, building, buying stock and paying living expenses. Sir William Herbert, for example, spent £1,738 in settling his estate in Kerry by 1591. The major item of expenditure of the undertakers was on building large residences for themselves or else restoring some of the substantial but ruined Desmond castles such as Askeaton and Castleisland. By contrast, the houses of tenants on the estates were of wood and thatch, built mostly at their own expense. Town-dwelling in Munster received a modest fillip, with Tallow, County Waterford, for instance, reviving from its ruined pre-plantation state. Some undertakers transported cows, sheep and horses from England to develop their own breeds, and by the mid-1590s there were signs on some of the better-managed estates that the land had been well settled and was beginning to be worked profitably.[35]

In early October 1598 a general uprising of the natives of Munster led to the destruction of the plantation within two weeks. The minority of settlers who had not fled to the towns or provincial strongholds before the rebels arrived were driven from their estates, and there was some loss of life. The thinness of the spread of the population of newcomers caused their vulnerability. The regional insurgency was resonant of the revolt of the Ulster confederates led by Hugh O'Neill, Earl of Tyrone, who dispatched the midland chief, Owney MacRory O'More, into Munster at the height of the campaign. A provincial leader emerged in the form of James FitzThomas, nephew of the attained Earl Gerald, who claimed the title of Earl of Desmond. While rallying to the cause of Hugh O'Neill, the participants had a variety of reasons for joining the rebellion. Individuals such as Lord Barry did so for reasons of immediate self-preservation. Some undoubtedly were members of the group of dispossessed who used the revolt as an opportunity to get back their lands. Even before 1598 there had been an upsurge in anti-plantation activity, with some settlers being killed. But while antipathy to the plantation and its agents may have been cited by some, the official response to native land claims had been generally sympathetic since the early 1590s, many of the settlers indeed regarding it as overgenerous. Perhaps more unsettling was the very lack of consistency in government policy which vacillated between rigour and lenity. This indetermination allowed scope for the activities of opportunistic minor officials who made use of fraudulent legal practices to discover and claim lands to which natives had defective titles. While senior crown personnel might berate such improper behaviour, their own administration had veered between upholding the rights of ownership of those on the chargeable lands of the Earl of Clancare and denying them in the case of those on similar lands in the earldom of Desmond. Problems of inconstancy also bedevilled attempts at reform in the two other provinces to be studied, Connacht and Ulster.[36]

Connacht: Council and Composition, 1569–95

ONLY a few of Admiral Recalde's fleet of twenty-seven ships from the scattered Spanish Armada which attempted to round the island of Ireland in the autumn of 1588 eventually reached their home ports. About half foundered on the craggy coastline of Connacht, then incorporating Clare. From Streedagh Point in Sligo around to Carrigaholt in the Shannon estuary many disasters befell the almost parched and starved crews of sailors and soldiers who were to have been the shock-troops in Philip II's proposed invasion of England. Between 6,000 and 7,000 may have drowned off the coasts of the province, and the much smaller number of survivors faced grim and uncertain fates ashore. In the more pacified southern half of Connacht officials such as Boetius Clancy, sheriff of County Clare, carried out mass executions, and Gaelic clans loyal to the civil authority such as the O'Flahertys of Iar-Chonnacht handed over hundreds of prisoners for dispatch by the provost marshal. Lords in the northern part of the province, less amenable to government control, acted in a variety of ways towards the shipwrecked foreigners: Dubhdarach Roe O'Malley slew the survivors from Don Pedro de Mendoza's ship on Clare Island for their gold, and the scavengers at Streedagh stripped naked the living and dead, whereas chiefs such as O'Rourke and MacClancy in Leitrim gave shelter and sustenance. The motivations for native behaviour towards the hapless crews ranged from fear of government retribution through feelings of politico-religious solidarity with Spanish Catholics to sheer greed or compassion.[1]

The evidence of alarm caused by the Armada's appearance off Ireland's Atlantic coast in 1588 underscores the English perception of the vulnerability of the north and west of the island to external influence. At the time of crisis in 1588 the effective extension of English administration west of the Shannon had been in train for less than two decades. The events of that year triggered a serious revolt in northern Connacht which threatened to sweep away the still fragile institutions of the presidency in the region. Yet the potential for the destabilising of internal political arrangements from extra-provincial broils had already lent added urgency to the establishment of English law and norms. The perception of Connacht as thoroughfare between the provinces of Munster and Ulster was a factor in the political advances made, and the danger was intensified in the time of the FitzMaurice revolt and later in the Nine Years' War. Apart from illuminating the sense of insecurity of the defenders of the western maritime zone, the experiences of the stranded foreigners help to show the contrasts between the policies of individual leaders. The progress of the presidency as imposed in Connacht since 1569 was governed to a large extent by the difference between southern and northern lordships. Changes in taxation and military organisation were already well under way, and these prefigured social and economic transformations at varying rates throughout the province.

An examination of events in Connacht during the years from 1569 to 1595 reveals a significantly different pattern of English institutional advance and native response to that seen in the cases of Leinster and Munster. As with the southern province, that deeper administrative engagement had its genesis in Sir Henry Sidney's programme of reform through regional presidency councils as elaborated in the later 1560s. The first President, Sir Edward Fitton (1569–74), who had the task of laying foundations for English administration mainly in Thomond and Clanricard, met with resistance, albeit less coordinated than that with which Gilbert and Perrot had to contend in Munster. By the time of Sidney's relaunching of the presidency under Sir Nicholas Malby (1579–84) the scheme for governmental fiscal and military control over the greater lords seemed to be proceeding satisfactorily with again only sporadic opposition. These innovations foreshadowed the centralised system of commutations generally known as the 'Composition of Connacht', worked out in 1585–6 at the start of Sir Richard Bingham's presidency (1584–96). In contrast with the previous scheme, however, the Composition boosted the status and authority of the Earls of Thomond and Clanricard, who were now in a position to capitalise on conditions of increased stability and economic promise, in southern Connacht at least. Both presidency and Composition acted as agents of anglicisation there to the mutual benefit of natives and English officials.

In the northern areas—of Mayo, Sligo and Roscommon, on the other hand—the meshing of the two systems was complicated by the more fractious nature of Gaelic and gaelicised society and the more aggressive social and economic ambitions of newcomers. By the mid-1590s, then, many elements in northern Connacht were susceptible to the claims of Hugh O'Donnell of Tyrconnell for overlordship of the region, as part of his war against the crown.

The establishment of the presidency council

By the 1560s the administrative mind was conceiving of Connacht as a province with a distinct identity, ready for treatment as a coherent unit. Since political reform had been broached in the earlier part of the century there had been calls for a regional council to govern the west as well as the south and north of Ireland. In the late 1560s the way was cleared for presidents with councils to be appointed, but the new institutions had even less of a foothold in the western province than in Munster. Athlone rather than the municipality of Galway was to be chosen as the presidential seat, as the garrison already installed there could patrol the extended western Pale as well as the Shannon's right bank. Political agreements reached with the Connacht lords in the mid-century years had helped in some ways to prepare for a new provincial governor but in other ways had created complications for his work. While some of their vassal lords such as MacNamara and O'Shaughnessy had been knighted in 1543, the two newly created Earls of Thomond and Clanricard had forged near-palatine authority for themselves in Clare and Galway respectively under the auspices of benign surrender and regrant agreements, making them formidable rivals for a provincial ruler. Also the succession arrangements to some lordships, especially Thomond, had heaped up fuel for serious disputes. When, in a departure from the practice of primogeniture, the government identified Donough O'Brien, nephew of the first Earl of Thomond, as heir apparent, it seemed to condone the system of tanistry among the clan. But Donough's brother and murderer, Donal, elected as O'Brien, was bitterly disappointed to be rejected as earl in favour of Donough's eldest son, Conor. The resulting dispute between rival O'Briens was serious enough to bring the traditional factional heads into near-confrontation in Thomond in 1564: the Earl of

Desmond crossed the Shannon with a large force of galloglas and kerne on behalf of Donal to attack the Earl of Thomond, who was saved with the assistance of the Earl of Clanricard and with the Earl of Ormond on stand-by.[2]

To prepare the ground for a president and council in Connacht, Sidney included the northern and southern segments in his two separate sweeps of the country in late 1566 and early 1567. The Lord Deputy's concern during his tour of the north-west in late 1566, taking in Sligo and Boyle, was the consolidation of the O'Donnell lordship there as a counterbalance to O'Neill. In turn, the regional authority of Donal O'Connor Sligo was ratified by a surrender and regrant agreement and his subsequent trip to Queen Elizabeth's court. Sidney took in the two provincial earldoms during his swing through the south of Ireland in the spring of 1567. At Limerick the viceroy attempted to inspirit the citizens, oppressed not only by Desmond but also by Thomond. Of the latter Sidney formed an unfavourable impression, describing him as having 'neither wit of himself to govern, nor grace or capacity to learn of others', but he nevertheless realised his potential for trouble in pursuit of aggressive overlordship of clans in Clare. Of Clanricard the governor came to have a better opinion, but the earl's two sons, John and Ulick, were recognised as being unmanageably fractious. They were therefore consigned to detention in Dublin. Galway, the target of many Burke attacks, was seen as a 'town of war', but no doubt the pacification of Murrough na Doe O'Flaherty of Iar-Chonnacht was of comfort to the hard-pressed townsfolk. Overall, the urban presence in Connacht was extremely tenuous at that time, the only other town of note, Athenry, barely housing a few families. Although some auspicious signs of economic advancement were seen in O'Shaughnessy's country, bordering Clanricard and Thomond, where the lands were 'rich, plentiful and well ordered', Sidney's message to Queen Elizabeth on the state of the western province in April 1567 stressed the need for state-sponsored reform.[3]

In this prelusive period to the presidency Sidney contented himself with St Leger-style surrender and regrant pacts with O'Connor Sligo and MacWilliam Iochtar, ceding to them captaincy of their clans' lands. As was soon to be manifested in Upper Connacht and Thomond, however, the new type of agreement with local lords entailed the dismantling of the power of the overlord and diffusing it through the ranks of the collateral branches and vassal chiefs. For example, the Lord Deputy was determined to encourage the lesser O'Briens and other sept heads to pursue freehold status to undermine the Earl of Thomond's proprietorial claims. Political power would eventually be shared through advancing the earls' rivals to the offices of sheriff in Clare and Galway. The shiring process itself represented a key stage in the spreading of English law and administration throughout the province, with the hope that county institutions of justice and government would offer avenues of patronage to locals within an English shrieval system. Throughout Connacht (as in Munster) all power would ultimately be centred on the president and his officials, as the focus of justice, law and order, taxation and social reform. A further erosion of the magnates' power would thus occur by the weakening of their military organisation based on coign and livery and the use of Scots mercenaries. The financing of the presidential army would eventually entail an innovative system of taxation, but initially Sidney believed that unexploited crown land in the province such as former monastic property could help to pay for the establishment. In the wake of freeholding and martial reforms among the clans, it was hoped that agriculture could be fostered and trade stimulated through revived towns. The ultimate aim of anglicisation through the sapping of the native polity, society and economy would also embody inurement in the state religion.[4]

Sidney's analysis having been cautiously accepted at court, the appointment of a President of Connacht went ahead, with the Englishman Sir Edward Fitton holding the office from December 1569 to March 1574. Fitton, who brought with him Sir Ralph Rokeby and Robert Dillon as justice and second justice respectively, had as his brief the setting up of a new kind of civil and judicial administration in the province with the backing of the army already stationed at Athlone. Although this aim would inevitably mean encroachment on the autonomy of the leading lords, it was hoped to win their support for the presidency through relieving them of the wasteful system of private armies sustained by coign and livery, and through the impartial settlement of disputes. By early 1570 Fitton had completed a circuit of the newly shired Galway and Roscommon, holding assizes there and beginning the establishment of English law. The city of Galway was a mainstay of civility. Initially at least Clanricard and the other lords of that area were acquiescent enough in the lifting of 'all unreasonable exactions and lewd Irish customs', giving pledges and recognizances totalling £9,000 as an assurance of

good behaviour. Extending the curbing of Gaelic customs to under-
pin order, the President banned the Irish glib or fringe in his presence
as a 'first token of obedience' and followed Gilbert's lead in Munster
by insisting on the booking of all retainers of the provincial lords on
pain of their being hanged by the provost marshal. Fitton also took
seriously his duty of furthering the Reformation in Connacht by
his iconoclastic attack on Catholic churches and expulsion of
communities of friars, including the Dominicans at Athenry and
Franciscans at Kilconnell, during his first tour of the province.[5]

Conor O'Brien, Earl of Thomond, was an unlikely rebel against
the English presence in his lordship in 1570, as his pre-eminence owed
everything to crown backing against his rivals within the clan. Yet he
was the first to defy the new Lord President when, on 1 February
1570, he refused to attend Fitton's assizes at Ennis in his Thomond
heartland. Later he detained Captain Apsley and his soldiers on their
return from Kerry, where they had been quelling the FitzMaurice
rebellion. Thomond's immediate irritation may have stemmed from
the promotion of a rival, Sir Tadhg MacMurrough O'Brien of
Leamaneh, to the office of sheriff of Clare. More fundamentally,
however, he was antipathetic to the regime of Sidney and its
English court faction led by Leicester. The earl proclaimed 'openly
at his table that he would do nothing with the Lord Deputy nor Lord
President but as the Duke of Norfolk would say'. Contemporaneous
with Thomond's uprising was the northern rising in England in
support of Norfolk's old aristocratic party at court. Thomond
posed as a champion of the poor people of his country in the face of
presidential oppression and adopted the dress of a Gaelic chieftain.
The tactics used were the denial of food supplies to the President
and his army throughout Clare, forcing their withdrawal, the capture
of officers such as Tadhg MacMurrough and the principal rival,
Donal O'Brien, and raids on the lands of the loyal O'Shaughnessys.
In the late spring the Earl of Ormond was deputed to cross into
Thomond to placate his rebellious cousin. In sympathy with his
pro-Norfolk leanings and having drawn his own brothers out of a
similar imbroglio, Ormond received Thomond's submission in
April 1570 on the understanding that he (Ormond) would have
custody of his country and castles. Thomond asked to be allowed to
receive a pardon from the queen in person, not trusting the clemency
of Sidney or Fitton. His flight to France from the Shannon estuary
was to negotiate an audience with Queen Elizabeth through the

mediacy of the English ambassador at Paris. Eventually he was received at the court in London, pardoned and bound over on £10,000 Irish for his future good behaviour. Ormond received the surrender of the principal O'Briens, as well as O'Loughlins and O'Mahons, sparing all but a few, and wrote that 'the queen hath many good subjects here if they were but cherished and not overpressed'.[6]

Meanwhile Sir Edward Fitton was forced to deal with more outbreaks of disorder, particularly among the MacWilliam Burkes of Mayo, who skirmished with the President's reinforced army before Shrule castle in the summer of 1570. As rebellion spread in resonance with Thomond and James FitzMaurice in Desmond, Fitton and Justice Rokeby employed ruthless tactics against belligerent and civilian alike, martial law was continuous, and extra English troops were billeted and cessed on the Connacht populace. By 1572 the thitherto co-operative Earl of Clanricard had become restive under Fitton's increasingly draconian style of presidency. He objected to his cousin and rival John Burke's appointment as sheriff of County Galway, execrated the use of martial law against his followers, and was put out at the proposal for a new tax on each ploughland of Clanricard. John and Ulick Burke, the earl's sons, sometime prisoners under Sidney, were now free to revolt, unbridled by their ineffectual father. In fact Clanricard was himself held in Dublin for two spells of captivity in 1572, dispatched by Fitton on suspicion of abetting his sons, and became a pawn in a power struggle between the President and the new Lord Deputy, Sir William Fitzwilliam. Stressing the Gaelic dimension of their heritage, the 'Mac an Iarlas', as they were known, burnt the towns of Athenry and Athlone and menaced Galway. For a time in the summer of 1572 they dominated the right and left banks of the Shannon, seizing many castles with the aid of up to 2,000 mercenaries and supporters, and assisted for a time by James FitzMaurice. Fitton's discomfiture was complete when, having helplessly witnessed the firing of Athlone, he saw the Earl of Clanricard restored with full powers and his sons submitting in November 1572 with every hope of a pardon.[7]

The year 1573 witnessed the Lord President's withdrawal from Connacht, first to Dublin and then to London. On his return to Ireland, Fitton was appointed Vice-Treasurer, in which position he served as joint commissioner for the province with Thomond and Clanricard. The presidency council was suspended but not abandoned as the experiences of the previous four years were absorbed. Certainly the institution as it evolved since December 1569 had proved to be much more costly than had been anticipated, and martial functions had paramountcy over civil. The bulk of the extra expenditure had been incurred in quashing rebellions caused by the activities of the President himself. Despite judicious submissions at appropriate junctures, chieftains such as MacWilliam Burke of Mayo continued their inter-clan feuding, even immersing the President in their rivalries. For every winner under the new regime, there were several potential losers whose hopes of succession to chieftaincy under the Gaelic system were stunted. For example, while the ambitious but junior O'Flaherty, Murrough na Doe, was advanced to the headship of his clan on submission to the crown in 1569, Donal Crone, the chieftain, and Donal an Chogaidh, the *tánaiste*, were ousted. These men fought with the disaffected MacWilliam Burkes against Clanricard and Fitton at Shrule in 1570. The MacWilliam who was elected in 1571, Shane MacOliverus Burke, identified the dilemma of many insecure Connacht lords when he contraposed the burden of maintaining his traditional title by spoiling his country with that of paying the expenses of the new English administration in the province. For the more secure lords like Thomond and Clanricard the choices were equally difficult: the attractions of jettisoning coign and livery in favour of fixed rents were considerable, but surrendering their martial dues unilaterally rendered them vulnerable to their provincial enemies.[8]

Positively for the government, most Connacht lords had been brought into contact with Englishmen, and there was no implacable hostility in their response. Clanricard, for example, professed himself willing to welcome any impartial Lord President as long as he was not Sir Edward Fitton. For all his personal failures, Fitton had adumbrated a solution to the major problem of sustaining presidential costs by his 1571 scheme for taxing annually the 360 ploughlands surveyed in Clanricard and Thomond at the rate of one mark (13s 4d). Although never brought to fruition, this regularising of cess and billeting charges was to establish the principle of commuting military levies of coign and livery in return for fixed annual rents, the President with his force taking the place of the provincial magnates in protecting the inferior lords. Refined into a project for universal composition, the scheme was embodied in the new programme of government launched by Sidney on his return to

Ireland in 1575. Characteristically the deputy set out on another tour of the island, during which he visited Thomond and Connacht in the spring of 1576. His sojourn in the former territory prepared the way for its transfer to the jurisdiction of a new President of Munster. A convocation of provincial landowners at Galway brought forth not only the magnates and bishops of the region but the lesser lords of Clanricard and north Connacht, including some, such as the heads of the Clandonnells of Mayo and the O'Malleys, who had never before made submissions. All including the MacWilliam were bound by oath and indenture to hold their lands of the queen in return for specified rents. The shiring of Connacht into four counties—Galway, Mayo, Roscommon and Sligo—was formalised, assizes were held at Galway, and plans were announced for granting freehold status to lesser lords and chieftains. As was his wont, Sidney attempted to boost the morale of the towns, most notably Athenry, which had been almost destroyed by the Mac an Iarlas: a levy was decreed on the earldom for its rebuilding. Finally, in withdrawing across the Shannon, Sidney brought with him as prisoners the destructive brothers, and the surrenders of the clan heads of east Connacht, including O'Connor Don and MacDermott.[9]

Sidney hoped for the speedy appointment of a new President for Connacht to co-ordinate the political and financial developments which he had set in train during his provincial tour. A dispiriting delay ensued, however, during which the Lord Deputy found himself engaged in tasks proper to a President, as, for example, when Brian O'Rourke of west Breifne came to Dublin to submit. Procrastination led to disaster in June 1576, when the Mac an Iarlas broke out of prison and, donning Gaelic clothes once west of the Shannon, attempted to rouse the province again. Athenry bore the brunt of their anger, the few rebuilt houses being razed and the masons killed. Their father, Clanricard, wrote with weak excuses to Ormond, saying that the financial burdens imposed on his earldom by the administration had been insupportable. Sidney reacted with great haste and determination, fearing for the security of Galway. Within four days of having heard the news of the revolt he was at Athlone with his officers, where he received Clanricard's surrender. The Lord Deputy had taken hostages from leading landowners in the province, and his recently acquired knowledge of networks there allowed him to isolate the Burke brothers. Sir Nicholas Malby, who was appointed colonel and subsequently President of

Connacht, was deputed to quell the rebellious brothers with 300 troops. The Mac an Iarlas had about 2,000 Scots mercenaries at their command, and they ranged up and down east-central Connacht. Although the leaders, John and Ulick Burke, proved to be elusive, their Scots supporters were chased through Mayo into Ulster. Malby then systematically wasted the brothers' territories upon their refusal to come in to him. 'I spared neither old nor young,' wrote the new President in his description of the campaign of attrition in the brothers' strongholds. By early 1577 Connacht had been pacified by these severe measures.[10]

Sir Nicholas Malby had had previous experience of Ireland as soldier and prospective colonist in Ulster. A strict disciplinarian, he was nevertheless prepared to extend to the local population the justice which, according to him, most of them earnestly sought. To that end he took to civil administration as a means of political and social reform, and was well attuned to the thinking of Lord Deputy Sidney. With the Earl of Clanricard in prison at pleasure and his sons cowed, the opportunity was there for using composition policy throughout Connacht not only to boost presidential income but also to impose a new political order on the province. The President with his force would be protector of all ranks of lords, and the arbitrary system of cessing and levying of martial dues and services, by state and overlord alike, would be subsumed within the new fixed annual rent. Malby contracted with landholders to pay a sum in lieu of billeting and cessing charges which were due both to the President and to the magnate. Agreements were negotiated with sometimes reluctant lords, in the Clanricard baronies, for example, by which money was provided for the presidency, which in turn undertook to give them protection from their enemies. This composition of 1577 initially raised an income of £1,137 for the President, with the prospect of more to come in from monastic and concealed land, surveyed the previous year. The Connacht administration thus became self-supporting by the early 1580s, and Malby could command a force of 1,000 to enforce his authority in north Connacht. Sidney was content as his term in Ireland ended that at least in the western province there had begun the dismantling of the oppressive mode of lordship based on exaction of military dues from inferiors by overmighty magnates.[11]

Being assured of an army and relieved of responsibility for Thomond, Malby was able to respond more directly to events in north Connacht from 1578. Although Fitton, the first President, had had little to do with the region, he did become embroiled in factional and inter-sept rivalry in the clash between Burke families at Shrule in 1570. During Sidney's two visits to the west in 1576 he received submissions from the principal ruler in Mayo, Shane MacOliverus, the MacWilliam Iochtar, lesser gaelicised families such as the MacEvillys, the hereditary galloglas, the Clandonnells, and the principal Gaelic family, the O'Malleys. Malby's task was to assert English authority while maintaining political stability and ridding the county of Scots mercenaries. His first challenge came with a revolt of Richard-in-Iarainn Burke in early 1580, apparently in sympathy with the Earl of Desmond. He was the *tánaiste* to the MacWilliam Iochtar, who himself refused to become involved but backed the President. The rebels, including Clandonnell, Clangibbon, and some O'Flaherty and O'Malley septs, raided as far as south Galway, and Malby acted with vigour against them. Having captured Donamona castle and killed the garrison, he marched to Burrishoole, which he garrisoned in February 1580, much taken with the site as location for a borough town of Mayo. Although officially outlawed, the MacWilliam title had been condoned by Malby in the person of Shane MacOliverus. On his death in November 1580, Richard-in-Iarainn, fearing that his claim under Gaelic law would be bypassed by Malby, prepared to resort to arms against his principal rival, Richard MacOliverus, Shane's brother, in the traditional mode with a largely mercenary army. Malby again reacted quickly, marching from Athlone to counter this threat. In a notable compromise Malby accepted Richard-in-Iarainn as MacWilliam, MacOliverus being appointed sheriff. In return, Richard-in-Iarainn had to disband his Scots mercenary force, but was allowed to remain in receipt of his chiefry rent as MacWilliam from a wide area of north Connacht. Although the Gaelic succession was here upheld, the precedent for English presidential power-broking was set with ominous implications for the future of native autonomy.[12]

Whereas Sir Nicholas Malby was content to infuse English influence gradually through the existing Gaelic political and social structures in Mayo, he tried to reshape relations more radically in County Sligo. The President's main concern in that region, however, transcended internal provincial factors: the O'Donnell lordship in the north-west had to be boosted to counterbalance the O'Neill threat in central Ulster. Thus while Sir Donal O'Connor Sligo sealed a surrender and regrant agreement with Queen Elizabeth at court in 1568, the question of the overlordship claims of O'Donnell in the new County Sligo remained to be addressed, particularly in view of the failure of letters patent to issue from the pact. The government continued to cosset Hugh O'Donnell through the late 1570s and early 1580s, allowing his claims over part of Sligo. In relation to O'Connor Sligo's own position within the old lordship area, Malby shared the prevailing antipathy to overlordship claims upon subordinate lords and disapproved of the measure of control accorded O'Connor in 1568 over families such as the O'Dowds and O'Haras. The President was unsympathetic to O'Connor Sligo's petitions for independence of O'Donnell, and so the Gaelic lord suffered the fate of similar county lords who wished to gain crown protection from regional magnates' power: his own lordship ambitions were curtailed at the very time when he most needed to be defended against overbearing lordship.[13]

When he died on 4 March 1584, Sir Nicholas Malby merited an obituary in the Gaelic annals. Described as learned, brave and victorious, he was perceived as a successful provincial ruler who benefited personally from his service. He had achieved self-sufficiency for his administration in Connacht through the composition agreements with many lords in 1577. In the absence of the Earl of Clanricard, these vassals had been content to substitute for state and overlords' impositions a regular rent to the crown in return for presidential protection. But when death removed his domineering personality, the rather informal composition which he had operated broke down. His successor as President was Sir Richard Bingham, a naval captain off Munster in 1580, who arrived in Connacht in the company of the new Lord Deputy, Sir John Perrot. Between these two officials there was discord not only over jurisdiction within Connacht but also over a fundamental issue of policy. Bingham would have continued the approach of Sidney and Malby in subjecting the principal Connacht lords to the presidency, withdrawing from them all claims to superiority over lesser lords. On the other hand, Perrot, in close consultation with Pale officials rather than New English advisers, engaged in a *volte-face* from his governance in Munster in the early 1570s: he was now prepared to countenance the involvement of local magnates such as Clanricard and Thomond in the forging of a new, pan-provincial compact. More auspicious circumstances in the west encouraged such a venture: old Clanricard died in 1582, to be replaced by his now-pacified son Ulick as third earl, while in the previous year the court-educated Donough O'Brien succeeded his doughty father as an exemplary inheritor of the earldom of Thomond. Perrot was ready for the launching of what became his most successful initiative while governor: the Composition of Connacht.[14]

The Composition and communal relations within Connacht, 1585–95

The key principle underpinning the Composition of 1585 was the compounding of taxes and dues for fixed rents. It differed from former schemes in its geographical and political comprehensiveness, and in having the framework of a well-established presidency to organise and synthesise the elements. Every tract of inhabited and worked land was to be rated for a set rent to the crown payable by the occupiers in lieu of all impositions which had been demanded in the past, whether by the President for his administration and army, or by the lord of the soil in payment of his own chiefry and martial dues. In return, the presidency undertook to defend the rent-payers from enemies, assuming the role which the overlord had played as protector in return for forced levies. Those same overlords would not now have to forage for their dues or employ Scots, as they too were under the President's protection. Also they were entitled to a separate rental income, again charged on the inhabited areas, this amount varying in accordance with the customary power wielded at local level. For the lesser lords, freeholders and tenants, the certainty of fixed charges compensated for the previous arbitrary forms of coign and livery, while the provincial administration benefited through the support of guaranteed revenues without having recourse to central funds. While the consolidated programme of agreements had as its main aim the rationalising of taxation for defensive purposes, it settled political relations in their existing form in Connacht. Inevitably, it was thought, the presidency would be strengthened as a vehicle of reform, inculcating law, civility and social change, but within the framework of settlement already established. Plantation was thus being ruled out, but not the introduction of phased New or Old English migration, and hence the enthusiasm of the now ascendant Pale officials for the composition plan.[15]

The first step was the appointment of commissioners to convene the nobility of Connacht for the purpose of making a new composition with the inhabitants to replace the old one of 1577. Significantly among the commissioners, besides Bingham, were the leading aristocrats of the province, including the Earls of Thomond and Clanricard, the MacWilliam Iochtar, Sir Richard Burke of Mayo, Sir Donal O'Connor Sligo and Brian O'Rourke. The main proposal was that each quarter of land (120 acres) of inhabited arable or pasture should yield a composition rent of 10s to Queen Elizabeth. The land was to be surveyed, barony by barony, through the holding of local inquisitions to establish the number of chargeable quarters. Annual payments could be in the form of cash or cattle, and failure to contribute would lead to seizure of goods. Freeholders were required to attend provincial hostings every year, and also general hostings when necessary. By accepting these terms the inhabitants were committing themselves to the presidency of Connacht, which undertook to protect them from 'common malefactors and spoilers'. All former cesses and charges on the populace from whatever quarter were now deemed fully commutable for the new rental payments. All Gaelic titles such as *taoiseach* and *tánaiste* were to be abolished, as were Gaelic succession and landholding customs. In return for the putative loss of status, the lords within the existing system received compensation in two ways: certain lands which were adjudged to be the demesne holding of the lords were declared free from composition rent, and a further yearly rent-charge was payable to the chief lord out of every quarter of inhabited land 'in full recompense of all duties, rents, exactions and spendings by him claimed of the freeholders'.[16]

The arrangements thus worked out were incorporated in a series of individual indentures or tripartite agreements between the queen, represented by Perrot, the lords, spiritual and temporal, and the freeholders (significantly so-called) and inhabitants of the various lordships. The Thomond indenture illustrates the characteristic form of these agreements, normally divided into five sections. In the first a survey of the eleven Thomond baronies named blocks of inhabited lands, comprising over 1,200 quarters, but not the individual owners. The second section agreed the annual rent-charge of 10s per quarter, to be paid to the President instead of all arbitrary exactions and cesses. By the terms of the third section all the lords and chiefs of Thomond agreed to give up their Gaelic jurisdictions, titles and practices, in compensation for which certain 'freedoms' were specified for the magnates to be held free from composition rent, and an extra annual rent of 5s per quarter was imposed on the lands of freeholders, payable to the earl. In addition to the earl, two branches each of the MacNamara and O'Mahon families, O'Loughlin of the Burren, Sir Turlough O'Brien of Corcomroe and the Baron of Inchiquin were granted 'freedoms'. In the fourth section, apparently a later addition, the grants to the lesser lords mentioned in the third were improved upon. Collaterals such as Sir Turlough and Lord Inchiquin were to receive the extra rents, following earlier grants of independent lordship, the price of their acceptance of primogeniture within the main O'Brien branch under surrender and regrant. The final section made provision for certain individuals such as Boetius Clancy, sheriff of Clare, and Edward White, clerk of the council in Connacht. The indenture with the other magnate of south Connacht, the Earl of Clanricard, ran along very similar lines, except for the variability of the earl's own rent, ranging from 3s to 13s 4d from the baronies surveyed, and the fact that most of the lesser families referred to in the indenture were not granted any special terms such as 'freedoms'.[17]

While the lords of northern Connacht also acquiesced in the new Composition without demur in 1585, there were some important differences in the nature of the arrangements there. A salient feature in the south was the centrality of the two earls, lesser lords being accommodated within the ambit of the indentures made for Thomond and Clanricard. In the north, by contrast, many individual lords, who were to be brought into the rent-paying system, subscribed to the agreement on terms of equality. In Mayo, for example, leading Burkes, O'Malleys and others signed in the expectation not only of alleviation of expensive exactions but also of recognition of their position in local society. Some lords, such as Owen and Murrough O'Flaherty of Iar-Chonnacht, were promised letters patent for allotted lands and the freedom of their demesnes from composition rent. Although Gaelic political and landholding customs were abolished, and transmission of lands by primogeniture was enjoined upon the lords (now freeholders in baronies), the commissioners for the Composition recommended in some cases that former overlords should have the right to transfer rent-charges of the lordship to the eldest son, thus residually perpetuating the old chiefly regime. In Sligo the Composition resolved the long struggle of Sir Donal O'Connor for security of title for himself and his heir. His own lands were discharged from the payment of the tax to the crown, and his rent-charge was £420 annually, to be drawn from the lords over whom he had claimed supremacy. This was the only rent-charge allowed for County Sligo, and was higher than that allowed to any other Connacht lord except for O'Rourke of the new County Leitrim. Thus, three years before his death, O'Connor Sligo was satisfied that he had secured his estates and had seen off the menace of O'Donnell in Connacht, no provision being made for the Tyrconnell chieftain in the Composition.[18]

Unlike the Malby scheme of 1577, the innovatory programme of 1585 won the staunch support of the major lords in Connacht, especially the southern earls, thus facilitating the full acceptance of the presidency regime in all its aspects. Undoubtedly the granting of freedoms to the leading landowners was the key to this widespread approval for the Composition. Throughout the province the demesne lands of the big landlords, measured in quarters, were declared exempt from the payment of composition rent. In Thomond, for instance, eighty-one quarters in three baronies were all 'freely exonerated and discharged of composition', for the 'supportation and maintenance of the place and dignity' of the earl. He was thus saved about £40 in rent to the crown. Besides this benefit, there was an additional bonus in that these lands proved to be attractive for leasing to tenants. As much of the province of Connacht in the later sixteenth century was underpopulated, there was competition among landlords for the services of farmers and tenants, rental income being less important for them than actual inhabitants of the soil. As the freedoms attracted no outgoings in terms of rent due to the crown, the lords could lease portions thereof at highly appealing rents and undercut their neighbours whose lands were burdened by composition charges and possibly rent-charges also. Sir Richard Bingham, the President, was highly critical of this feature of the Composition, pointing to a drift of tenants away from estates liable to composition towards the 'great freedoms'. Newcomers to Connacht were to complain frequently of being at a disadvantage when attempting to lure farming families to their settlements.[19]

The planned anglicisation of society in Connacht which was to accompany the composition scheme achieved varying degrees of success in different parts of the province. Overall, the jettisoning of the burdens of collecting and paying military dues and services proved to be the biggest attraction for the inhabitants, particularly in the northern region, where military activity in support of political claims was most intensive. The change in status of lords, *tánaistí* and *taoisigh* under the Gaelic system was borne with, especially when the inducements of rent-charges and 'freedoms' were written into the agreements. While a greater certainty may have been infused into landlord–tenant relations as they existed in the mid-1580s, the issue of ownership of the lands did not really arise. Certainly some lords sought and were promised letters patent to confirm their titles to lands, but the failure of these to materialise did not substantially alter the force of the indentures. As no plantation was contemplated in Connacht at that juncture, the question of common law titles to estates was not significant. The acceptance of composition arrangements among the northern Connacht lords did not in the short term lead to widespread success for the presidency regime, as strife over succession to the MacWilliamship broke out with renewed ferocity in the later 1580s. In southern Connacht, on the other hand, the amenability of Thomond and Clanricard to the Composition gave an impetus to the anglicising thrust of the President's rule. In fact the freedoms, rent-charges and settlement with collaterals reinforced the peaceful tendency initiated by the extirpation of coign and livery (the fundamental aim of composition), so that by the 1590s the two earls had a vested interest in the smooth operation of the arrangements, attested by the loyalty of both during the upheavals of the Nine Years' War.[20]

Lord President Bingham's criticisms of the overgenerous granting of 'freedoms' were compounded by his annoyance at the lack of clear responsibility at local level for the collection of the composition rent, owing to the failure to establish ownership titles. But Bingham was willing enough to accept credit for the manifest successes of the programme, and worked it to full effect when pursuing his provincial objectives. Above all, the Composition yielded him a handsome revenue, as it was designed to do. The total income from composition rents was £3,645 in 1586, while the outgoings on the presidency council's administration during the later 1580s were £3,167. Bingham had to hand a local force and was able to pursue the Scots and native antagonists with vigour. The way was also open for the encouragement of English, New and Old, to settle in the province. Already by 1585 there were over two dozen newcomers holding land in Connacht from the Pale and England who were attracted to waste lands or former monastic estates. The establishment of firm English governmental structures was an incentive for men such as John Browne to set up in south Mayo and Theobald Dillon to take up residence among the MacCostellos. Bingham had mixed feelings towards these *arrivistes*: he was obviously committed to facilitating their settlement, being involved in carving out a holding for himself at Boyle, and his brother George and other relatives also settling in the region. He was, however, harsh in his criticism of those 'supposed reformers of the commonwealth' who requested exemption from the terms of the Composition. The Lord President could not deny, however, that the Composition had laid the groundwork for moderate political, social and economic reform in Connacht.[21]

Faced with the problem of working the agreements after 1585, Lord President Bingham used whatever methods, legal or illegal, he thought necessary to establish his rule. Brooking no interference from central government within his provincial bailiwick, he became a figure of great controversy with English and Irish alike down to his final departure from Connacht in 1596. Almost immediately after the conclusion of the indentures a protest occurred in Mayo over issues which remained unresolved for many years. Some of the Mayo Burkes absented themselves from sessions at Galway where seventy people were hanged in early 1586. Bingham's seizure of Hag's Castle on Lough Mask assumed greater significance when Sir Richard MacOliverus, the MacWilliam, died and the *tánaiste* under Gaelic law, Edmund Burke, claimed the title. The English administration, which had banned the title, declared that the bulk of land associated with the position was to go to the late MacOliverus's son, William, regarded by all the Burke septs in Mayo as unsuitably young. Their response was outright rebellion in which they were joined by their traditional allies, including the O'Malleys, Joyces and Clandonnells. Bingham prepared to take the field against the rebels, and when truce negotiations broke down in July he executed some leading Burkes whom he held as hostages. Going on the offensive, he and his brother John captured castles and cattle, and by August the internal revolt was broken. A new threat to the security of Connacht developed with the mustering of a force of 2,000 Scottish mercenaries invited into Connacht by Richard Burke, known as 'the Devil's Hook'. The Scots under their MacDonnell leaders attempted to cross over the River Moy into Mayo, but on 22 September 1586 they were surprised at Ardnaree by Bingham's army of 600, and a fierce slaughter of the invaders followed.[22]

Against the wishes of the President, Lord Deputy Perrot had ventured westwards with an army and arrived in Galway shortly after Bingham's rout of the Scots. There he heard evidence of the Burkes' chafing both under the Composition and at the abolition of the name and power of the MacWilliam. The bitter rift between the two English officials deepened as Bingham accused Perrot of breaking the Composition's terms by cessing the inhabitants to support his expedition, and Perrot countered later by bringing charges against the President to the council board. Eventually in 1587 Bingham was dispatched to serve in the Netherlands against the Spanish army, and he remained out of Ireland until the spring of 1588. During his absence Sir Thomas Lestrange was Acting President and George Bingham served as Vice-President. When Sir Richard resumed his office, Perrot was being replaced as Lord Deputy by the veteran administrator, Sir William Fitzwilliam, who served until 1594. Within months the new Lord Deputy and the restored President had to face the crisis of the Armada's rounding of the northern and western coasts of Ireland. Fitzwilliam issued a proclamation, making it punishable by death to harbour or aid Spanish castaways. In Connacht and Thomond Bingham oversaw the carrying out of the proclamation with grim efficiency. He was to report that twelve ships foundered off his province and that 6,000 or 7,000 men perished, his brother George having executed more than 700 or 800 during the autumn of 1588. While most of the lords co-operated with the presidency by handing over Spaniards, a few in the north of the province did succour crew members of wrecked ships. Among these were Richard MacRickard Burke ('the Devil's Hook'), Murrough na Doe O'Flaherty of Iar-Chonnacht and Brian O'Rourke of Leitrim.[23]

The destabilising impact of the Armada crisis on the western province caused the most serious rebellion to date in northern Connacht in the spring of 1589. Although the authorities' fears had proved to be ill-founded, Bingham was dissatisfied with the level of support which he received from the Burkes in particular. In January 1589 he commissioned John Browne, an Englishmen who had settled at Neale in Mayo and had been appointed sheriff of that county, to raise levies and prosecute the Burkes and their allies. As Browne was proceeding into north Mayo with 250 men he was attacked and slain by Richard MacRickard and Walter na Mully Burke. Among the reasons given by them for the slaying were the general excesses of Bingham in Connacht and the specific action of Browne in taking cattle and spoiling the area to the north-west of Clew Bay. In the ensuing muster of rebels, the leading Burkes, including Richard MacRickard, William (the 'Blind Abbot') and Tibbott na Long, with his mother, Gráinne (Grace) O'Malley, were joined by the Clandonnells and Clangibbons from Mayo, and Murrough na Doe O'Flaherty, whose son, a hostage held by Bingham, had been executed. Their campaign took the form of burning villages, plundering cattle-herds and spoiling the country-side. Alarmed that this outbreak, unlike the previous ones, was threatening to engulf the Sligo and Leitrim region, the government attempted to negotiate with the Burkes, who responded by insisting that a MacWilliam be appointed and that Bingham be removed. Lord Deputy Fitzwilliam set up a commission of inquiry into the President's rule. Complaints drawn up against him were brought before the Irish council in Dublin, but once again in late 1589 Bingham was vindicated and resumed his operations unrestrainedly.[24]

Among the complainants against the grasping trend among newcomers in Connacht in mid-1589 were leading landowners in Sligo, some of whom had joined in the revolt in the spring. The hysteria engendered by the Spanish Armada landfalls may have exacerbated already existing tensions. In the scramble for salvage-able goods from the wrecks, native inhabitants were in fierce competition with English officials. George Bingham, sheriff of County Sligo, for example, fought vigorously with the O'Hartes of Grange for goods washed up on their lands, of which he was acting landlord. George Bingham and other lesser officials had taken over the former lordship of Donal O'Connor Sligo, so that the latter's nephew and heir, Donough, was forced to go to London for an extended period to prove his questioned legitimacy. As occupant of Sligo castle and custodian of O'Connor's lands, Bingham was entitled to collect the rent-charge from the former Gaelic lordship; he received the composition rent in his capacity as sheriff and was agent also for rents from monastic lands in Sligo. Inhabitants of the area were having to pay an increased number of charges under the new regime, while winning little alleviation of the old-style burdens of distraint of goods, billeting of soldiers and purveying of food to garrisons. If, as seems to have been the case, the spring of 1589 was a time of dearth and economic crisis in the north-west, grievances arising from these conditions would have been all the more deeply felt, and the activity of rebels in seizing cattle could have been motivated by hunger. There were raids on herds in east Sligo and an onslaught by Brian O'Rourke on Sligo castle in April 1589. The free hand which the President gained on his vindication was to be turned very forcefully against this leading lord of Leitrim.[25]

The incursion by newcomers into the province under the auspices of the presidency council set the context for the consolidation of the Bingham family lordship in north Connacht down to 1595. In Sligo alone by that year there were twenty-four landowners and leaseholders of Old and New English origin. Significant settlement of New English people in Connacht had begun under the presidency of Sir Nicholas Malby. He himself had switched his colonial ambitions from Ulster to Roscommon, where he received a grant of 17,000 acres of crown and monastic land around the town. Besides rebuilding Roscommon castle, Malby introduced several dozen settlers, mostly of English stock, on estates within a radius of four miles of the town. By 1593 Bingham was able to report that the area between Athlone and Roscommon was 'well peopled with English', though it was overrun by Gaelic rebels shortly afterwards. As President, Malby had the power and the resources to ensure the success of a colonial venture, albeit based on private enterprise on crown land. Elsewhere in the province the density of newcomer settlement was thin until the later 1580s. Generally the Earls of Thomond and Clanricard were strong enough to resist colonial ingresses into their counties of Clare and Galway. The ill-fated Sheriff Browne of Mayo, who described himself as 'the first Englishman in the memory of man that hath settled himself to dwell in the country of Mayo' had acquired an estate at Neale in the south of the county and planned elaborate schemes for developing the economy of the region which did not come to fruition until the following century.[26]

It was in County Sligo that the most successful settlement of newcomers occurred by the end of the sixteenth century. This was because of the strategic importance attached to the area and its focal point, Sligo castle, by Lord President Bingham. In the process of setting up an alternative lordship system to the Gaelic one under the Composition, Bingham and his connections revealed how the presidency could be used to further colonialism without plantation, through the exploitation of existing law and custom. George Bingham's collating of the various forms of tax in Sligo, some new and some old, to found his fortunes depended on acquiring titles by a variety of means. Most significantly, he undermined the power of the O'Connor Sligo family by gaining custody of the castle and lands, while the hapless Donough was forced to argue his case for proprietorship at court. He also gained custody on his brother's behalf of the Sligo lands of Boyle abbey. George Bingham's own residence was appointed at Ballymote, seized in 1584 by the President from the MacDonaghs as crown property, and the demesne lands of the castle were leased out by George at maximised rents. The tenants also had to pay him the rent-charge due to the MacDonaghs, Bingham thereby appropriating the rights of the former lords. The other methods of acquiring land through transfer from the existing owners—inheritance through marriage, wardship and mortgaging—were to become features of the consolidation of newcomers by the early seventeenth century. On their estates a new, efficient type of management was evident, many of the prime grazing and timbered lands of Sligo being the first to be absorbed. With the emergence of a more market-orientated economy, the importance of urban centres such as Sligo, Ballymote, Boyle, Roscommon and Castlebar in northern Connacht was increased.[27]

Besides the New English, members of the older English community, both native to the province and from outside, made much of opportunities for aggrandisement under the Connacht presidency and Composition in the last three decades of the century. Indeed, a report of 1592 stated that 'the country came to be much better inhabited, and especially the counties of Galway and Roscommon, for divers came from the English Pale to dwell there'. In the earlier Elizabethan period Old English people such as Thomas and Robert Dillon served as office-holders in the presidency council. There were also settlers in Roscommon and Galway on crown or monastic lands, such as Thomas Lestrange (sometime Acting President) at Athleague, George Cusack, who purchased lands in Thomond, and Alderman Nicholas Fitzsimon of Dublin, who was granted leases of former abbey lands west of the Shannon. While the settling of these individuals in southern Connacht took place within the overall jurisdiction of the great earls, the ingress of newcomers to the areas of weaker lordship in northern Connacht exacerbated problems for the provincial administration. Theobald Dillon, who became collector of composition rents in Connacht, managed to acquire ownership of the entire barony of Costello in Mayo from the MacCostellos by exploiting features of the Gaelic and English legal systems. Dillon was the target of the resentment of Richard-in-Iarainn Burke and his wife, Gráinne O'Malley, in 1583 at their having to pay £600 to the crown due in rent under a pre-Composition compact. William Taaffe from the north of the Pale became a major landholder in County Sligo through vigorous legal machinations which eventually led to his family becoming the most wealthy of all settled newcomers by the 1630s. Taaffe's activities contributed in some part to the rebellious demeanour of the O'Dowds and O'Garas in 1589, who complained at the sub-sheriff's seizure of lands of imprisoned inhabitants, and his enticing of tenants from their imprisoned proprietors' estates. Both Dillons and Taaffes benefited from wardship and marriage ties with local Gaelic families.[28]

Many Gaelic and gaelicised landowners in Connacht accommodated themselves to the anglicising trend in society and politics under the presidency and Composition. While rebellions could flare up amongst them over short-term issues such as the Armada crisis, some families, including the O'Dowds and O'Garas, were reconciled effectively to the English common law. On the other hand, others, such as many of the Burkes of Mayo and the O'Rourkes of Leitrim, proved to be inveterate opponents of government policy. The gamut of responses bespeaks many gradations of flexibility and inflexibility which were contributed to by factors other than the actual series of events of the later 1580s. In Clanricard and Thomond the earls proved to be strong and adaptable enough in the milieu created by the Composition to set their lands on a commercial basis with the advice of Old English kinsfolk and lawyers. Both lords remained loyal during the Nine Years' War. The court-educated fourth Earl of Thomond was later described as 'as truly English as if he had been born in Middlesex', and Clanricard was to become a regular attender at the English court. In other parts too those native lords, who were strong enough to channel the effects of the compact while benefiting from the trend towards demilitarisation, could exploit English inheritance, landholding and land-use practices for their aggrandisement. But some prior inurement in these customs, as well as a modicum of good fortune, were essential for Gaelic survival and enhancement in late sixteenth-century Connacht.[29]

In theory, the setting up of a system to substitute rents for martial levies worked to the economic advantage of landlords, especially those below the rank of regional overlord. In practice, as is clear from the book of complaints compiled in 1589, officials including the President himself were seen to be imposing a new kind of military oppression and reverting to many of the ills of the old regime. A *modus vivendi* did emerge after 1590 in Sligo, where the landholdings of the Gaelic lords were compact and economic and could therefore be brought efficiently into the new style of estate management dictated by the Composition culture. Helpful was the fact that among branches of families such as the O'Haras and O'Garas, even before the later sixteenth century, inheritance was by the continuous transmission of land through male heirs within the stem families, and not by partible division. If heirs were produced, the system worked to the advantage of Gaelic lords already used to the tightly controlled inheritance scheme, but failure of progeny could lead to misfortune, as happened most notably among the O'Connors of Sligo. In Mayo the problem of uneconomic units caused by excessive subdivision was compounded by the devastation wrought by the attritional campaigns of Bingham during the revolts. Moreover, the underlying bitterness about English interference in the MacWilliamship prevented ordered succession practices from emerging within lordships, and the result was large-scale impoverishment and mortgaging of lands. The pattern was repeated not just in the poor regions of the north-west of the province but in richer areas where landowners found their estates encumbered by increased rents and widows' jointures, as well as by litigation costs in cases of questioning of land titles by outsiders. Mortgaging was equivalent under the prevailing custom to transferring effective ownership to the lender, pending the unlikely event of the repayment of the advance, though the mortgagor could remain on as tenant of the mortgagee. The main agents of cash advances were the merchants of Galway who operated throughout most of the province, including Thomond, Mayo, Roscommon and Sligo. In the case of the latter county, New English settlers as well as the Crean merchant family of Sligo town were prominent mortgagees for impecunious landowners and thus advanced their own proprietorship there.[30]

During the early 1590s Sir Richard Bingham had total freedom under the complaisant regime of Lord Deputy Fitzwilliam to impose a strong military rule in Connacht. As well as pursuing a rigorous campaign against the Burkes of Mayo, he was most anxious to secure the northern and eastern frontiers of his provincial bailiwick. Sir Brian O'Rourke of west Breifne had been supported by Perrot in his disputes with Bingham in the mid-1580s, but now the Gaelic lord was vulnerable to the President's attack. O'Rourke's succouring of the Spanish castaways, his non-payment of composition rents and his onslaught on Sligo in 1589 compounded the perception of him as a rebellious malcontent. In the spring of 1590 his lordship was invaded and occupied. O'Rourke fled to Scotland, seeking James VI's protection and also more mercenary soldiers. The Scottish king surrendered Sir Brian to Queen Elizabeth, and in late 1591 he was executed as a traitor at Tyburn in London. O'Rourke's lordship, which had been shired as County Leitrim, became the object of a debate between Bingham and New English officials who proposed the confiscation of all or most of the lands and their redistribution among the freeholders or chief lords, or else a plantation by New and Old English colonists. Bingham, on the other hand, wished to have Leitrim retained fully within the jurisdiction of the President of Connacht, and thus advocated the consolidation of the Composition there, based on a proper scheme of rents. His view prevailed, and Leitrim was not radically reorganised as Monaghan had been in 1589. To fortify the approaches to County Sligo, the President built a new fort at Ballinafad in the Curlew Mountains and also seized Bundrowes castle and warded it for the crown. With these fortifications and also the existing strategic strong points of Sligo, Ballymote and Boyle, the north–south route within the county was secure.[31]

In encouraging his friend, Sir Ralph Lane, the muster-master of the army and a fortifications expert, to settle in the Sligo–Donegal borders, Bingham may have had a dual purpose. By aiding Lane's suit for a grant of Sligo, Bundrowes and Belleek castles, the President was hoping to stiffen the provincial defences. He was also assisting the plans of Sir William Fitzwilliam, the Lord Deputy, for stabilising west Ulster, the turbulence of which threatened his own settlement of northern Connacht. Raids were launched by Bingham's connections into Donegal and Fermanagh in pursuit of fugitives from the President's jurisdiction and also the Catholic archbishops, James O'Hely and Edmund Magauran, who were engaged in forging a conspiracy of northern chieftains against the crown. In May 1593 a counter-attack led by some of the principal Maguires of Fermanagh took place in Sligo, the town and district of Ballymote, base of Sir George Bingham, being burned. Hugh Maguire, the lord of Fermanagh, explained that the raid was in retaliation for the attacks on his territory by the Binghams and other government officials, and there was an added motivation in the harassment of Brian Óg O'Rourke for composition rents by the President. Maguire and Hugh Roe O'Donnell, the lord of Tyrconnell, were now united in their hostility to the government, feeling threatened by Bingham's activity in the north-west. In the summer of 1595 Ulick Burke, a servant of Captain George Bingham, cousin of the President, turned on his master in Sligo castle and stabbed him to death. Burke seized the castle and handed it over to Hugh O'Donnell, who now had possession of the 'very key of the province [of Connacht] and passage from Tyrconnell'.[32]

Sligo became pivotal for O'Donnell's overlordship of northern Connacht in the years that followed. As well as destroying Sligo and Ballinafad castles, he razed three O'Connor Sligo castles in Carbury to prevent their being used against him. Hugh Roe also asserted his power in the traditional Gaelic mode by nominating his candidates to the MacWilliamship and headship of the O'Dowds and other native families. O'Donnell was able to extend the war in Ulster into all of Connacht except Counties Galway and Clare, the northern part of the province being ripe for rebellion for a number of reasons. While many lords had welcomed the opportunity presented by the Composition to normalise their economic and social relations, the actual implementation of the agreements after 1585 was fraught with difficulty. Certainly Bingham worked energetically to bring in the rents and, the hostility which he aroused among Gaelic and English notwithstanding, his rule was firm but fair. Not so equitable were the activities of his family and friends who took to using many of the old forceful methods to collect a range of levies, including, for example, the chiefry charges of the O'Connor Sligo. Bingham was also thrown back on cessing and billeting of military garrisons on the local population in his efforts to counter the military activities of O'Donnell and Maguire in the early 1590s. Undoubtedly the alienation of some of the northern Connacht clans such as the Mayo Burkes as a result of the abolition by Bingham of Gaelic titles and lordship contributed heavily to the success of O'Donnell as patron. Also irksome, especially to many of the smaller landlords in the area, was the relentless search by adventurers for concealed lands in Connacht. These properties were discovered by dubious means to be crown property and were often acquired by the opportunistic officials at low rents. Above all, the Armada crisis of 1588 compounded feelings of disaffection, resulting in the 1589 rebellion in Sligo and Mayo, which in turn provoked hostilities right to the borders of Ulster and beyond. After 1595 these areas of Connacht were engulfed by the war which had its genesis in the northern province.[33]

Ulster and the General Crisis of the Nine Years' War, 1560–1603

HUGH O'Neill, Earl of Tyrone, and Robert Devereux, Earl of Essex, met and parleyed at Athclynt, a ford south of Carrickmacross, County Monaghan, on 7 September 1599. O'Neill was on horseback in midstream, while Lord Lieutenant Essex remained on the bank. Both men, commanders of their respective sides in the war which had been waged since 1594, had large forces on higher ground out of earshot. The location of the conference was on the fringe of the northern Pale, whose integrity and defences O'Neill had been careful not to breach. No doubt the Irishman used the occasion of that half-hour meeting with the English courtier to explain his political claims within Ulster as chief of the O'Neills and Earl of Tyrone. It was the latest in a series of attempts by O'Neill to keep the channels of communication with the English government open despite the intensification of the fighting. There was a personal connection with the Englishman through O'Neill's having served Essex's father during the latter's ill-fated attempt to found a colony in Antrim. While the topics discussed at Athclynt are not known, it has been speculated that the question of the succession to the aged Queen Elizabeth was broached. O'Neill had committed himself to the Spanish regime with his embassies in the preceding period, and his European profile was high after his victory at the Yellow Ford in the previous year. Essex had been a key figure in the factional rivalries of the English court, but his political credit was now at a low ebb. Nothing tangible except a shaky truce came of the O'Neill–Essex colloquy, and the two earls separated, each to follow different paths of ill fortune.[1]

Given the precipitous decline in his position in the years after 1599, it may be tempting to see the episode at Athclynt as a vain effort by Hugh O'Neill to stave off an uncertain end to the struggle.

But his military strength showed no signs of weakening at that time. Nor was the Nine Years' War itself an inevitable outcome of English intrusion on the intensely Gaelic and geographically hostile territory of Ulster. English soldiers and officials and Irish chieftains had engaged in negotiation at such close quarters for the previous fifty years and more. The main thrust of Tudor policies towards Ulster was broadly in line with that directed towards the other provinces: reform of native society and polity within an anglicising framework of laws and structures by conciliatory means. Some success attended this initiative within the northern lordships, as is shown, for example, by the duality of O'Neill's own political power as Gaelic- and crown-approved ruler of Tyrone. Yet the limits of pacification may also be gleaned from the reference above to the senior Earl of Essex's colonial enterprise, one of two such ventures in the 1570s. While great antagonism was caused among resident leaders whose lands were claimed by colonial venturers, Gaelic responses to English advance were not marked by universal resistance. Hugh O'Neill is only the most important of many chiefs who responded positively to placatory deals on offer from the mid-century, in a context of openness to change from a variety of sources. Innovation was transforming many aspects of life in the province during the later century, much of it coming from the continent through Scotland. It was perhaps the European, and especially the Spanish, dimension of events in the late 1590s which made the ritual of diplomacy mixed with martiality qualitatively different from anything that had gone before, hastening the ultimate breakdown of reform attempts.[2]

In order to explain the failure of Tudor reform in Ulster and the outbreak of a major war which was to engulf much of Ireland, the evolution of an essentially conciliatory English policy from mid-century should be examined. An analysis of the botched efforts to deal with Shane O'Neill, who symbolised resistance to reform, highlights many of the weaknesses faced by officials in implementing change within Gaelic lordships. These came into focus in slightly different ways during the chieftaincy of Turlough Luineach O'Neill, whose period coincided with the fostering of fruitless private colonial ventures in the north-east. The inconsistency of government policy as manifested in these conflicting approaches helped to undermine the credibility of its agents and also speeded up some important military and economic changes already emerging among the clansmen. For example, the migration of Scots to the province was of deep concern to the government, and the social changes being wrought among lesser landowners under the impact of English laws of tenure and succession were also significant. Many of these themes come in for scrutiny in the discussion of the 1580s and early 1590s, when Perrot and Fitzwilliam were pursuing active policies in some of the southern Ulster lordships, and as Hugh O'Neill was becoming a pivotal figure in the politics of the region. Late surrender and regrant agreements embracing reorganisation of lordships such as that of the MacMahons were overtaken by complex political rivalries, leading to revolt. The decisive break came when O'Neill committed himself to the rebel cause after a period of considerable equivocation. During the earlier part of the Nine Years' War it is evident that O'Neill tried to leave options open for co-operation with the English administration, but his propaganda and Spanish overtures caught up with him and impelled him into a full-scale national campaign for which he felt himself unready.

Sussex, Sidney and Shane O'Neill

While a presidency council was the ultimate aim of Tudor policy towards Ulster, successive governors from the mid-century acknowledged that at least some loose control over the Gaelic lordships was a prerequisite for its attainment. Unlike the other provinces, Ulster about 1550 did not have any ready-made foothold to sustain the activities of English officials and soldiers, apart from the beleaguered town of Carrickfergus. Nevertheless, the process of winning over the Ulster lords, great and small, to the norms of English tenure and succession within a unified Irish kingdom was set in train by St Leger and continued by his successors. In the decades after 1541 regular visits to the province were made by English viceroys, who made persistent efforts to gain the chiefs' fealty to the crown and to enforce the terms of the surrender and regrant agreements. Not only did they hope to reform the political and military systems of the Gaelic leaders, but they also aspired to effect economic and cultural changes in the longer term. But while there was a commitment to releasing *uirrithe* such as O'Reilly, Maguire, Magennis and MacMahon from the overlordship of the O'Neills, for example, and encouraging their freeholding status, it proved impossible in the short term to achieve a dismantling of the Tyrone power bloc. Moreover, disappointed contenders for the chieftaincy whose succession was now obstructed by the operation of primogeniture within the main lineage could restively combine forces with disaffected swordsmen made redundant by the attempted demilitarising of the lordships.[3]

Another destabilising factor was the settlement in the north-east of increasingly large numbers of Scots from the Western Isles and Argyll whose presence threatened the balance of relations between clans. By the 1550s James MacDonnell and his brothers had occupied the Glens of Antrim and later evicted the MacQuillans from the Route, while another branch took over the Dufferin from the White family. The collapse of the Clandeboye O'Neill lordship east of the Bann was hastened by this marauding, and even Conn O'Neill of Tyrone was affected by James MacDonnell's power when his second wife, son and grandson were held prisoner in Scotland in the late 1550s. Croft's unsuccessful expedition against the MacDonnells in 1551 was the first of three in that decade to try to dislodge the Scots. Under the Earl of Sussex the routing of the MacDonnells became a priority of the administrative programme owing to the parlous international situation in which England faced a hostile French nation in alliance with Scotland. A vain hosting into Antrim in 1556 was followed by a disastrous amphibious operation against the MacDonnells in the North Channel and the Isles two years later. Although the peace of Câteau-Cambrésis in 1559 removed the immediate threat of a French invasion of Ireland through the Scottish bridgehead, the menace of the MacDonnells continued to haunt the English in Ulster, particularly as they served as conduits for the recruitment of mercenary troops. A start was made on the ringing of the north-east with forts with the garrisoning of the borders. Under Bellingham, Nicholas Bagenal had been granted Newry and Andrew Brereton Lecale, and later Carrickfergus was fortified under Captain William Piers and Armagh under Bagenal, the latter site being designated by Sussex in 1562 as a likely seat of presidential government in the province when circumstances proved suitable.[4]

The most fundamental problem which faced Sussex during his governance of Ireland was the usurpation, as he saw it, by Shane O'Neill of power within Tyrone and Ulster. The very principles underpinning the reform programme seemed to the viceroy to be at stake in the dogged struggle between the government and O'Neill.

The agreement reached between Conn O'Neill, Shane's father, and Lord Deputy St Leger, in 1542 had boosted the authority of the former, thereafter styled Earl of Tyrone, within that demesne territory, and his sway over the lesser lords in the province was left deliberately undefined. Conn contracted to settle the succession to the earldom on his adopted natural son, Matthew, created Baron of Dungannon, who was senior to Shane, the eldest legitimate son. Both sides stood by this quixotic decision throughout the later 1540s and 1550s, causing the bitter dispute between Conn's sons. The collateral branches of the clan resented their exclusion from the succession to the O'Neillship as a result of the adoption by Conn of English law, and the nomination of Matthew, his son by the wife of a Dundalk blacksmith named Kelly, was fiercely opposed by Shane. Backed by the state (which in other cases after the 1540s was quite prepared to set aside primogeniture as the route to succession in Gaelic clans), Matthew fought for his inheritance to the earldom of Tyrone against Shane, the clan-elected *tánaiste*, whose claims were to the traditional, pan-provincial overlordship of the O'Neills. In 1558 Matthew was killed in a fight with Shane's supporters, and in the following year Earl Conn died. Rather than accept the new political reality in Ulster, Sussex was determined to bring Shane down and to effect the succession to the earldom of one of Matthew's sons, first Brian, and then Hugh, successive Barons of Dungannon. For his part, Shane may have been prepared to accept the title of earl, with the changes in property and succession law that it implied, but the implacable hatred of Sussex for him, coupled with his own ambitiousness, served to propel O'Neill into dynamic militancy.[5]

That militancy manifested itself in the late 1550s and early 1560s in Shane's aggression towards those whom he saw as the traditional O'Neill *uirrithe*, the other major lords in Ulster and extra-provincial targets in the northern Pale and northern Connacht. Maolmórdha O'Reilly, chief of the east Breifne clan, was harassed by O'Neill because of his support for the governor, while the heads of the MacMahons and Maguires in Monaghan and Fermanagh also came under severe pressure for their countenancing of English reforms. The traditional rivalry of the O'Neills and O'Donnells was exacerbated by Shane's attempt to undermine the Tyrconnell chief's overlordship of his (O'Donnell's) vassals, and the bitter feud culminated in Shane's capture of Calvagh O'Donnell and the seduction of his wife, Catherine MacLean, the Dowager Countess of Argyll, in 1561. Government policy attempted to drive a wedge between the MacDonnells and O'Neill, with Sussex manoeuvring, in return for recognition of their territorial claims in the north-east, to deploy the Scots against Shane, who responded by warring against them. Sir Brian MacPhelim O'Neill of Clandeboye suffered devastation of his lands east of the Bann at the hands of Shane O'Neill's supporters because of his loyalty to the government. To stress his claims to the widest jurisdiction, Shane raided villages in the Pale, burned Carlingford and placed Dundalk under economic blockade for not supporting long-standing trading rights of O'Neill-favoured merchants. Shane also mounted an invasion of Connacht to regain control of those clans who had in the past paid tribute to the O'Neill.[6]

The Earl of Sussex staked his reputation as governor on the destruction of O'Neill, claiming that 'if Shane be overthrown, all is settled; if Shane settle, all is overthrown'. By degrees the number of troops under his command was raised to over 2,000 by 1560, and subventions, albeit irregularly received from England, amounted to over a quarter of a million pounds over ten years as the relentless struggle was waged. The uneven rate of deployment of resources from England was due in part to the unwillingness of Queen Elizabeth to authorise an all-out war against O'Neill down to 1560, and even afterwards there were reversals of policy. In Ireland a party headed by the Earl of Kildare and Sir Thomas Cusack opposed Sussex's bellicosity, arguing that Shane could be pacified through diplomacy. Eventually, having had reports of a foreign-backed conspiracy, the queen was persuaded by the Lord Lieutenant to approve intervention, and the first major expedition took place in July 1561. Before the march of Sussex's forces to Armagh, which was garrisoned with 200 soldiers, Shane O'Neill's army fell back to the borders of Tyrconnell. Shane repelled an attempt by the English captains to plunder cattle in the Monaghan area, and Sussex was forced to withdraw with nothing to show for the foray except the loss of dozens of men. After an abortive attempt to secure O'Neill's assassination, the Lord Lieutenant mounted another onslaught with extra troops in the autumn of 1561. Accompanied by the Earls of Ormond, Kildare, Desmond and Clanricard, Sussex rapidly led a party northwards and westwards through Tyrone, driving 4,000 cattle and forging a passage through to Lough Foyle. Disappointed by the failure of a provisioning fleet to rendezvous with him there, the governor returned to Newry with only a fraction of the booty and without having engaged Shane O'Neill.[7]

The growing resentment of the Pale community at Sussex's burdensome and unsuccessful regime gave a fillip to the peace party led by the Earl of Kildare to press for a treaty with Shane in late 1561. Commissioned to negotiate with O'Neill, Kildare agreed to terms which included a pardon, a safe conduct for Shane to visit the court in London, and a loan of £2,000 for his travelling expenses. For Sussex the articles represented a shameful capitulation, and he prepared to follow O'Neill to England. Shane left Ireland in December in the company of the Earls of Kildare and Ormond and arrived at the court of Queen Elizabeth on 6 January 1562. There, before an audience which included foreign ambassadors, O'Neill, attired in his native dress and surrounded by his galloglas, prostrated himself before Elizabeth and in the Irish language confessed his rebelliousness. In the following weeks Sir William Cecil examined O'Neill's claims in Ulster and his complaints against Lord Lieutenant Sussex, who replied in his own defence. Meanwhile Shane was being entertained by the Earl of Leicester, who supported the faction within Ireland opposing Sussex, and he also made contact with Spanish diplomats in London. Fearing that his standing in Ulster would be eroded by a protracted absence, Shane begged leave to return in the late spring. Events at home showed that he was right: the O'Neill *tánaiste*, Turlough Luineach, secured the murder of Matthew's young heir, the main claimant of the earldom, Brian, Baron of Dungannon. Before departing, Shane secured an indenture which recognised him as *taoiseach* of Tyrone, with a reservation concerning the rights of Hugh, the late Brian's younger brother (who later became Earl of Tyrone). His overlordship claims over most of Ulster were tacitly rejected, and his disputes with O'Reilly and O'Donnell were remitted to arbitrators.[8]

Back in Ulster by the end of May 1562, Shane had ample scope to consolidate his position without being checked by crown forces. While professing loyalty, he continued his drive to overlordship of the north. Once again the lordships in the southern region bore the brunt of his need for tribute and military support. From Tyrconnell and east Breifne O'Neill drove 30,000 cattle into Tyrone, and Fermanagh was invaded with great rapine and slaughter. While his aspiration was a traditional one for the O'Neills and the wonted methods of intimidation and extortion were used on all fronts, there were aspects of Shane O'Neill's operations which were innovative. Although he himself had risen to the top by tanistry and was prepared to carry on the system of succession through election of Turlough Luineach, his first cousin, Shane's Tyrone showed definite signs of novelty in terms of military, social and economic organisation. Already the recruitment of Scottish mercenary troops had become a salient feature of Ulster warfare by the mid-sixteenth century, and Shane certainly contributed by hiring large numbers of Scots fighters for his struggle with Matthew. Moreover, by his marriage to Catherine, daughter of James MacDonnell, and his liaison with Catherine MacLean, he secured supplies of mercenaries for his later campaigns. Much commented upon has been his arming of the peasantry of his lordship. Normally the privilege of the free, or *grádh fhéine*, the right to bear weapons was extended to all, adding to the predicament of the lowest class, which was in a particularly weak position already. Down to the early 1560s O'Neill had attracted significant numbers of peasant migrants from the Pale to work the land in Tyrone where they found that conditions were less oppressive. When the demands of war became too onerous, O'Neill forbade these settled farming folk to return to the Pale shires. He also forced the tenants of ecclesiastical lands in his lordship to contribute to his rents, although this was contrary to custom. Contemporaries reported that Shane succeeded in increasing cultivation in Tyrone, which was 'never so rich nor so inhabited'. Overall, the lordship created by O'Neill was geared to military expansion and not peaceful civil administration, but its strength attested the potential of the unreformed Gaelic polity.[9]

Sussex's ineffectuality in dealing with the challenge from Shane O'Neill during his final two years in Ireland was the main cause of the failure of his regime. Attempts to negotiate on the basis of the indentures agreed at court in early 1562 were marred by bad faith on both sides. In 1563 the Lord Lieutenant led two more military expeditions against O'Neill, in April and June. Both turned out to be no more than glorified cattle-raids across the Blackwater from Armagh, with Shane avoiding any direct confrontation. An alternative peaceful strategy was ratified under Sir Thomas Cusack and the Earl of Kildare. In September 1563 Shane was granted almost all of his demands in a treaty: his powers as O'Neill were fully acknowledged, the *uirrithe* being effectively abandoned to his jurisdiction, and the Armagh garrison, a provocation to Shane, was to be withdrawn. Fatally undermined by this initiative, which was fostered by the bitter criticism of the Pale community's leaders for his policy of high taxation, and outmanoeuvred at court by the Earl of Leicester's faction, Sussex bowed to the inevitable and resigned his commission in 1564. His inglorious end was more than just a personal reverse: its circumstances raised pressing questions about the commitment of the government to reform of the Gaelic lordships in a coherent and consistent manner. The lack of protection for lords such as Shane Maguire, Maolmórdha O'Reilly and MacMahon in the face of O'Neill's aggression was embarrassing enough. It was compounded, however, by the continuing humiliation at Shane's hands of the captive Calvagh O'Donnell and the murder of the loyal Alaster MacRandal Boy MacDonnell by Sir Andrew Brereton, an English planter in Lecale. The brief lord justiceship of Sir Nicholas Arnold was buoyed up by political support from the Pale, and in 1564 and 1565 Shane strengthened his position, notably by gaining control of Lifford in Tyrconnell and going on the offensive against the Scots.[10]

By the time Sir Henry Sidney was installed in Ireland as Lord Deputy in early 1566 Shane O'Neill had further strengthened his position with a crushing defeat of the MacDonnells and their allies at Glenshesk, County Antrim, in the previous May. Two of the MacDonnell leaders, the brothers James and Angus, died as a result of the fighting, and a third, Sorley Boy, remained Shane's captive. Despite his representing this exploit as service of Queen Elizabeth, Shane was regarded by Sidney as the greatest single obstacle to his plans for the anglicisation of the northern province. To achieve the objective of overthrowing O'Neill, Sidney believed that garrisoning the borders for wearing down the Tyrone chief's power would be essential. Once that was attained, the ultimate aim was the break-up of the O'Neill lordship by dividing the clan territories among the collateral heads to hold of the crown, and the establishment of civil and military colonies to inure the native inhabitants to English common law and customs. With the backing of Sir William Cecil for the programme, Sidney went through the motions of trying to negotiate with Shane, but found that 'Lucifer had never been more puffed up with pride and ambition' than O'Neill who boasted that he 'never made peace with the queen but by her own seeking'. Before finally committing herself to the expense of all-out war, however, Elizabeth dispatched her vice-chamberlain, Sir Francis Knollys, to Ireland to discover if Shane O'Neill could be removed by 'any other way than by actual and open war'. Knollys agreed with Sidney's assessment that this was the only realistic approach.[11]

Once Sidney was free to deal exclusively with Ulster in 1566, he formulated an elaborate plan with Knollys's approval. As a first stage in garrisoning, there was to be a fort at Derry on Lough Foyle. This would have the effect, it was hoped, of wresting domination of the O'Donnells from O'Neill and allowing the restored Tyrconnell chieftain to flourish as a counterweight. Shane's enemies within Ulster were encouraged to befriend the government, and a blockade of shipping in the North Channel was to forestall the landing of more Scots mercenaries for O'Neill's army. As an earnest of her intention to let Sidney deal decisively with the situation, Queen Elizabeth granted £6,000 and more troops under Captains Horsey and Gilbert. Colonel Edward Randolph was charged with bringing 1,000 soldiers from Bristol to Lough Foyle to establish the garrison there, a feat achieved by the early autumn of 1566. Once apprised of this, Sidney set out on a march from the south across the Blackwater and into Tyrone. With his force Sidney passed by Benburb and Omagh and on to Lifford and Derry, destroying the recently gathered crops, confirming the lesser chiefs such as O'Reilly, Maguire and MacMahon in their loyalty, and restoring Calvagh O'Donnell to his lordship. Having linked up with Randolph and given him six weeks' supplies, the Lord Deputy continued through the north-west by Donegal across the Erne. Sidney's two-month progress through Ulster, including Shane's heartland of Tyrone, was hailed as the long-awaited breakthrough, and during the winter months which followed O'Neill was in the unfamiliar position of being under pressure. He therefore planned a break-out for early 1567.[12]

With his wide-ranging overlordship claims at the heart of his political ascendancy, Shane's loss of vassal chiefs as military support-ers and the physical restraint through the garrison were grievously felt. Thus his first target was the Lough Foyle fort, which he attacked unsuccessfully in early 1567. Colonel Randolph was the one English casualty, however, and in April the demoralised garrison suffered the loss of thirty men as well as its buildings in an accidental explosion in the magazine. The evacuation of Derry allowed Shane to march on Tyrconnell to try to re-establish control over the O'Donnells, now led by Hugh Dubh, brother of the recently deceased Calvagh. In May, with a large force, O'Neill crossed the

Swilly at Farsetmore near Letterkenny, where O'Donnell was ready for a confrontation. The result was a rout of Shane's army with heavy losses, the leader himself escaping with difficulty back over the swollen ford. He then risked his position by gambling on an alliance with the MacDonnells which would yield at least 1,000 mercenaries for his much-depleted army. The background to the fateful negotiations in Antrim between Shane and Alexander Óg MacDonnell in June was the open-ended diplomacy of the latter, whose aim was the consolidation of the Scottish presence in north-east Ulster. Although two of his brothers had been killed as a result of Shane's onslaught at Glenshesk in 1565, and a third, Sorley Boy, was held under restraint since then, Alexander Óg was not averse to a possible alliance with O'Neill were his brother to be released. MacDonnell was also open to a deal with Sidney which would secure the clan's settlements in the Route and the Glens of Antrim. At a crucial juncture in the talks with O'Neill near Cushendun Captain Piers may have made a more attractive offer to Alexander on Sidney's behalf, and Shane and his close associates were knifed to death. O'Neill's head, preserved in salt, was sent to Dublin Castle, and Lord Deputy Sidney was able to claim a great triumph. Within months, however, all talk of state recognition of the Scots was abandoned, and eventually an account of Shane's death in the course of a drunken brawl was concocted in order to convey the savagery of Gaelic and Scottish enemies of the crown. Such duplicitous dealings, however, served merely to undermine further among the inhabitants of Ulster the government's credibility as a reforming and placatory agent there.[13]

Colonial schemes and their aftermath

Although he applied himself strenuously to planning a major reform scheme in Ulster after the killing of Shane O'Neill, Sidney was unable to seize the opportunity in the short term. Within days of the Tyrone chieftain's death Turlough Luineach O'Neill had himself quietly inaugurated as the O'Neill. Among the participants were vassal lords such as O'Cahan and O'Hagan, as well as some MacDonnells, but the O'Neill family collaterals were opposed to this succession. The latter included Turlough Brasselagh, Hugh MacNeill Mór of the Fews, the sons of Shane, the MacShanes, and the sons of Matthew, most notably Hugh. The latter had been raised by the Hovendon family in the midlands and brought to court by Sidney in 1567 to be invested as Baron of Dungannon. Despite the chronic instability within the O'Neill clan during his chieftaincy, however, Turlough managed to survive for over twenty years with a judicious blend of compromise with and intimidation of Gaelic, Scottish and English. Sidney reacted initially to this 'hydra-like' phenomenon in 1567 and 1568 by coming to terms with O'Neill, who was pardoned and promised to keep the peace. But in spite of agreements forged between the lesser lords within the province and the crown, Turlough Luineach O'Neill's rise to prominence in place of Shane after 1567 hindered the course of tenurial reform in central and southern Ulster. Unmoved by government overtures in this regard himself, Turlough effectively blocked the operation of such advances among those whom he claimed to be his *uirrithe*. And without his approval any unilateral compacts made between native leaders and government officials were doomed to failure.[14]

His insecurity based on internal clan rivalry and external threats impelled Turlough Luineach to become involved in massive recruitment of Scottish mercenary soldiers, and other chiefs of various rank pursued the same course. In 1569 O'Neill married Lady Agnes Campbell, the widow of James MacDonnell and sister of the Earl of Argyll, who brought a dowry of 8,000 Scots with her. Although the hiring of heavy Scottish infantrymen, or galloglas, was not an innovation, the deployment of thousands of fighters or 'redshanks' on three-month contracts for summer campaigns in Ulster and elsewhere in the later sixteenth century led to an increase in militarism, an inflation of levies on tenantry, and a qualitative change in fighting techniques. In order to maintain such numbers, the scope of billeting and provisioning levies, or bonaghts, was expanded. In this respect the lordship of Oireacht Uí Chatháin was subjected by O'Neill to the imposition of Scottish mercenaries in an effort to assert a traditional jurisdiction as well as compensate for his loss of power south of the River Blackwater. In 1573 O'Cahan wanted to move his possessions across the Bann into Clandeboye, where he might hold land of the queen for a certain rent and 'be rid of Turlough and the Scots'. A similar pattern of aggrandisement was evident in the O'Donnell lordship of Tyrconnell. In the same year as her mother's marriage to Turlough Luineach, Finola, known as 'Iníon Dubh', daughter of James MacDonnell and Lady Agnes Campbell, married Hugh Dubh O'Donnell. She brought her new husband a substantial private army of Scots, and with their help Hugh could buttress his disputed position within the O'Donnell lordship. For the chief, Inishowen was the most convenient territory in which to quarter his new recruits, and this once autonomous area was absorbed more fully into his lordship. As a response to the growth of the overlords' armies, lesser lords and collaterals also employed large Scottish forces, thus increasing the potential for bellicosity within the province during the 1570s and 1580s.[15]

Sir Henry Sidney pressed on with his radical plans for a reformed Ulster despite the emergence of Turlough Luineach and the increase in Scottish recruitment after 1567. The scheme was to divide up the Tyrone lordship among all the collaterals and vassals as freeholders of the crown (to be represented in the region by a president). Sidney was more determined than ever to expel the Scots from the north-east in spite of their killing of Shane O'Neill; in place of the marauders would be established English colonists living in nucleated settlements. The area east of the River Bann to the coast would thus become an exemplary zone of civilisation, protected by fourteen strategically placed garrisons and provisioned by the agriculture of the colonists. For the native lords the captains would serve the function of the seneschals in Leinster. While Humphrey Gilbert and bands of soldiers governed Ulster in 1567–8, Sidney in England elicited the support of prominent Privy Councillors for his schemes, most notably Sir William Cecil. Extremely well briefed on the political geography of Ulster, with the help of specially commissioned maps, Cecil endorsed colonisation with military support in an Ulster where the crown's title to lands would be reclaimed in a forthcoming Irish parliament. While Queen Elizabeth approved in principle, she ordered a reduction in expenditure on Ireland now that Shane O'Neill was dead, and this insistence effectively ruined the hopes of some who hoped for a state-sponsored enterprise of Ulster. Already a number of schemes for colonial ventures had been canvassed, the most significant perhaps being a project of 1565 in which a corporation of twelve, probably including Sidney, envisaged the settlement in north-east Ireland of 4,000 English people from the West Country with material aid from the government.[16]

The vetoing of increased martial expenditure in Ireland led to private colonial ventures in Ulster in the 1570s with little or no success. While minor figures such as Thomas Chatterton and

Captains Thomas Browne and Thomas Borrow offered to settle in Down and Armagh, the major projects were undertaken by Sir Thomas Smith and Walter Devereux, the Earl of Essex, in Ards and Antrim. Smith, an English Privy Councillor, was the most articulate theorist of the private colony, offering to settle Clandeboye and Ards with English at his own 'charge and perils'. Already on record as an advocate of the reconciling of public and private interests in individual ventures for the common weal, he proposed to make good Queen Elizabeth's title to the lands in Ulster. Arguing that much land was waste and desolate in the region, he undertook to develop it through the labour of native 'churls' liberated from oppressive Gaelic lords by English adventurers. These latter would comprise a corps of younger sons of gentlemen who were without prospects in their own overpopulated home regions. Based on nucleated village and town settlements, the colony would enshrine the plough as the engine of advancement, weaning the natives from shiftless pastoralism and making newcomers proof against nativation. Although set within a framework of a private seignory exercising quasi-feudal rights, the colony would foster market-orientated commercial activity in the extraction and export of native resources such as timber and fish. Once Smith's grant of the Ards (and 'adjacent' places including Tyrone) was received from the queen in November 1571, the innovative step was taken of publicising the venture in a broadsheet and pamphlet. By the spring of 1572 Smith's son, also Thomas, had collected up to 800 men at Liverpool. Between then and his arrival in the Ards on 31 August the youger Smith was left with a force of only 100.[17]

Smith's position was not aided by the unsupportive attitude of Lord Deputy Fitzwilliam, Sidney's successor. Fitzwilliam resented the lack of consultation about the proposed colony and the dark rumours spread among the Irish in Ulster by the propaganda issued to advertise the project. Not only was he expected to operate with reduced forces in circumstances likely to provoke Gaelic military reaction, but he was also 'overcrowed' by the Smiths at court and their allies among the English captains and officials in the north-east. Among these were Sir Nicholas Malby, who put his entire band at Thomas Smith's disposal in the Ards until countermanded by Fitzwilliam to defend Newry. Most feared of all reactions to the planned colony there was that of the thitherto loyal Sir Brian MacPhelim O'Neill of Clandeboye. Protesting vehemently that he had aided successive deputies and defended Carrickfergus, Sir Brian claimed that his rights in south Antrim and north Down were sanctified by fourteen generations of tenure, and that his lands were too poor to sustain newcomers. Although Queen Elizabeth was disposed to uphold his case, the grant to Smith overrode O'Neill's right to customary possession, and the chief engaged in resistance. Securing the encouragement of Turlough Luineach O'Neill, Sir Brian used force and diplomacy to undermine the designs of Smith and his followers. He burnt the abbeys in Ards and drove away large cattle-herds, depriving the English newcomers of shelter and food for the winter of 1572–3. There followed feints of peace and defections, but Thomas Smith and Malby could make little headway against the virtually united opposition of natives in the area, including the Savages of Ardkeen. With the burning of Carrickfergus by Sir Brian in the spring of 1573, the Smiths' enterprise unravelled, and the fatal shooting of Thomas junior by a retainer of Niall MacBrian Fertagh at Comber in October 1573 overshadowed two later, futile expeditions sent by Sir Thomas to reactivate his grant of the Ards.[18]

The third and last of these in August 1574 was led by Sir Thomas's brother George and Jerome Brett, already involved in the Munster enterprise of the late 1560s. Although elaborately planned according to classical Roman principles of colonisation, the venture to Ards proved to be ineffectual and was subsumed within the more ambitious plan of the Earl of Essex for settling Antrim. The whole of the area from Belfast to Coleraine and from the Bann and Lough Neagh to the sea was granted with wide political and economic powers to the dashingly successful soldier-earl in 1573. Essex hoped to attract to Antrim the younger sons of distinguished houses, and the plots of land to be occupied by the gentlemen adventurers were delineated in advance. Only Carrickfergus and its environs were excluded from the colonial project. Although the project was a private undertaking on Essex's part, the queen promised to match his 200 horse and 400 foot, and in order to raise money to finance the scheme the earl mortgaged his estates in England to Elizabeth for £10,000. With the backing of leading Privy Councillors, Essex departed for Ireland in the summer of 1573 and arrived near Carrickfergus, with numbers well short of those which he had anticipated to command. He had the assistance of officers and soldiers experienced in Irish conditions such as Nicholas Malby and Thomas Chatterton, as well as Francis Drake, the captain of the *Falcon*. Initially the members of the expedition staked out the ground, the Scots remaining elusive and Sir Brian MacPhelim O'Neill apparently submissive. By late September, however, resistance had emerged, with Sir Brian driving his huge cattle-herd out of Essex's security and linking up with Turlough Luineach and a party of Scots. The morale of the new-comers declined sharply, sapped by the inhospitable conditions and low food supplies and severely jolted by the killing of the younger Smith. There were many desertions among the adventurers and soldiers, and Essex complained of the lack of co-operation of Captain Piers and Lord Deputy Fitzwilliam.[19]

By the spring of 1574 efforts were under way to bale out the Earl of Essex, whose venture had manifestly failed. He was appointed governor of Ulster and mandated to pursue Turlough Luineach, Sir Brian MacPhelim, the Scots and other rebellious figures in the province. Queen Elizabeth agreed to more loans to Essex and ordered Fitzwilliam to be more supportive. Although much weak-ened by hunger, the soldiers at the governor of Ulster's disposal managed to cow Sir Brian MacPhelim into surrendering Clandeboye to the queen in May. After his diplomatic efforts with the Earl of Desmond in Munster during the summer, Essex returned to lead a foray against the O'Neills of Tyrone with the enthusiastic support of Hugh, Baron of Dungannon. Marching through the lordship of Turlough Luineach from Benburb to the Foyle, the army destroyed a bountiful corn harvest worth, Essex claimed, £5,000, and contact was made with the O'Donnells at Lifford. The earl's frustration at the perceived lack of progress in fostering his original enterprise came to a head in the months which followed, and issued forth in callous massacres. First Sir Brian MacPhelim O'Neill, his wife and kinsmen were seized by Essex at a Christmas feast in Clandeboye and 200 of his followers slaughtered. Sir Brian, his wife and brother were sent for execution to Dublin, presumably for treachery. Then in July 1575 a raid led by John Norris and Francis Drake on the Scottish base of Rathlin Island led to the killing of all 600 of the inhabitants. Such deeds, while justified to the crown by Essex's servitors on the grounds of the unreasonableness of their enemies in Ulster, reflected the desperation of a sinking adventurer. Queen Elizabeth gave up trying to let Essex save face by building a fort on the Blackwater and effectively ordered his withdrawal. The earl spent some months in England before returning to Ireland, where he died in September 1576.[20]

The effects of the colonial irruptions into Ulster were far-reaching, both within the province and throughout the island. When Sir Henry Sidney visited the north on his return as Lord Deputy in the autumn of 1575, he saw the signs of disaster at first hand. Those areas which had been earmarked for settlement by the adventurers were mostly in a dire state. Carrickfergus was 'much decayed and impoverished', the inhabitants 'fled, not above six householders of any countenance remaining'. The rest of Antrim was held by the reinvigorated Sorley Boy MacDonnell, and Rathlin was abandoned by the English as a liability. Orior or south Armagh, granted to the Chatterton brothers, was totally out of their control, and Kinelarty, bestowed upon Nicholas Malby, was 'desolate and waste'. Clandeboye was found to be utterly 'disinhabited'. Only Lecale and Ards were in any way reasonably peopled. Sidney was not discouraged, however, claiming that the resources at Essex's disposal had been sufficient for success, but that they had not been well employed. But private venturers were never again given licences for colonies outside state-organised plantations, such as that of Munster ten years later. The military failures of the early 1570s in Ulster, coming on top of those against Shane O'Neill, were a sobering reminder to the government of the intractable problems of warfare against natives exploiting the features of their own terrain. The urgency of having well-supplied garrisons strategically ringing Gaelic Ulster was clear, reinforcing the plans of Sidney and Lord Burghley. While their construction and the deployment of troops would have to await a commitment to proper funding of the Irish service, many English had become convinced of the unreasonableness of the Gaelic people in the light of the experience of the 1560s and 1570s in Ulster and elsewhere. For them such obstinacy warranted the use of extra-legal means, including violence and retribution, such as were evident in the Clandeboye and Rathlin massacres.[21]

While there were some among the Gaelic Irish and Scots of Ulster who benefited by the arrival of new colonials in the province, the overall impact of English policy in these years on native society was negative. Once again the inconsistency of the English approach served to undermine the credibility of its commitment to peaceable reform, as did its inefficient military show and its skimpy finances. From being sometime subjects for compromise with the crown, both Sir Brian MacPhelim O'Neill and Sorley Boy MacDonnell were singled out for extreme treatment, if in different ways.

Mounting violence against the natives was reciprocated with increased ferocity. Thomas Smith was stabbed to death by his Irish servants and his corpse fed to dogs after being boiled. Essex reported that into the severed heads of slain English soldiers were stuffed their private parts by their enemies. Justification for resistance by the Gaelic clans was based on the argument that rebellion was not in question, as the war was not the queen's but that of private individuals. Divisions between spheres of responsibility were, however, blurred by the participation of English captains and troops in the campaigns of the adventurers, some of whom were desirous of making good grants of land in south-east Ulster. One beneficiary of the struggle against perceived aggressors was Turlough Luineach O'Neill, who forged a defensive alliance including the O'Donnells and MacDonnells based on central Ulster, prefiguring Hugh O'Neill's in the 1590s. The latter also benefited through his service of Essex, managing to establish himself south of the Blackwater through his assertiveness against other O'Neill collaterals and vassal lords such as the Magennises. By and large, indeed, the colonial years were not good ones for the sub-lords such as O'Reilly, MacMahon and Magennis, whose reliance on crown support could easily be found to be shaky and misplaced.[22]

The collapse of the schemes, besides deferring the hoped-for transitional arrangements from the 'feudal' to the capitalist mode, also served to point up the indomitability of the native Irish economy. Both pastoralism and tillage proved to be adaptable in the face of the challenge of the new, but the framework within which production was organised was that of military lordship rather than capitalist enterprise. The traditional herding system of the 'creaghts', whose essential feature was the mobility of thousands of cattle and sheep with their herdsfolk, certainly stood the Clandeboye O'Neills in good stead as a tactic in the initial phase of resistance to the colonisers. The productivity of the arable lands proved to be a mainstay of lordships such as Turlough Luineach's Tyrone: Essex encountered corn in 'great plenty and in great reeks' in that country, estimating that a harvest worth £5,000 was burnt by him in 1574. Sir Brian MacPhelim claimed that in his lordship of Clandeboye there were more ploughs than there were at any time 'this hundred years'. During Shane O'Neill's lordship migration across the borderland from the Pale into south Ulster had sustained agriculture, and more advanced techniques were introduced by the Old English allies of Shane, the Flemings, who in 1565 claimed expenses for 'putting ploughs after English sort agoing in Tyrone and in building after English sort'.[23]

With the failure of colonialism there disappeared for the time being the possibility of founding settlements which might evolve into nodal towns. Apart from Carrickfergus and Ardglass, Ulster had only a few moderate concentrations of population, for example those at Donegal, Lifford, Strabane and Armagh. Overweening lordship of the clan leaders may have precluded normal market and fair development, though the O'Reillys of east Breifne were exceptional in fostering the growth of Cavan, a 'great town and castle', according to Sidney. Mercantile traffic was otherwise very tightly controlled by the regional and local lords, who laid heavy impositions on trade. Carrickfergus in Antrim and Dundalk in the Pale borderland, both independent corporate towns, came under intense pressure from the O'Neills of Clandeboye and Tyrone respectively to yield taxes and to recognise their commercial mastery. The development of Newry during that era was significant, both for sustaining an urban infrastructure and the maintaining by a New English family of a quasi-independent jurisdiction over the Gaelic clan of Magennis and others. Sir Nicholas Bagenal had established a fairly thriving town there by the mid-1570s in the face of the hostility of both Shane and Turlough Luineach O'Neill. When Lord Deputy Sidney visited it in 1575, he found that Newry was 'well built and increasing fast, and the lands well cultivated'. The price for such improvement, however, was Bagenal's, rather than the government's, direct exercise of lordship over Hugh Magennis of Iveagh, who had gained protection from his O'Neill enemies from Marshal Nicholas.[24]

In 1577 Marshal Bagenal was appointed chief commissioner of Ulster by Sir Henry Sidney, charged with enforcing law and order in the province. His jurisdiction was effectively restricted, however, to his own lands and clients in south-east Ulster. The major obstacle to any plan to erect a working presidency in Ulster within which political and social reforms could be accomplished was the lordship of the O'Neills in the centre of the region. Turlough Luineach had come to terms with Essex in June 1575, agreeing to confine himself to Tyrone, to give up his claim to superiority over his neighbours, to keep peace with O'Donnell and other subjects of the queen, and to contribute to all hostings. In return, he was granted certain concessions, including the right to keep 300 Scots. Sidney received

Turlough Luineach at Armagh later that year and recommended to the Privy Council in London that he be granted a peerage. While Turlough may have been an unexpected choice as the O'Neill in 1567, coming as he did from a junior branch of the family based at Strabane, his survival as head of the clan for over two decades in conditions of great internal and external strife was no mean feat. Through his exploitation of government weakness, especially during rebellions elsewhere in Ireland and the local colonial ventures, he managed to assert the traditional O'Neill overlordship over areas outside Tyrone. His formidability was greatly added to by his importation of thousands of Scots mercenaries and his billeting them on his vassal lords. Turlough's greatest problem in the longer term, however, proved to be his second cousin, Hugh, Baron of Dungannon.[25]

The rise of Hugh O'Neill

Brought up among the New English Hovendons in the Pale and introduced to the court by Sir Henry Sidney in the late 1560s, Hugh was emerging a decade later as the most influential personality among the disunified O'Neills. Certainly the English crown looked upon him as the great hope for introducing legal and social reform into Tyrone and Ulster, and had set him up with part of Oneilland barony south of Lough Neagh after Shane's death. Hugh's initial and abiding objective was to attain the succession to and inheritance of the patrimony which was his by descent from his grandfather, Conn, and his father, Matthew, Baron of Dungannon. In order to establish himself, however, the younger baron had to tread carefully through the fissiparous world of O'Neill dynastic politics. His activities in support of the government through his assistance for Smith and Essex in east Ulster consolidated his position in official eyes, and he made the most of opportunities during their campaigns to assert his power at the expense of Turlough Luineach's in south Tyrone. His support among the freeholding septs of Tyrone, such as the O'Hagans, O'Devlins, MacCanns and O'Quinns, was strong and augured well for a future earldom. By the late 1570s Hugh had grown wary of the efficacy of government support owing to its agents' unreliability and was pursuing an independent line which now encompassed the acquisition of the

O'Neillship as well as the earldom. A chance for him to challenge the existing regime within central Ulster came with the crisis provoked in 1579 by the near-fatal illness of the sitting O'Neill, Turlough Luineach.[26]

The succession to the O'Neillship at that time was regarded as resting between four branches of the family: those of the O'Neills of the Fews, represented by Turlough MacHenry, Turlough Brasselagh, the sons of Shane (the MacShanes), and Hugh, son of Matthew. Of these the strongest were the MacShanes and Hugh in terms of support, resources and geographical location. While the sons of Shane had the more forceful claim to the chieftaincy, the failure of a strong individual to emerge was detrimental to their hopes of succeeding. Turlough Luineach did, however, nominate Shane Óg as his *tánaiste* in 1579, and the brothers prepared to fight their corner with the aid of their loyal Tyrone sept, the O'Donnellys, and substantial Scots recruits. Against their challenge, Hugh, the baron, had the backing of most of the freeholders of Tyrone, and he also won over most of the traditional *uirrithe* of the clan in greater Ulster, such as the Maguires and MacMahons, who had been enemies of Shane. Matrimonial ties were used skilfully by Hugh to weave a web among these vassals, as in the case of Hugh Maguire, and with the other provincial ruling family, the O'Donnells, Baron Hugh marrying a daughter of Sir Hugh O'Donnell, and his own daughter marrying Hugh Roe, his brother-in-law. The main obstacle to Hugh's ascendancy then and later were the collateral O'Neills, who regarded him as an outsider and who began to look to the crown themselves for independent tenurial arrangements once succession seemed cut off from their families. Meanwhile a rapprochement was arrived at between Hugh and Turlough Luineach, who agreed that Hugh should succeed him; however, the understanding quickly broke down. The O'Neill chief survived his illness and continued his rule into the 1580s, but by the middle of that decade Hugh was seen as being the centre of a powerful provincial network which aimed at Turlough's overthrow.[27]

Sir John Perrot's assumption of the deputyship in June 1584 marked the start of another sustained attempt to introduce an integrated policy for all of Ulster. Although unofficially intending to 'look through my fingers at Ulster as a fit receptacle of all the savage beasts of this land', Perrot was soon forced to march northwards to deal with raids by the MacDonnells and MacLeans of the

Scottish Isles on Tyrconnell and other places. Foiled in his efforts to defeat the Scots on land and at sea in 1584 and 1585, the Lord Deputy eventually received Sorley Boy MacDonnell into submission in June 1586. Sorley became a naturalised subject, received a grant of the lands between the Rivers Bann and Bush, and was appointed constable of Dunluce castle. Already much of the Glens of Antrim region between Larne and Ballycastle had been granted to Sorley's nephew, Angus. The settlement with the MacDonnells in Antrim was to be the keynote of the years of Perrot's administration, as he tried to come to terms with all of the local interests in Ulster. Essentially he envisaged a framework of surrender and regrant agreements to secure tenurial rights of lords and freeholders. Complementary to this policy would be the implementation of a comprehensive composition to effect the demilitarisation of the province. And a system of permanent castellated garrisons linked to a network of seven walled towns and seven bridges would be needed to secure a pacified and reformed province.[28]

An important administrative step was to be the shiring of the province in readiness for the introduction of English-style officials such as sheriffs. While the transmutation of east Breifne into County Cavan was the most successful initiative in this regard, Monaghan, Tyrconnell and Fermanagh were also to receive sheriffs. The local chiefs were appointed to commissions for shiring, and boundary disputes were to be settled by inquisition. During gubernatorial tours of the province between 1584 and 1587 previous surrender and regrant agreements with O'Donnell, O'Reilly and Magennis were confirmed and renewed, and new ones made with Maguire and MacMahon. In all of these indentures the rights of the freeholders under the chiefs were to be upheld. The groundwork was being laid for an English county style of landholding and inheritance. An integral part of such legal, social and, it was hoped, economic reforms was the lifting of the incubus of militarism from all, of high and low station. Thus a Connacht-style composition rent was charged on the landowners, in return for which they could look to a garrison of 1,100 English soldiers for protection, thus enabling them to dispense with their Scottish mercenaries. Without forts of their own, however, these soldiers were under the lords themselves and were used by them in place of the mercenaries. The mainstay of this new order in Ulster was the settlement of the central zone. An agreement was negotiated by Perrot whereby Turlough Luineach O'Neill would occupy the northern part of Tyrone, with his son Art based at Strabane, and the southern part was to be leased by Hugh, the Baron of Dungannon, from Turlough for 1,000 marks. As a sign of his approval of Hugh's loyalty and his aspirations for seignorial rule in mid-Ulster, Perrot had him formally nominated second Earl of Tyrone by parliament in 1585. Symbolically Turlough Luineach attended sessions of that parliament dressed in English apparel.[29]

Despite the good omens of 1585 and 1586, however, the programme of Perrot for Ulster fell to pieces thereafter, and its failure contributed to his recall in disgrace in 1588. Undoubtedly his own tempestuous personality caused great difficulties, and specifically in Ulster, where Marshal Bagenal, whom Perrot had struck at the council board, opposed his designs at every turn. Bagenal attempted to interpose his authority between the Lord Deputy and the chiefs of south-east Ulster, such as Sir Hugh Magennis, whom Bagenal looked upon as his own client. Well-connected in Dublin administrative circles and through them at court, Bagenal steadily undermined Perrot's position. Nor were the governor's requests for funding for his schemes, especially for the fortresses, acceded to by a queen whose main attention was focused on the worsening of Anglo-Spanish relations over the Netherlands. Local instability occasioned by bitter dynastic disputes within Tyrone and Tyrconnell compounded the problems, but the fundamental causes of breakdown were a lack of consistency and comprehensiveness in the application of policy. In order to consolidate his political arrangements, Perrot used forceful methods such as kidnapping and imprisonment of popular rivals to approved leaders. Hugh Roe O'Donnell was seized on board a wine ship in Lough Swilly in 1587, and Pilib O'Reilly was captured by Perrot to be lodged in the prison of Dublin Castle for seven years. While their removal may have eased tensions within the O'Reilly and O'Donnell lordships, the returned swordsmen would eventually play a significant role in the 1590s. Moreover, despite his energetic approach, Perrot never solved the problem of dealing with all levels of Gaelic landholders from overlords through vassal lords to freeholders simultaneously.[30]

His most successful venture, at least in the short term, was the settlement reached with the O'Reillys of east Breifne, now County Cavan. In its operation the scheme was a mature version of surrender and regrant. The O'Reillyship of east Breifne was abolished, and instead the county was divided up between the branches of the clan.

The principal lords, including the elected *taoiseach*, Sir John, and the *tánaiste*, Eamonn, were granted seignorial control over certain baronies, with the freeholders' rights to be enshrined. Former military exactions or 'cuttings' were commuted to fixed payments, and a levy of 330 cattle from the county represented the composition rent. A sheriff, Henry Duke, was appointed, and the apparatus of English shire government was set up in the new county. Apparently the Cavan settlement was to be a model for procedure in other lordships which were now shires. Yet Sir John O'Reilly's position as liaison functionary between the inhabitants of Breifne and the English exposed him to great risks. Although support for his principal rival, the old-style Gaelic leader, Pilib, was curbed through the latter's imprisonment, the volatile nature of south Ulster politics made Sir John's relinquishing of traditional O'Reilly military defences premature. As long as instability reigned within the O'Neill lordship, and between the O'Donnell and O'Connor Sligo, the probability was that the O'Reillys would be drawn into a provincial war. And this was all the more likely once Perrot had been replaced by Sir William Fitzwilliam as Lord Deputy in the summer of 1588. Fitzwilliam's choice as Cavan sheriff, Edward Herbert, lacked his predecessor's sensitivity, and the Lord Deputy's action in billeting soldiers on the county in 1590 cut across the composition agreement of 1585.[31]

Inured to the realities of provincial politics after four decades of service in Ireland, Fitzwilliam was concerned to allow the natural balance of power to emerge in each Gaelic lordship in Ulster over time. Yet despite his natural instincts, he found himself applying a system in which his treatment of individual lordships formed a pattern of legal and administrative reform. His actions in this pursuit, however, were perceived locally as contradictory and vindictive. Within a few months of his assuming office in June 1588 Fitzwilliam marched into the north-west to restabilise the region after the shock of the Armada landings. Two lesser chiefs within the O'Donnell sphere, Sir John Gallagher and Sir John O'Doherty, were taken prisoner. Within Tyrconnell, the eldest son of the chieftain, Donal O'Donnell, was made sheriff, Hugh Roe remaining in custody in Dublin. In Leitrim (under Lord President Bingham's jurisdiction) the aftermath of the execution of Sir Brian O'Rourke in 1591 was the embitterment of his son, Brian Óg. The settlement of Leitrim was not as radical as that proposed for the MacMahons of Monaghan in 1591. There the death of the old chief, Sir Ross MacMahon, in 1589 occasioned a dynastic struggle between his brother, Hugh Roe MacMahon, and Brian MacHugh Óg. Fitzwilliam, who favoured a division of the county between the principal landholders, backed Hugh Roe and sent him military support against his rival. But Hugh Roe behaved in the manner of a traditional chieftain, raiding his enemies' lands and defying the newly installed sheriff. Reversing the wonted approach of pardoning an errant Gaelic warlord who was finding the change to landlord difficult, the Lord Deputy secured MacMahon's arrest and had him tried for treason, convicted and hanged in Monaghan town in October 1590.[32]

The way was now open for the reorganisation of the former MacMahon lordship along lines of English tenurial and inheritance laws. Although the settlement took place within the framework of the Gaelic landholding pattern in Monaghan (excluding the barony of Farney, already granted to the Earl of Essex), the changes facilitated new attitudes towards ownership and investment. The key was the abolition of the MacMahon overlordship with its nexus of economic and military services, and the setting up instead of individual major landlords (the existing principal sept leaders) and over 250 lesser freeholding families, all holding of the crown in return for annual rents. The 1591 survey identified the landholding units, as well as their ownership by the lineage groups. All collective ownership was abolished, and individual independent landowning families were established as the norm. The major MacMahon sept leaders owed a rent of 7s 6d per tate (or townland) to the crown and held in tail male by knight's service *in capite*. The lesser lords, the backbone of freeholding family heads, were set up to hold of the crown (by fee simple in free and common socage), to which was due a rent of 7s 6d. To the local principal landlord there was payable an annual charge of 12s 6d. Thus the Gaelic socio-political system was not completely jettisoned, but was on its way to being subverted. The enthusiasm of so many landowners for the new order suggests relief at the abandonment of the oppressive lordship of the MacMahons. The primogeniture system of succession was copperfastened after 1591. Fitzwilliam, who won much acclaim for his settlement, was now in a position to introduce a seneschal and a sheriff, and with the break-up of the church and mensal lands, originally pertaining to the MacMahon office, grants were made to incoming settlers such as Captain Humphrey Willis and Christopher Fleming, a Newry merchant.[33]

English penetration of the north-west was to bring confrontation with the O'Donnells of Tyrconnell. Down to the mid-1580s the Dublin government had tried to bolster the Donegal clan in geo-political terms to counteract the adverse effects of O'Neill hegemony in central Ulster. But the terms of the Composition of Connacht signalled the end of the countenancing of any O'Donnell overlord-ship claims in the north of that province. Then the militaristic designs of Lord President Richard Bingham in his fortification of Sligo and his attempted settling of muster-master and fortifications expert, Ralph Lane, at Bundrowes from 1590 dovetailed with Fitzwilliam's constrictive policy. A dynastic struggle was under way in the Tyrconnell lordship, where Sir Hugh, the chieftain, had manifested signs of weakness. Fitzwilliam appeared to recognise the claims of the eldest acknowledged son of Sir Hugh, Donal, when elevating him to the shrievalty of Donegal in 1588. Iníon Dubh MacDonnell was insisting that Sir Hugh's son by their marriage, Hugh Roe, should succeed to the O'Donnellship, and her force of Scots defeated and killed Donal in 1590. Hugh Roe, who had been seized by agents of Lord Deputy Perrot in 1587 and held as hostage for his father's good behaviour in Dublin, had married a daughter of the new Earl of Tyrone. After one abortive attempt Hugh Roe escaped from Dublin Castle, possibly with Fitzwilliam's connivance, at Christmas 1591 and made his way back to Donegal with Tyrone's assistance. If the Lord Deputy hoped that the returned swordsman, now O'Donnell-elect on his father's retirement, would be a conduit for reform, he was to be disappointed. Lacking strength among the major O'Donnell freeholders but possessing powerful military support through his mother, Hugh Roe needed to oppose reform by composition in order to assert himself. An immediate target was Captain Willis, appointed by the governor as sheriff on Donal's death. Willis, who had occupied Donegal friary, was driven out of Donegal in February 1592, and the newly inaugurated O'Donnell was brought by his brother-in-law Tyrone to submit to Fitzwilliam in the summer of that year.[34]

Willis was also responsible for stirring up resistance to govern-ment designs in another part of western Ulster in the early 1590s. In Fermanagh Lord Deputy Fitzwilliam had imposed his captain on the newly shired territory as a prelude, he hoped, to effecting a reorganisation of the lordship. Like his future ally, Hugh Roe O'Donnell, Hugh Maguire, recently elected chief in succession to his father, had married a daughter of Hugh O'Neill, Earl of Tyrone. He was anxious to resist the dismantling of his lordship, as his position, like O'Donnell's, was vulnerable owing to restive freeholders and a rival to the succession, Conor Roe. Hugh's pretext was the unruly conduct of Sheriff Willis in concert with George Bingham within his area. Emulating Brian Óg O'Rourke, who plundered the country around Ballymote in his dispute with the Binghams over composition rents, Maguire went on the rampage in May 1593 across the Erne into Sligo and Roscommon, where he came into conflict with Sir Richard Bingham. Although gaining booty of many cattle, the raids resulted in the death of Archbishop Edmund Magauran of Armagh, who was in Maguire's company. The Primate had been canvassing a Catholic confederacy led by O'Donnell under the patronage of the Spanish king, Philip II. Maguire then turned to Monaghan and attacked the garrison there in September 1593. The onslaught was repelled by forces led by Marshal Henry Bagenal and Hugh, Earl of Tyrone, who defeated the Fermanagh chief at Belleek. Maguire was forced to flee, driving his cattle before him, but his stronghold of Enniskillen was captured by Bingham in early 1594.[35]

In retrospect, the joint action of O'Neill and Bagenal in the autumn of 1593 can be seen as a charade. Their standing enmity had been exacerbated by Hugh O'Neill's elopement with Bagenal's sister, Mabel, in 1591 and her subsequent humiliation due to the earl's infidelity. Predating this personal spleen was a bitter clash between the two over jurisdiction in south Ulster. Bagenal attempted to keep lords such as Sir Hugh Magennis and Conn MacNeill Óg free from subjection to O'Neill, while the earl resented any claim of the marshal to the lieutenancy of Ulster. By 1593 Henry Bagenal had become a focus for all plaintiffs to the government for redress of grievances against O'Neill. But Lord Deputy Fitzwilliam had been supportive of Tyrone's ambitions within the province. He encouraged the earl's territorial aggrandisement and condoned his weaving of a web of dynastic marital ties. The state-sponsored agreement with Turlough Luineach in 1587 gave the earl effective control over southern Tyrone around Dungannon, to go along with his mastery of Oneilland and Tiranny to the south-east of the River Blackwater. Besides his links to the families such as the O'Quinns and O'Hagans, traditional household clans of the O'Neills, Hugh had connections through marriage to a wide-ranging group of lineages throughout all parts of Ulster, including Inishowen, south Derry, Fermanagh, Tyrconnell, Monaghan, Armagh and Antrim. Ranged against him were many of the O'Neill collaterals who were in contention for the O'Neill title when the failing Turlough Luineach would eventually pass on. Most antagonistic of all towards the earl were the MacShanes, who sought power through confrontation. O'Neill staged a public execution of the captured Hugh Gavelagh MacShane near Dungannon in 1590 on the pretext of his being a thief and a murderer, but despite the transparency of his strategy in wiping out his dangerous rival, Fitzwilliam effected Tyrone's exculpation after an investigation in London and Dublin.[36]

By the time old Turlough Luineach resigned the O'Neillship in May 1593 in favour of Hugh, Fitzwilliam's perception of the earl had changed. Influenced by Bagenal's reports to the council in Dublin of O'Neill's aggression against his neighbours, Fitzwilliam heard corroborating sentiments at a two-week session of the council at Dundalk in June 1593. The realisation of the implications of the O'Neill–O'Donnell axis in the north after 1592 raised suspicions that Hugh's ultimate aims transcended English-style proprietorship of his earldom. With his friends on the English Privy Council, such as the Earl of Leicester, dying off and the trust of his New English admirers in Ireland being eroded, Tyrone's protestations of allegiance were wearing thin. Then evidence of tacit support for his restive sons-in-law, Hugh O'Donnell and Hugh Maguire, began to mount. The later backing given by the earl's brother, Cormac MacBaron, to Maguire was taken to prove Tyrone's prior complicity. O'Neill himself was coming under severe pressure to clarify his position in the aftermath of the offensive of October 1593 at Belleek. While wishing avoid a war, he saw that the extension of English shrieval administration and military garrisons to the new Ulster shires was bound to be resolutely resisted by the Tyrconnell and Fermanagh leaders, who feared the dismemberment of their lordships along Monaghan lines. Moreover, he had become aware of the appeal made to King Philip II in 1593 by the north-western chiefs and bishops for assistance for a crusade against the English. To join a struggle meant the possibility of visiting upon his province the devastation which he had witnessed in Munster in the Desmond war. If Tyrone were to co-operate with the anglicisation process in Ulster, he might have a role like that of the Earls of Thomond and Clanricard to play in the socio-political life of the province. But the operations of English settlers in the province did not augur well for his continued ascendancy, let alone a presidential function. And in siding with the English against his kinsmen, he could jeopardise his newly won authority over the O'Neill lordship, as landowning septs there would desert him for one of his O'Neill rivals who might promise outright resistance to change.[37]

The Nine Years' War

The first salvo in the Nine Years' War was fired with the besieging by Hugh Roe O'Donnell and Hugh Maguire of Enniskillen fortress in June 1594. In August an army bringing food supplies led by Sir Henry Duke and Sir Edward Herbert was cut off by Maguire and Cormac O'Neill at a place nearby (afterwards known as the 'Ford of the Biscuits') with the loss of fifty-six English soldiers. Thus was established the pattern of warfare in which under-strength English garrisons in the southern approaches to Ulster were taken and retaken, and armies sent in assistance became vulnerable to attack. Contemporaneously, the ailing Sir William Fitzwilliam gave way to Sir William Russell as Lord Deputy. Within a day of the latter's swearing-in, the Earl of Tyrone appeared submissively in Dublin, promising to expel the Scots mercenaries, pay a composition rent, receive a sheriff, and send his son to England for a university education—provided that Armagh and Tyrone were not separately shired. The inexperienced Russell was upbraided by Queen Elizabeth for letting O'Neill return unshackled to Ulster. It seemed that Tyrone wanted for himself an exclusive commission to govern Ulster, but when this was withheld he determined to join the rebellion. The occasion arose in the context of assaults on forts ringing the south of the province in the first half of 1595. Blackwater fort had been captured by O'Neill's brother, Art MacBaron, in February, and Enniskillen was retaken by Maguire in May. In June Captain George Bingham, the President of Connacht's cousin, then in charge of Sligo castle, was slain by a servant, who handed the fortress over to Hugh O'Donnell and with it access to northern Connacht. In the same month the Earl of Tyrone himself ambushed an army under Marshal Bagenal which had marched from Newry to relieve the besieged Monaghan fort. This encounter at Clontibret, which resulted in a severe defeat for the marshal, was a rallying-call to the emergent northern confederacy.[38]

Clontibret heralded the birth of a formidable new Gaelic Irish army, well trained and equipped. O'Neill's time of deliberation down to mid-1595 had afforded him the opportunity to reach a state of supreme military preparedness. By that time the lordship of Tyrone had 2,500 horse and foot, rising to 4,000 by 1601. O'Neill's force comprised native mercenary soldiers based on the bonaght system and was less heavily reliant on imported Scots fighters. The recruits were enlisted by regular proclamations and formed into English-style companies. Their training had been carried on to a large extent under the guise of the peace-keeping force allowed to the earl during his years as loyalist. As instructors and commanders he had veterans of the English and Spanish armies; these were responsible for the 'skill and practice' and 'orderly carriage' displayed by cavalry and infantry at Clontibret. Martial readiness in the mid-1590s also encompassed the use of the most advanced weapons — muskets, calivers and pikes — to supplement the traditional axes, javelins and bows. At the start of O'Neill's campaign in 1595 a third of the army of Ulster fought with guns, up from an eighth a generation earlier. Supplies of munitions were brought in mostly from Scottish Lowland ports through the mercantile network established by O'Neill. To support such large armies in the field, the economic system had been geared to the production of substantial resources of food, and it successfully maintained the war effort until 1600. Demesne agriculture had been extended by O'Neill throughout the lands annexed by him down to 1593, and his income out of Ulster was £80,000 per annum. With this military capability, O'Neill was able to confront the English armies in the field, making much use of the advantages conferred by the Ulster terrain for planning ambushes and attacks.[39]

Hugh O'Neill was also careful to leave diplomatic channels open, even after his outright commitment to arms and his proclamation as traitor in late June 1595. For four years he sporadically engaged in what English observers increasingly saw as 'deluding parleys'. He reacted only against invasions of Ulster and refused to bring the war into other provinces. During protracted negotiations in the period of truce for almost two years after Clontibret, O'Neill demanded liberty of conscience, retention of his own overlordship in Ulster, and freedom from shrieval intervention in Tyrone and Armagh. He was, however, manoeuvring for royal recognition as both earl and O'Neill, a mediator who could promote social and political reform west of the Bann. With Ulster comparatively quiet down to 1597, the English administrators were for their part relieved to be able to strengthen their position, though unrest was widespread in Connacht and parts of south Leinster controlled by Feagh MacHugh O'Byrne. The English effort was hampered by a number of difficulties. In a weak chain of command, the appointment of Sir John Norris, President of Munster, as general in Ulster caused friction with Deputy Russell, and Bingham's continuing presence in Connacht was seen by his enemies as a constant incitement to rebellion. Moreover, reinforcements for the army were slow to arrive from England, and when they did there were problems of inexperience, indiscipline, sickness and shortage of money. By late 1596 650 horse and 4,000 foot were available to the government, but deploying troops in garrisons was proving to be counterproductive in view of the isolated locations and problems of supply. Sir Conyers Clifford eventually replaced Bingham in the Connacht presidency, and Russell's regime scored a rare success with the hunting down and beheading of Feagh MacHugh in a Wicklow cave in May 1597.[40]

Thomas, Lord Burgh, a seasoned campaigner in the Low Countries, took over as Lord Deputy in that month and determined to go on the offensive against Hugh O'Neill. He planned a two-pronged assault on southern Ulster, in which he himself would lead an army from Newry through Dungannon to Lifford, where Sir Conyers Clifford, having broken through across the Erne at Ballyshannon, would link up with him. Burgh's force managed to regarrison Armagh, and then part of it marched on the Blackwater, where a defended earthwork was captured from O'Neill. Further progress was seen to be unfeasible, however, and Burgh withdrew, having attempted to come to terms with Tyrone. Clifford's invasion from Connacht was delayed, and eventually, with the support of leading Connacht lords such as Thomond and Clanricard, he attempted to cross the Erne at Belleek. The onslaught on the O'Donnell-held Ballyshannon failed, and in the incursion Lord Inchiquin was killed. An ignominious retreat back into Connacht followed. The Lord Deputy made another sortie northwards in October 1597 to victual and strengthen the Blackwater outpost, and, having accomplished this, Burgh was taken ill and carried on a litter to Newry, where he died within days. This was just over a month after the death in Munster of the leading soldier in Ireland, Sir John Norris. The loss of two senior administrators was a grievous blow to the government, which was taken over by Archbishop Adam Loftus and Chief Justice William Gardiner as Lords Justices. The sixty-six-year-old Earl of Ormond was appointed lieutenant-general with supreme military command.[41]

The burden of sustaining the war effort in the 1590s and early 1600s fell disproportionately on the community of the Pale. While complaints of the county communities about the depredations of the soldiery were perennial, the volume of grievances rose substantially as the numbers of troops escalated. Lord Deputy Burgh commented on the shortage of all commodities on his arrival in Ireland in early 1597, with prices unconscionably high. Moreover, there were many reports of dearth of food in the middle years of the decade, as the growing seasons were cold and wet and harvests late, compounding the problem of feeding the large army of the crown. Besides near-famine conditions in parts of the Pale, there was the added risk of infectious disease caused by malnutrition and contagion spread through the marauding of troops. The problems posed were to be found in microcosm in Dublin in the later 1590s. There the requirement that troops be billeted in city households occasioned much resentment. Sick and wounded soldiers were forced to lie under stalls in the streets in the absence of a suitable hospital, and the increased demand for food caused prices to soar. Then in March 1597 a massive explosion of barrels of gunpowder stacked at the quayside caused terrible loss of life, with 126 killed, and massive destruction of property. Although subsequent inquiries laid the blame on inadequate casking in the Tower of London, compensation for the citizens was not forthcoming. And even though some merchants would have benefited from supplying the army with food and other commodities, warfare was a major deterrent to trade. As a means of dealing with currency shortage, the administration authorised the circulation of copper coins, in which, however, the merchants of the towns had little faith. Not surprisingly, then, fears of rebellious outbreaks on the part of the quintessentially loyal civic populations were voiced by English officials, unable to do much to alleviate their distress.[42]

The events of later 1598 strongly increased the pressure on relations between the state authorities and all the inhabitants of Ireland. The Earl of Ormond's hopes that a truce made with O'Neill would lead to the restoration of order in Ulster were dashed with the renewal of hostilities in June, and subsequent disasters shattered irrevocably the plausibility of the Butler leader as power-broker. The focus of attention of the regime that summer was the parlous condition of the Blackwater fort, which Burgh had revived the previous year. The 150 near-starving English soldiers there were besieged by O'Neill's forces, and urgent debates at the council board in Dublin centred on whether to withdraw the garrison or mount a relief exercise. Ormond and the two Lords Justices were persuaded against their better judgment by Marshal Henry Bagenal that the latter course should be pursued. The marshal proposed to march with an mixed army of 4,300 veterans and raw recruits from Dundalk through Armagh to the Blackwater. He could point to his topographical knowledge of south Armagh, and he was motivated by his animus towards his brother-in-law. The expedition progressed without undue incident until the River Callan was crossed at a place known as the Yellow Ford on 14 August. Then the combined forces of O'Neill, O'Donnell and Maguire used the advantages of the prepared ground with the natural features of the environment to attack Bagenal's army. Obstructed by a mile-long ditch, the vanguard suffered severe losses, including that of the marshal himself, who was shot through the head. Although the rearguard managed to conduct a retreat to Armagh, the toll of casualties was 830 killed and 400 wounded, with 300 deserting to Tyrone. The latter was cautious in his following through of the victory because of his fear of an English landing at Lough Foyle, and the beleaguered defenders of Blackwater fort were allowed to leave without colours, drums and firearms.[43]

While the Dublin authorities tried to come to terms with the shock of the débâcle, Hugh O'Neill's stock as leader in Ireland and elsewhere rose to the point of embarrassing him with success. The credibility of any Spanish landing in the country would now have to be taken extremely seriously. Within Ulster the struggles of the swordsmen in the lordships—for example, east Breifne—against those kinsfolk who had accepted reforms took on a new confidence. Most significantly, and potentially dangerously for Tyrone, he was now looked to by those alienated by anglicisation in all provinces as a messianic figure who would supply contingents of troops to boost local and regional uprisings against recent socio-political arrangements. In the midlands area of Leinster key plantation strongholds at Croghane and Stradbally were captured by the O'Connor and O'More attackers, Athy was surrendered to Owney

MacRory O'More, and the partisan leader Captain Richard Tyrrell ranged the countryside in O'Neill's name. In October 1598 a major uprising took place in Munster when Owney MacRory and Tyrrell were dispatched by Tyrone into County Limerick, and, beginning there, assaults on the plantation settlements spread rapidly through the counties colonised by newcomers, causing most of them to flee to the walled towns of the province for safety. Some of the unlucky ones were killed or mutilated. Estates such as Sir Walter Raleigh's at Tallow and Edmund Spenser's at Kilcolman were abandoned to the repossessing native claimants, whose pre-plantation rights were upheld by O'Neill. A nephew of the late Earl of Desmond, James FitzThomas, was set up by the rebels as his successor, though his enemies dubbed him the '*súgán*' ('straw-rope') earl. The Earl of Ormond managed to salvage a tenuous foothold in Munster for the government, but questions were raised about the efficacy of the local militia. Connacht was also disturbed in the wake of O'Neill's victory. The English-backed leader of the Mayo Burkes was ousted by the O'Donnell's choice of MacWilliam with the help of Tyrconnell troops. Clanricard held out as a source of assistance to Lord President Conyers Clifford, but Thomond was overrun by the Earl Donough's brother, Tadhg, who called himself 'the O'Brien'. Hugh Roe O'Donnell later raided the baronies of north Clare, before the earl returned to restore order and punish those who had defied his authority and that of the English government.[44]

Robert Devereux, second Earl of Essex, was appointed governor of Ireland in March 1599 with the prestigious title of Lord Lieutenant. On arrival in Ireland in April with a huge army of 17,300, the thirty-one-year-old Essex vowed that he would 'beat Tyrone in the field'. His lack of military nous was soon evident, however, as he dispersed over half of that force into garrisons and marched southwards, exposing the rest to harrying raids by rebels such as Owney O'More and the followers of the '*súgán*' Earl of Desmond. The eight-week circuit of Munster, while gaining very little for Essex except a few castles and submissions of rebels, resulted in the exhausting of his troops. Two major reverses for ancillary armies under his jurisdiction caused further erosion of Essex's credibility as military strategist. Near Wicklow in late May 1599 Phelim MacFeagh O'Byrne routed the soldiers of Sir Henry Harrington and Captain Adam Loftus, who was killed in the encounter. Later that summer Sir Conyers Clifford attempted to relieve Sir Donough O'Connor Sligo in Collooney from a siege by Hugh Roe O'Donnell, but was killed in a battle in the Curlew Mountains which saw the loss of hundreds of the President's army. Eventually, after a dilatory council of war in Dublin, Essex was ordered to go north by Queen Elizabeth. In early September the earl set out with 4,000 men, but found O'Neill on the Monaghan–Pale border with a force more than twice as strong. The result was the private parley at Athclynt between the two earls on 7 September which issued in another truce, beneficial to the insurgents. Realising the shameful implications of his negotiations with the arch-rebel, Essex left Ireland abruptly within a fortnight without royal permission and hurried to London to explain himself to a suspicious court. Faced with ruin, Essex attempted a futile court putsch in 1601 and was executed as traitor shortly afterwards.[45]

The aftermath of the Essex episode was momentous for Hugh O'Neill as, under the impetus of internal and external events, his aspirations rose ever higher. Convinced by the purposefulness of the English war effort from late 1599 and buoyed up by support inside and outside Ireland, O'Neill was galvanised into pushing his war into the other provinces in the hope of gaining substantial Spanish aid. As symbolic of this expansive role as national leader, O'Neill for the first time took on a progress through the midlands and the south in early 1600. He punished opponents such as Sir Charles O'Carroll of Ely and held court at Iniscarra on the River Lee, confirming James FitzThomas as Earl of Desmond and Florence MacCarthy as the MacCarthy More. Tyrone demanded in a letter that David Barry, Viscount Buttevant, support the struggle for the Catholic religion and the relief of the country. This injunction— which proved fruitless—was only one of several issued by O'Neill from 1596 either in proclamations, personal letters and manifestos, outlining the basis for peace-making. In its elaborated form in November 1599, O'Neill's programme incorporated the restoration of Catholicism and the assertion of full political and economic privileges for Irish people. His cause was that of the Catholic faith and the fatherland of Ireland, appealing to Old English as well as Gaelic in the mode of the commonwealth reform treatises of the mid-century years. To acquire both papal and Spanish support, O'Neill needed to be able to show his religious and political legitimacy. A key question was the affirmation of the Catholic dimension, and this was addressed very fully in the work of the Waterford cleric, Peter Lombard, deputed by Tyrone to present his case to Pope Clement VIII at Rome. But while Clement was prepared to grant an indulgence for those taking up the cause in Ireland as in James FitzMaurice's time, he did not yield to the confederates his official excommunication of the recalcitrant. The pope was wary of boosting a Spanish enterprise in Ireland and was also warned by other Old English clergy that such a move would be self-defeating. Thus, while the authorities were genuinely fearful of a revolt of the older colonials in the Pale and elsewhere, the vast majority of members of the community themselves remained aloof from any pro-confederate feeling, preferring the *de facto* religious toleration already enjoyed and eschewing any traitorous contacts with the Spanish monarchy.[46]

The appointment of Charles Blount, Lord Mountjoy, as Lord Deputy in early 1600 ushered in a phase of determined pursuit of an ending of the war. Although Mountjoy was new to high military command, he quickly showed that he would use his army of 13,200 to great effect, and, unlike Essex, he worked harmoniously with his military subordinates. His attritional methods included the establishment of provocative garrisons, campaigning in winter, and the winning over of disaffected followers of the confederate leaders. Reflective of both aims and method was the regime of the new President of Munster, Sir George Carew, a cousin of Sir Peter. His tenure began in April 1600 just after O'Neill withdrew from the southern province, chastened by the loss of his son-in-law, Hugh Maguire, in a skirmish in Cork. Carew quickly set about establishing a network of control with his 3,000-strong army, using diplomacy and the threat of force. This policy proved to be successful, as the mercenary army left by Tyrone departed, and of the recently established leaders, James FitzThomas was undermined and captured, and Florence MacCarthy was brought back to allegiance by the autumn. The province was secured by the time of the Spaniards' arrival a year later. Mountjoy's attention was firmly focused on Ulster, where his first priority was the planting of a garrison at Lough Foyle. Under Sir Henry Docwra, 4,000 men were landed near Derry in May with the help of a feint by Mountjoy towards the Blackwater. Docwra dug in during the summer and suborned Sir Art O'Neill, son of Turlough Luineach, and Niall Garbh O'Donnell, cousin of Hugh Roe. Having successfully campaigned against the O'Mores, kidnappers of the Earl of Ormond, during the summer, the Lord Deputy turned to tighten the noose around Tyrone in the autumn. Foiled in his attempt to regarrison Armagh, Mountjoy instead built a new fortress at Mountnorris, eight miles beyond Newry, and established a new Blackwater fort. Across Lough Neagh came Sir Arthur Chichester, raiding from Antrim.[47]

As the year 1601 began King Philip III was very interested in dispatching an expedition to Ireland as a means of opening a new front in the Anglo-Spanish war. Since the reconnaissance missions of the late 1590s, however, the efficacy of a landing outside north Connacht or Ulster had decreased, with implications for the manning of the enterprise: the farther away from the confederates' northern base, the more troops which would be required. When on 21 September 1601 some 3,400 Spaniards landed at Kinsale under the command of Don Juan del Águila, the force was proportionately small in relation to the prevailing military situation. Immediately, however, Mountjoy hurried southwards from Dublin, ordering reinforcements to follow him from the garrisons. His army, eventually mustered at 7,000, besieged Kinsale in the hope of defeating the invasion force before O'Neill arrived. Although the time and place were inexpedient, Tyrone knew that with Spanish help final victory was close, but that meant taking on the English in the open field. So he and O'Donnell planned to journey to County Cork, the Tyrconnell chief leaving on 2 November, a week in advance of Tyrone. Hugh Roe marched by Roscommon, Galway and Tipperary, eluding Carew's army of 2,500, before reaching Bandon Bridge. There he was joined in early December by O'Neill, who had taken a route through the midlands. Sandwiched in between the Spaniards in the town and the surrounding Irish forces, the army of Mountjoy was reaching the extremity of exhaustion and sickness. Yet O'Neill was persuaded to gamble on a joint operation, with Águila and his own forces attacking the English camps simultaneously. The offensive at dawn on Christmas Eve was met resolutely by the cavalry of Mountjoy who surprised the 'surprise' attackers. The confederates' army, whose formation was incomplete, was thrown into disarray with considerable losses being sustained, and the Spaniards did not venture out of Kinsale because of the failure of the attackers to approach the appointed rendezvous.[48]

Although Águila and the Spaniards were allowed by Mountjoy to surrender Kinsale and their other coastal outposts and return home, the effects of the battle for the other belligerents were critical. Hugh Roe O'Donnell also fled to Spain to seek more aid, but he died there within a short time. The remainder of the confederate army split up into its component parts, each fending for itself either in retreat or in desperate delaying tactics. While O'Neill led his battered forces back northwards, Lord President Carew spent the first half of 1602 quenching the rebellion in west Munster, eventually in June storming Dunboy castle, which had become a symbol of southern resistance under O'Sullivan Beare. Mountjoy meanwhile returned to the fray after some weeks' rest, intent on effecting the final reduction of O'Neill's position in Ulster. Tyrone was suing for peace against a backdrop of fluid relations between Spain and the ailing Queen Elizabeth. His hopes may have been pinned on holding out until James VI achieved his expected succession to the English throne, as he had had diplomatic relations with the Scottish monarch in the earlier years of the war. While gambits for peace were being exchanged during late 1602, Mountjoy aimed at the abject submission of O'Neill in the field. Tyrone itself was constricted by the spoiling tactics of the armies of the Lord Deputy from the south, Docwra to the north-west and Chichester from the north and east, with famine conditions resulting during the winter of 1602–3. New fortresses were built on Lough Neagh and the River Blackwater, and symbolically Mountjoy broke up the O'Neill inauguration stone at Tullaghogue. O'Neill himself took refuge with a band of intrepid followers in the forest of Glenconkeyne, prepared if necessary to take flight to the continent through Scotland. By the end of 1602 Rory O'Donnell, Hugh Roe's brother and successor as O'Donnell, had submitted to Mountjoy, being undermined by the favour shown to Niall Garbh, the loyalist. In the early months of 1603 it was evident that Elizabeth was dying, and Mountjoy felt authorised to offer to the Earl of Tyrone the terms of life, liberty and pardon tacitly agreed in the previous year.[49]

The surrender of Hugh O'Neill to Mountjoy took place at Mellifont on 30 March 1603. Unknown to O'Neill, Mountjoy had received news three days earlier that Queen Elizabeth had died on 24 March, and he was anxious to press ahead before the demise was officially proclaimed. Kneeling before the governor, O'Neill submitted to the dead queen, renouncing all dependence upon foreign rulers, the title of the O'Neill and overlordship rights over the chiefs in Ulster traditionally regarded as the O'Neill's *uirrithe*. In return, the earl was granted a royal pardon and a patent for nearly all the lands he held before the rebellion, with the exception of those needed to support the two new garrisons. Within Tyrone his power was made absolute over the inhabitants of all ranks and over Donal O'Cahan, traditionally principal vassal of the O'Neills, whose lordship was incorporated within Tyrone. Thus O'Neill was accorded virtual palatinate powers in his territory with the backing of English law, the outcome he had sought more or less at the beginning of his campaign in 1595. Rory O'Donnell was also granted outright ownership of his ancestral lands and was created Earl of Tyrconnell. Peace was restored, but at a very high price: the expenditure of £2 million by the crown and £500 a day at the height of the war by O'Neill, and the slaughter and injury, and deaths from starvation and disease, of thousands of soldiers and civilians. Ominously, the thrust of the pre-war political and economic reforms was resumed by determined officials in Dublin, and the Ulster leaders were dependent on Mountjoy as a point of contact at court. Within four years of Mellifont the apparent gains of the earls in 1603 were seen as so tenuous as to warrant their precipitate flight from the country.[50]

From Reformation to Counter-Reformation, 1560–1600

IN February 1542 Fathers Paschal Broet and Alfonso Salmeron of the newly founded Society of Jesus landed in the north of Ireland, probably near Derry. The local bishop had transmitted an appeal from the northern lords to the pope for immediate action to prevent a total eclipse of Roman ecclesiastical jurisdiction. The mission of the two Jesuits was to confirm the allegiance of the leaders of the region to the papacy through the delivery of letters from Paul III in Rome and to catechise the local populace. That Ireland was regarded as a priority for intervention on the pope's part is attested by the fact that the general of the Society of Jesus, Ignatius of Loyola, was asked to supply missionaries for that country so soon after the ratification of his order. In Ulster in the early 1540s, however, the time was not ripe for such activity. Broet and Salmeron spent several fruitless weeks awaiting an official reception by the provincial chiefs, Conn O'Neill and Manus O'Donnell, but were rebuffed. The pacificatory strategy of Lord Deputy St Leger had created a climate of goodwill for relations between the government and the native lords. Because the Jesuit embassy to Ireland was facilitated through the French and Scottish monarchs, it was evident to rulers such as Conn O'Neill that there was a political dimension to the initiative, and thus they remained aloof. The two priests were forced to withdraw to Scotland after four months. In their report to the general they expressed their conviction that the northern chiefs were committed to King Henry VIII as head of the church in Ireland and that the entire country was on the point of being lost to the Roman Catholic Church.[1]

By contrast, when the next major Jesuit mission to Ireland was launched in 1596 the reception accorded the priests was enthusiastic, even within the heart of the capital city. Father Henry Fitzsimon,

S.J., a native of Dublin, celebrated high mass at Easter 1597 in the house of a local patrician at which hundreds of citizens attended. During the months of his active mission Fitzsimon administered the sacraments to large numbers of Catholics, his work being facilitated through a local network of kinsfolk and friends. Within a few years a successful Jesuit residency had been established, and soon seminary-trained priests and bishops, both secular and religious, were engaged in reorganising the Catholic Church in Ireland. In this they were entering into competition with the agents of the official state church who were attempting to relaunch the evangelical programme which had languished since the early Reformation. The failure of the Church of Ireland to make significant progress in converting the majority of the island's population was not unconnected to the forming of a receptive community for the agents of Catholic reform, but the link must be considered with care. Why was the impetus towards change in the first decade of state-sponsored religious reform not sustained in those that followed to the end of the century? How did intrinsic weaknesses within the ecclesiastical structures as well as aspects of civil and religious policies bring religious continuities into sharp focus for the communities in Ireland and orientate them increasingly towards the Counter-Reformation?[2]

In order to essay an answer to these questions, the pattern of reform during the mid-Tudor period and the communal response thereto must be outlined first. With the establishment of the Elizabethan settlement in 1560 the civil and ecclesiastical author-ities were poised to apply the Reformation statutes throughout the area of their jurisdiction. Despite the expansion in governmental outreach, however, severe structural problems obtruded. Most grievously lacking were educational facilities, a sufficient ministry, and control over vital church temporalities and appointments. The crucial role of the community leaders in relation to ecclesiastical resources must also be explored. In the mid-Elizabethan period the crisis of the revolts in the name of religion with links to the continent and the subsequent convulsions caused a defining of ideological positions among all groups in Ireland. For the New English a radical form of Protestantism tied to a colonial mentality tended to gain ascendancy by the later years of the century. Contending approaches among the long-settled communities ultimately caused a divergence within their Catholicism. The Old English opted for a religious position which, while not within the law, was, they felt, compatible with loyalty to the crown, though their leaders were to deploy their ecclesiastical perquisites in favour of the Counter-Reformation. By comparison, the Gaelic leadership during the Nine Years' War was prepared to canvass Spanish-backed Catholic militancy based on an ideology of faith and the fatherland of Ireland.

Structural weakness of the church and problems of evangelisation

Credit for the amicable absorption of the Henrician ecclesiastical reforms lay with Sir Anthony St Leger, Lord Deputy from 1540 to 1548. He set a pattern for state policy in church matters which derived from an anxiety to push forward with political and social reform, without religion proving to be a discordant factor. In this context are explainable, for example, his actions in reconciling papally appointed bishops to the regime and in distributing substantial grants of former monastic estates to members of the local lay elites. Under the royal ecclesiastical aegis from 1547 onwards, the Reformation embraced doctrinal changes inspired by continental Protestantism. Faced with implementing the reforms set out in the Book of Common Prayer as applied in Ireland in mid-1549, St Leger continued to play the part of conciliator when reappointed in the following year. Such an approach was seen to be all the more pressing as the papal Archbishop of Armagh, Robert Wauchop, arrived in the north in 1550, seemingly preparing a campaign of Catholic revival in Ireland with French backing. Thus the Lord Deputy attempted to secure the appointment of native-born bishops to vacant sees and won approval for a Latin version of the Prayer Book, an Irish-language edition not being practicable at that time. A notable failure of his policy was the defection of the royal appointee as Archbishop of Armagh, George Dowdall, to the continent for reasons of conscience. St Leger's replacements as Lord Deputy, Sir Edward Bellingham and Sir James Croft, preferred a more stringent approach to spreading the religious innovations, but were also largely constrained by the urgent political and military demands of governance. It was during the latter's term of office that the Englishmen Hugh Goodacre and John Bale were prevailed upon to take up Irish episcopacies. While Goodacre died prematurely, Bale did take up residence in Kilkenny, where he had a chequered career as Bishop of Ossory.[3]

The occasion of Bishop Bale's being harried out of his see was the popular restoration of Catholic forms of worship on Queen Mary's accession in the summer of 1553. Once again St Leger as Lord Deputy was charged with overseeing changes in liturgical practice, including the restoration of those rites 'of old time used'. Retaining her supreme power in the church temporarily, the queen appointed bishops to the sees of Ossory, Cashel and Armagh (to which George Dowdall was returned as Primate). In 1554 a number of bishops were deprived of their offices on grounds of their having married, including Staples of Meath, Lancaster of Kildare and Browne of Dublin. In their places were appointed William Walsh, Thomas Leverous, and Hugh Curwin respectively. Relations with the papacy were normalised so far as Ireland was concerned in June 1555 when Pope Paul IV erected Ireland into a kingdom ruled by Queen Mary and her husband, King Philip. Cardinal Pole, papal legate to England, was appointed to a similar position for Ireland. In 1557 parliament repealed all the anti-papal statutes of the Henrician reign, as well as discharging first fruits of ecclesiastical benefices and reviving anti-heresy laws. Although commissioners were appointed in late 1557 to inquire into church properties, no attempt was made to revive the monastic establishment. The only restoration was of the priory of the Knights Hospitaller of St John at Kilmainham in 1558, along with the re-erection of St Patrick's, Dublin, into a cathedral church. In Ireland, where little doctrinal ferment occurred, there was no replication of the punitive measures against Protestants seen in England, and no proceedings under the heresy statutes. In general, the appearance of continuity with the past in church practice was maintained until the end of Mary's reign.[4]

The effects of the Marian restoration of Catholicism were not positive enough to have instilled proper Counter-Reformation devotion. They may have been sufficient, however, to stabilise the confused situation brought about by events in the ecclesiastical sphere in the previous twenty years, especially by leaving untouched lay property gains. The evidence suggests that the leaders in town and county acquiesced in the changing jurisdiction over the church in the early Reformation but that doctrinal changes under Edward VI had been generally resisted. The failure to convene a parliament in Ireland in that monarch's reign precluded a consensual approach to the Reformation measures being undertaken among the political community. Moreover, the beneficiaries of the sharing-out of church property were not given an extra incentive to adopt the substance of theological change as were their gentry and patrician counterparts in England. There the suppression of the chantries and religious guilds under Edward made available additional largesse for the lay communal leaders at the crucial juncture of the introduction of Protestantism. In Ireland no such suppression occurred. Instead the solid if unspectacular rolling back of doctrinal innovation in Ireland under Mary was facilitated by the preservation of the status quo among the landholding elites. Although a small coterie of committed native Protestants had emerged in the years around the mid-century, most of the gentry and merchants occupied a position of benign neutrality in matters religious.[5]

The team of officials which had supervised the parliamentary proceedings under Mary in 1557 was retained to manage the passage of the legislation for the Elizabethan settlement in January 1560. This was in order that the maximum degree of continuity be achieved in effecting the religious reforms. The Houses of Commons and Lords were presented with laws very similar to those which had been passed in the English parliament in the previous year. Although Catholic apologists writing later from their stance of certainty in the Counter-Reformation era attempted to exculpate their gentry and merchant forebears from having acquiesced in the introduction of heterodoxy as they saw it, the reports of intimidation and subterfuge on the government's part were evidently very much *post factum*. Within three weeks the key Acts of Supremacy and Uniformity were on the statute book. The first of these, declaring that Queen Elizabeth was the supreme governor of the Church of Ireland, against whose authority it was potentially treasonous to preach, incorporated an oath to be sworn by principal ecclesiastical and civil office-holders. The second ordained that liturgical practice in Ireland should be in keeping with the norms laid down in the 1552 Book of Common Prayer. It further enjoined attendance at divine service on all subjects on pain of fine, mayors of towns and other justices of the peace being authorised to determine offences specified. There were, however, at least two significant departures from the counterpart English act. A Latin version of the set prayers could be used in areas where English was not spoken or understood, and also church ornaments and clerical vestments as allowed at the outset of King Edward's reign were to be permitted in Irish churches. Thus, far from brow-beating the parliamentarians, the government aimed at ensuring the appearance of continuity with late medieval practice.[6]

In theory, the liturgical changes under the Act of Uniformity were due to come into effect in parishes on 23 June 1560. In practice, however, the new rites could only be introduced by co-operative clergy acting with the approval or complaisance of local lay elites. The key to clerical reform lay in the provision of a willing episcopacy and a well-trained ministry. Of the four bishops who were presented with the Oath of Supremacy in February 1560, two, Archbishops Bodkin of Tuam and Curwin of Dublin, swore, while the other two, Bishops Leverous of Kildare and Walsh of Meath, demurred and were deprived of office. By 1564 eight of the bishops appointed during Queen Mary's reign had accepted the Anglican reforms. Moreover, key appointments to the dioceses of Kildare (Bishop Alexander Craik and, on his death in 1564, Robert Daly), Armagh (Archbishop Adam Loftus), Meath (Bishop Hugh Brady) and Dublin (Archbishop Loftus translated) were designed to buttress the Protestant administration of the core sees of the *ecclesia inter anglicos*. A start was made on setting up a body of conforming clergy by numerous appointments to vacant benefices in the early 1560s, but obtaining the compliance of the already beneficed priests was to represent a major challenge for the Church of Ireland authorities. Several lay officials of the executive and judiciary accepted the tendered Oath of Supremacy in 1560, but most local government agents were not requested to swear. A series of regional ecclesiastical commissions was issued between 1561 and 1564, empowered with enforcing the religious settlement in the midlands, south and west, and Armagh, and a Court of High Commission was established in October 1564 to impose lay uniformity in the Pale. As even within this zone of political conformability the commission was inoperable, acceptance of the Reformation statutes in remoter regions was highly problematic. For the reformers priority had to be given to evangelising through educational advances and supplying qualified clergy.[7]

All who were engaged in advancing religious reform in Elizabethan Ireland were agreed on the need for pedagogy to inculcate belief and to train up native candidates for church posts. In the early 1560s grammar or second-level schooling was mostly in the charge of masters or tutors employed by aristocratic or patrician families or by municipalities such as Dublin. Then and later the perception was that most of the teachers were conservative in their religious beliefs, and accordingly new initiatives were required to further the Protestant Reformation through education. Bishop Hugh Brady, a native-born reformer, for example, endowed a school for producing Irish-speaking students who might go on to university. In 1569 a bill for the erection of free schools came before the Irish parliament. This measure would have provided for schoolhouses at the expense of the counties, staffed by English schoolmasters appointable by the Lord Deputy and partially paid by the bishops and clergy. The bill was lost because the bishops wished to appoint masters, and they also resented the exclusion of impropriated lands within the dioceses from bearing a share of the salary costs. In the following year amended proposals were passed into law whereby schools were to be founded in every diocese, with patronage in four key dioceses, namely Armagh, Dublin, Kildare and Meath, being under episcopal control. The results of the legislation were to prove very disappointing for the planners of religious reform through secondary schooling. Most dioceses were too poor to bear the added costs, and the problem of the unavailablity of large amounts of income because of lay impropriations was not solved.[8]

Even more controversial were the various schemes to found a university in Ireland, all of which came to nothing before the 1590s. Originally mooted by Archbishop Browne in 1547, the proposal for an Irish academy of higher learning was fraught with difficulty. The most contentious issue in the early Elizabethan decades was that of the site for a college. In the 1560s and 1580s strongly backed projects were canvassed for the transformation of St Patrick's Cathedral, Dublin, into a university, its valuable livings being designated as income to support the facilities and staff. Successive Archbishops of Dublin set their faces doggedly against such proposals of ecclesiastical and lay advocates. In the mid-1560s, for example, Bishop Brady of Meath was signally vocal in recommending the conversion of the cathedral to academic use, but first Archbishop Curwin and then more notably Archbishop Loftus argued for the status quo. In 1570 the Brady project culminated in an abortive move in Sir Henry Sidney's parliament. In that connection, the prominent English scholar Edmund Campion, a protégé of Sidney's patron, the Earl of Leicester, was attracted from Oxford to Dublin in the hope of gaining the mastership of the college, for which funds and a name ('Plantolinum') had been assigned. At the time of this unsuccessful attempt the concern of the local community for convenient access to third-level training as an alternative to expensive migration and as a vehicle of anglicisation meshed with the ecclesiastical authorities' desire for the training of a reformed ministry. The prevailing atmosphere was not ideological but was influenced greatly by strains of Christian humanism. The venture spearheaded by Lord Deputy Perrot in the mid-1580s, which also met implacable opposition from Loftus, was more overtly sectarian as the Puritan view of university training for religious rather than secular ends had become entrenched. By the time of the foundation of Trinity College in 1592 the academic thrust was exclusivist and alien to most of the native population.[9]

The nature of the 'reciprocating connection' of human and material resources is glimpsed in the episodes of episcopal recalcitrance in the face of eminently desirable innovations such as a university and diocesan schools. Financial insecurity dogged the careers of Church of Ireland bishops, and they argued for the prior provision of adequate livings for the highly educated clergy which it was hoped the reforms would produce. An impoverished church would deter people of talent from coming from England to take up benefices and natives from entering the clerical profession. Archbishop Loftus, who ruled the diocese of Dublin from 1567 to 1605, had the patronage of seventeen of the twenty-four richest livings in the diocese, the vast majority of the incumbents of which were preaching ministers by the end of his period of office. This exceptionally high proportion of well-qualified appointees was tied to the attractiveness of the benefices. Although committed to the establishment of a university to train native Protestant graduates, the archbishop was totally opposed to divesting himself of the sources of patronage attached to St Patrick's Cathedral. Bishop Brady's credentials as a champion of educational reform are impeccable, but his money problems blighted his episcopate. The demands of the exchequer for payment of his first fruits and his clergy's twentieth part proved a crushing burden to him. This predicament arose despite the fact that Meath had the second highest income per annum of the Irish sees. In 1576 Brady reported that in the 224 parishes in his diocese there were only fifteen of his clergy who were both competent and reasonably provided for.[10]

Beyond the dioceses of the inner Pale the value of sees and benefices fell. While livings in the anglicised areas of Armagh diocese, north Kildare, Kilkenny, south Wexford and Waterford

city were modestly sufficient for maintaining clergy, the benefices
in the border areas of the Englishry returned very low incomes. As
the English administration extended its reach into the more Gaelic
and gaelicised regions, valuations of the dioceses carried out found
that the majority of livings were miserably poor. Even then, incomes
were vulnerable to rebellion and lay intrusion, as in the case of the
bishopric of Clonfert, for example, which was worth £100 in 1584
and only £25 three decades later. Almost two-thirds of clergy in the
better-endowed English areas earned less than half of the £10 per
annum needed to meet their expenses. In the west of the country
the income per annum could be as low as 5s. Small wonder that most
of the benefices were occupied by reading or non-graduate ministers
who were traditional in their religious outlook, able merely to read
the service book to their parishioners but not to preach. There were
many examples of clerical pluralism at all levels of the church as
incumbents engrossed benefices to boost their incomes. Irish
benefices presented few attractions for university-trained preachers
who would be able to communicate the new scripturally centred
doctrines. Church dignitaries, including Archbishop Curwin and
Bishop Craik, impeded the reform by leasing diocesan properties
for high entry fines and at low rents, and the state policy of whole-
sale granting of church possessions in the mid-Tudor years struck
at the roots of ecclesiastical assets. Not only did these pass out of
church control, but the associated tithes and advowsons magnified
the extent of lay involvement. Also counterproductive was the
granting by the secular authorities of church posts with their
income to lay persons such as Lord Chancellor Robert Weston,
who became Dean of St Patrick's, Dublin, in 1567.[11]

Communal responses to the Reformation

Despite the uncertain start to the evangelical campaign in the 1560s
and the structural weaknesses in the church itself, the reform leaders
hoped that the small but dedicated coterie of native Protestants
would have a leavening influence within their communities. For it
was from among the ranks of the gentry and merchant patriciates in
England that initiatives for the founding of grammar schools and
Puritan lectureships came. Although John Bale's episcopate in
Kilkenny in 1553 was brief and turbulent, he did leave behind a

group of enthusiastically Protestant youths. Some young people in Limerick were reported by the papal legate, David Wolfe, to have embraced the 'Lutheran leprosy' by 1574. In Galway too it was noted that the civic leaders and other townsfolk 'orderly repaired to church' after the reforming efforts of Lord President Fitton in the early 1570s. It was in Dublin that most was expected of the band of vociferous Protestant citizens. Among the small number of prominent families which had committed themselves to the Reformation were the Usshers, who produced two Church of Ireland archbishops in succeeding generations. Alderman John Ussher the elder, described by Archbishop Loftus as 'a rare man for honesty and religion', promoted an enterprising scheme for a university at Dublin and had also facilitated the printing in 1571 of the first book with a Gaelic typeface, a Protestant primer and catechism by John Kearney. Alderman Walter Ball, afterwards notorious for his prosecution to the death of his recusant mother, Margaret, oversaw the settling of two Protestant schoolmasters in Dublin in the 1580s and was a great champion of Trinity College. Along with Alderman John Challoner, uncle of Luke, founding fellow of the university, Ussher and Ball served on the Court of High Commission. Among the families of these Protestant patricians there was a tight nexus of marital ties, binding them more tightly together, and to New English families such as that of Loftus. While such endogamous links affirmed their religious convictions, they did serve to cut the members off from the municipal mainstream with its conservative majority leadership by the mid-Elizabethan years.[12]

Magnifying these hopeful auguries from the reformers' point of view was the tentativeness of the papal counter-thrust in the early Elizabethan decades. Problems of recruitment of fresh talent for Catholic bishoprics and of finding material resources were similar to those of the state church. The mission of Father David Wolfe, S.J., in 1561 is illustrative of the obstacles to and opportunities for a revival of the Roman allegiance. A native of Limerick and one of the first Irish entrants into the Society of Jesus, Wolfe was dispatched by the pope as his legate to Ireland to supervise clerical and lay religious practice and to propose names of candidates for Irish sees which were unoccupied by papal appointees. As with the Protestant campaign, a key element in the cultivation of such promise was to be the erection of a university and colleges. While these plans for Catholic reform were no more successful than those of their confessional counterparts, Wolfe's crucial proposal of his fellow-citizen Richard Creagh for the archbishopric of Armagh seemed set to challenge the unseasoned holding of the Anglicans. An impressive scholar and zealous teacher in Limerick, Creagh placed his deeply ingrained loyalty to the queen at the royal service as he defied the rampant Shane O'Neill in later 1566. Nevertheless, the archbishop was arrested in 1567 and accused of conspiracy with O'Neill against the crown. His protestations of mere spiritual purpose proving to be unavailing, Creagh was imprisoned in Dublin, tried and acquitted on a treason charge, and finally transferred to the Tower of London, where he was kept until his death in 1586–7. Among Wolfe's other nominees for episcopal rank were Andrew O'Crean for Elphin, Donal MacCongail for Raphoe and Eugene O'Harte for Achonry, all of whom attended the closing session of the Council of Trent. These bishops faced a massive task on their return to their western dioceses, given the institutional dislocation and social upheavals in the regions. Royally appointed bishops such as Christopher Bodkin of Tuam and Hugh Lacy of Limerick were close to traditional Catholicism in their rituals while remaining in harmony with the government. David Wolfe himself left Ireland in 1572, having spent five years in prison in Dublin Castle. In his report to Rome he presented the religious disposition of the population as being mostly traditionalist Catholic, 'heresy' being eschewed for the most part and church-papistry a feature of Dublin religious life especially.[13]

Church-papistry was not unusual among public figures of that generation in England and Ireland. Two gentlemen who benefited by the division of monastic lands, Patrick Barnewall of Turvey, County Dublin, and Roland Eustace of Ballymore-Eustace on the southern border of the Pale, both state officials, were said to have sheltered the displaced religious communities of Grace Dieu and Baltinglass respectively. Some gentry families continued to nurture local cults: the Luttrells of Luttrellstown in west County Dublin were closely identified with the famous well of St Mary at Mulhuddart, and the Fagans of Feltrim in the north of the county financed the decoration of St Doulagh's well. Individuals who were compliant in their public careers displayed Catholic convictions in private, including Sir John Plunkett of Dunsoghly, Chief Justice of the Queen's Bench for many years, James Stanihurst, Speaker of the House of Commons on three occasions, and James Bathe, Chief

Baron of the Exchequer. Private schoolmasters seem to have been employed by the heads of gentry and patrician families in their homes, and in some cases at least these were domestic chaplains, displaced from benefices by the Elizabethan settlement.[14]

The preservation of older religious devotions was not influenced to any great degree by the languishing state evangelism of the two or three decades after 1560, nor by the nascent Counter-Reformation (though there are references to Catholic clergy at work in the Pale and towns in the early to mid-Elizabethan years). Because of their social ascendancy, the gentry and merchant elites could have championed the reformed church despite the infrastructural weaknesses. Their material and cultural interests were intricately interwoven with the church at local level, most notably in County Louth. But the acquisition of great reserves of wealth and patronage in the form of tithes and advowsons served to stabilise and entrench the aristocratic holding within the ecclesiastical sphere without any persuasive arguments for a change of doctrine being offered by the state church. The lucrative perquisites in gentry and merchant possession originated in the transfer of huge amounts of monastic lands from religious to lay proprietorship after the late 1530s. The conveyances included a vast number of benefices given to the abbeys during the earlier centuries of benefaction. The monasteries had been in receipt of the tithed income from these holdings, and in return had had the right and duty of presenting clergy to minister in rectories or vicarages. On the secularisation of the monastic possessions, the crown, the new owner, granted away many hundreds of leases of the lands and estates to lay people. With these leases in return for rents went advowsons in most cases, that is, the right to appoint clergy.[15]

It appears that the proportion of impropriated benefices was much higher in Ireland than it was in England or Wales (60 per cent compared with 40 per cent). For the ecclesiastical province of Dublin, which included most of the Pale, the percentage was up to 70 per cent. In his diocese of Meath Bishop Brady found that, of 224 parish churches, 105 were impropriate and another 52 'pertain to divers particular lords', presumably manor churches, leaving only a quarter of the parishes which were directly endowed by the bishop. In 1576 many of the priests' residences and church buildings were in ruins in a region where much gentry patronage of church-building had been evident in the decades before the Reformation. It is possible that the economic decline of the inland Pale may have rendered the gentry unable to maintain their previous rate of subsidy for church-building. Yet it is very significant that so many of the parish churches which were impropriate and therefore in the gift of the gentry were ruinous. The supply of a Protestant ministry was related to the problem of advowsons. There is no doubt that some of the lay patrons would have been assiduous in their patronage of Protestant clergymen. But the fact that over 300 rectories and parsonages were in lay gift meant that there was a weapon to be wielded at some time against the state church. In all of the counties of the Pale, grants acquired by gentry families at the dissolution entailed advowsons, and for several generations the leading figures presented to the cures, as in the case of the Luttrells and the rectory of Donabate parish church. In Louth, which had a very intricate system of intertwined manors and rectories, advowsons were in the gift of gentry families such as Taaffe, Babe, Verdon and Dowdall down to the seventeenth century.[16]

Tightly-knit networks of intermarriages throughout the old colonial areas were mostly strong enough to prove resistant to the assimilation of Protestants and were protective of traditional devotions and legal interests. Thus older rituals were carried on, whenever necessary outside of the environs of the church buildings and grounds. In the towns of the east, south and south-west, which were notable bastions of the Counter-Reformation in the early seventeenth century, the practices associated with the religious guilds and chantries survived, and their not inconsiderable endowments remained intact, to be disposed of as the patrons and trustees saw fit. The maritime towns also proved to be conduits for the influence of Tridentine Catholicism from the continent and for the shipping of youths to seminaries in Catholic Europe.[17]

Religious conviction and political identity in a time of crisis, 1579–1600

At the end of the 1570s there occurred a series of events which brought to an end the practice and toleration of easy-going church-papistry. The backdrop was the international tension arising from Pope Pius V's excommunication of Queen Elizabeth in 1570, relieving her Catholic subjects of the duty of loyalty, and the outbreak of politico-religious conflicts in northern Europe. Events in France and the Netherlands were followed with avid interest in Ireland. Perhaps as a response to the increasingly vexed diplomatic situation, Protestant leaders such as Archbishop Loftus were more active in the prosecution of recusancy through the Court of High Commission. A religious dimension, residual in the earlier rebellion in Munster in 1569, became entwined with grievances in the Desmond revolt of 1579. James FitzMaurice used the medium of religion to propagate his campaign for redress, arguing that the plight of the traditional ecclesiastical order epitomised the threat to the old way of life in general. In this he had a precursor in Maurice MacGibbon, papal Archbishop of Cashel and emissary of Irish leaders to the Spanish court in 1569, who had lobbied Philip II unsuccessfully for aid for an Irish Catholic confederacy, with the backing of Pope Gregory XIII from 1572. After the Stukeley fiasco and the small landing of FitzMaurice in Kerry in 1579 Philip was persuaded to wrest his attention from the Netherlands and to send troops, along with papal forces, in the ill-fated expedition in 1580. FitzMaurice's death and the tepid response of southern and western leaders to his and Sanders's proclamation of a papal crusade set back the cause of militant Catholicism in Ireland, but the civil authorities were undoubtedly alarmed at its manifestation. Patrick O'Healy, Bishop of Mayo, was captured, tried by martial law under Lord President Drury and hanged at Kilmallock in August 1579 on a charge of treason. He was the most notable Catholic to that date to be executed for the exercise of what he claimed was an exclusively spiritual mission.[18]

The call to action in defence of Catholicism resonated in the borders of the Pale in the early 1580s. Here religious disaffection meshed with economic and constitutional grievances, notably the cess controversy, to produce revolt and conspiracy. The most prominent figure was James Eustace, Viscount Baltinglass, a lawyer who had spent some years at Rome in the mid-1570s. Imbued with zeal for the official restoration of the Catholic Church in Ireland, he enlisted the support of members of the gentry of Kildare and south Dublin, including young lawyers who had become committed to Catholicism during their studies at the Inns of Court in London or on the continent. Also giving sustenance to the burgeoning recusancy of the gentry households was a corps of priests, including Father Robert Rochford, S.J., who travelled about the countryside, being received by gentlewomen who confirmed the resolve of their spouses. After its initial success at Glenmalure in 1580 the revolt of Baltinglass fizzled out, undermined by the failure of the Earl of Kildare to rally to the cause. Interlinked with this insurgency was the conspiracy unveiled in 1581 revolving around William Nugent, the brother of the Baron of Delvin in Westmeath. Nugent was bent on avenging himself on the regime which had arrested his brother and the Earl of Kildare at Christmas 1580, and the motivations of his Old English and Gaelic following were mixed. There is no doubt about the commitment of some of the gentry conspirators, such as, for example, George Netterville, to the religious cause. About twenty gentlemen were executed for their parts in the rebellion and conspiracy, many of them professing their Catholicism on the scaffold. The judicial bloodletting was confined to these ringleaders, though many humbler folk may have been dispatched by martial law. Among the latter who were tried and convicted by common law were a company of Wexford sailors and a baker, Matthew Lambert, who declared at his trial that he knew nothing of religious controversy but that he was a Catholic and believed what the 'holy mother church' believed. The most notable victim of the sweep against Catholic activists was Archbishop Dermot O'Hurley of Cashel, who was executed for treason in Dublin in June 1584 after a trial by martial law.[19]

The events of the early 1580s were to have a significant impact on the religious attitudes of all groups in Ireland in the decades ahead. For the merchant and gentry elites in the Englishry the effect was to quicken the movement to more overt recusancy. A quiet drifting away from attendance at the state church services was noticeable in many places, led by the women of the community. Indeed, the more committed stance of women as regulators of the households is evidenced for example in the career of Margaret Ball (née Bermingham), widow of a Mayor of Dublin, whose home served as a school for Catholic youths and a refuge for priests down to the 1580s. She died in prison in 1584, having been lodged there for her recusant activities by her Protestant son, Alderman Walter Ball. For the majority of Ball's aldermanic colleagues and their gentry counterparts the path chosen was that of constitutional and legislative opposition to the programme of changes intended by Sir John Perrot in 1585–6, including the stronger anti-Catholic measures. It was at this juncture that Archbishop Loftus noted that the representatives of the counties and boroughs became entrenched in their Catholicism, having manifested openness at least to ecclesiastical change in the early Reformation period. Most traumatic of all during this era were the executions of relatives of heads of houses in the Pale shires for revolt and conspiracy. Among the Dublin patricians only a few were found to be directly involved in supplying Viscount Baltinglass, and they managed to evade the penalty for treason through their citizenship of Dublin. In the years after 1585 a salient feature was the quiet deployment by these elites of ecclesiastical resources and practices over which they had control—devotions, priests nominated through guilds and advowsons, income through tithes and guild rents, educational and marital networks—on the side of the Counter-Reformation.[20]

For the small Protestant community in Ireland also the occur-rences of the mid-Elizabethan years exerted a defining force on convictions and methods of evangelisation. A strain of Puritanism manifested itself increasingly in the actions and utterances of leading Anglican churchmen, and this tendency was often subsumed within the policies of lay officials in the provinces. Coming from an English background of rigid Protestant discipline, Archbishop Loftus of Dublin and Bishop Thomas Jones of Meath were freer from the early 1580s to give vent to their coercive approach to the enforcement of the religious statutes. For example, Loftus, in office as Lord Justice in 1584, took the initiative in the prosecution of Archbishop O'Hurley to the death. Conjoined with the archbishop in office was Sir Henry Wallop, Vice-Treasurer of Ireland from 1579 to 1599, who also had radical religious views. There is little doubt that their predestinarian Calvinism inclined men like Loftus and Wallop towards a harsh strategy *ab initio*, and experience of religious dissidence and civil disorder in Ireland reinforced the disciplinary approach. Indeed, the advocates of stringency in the implementation of the Reformation laws tended to argue that conformity was a necessary precondition for conversion. They further held that the preaching of the gospel should be delayed until amenable congregations were marshalled by the 'sword' or the deployment of disciplinary institutions such as the Court of High Commission. In the assessments of the failure of political reform in Ireland written in the later 1580s and 1590s emphasis was placed on the lack of progress in the propagation of the reformed religion, not just among the remoter Gaelic and gaelicised inhabitants, but among the Old English of the Pale.[21]

Although in spite of the wishes of the proponents of coercion there was no major onslaught on public nonconformity in the last two decades of the century, many incidences of rigorous dealings with noted Catholic activists marked the English push into the provinces. The underpinning of political programmes with religious principles by crown officials courted the rejection of Anglicanism on the part of the local communities because of its identification with arbitrary and harsh rule. In the Leinster area the purge of recusants from official positions was justified all the more because of the implication of gentry families in the Baltinglass and Nugent conspiracies. The redistribution of confiscated lands by Lord Deputy Grey to his supporters in the early 1580s was a blow aimed at Catholic proprietorship within the Pale. In 1591 Michael Fitzsimon, a Catholic schoolmaster of Dublin who was involved in the Baltinglass revolt, was executed for treason, recusant propagandists alleging that Bishop Jones was very interested in gaining possession of Fitzsimon's estate in County Meath. In Munster the punitive measures of Lord President Drury directed against Catholic clergy caught up in the Desmond revolt, were pursued by a successor in office, Sir John Norris. In 1585 he staged a raid on the house of a leading Clonmel merchant, Victor White, who had afforded protection to the Earl of Desmond's chaplain, Maurice MacKenraghty. The latter was subsequently tried by martial law and executed. Even before the hardening of attitudes in the later 1570s Lord President Fitton had conducted a campaign of official iconoclasm in Connacht as part of his policy of stamping his authority on that province. Later under Bingham the prosecution of Brian O'Rourke of west Breifne was due, in part at least, to his outspoken anti-Protestantism. And in Ulster the groundwork for the unpopular actions of Sheriff Willis against the friars in Donegal in the 1590s had been laid by Captain Randolph's expulsion of the Dominicans at Derry in 1566.[22]

Whatever their motivation, these administrators set the tone for a New English ideology from the 1590s onwards. Its theoretical expression was to be found in the writings of Munster planters such as Richard Beacon, Edmund Spenser and Sir William Herbert, and of Barnaby Rich, a retired soldier. As part of their argument for the use of expropriatory measures against the Irish landholders, these commentators pointed to the paganism of the Gaelic Irish and the unreconstructed popery of the Old English. The lack of true, reformed Christianity among the two native peoples rendered them either barbaric or less than civilised respectively, according to the English model, and therefore ripe for conquest. It was in the circumstances of this conjunction of strict Protestantism and the prevailing New English political mentality that the campaign for the foundation of a university finally came to fruition. After the unedifying squabbles over a site in the 1580s, Archbishop Loftus presented to the English court a ready-made location for a new college in 1591, and the proposal was accepted officially by Queen Elizabeth in the following year. The proponents of Trinity College were in no doubt about the primacy of religious aims for the academy: 'the seed and fry of the holy ministry throughout the realm'. This was despite the fact that local supporters, especially in the municipality of Dublin which donated the site, were appealed to on the basis that a native college would save the expense involved in overseas migration for education and would also prove financially lucrative for local businessmen. But the allurements of Catholic colleges abroad were specifically mentioned in the briefing documents, and it is clear that in the official church mind at least the academic environment was to be exclusively Protestant. The only Dublin parents to send their boys to Trinity in the early years were those who were of the small reformed coterie of families such as Ball, Money, Challoner and Ussher.[23]

Most families in the broad mainstream from whom these Protestants were isolated chose the option of overseas education and shunned the local college. Educational migration was one of a number of ways in which the growing recusancy of the older English community was reflected. Travel abroad for second- and third-level studies to places like Louvain was not a new phenomenon, but the number of scholars increased substantially from the mid-Elizabethan period onwards. Their destinations were Catholic colleges located mostly in Habsburg-governed lands of the Iberian peninsula and the Low Countries, as well as Italy and France. From the 1590s colleges were founded specifically for Irish students, at Salamanca in 1592, Lisbon in 1593 and Douai in 1594, for example. Financial support from the Spanish crown and the archdukes of the Netherlands was forthcoming, although the colleges were frequently very short of funds. Parents who chose to send their offspring to the continent for education in the 1580s and 1590s could have been in no doubt about the nature of the colleges: the curricula had at their core the theology of the Council of Trent, and their objective was the training of priests for the Counter-Reformation mission. A striking number of students enrolling in the colleges stated that their grammar schooling had been under the tutelage of Catholic schoolmasters. Despite the efforts of the administrators to halt this traffic, the exodus continued, and by the end of the century the returned priests were themselves organising the transit of Irish girls and boys to European seminaries and convents. There were also passages arranged through Irish ports for students from England travelling to the continent. The roots of the alternative Catholic Church which developed strongly in opposition to the state church in the early seventeenth century were established by this educational interchange.[24]

When they returned to their native places in Ireland the ordained graduates of the continental colleges found receptive communities awaiting their ministrations. The priests could utilise the mobility which the tightly-knit networks of gentry and merchant families straddling town and country allowed. The webs of intermarriage spun from the towns through the hinterlands provided protective systems for the missioners which were seen by state and church officials as almost impervious to Anglican penetration. As the parish churches became increasingly alien places for the Catholic community, the residences of patricians and gentry came to serve as places of worship or 'mass-houses' for recusant congregations. Many of these were presided over by women such as Margaret Ball and Anna Cusack of Dublin and Anastasia Strong of Waterford who acted as receptrices of their priest relatives. Besides providing them with the facilities and the moral support needed to maintain their ministry, the Old English Catholic leaders helped to finance the burgeoning Counter-Reformation among their community. In a large number of parishes in the Pale and elsewhere tithes were withheld from the established clergy, and instead the income went to sustain Catholic priests. In the case of benefices where advowsons were in the gift of lay recusant patrons, appointments of clergy were liable to be of their co-religionists. Some of the residual powers vested in the lay corporations of the religious guilds were used by the members to sponsor Catholic clergy. Funds from property rentals were applied by papal order to the employment of Catholic chaplains whose appointments were authorised by foundation charters.[25]

The survival of religious guilds for fifty years after their abolition in England and Wales is an indication of the divergence of patterns of religious practice on the two sides of the Irish Sea. In Ireland the fraternities provided a vital element of continuity between the pre-Reformation pieties of the Englishry and the new devotions of the

Counter-Reformation. Not only were property rights preserved intact in the hands of the members, but also regular meetings gave scope for retaining the rituals associated with the guilds. While the formal designation of obits may have ceased by the mid-century, evidence suggests that priests continued to operate under the aegis of the corporate powers of the guilds' brothers and sisters. In the case of one of the most significant, that of St Anne in the parish of St Audoen, Dublin, the guild chapel was refurbished in 1597 at the expense of the members, and the six priests whose appointment was permitted in the charter of 1430 were kept on in the guise of six 'singing men'. Despite complaints from the established clergy of St Audoen's parish and many investigations of its warrant, the Guild of St Anne survived as a Catholic institution in Dublin until the late seventeenth century. For the most part, the practice of Catholicism was carried on in a muted, non-ostentatious manner, based mainly on the private residences of the elites. The returning secular and reg-ular clergy—Jesuits, Franciscans, Capuchins, Carmelites, Dominicans and others—celebrated mass and administered the sacraments under domestic protection. Devotions at sanctified places such as holy wells and shrines were also still vibrant, perhaps to the chagrin of the Tridentine missioners. Down to the early 1600s the emphasis was on circumspect and quietist piety for the vast majority of the Old English. It was possible for them to hope for *de facto* toleration of their dissidence, and they had no difficulty in reconciling their loyalty to the state with their allegiance to the Roman Catholic Church.[26]

The time of greatest testing for this compromise was during the Nine Years' War. Hugh O'Neill was intent on obtaining from the pope a formal decree of excommunication of those who failed fully to support his cause. The most that Pope Clement VIII was prepared to grant was a plenary indulgence for participants similar to that accorded James FitzMaurice's force in 1579. Despite the proclam-ations and letters of the Earl of Tyrone, however, there is little evidence that townsfolk and Pale gentry were in sympathy with the Ulster chieftain's war, and in this they had the backing of leading Jesuits such as Father Richard Field, S.J. Whatever about the common commitment to Catholicism, the links with the Spanish monarchy were strongly eschewed by the vast majority of those of older English origin in Ireland. Contrarily, for the militant opponents of the English crown, the forging of diplomatic ties with the Escorial outside Madrid brought into focus the nature of the religious principle which was at issue. The background to such links was the preparatory continental phase for some bishops and religious who returned to labour in the west and north of Ireland. Bishops such as Eugene O'Harte of Achonry and Redmund O'Gallagher of Derry were interested primarily in fostering the spiritual mission of Tridentine reform. Other religious activists such as Archbishop Edmund Magauran of Armagh were convinced of the need for military force to bring about the restoration of Catholicism. Magauran galvanised the northern chieftains into action, and it was on his initiative that Archbishop James O'Hely of Tuam was dispatched to the Spanish court in 1593 to seek assistance for a Catholic crusade. Associated with this embassy were Hugh Roe O'Donnell, Brian Óg O'Rourke and Hugh Maguire, who asserted that they were taking up arms 'for the defence of the Catholic faith'. It was not until the entry of Hugh O'Neill into the war in 1595 that Spanish strategists began seriously to think of intervention in Ireland.[27]

Inurement in the Spanish Catholic environment was the basis of the ideology which sustained the militant confederacy in late 1590s. The bridge between the Catholic activism of the 1570s and that of the 1590s was the formation of a community of Irish people in exile on the continent. While the numbers involved at the earlier date were small—made up of some scholars, priests and miscellaneous migrants—they were swollen from the 1580s by the exodus of students to the Catholic colleges, religious refugees and especially soldiers and their families to the armies of the Spanish king. After 1586, for instance, several hundred Irish troops were conveyed to the Netherlands by Sir William Stanley to fight for the Dutch rebels, but they defected to the Spaniards with him at Deventer in 1587. Thereafter thousands of migrant swordsmen arrived for service in the army of Flanders, some of them permanent emigrés and some transient. Drawn from high and low ranks in society, most left Ireland for socio-economic reasons, driven by privations in the wake of the Desmond war and other broils. Of Old English and Gaelic background, they provided officers and rank-and-file in an Irish regiment which formed one of the 'nations' in the Spanish army of Flanders. There were also close ties with the seminaries where Irish students were enrolled, and priests from the colleges served as chaplains to their fellow-countrymen, raising their consciousness of the religious debates of the time. Accordingly, the soldiers were drawn into the wider world of the Counter-Reformation in which leading Irish refugees and diplomats joined with exiles from England, Wales and Scotland in attempting to influence the course of Spanish and papal policy towards their homelands. The thrust of the Irish cause at the courts in Madrid, Brussels and Rome was military action to support the campaign of Hugh O'Neill as his success culminated in 1598, and the Irish regiment was seen as having a vital role to play.[28]

At the height of the diplomatic gambit of transferring the kingdom of Ireland to Spanish rule with papal benediction the defining of a separate Catholic identity for the island was given added urgency. When Hugh O'Neill's cause was transmuted into a politico-religious one in the later 1590s, he sought retrospective justification in confessional terms for his revolt. His chief propagandist was Peter Lombard, an Old English priest from Waterford, who in a briefing document for the Vatican in 1599 presented Hugh O'Neill as the champion of Catholicism in succession to the doomed James FitzMaurice, upholding the institutions of an ancient Irish church which had been traduced by the Tudor monarchs. This unified perspective on an Irish Catholic nation had been prefigured fifteen years earlier in *De rebus in Hibernia gestis*, a work by Richard Stanihurst, also an Old English priest. The ethnic gulf had been bridged by Stanihurst when he had lauded the Gaelic Irish as being well-intentioned in their zest for religious reform. Another strand was the research by Stanihurst and others into the lives of the early Irish saints, especially St Patrick. In attempting to underscore the antiquity of Irish Christian traditions, the Catholic apologists contended with their Protestant counterparts such as James Ussher, who was also interested in the saint as exemplar for his creed. In direct line from the early Irish saints were the contemporary heroes and heroines who died for their faith under the Elizabethan regime and whose biographies were written up by Catholic martyrologists. Despite the coolness of the pope towards the depiction of Hugh O'Neill's campaign as a Catholic crusade, the elements of an ideology of Irish Catholic nationalism which emerged in the seventeenth century were being put into place.[29]

Abbreviations

Anal. Hib.	*Analecta Hibernica*
Archiv. Hib.	*Archivium Hibernicum*
Cal. S.P. Ire.	*Calendar of the state papers relating to Ireland*
Dublin Hist. Rec.	*Dublin Historical Record*
Eng. Hist. Rev.	*English Historical Review*
Hist. Jn.	*Historical Journal*
I.E.R.	*Irish Ecclesiastical Record*
I.H.S.	*Irish Historical Studies*
Jn. Ecc. Hist.	*Journal of Ecclesiastical History*
N.H.I.	*New History of Ireland*
N.L.I.	National Library of Ireland
R.I.A.	Royal Irish Academy
R.I.A.Proc.	*Proceedings of the Royal Irish Academy*
R.S.A.I. Jn.	*Journal of the Royal Society of Antiquaries of Ireland*
S.P. Hen. VIII	*State papers, Henry VIII*
Studia Hib.	*Studia Hibernica*
T.C.D.	Trinity College, Dublin

References

Introduction (pp 1–18)
1. Michael Haren and Yolande de Pontfarcy (ed.), *The medieval pilgrimage to St Patrick's Purgatory* (Enniskillen, 1988); for humanist writers see Denys Hay, *Annalists and historians: western historiography from the eighth to the eighteenth century* (London, 1977), chs 5–6; for Polydore Vergil on Ireland see his *Anglica Historia*, ed. Denys Hay (London, 1955), pp 78–80; Nicholas Canny, *The Elizabethan conquest of Ireland: a pattern established, 1565–76* (Hassocks, 1976), p. 62; Brendan Bradshaw, *The Irish constitutional revolution of the sixteenth century* (Cambridge, 1979), pp 32–57.
2. Robert Dunlop, 'Sixteenth-century maps of Ireland' in *Eng. Hist. Rev.*, xx (1905), pp 309–37; T. J. Westropp, 'Early Italian maps of Ireland from 1300 to 1600' in *R.I.A. Proc.*, xiii sect. C (1913), pp 361–402; Colm Lennon, *Richard Stanihurst the Dubliner (1547–1618) with his 'History of Ireland'* (Dublin, 1981), p. 141; J. H. Andrews, *Plantation acres: an historical study of the Irish land surveyor and his maps* (Belfast, 1985), pp 28–51.
3. Abraham Ortelius, *Theatrum orbis terrarum* (Antwerp, 1570); Gerardus Mercator (ed.), *Atlas, sive cosmographicae meditationes* (Dusseldorf, 1595); Michael Richter, *Medieval Ireland: the enduring tradition* (Dublin, 1988), pp 121–3; for the Irish emigré community in Flanders see Gráinne Henry, *The Irish military community in Spanish Flanders* (Dublin, 1992).
4. A. P. Smyth, *Celtic Leinster* (Dublin, 1982), pp 4–5, 109–16.
5. Eileen McCracken, *The Irish woods since Tudor times* (Newton Abbot, 1971), pp 15–37; Smyth, *Celtic Leinster*, p. 86; J. H. Andrews, 'A geographer's view of Irish history' in T.W. Moody and F. X. Martin (ed.), *The course of Irish history* (Cork, 1967), p. 18.
6. Smyth, *Celtic Leinster*, pp 71–2.
7. D. B. Quinn, 'The bills and statutes of the Irish parliaments of Henry VII and Henry VIII' in *Anal. Hib.*, x (1941), p. 156.
8. Richard Bagwell, *Ireland under the Tudors* (3 vols, London, 1885–90), i, 201; Smyth, *Celtic Leinster*, pp 109, 114 ; H. G. Tempest, 'The Moyry pass' in *Louth Arch. Soc. Jn.*, xiv (1958), pp 82–90; for information on Irish bridges see *Dublin Builder*, i–viii (1859–66) and *Irish Builder*, ix–xxxiv (1867–92).
9. Timothy O'Neill, *Merchants and mariners in medieval Ireland* (Dublin, 1987), pp 107–29; Colm Lennon, *The lords of Dublin in the age of reformation* (Dublin, 1989), p. 72.
10. *Cal. S.P. Ire., 1573–85*, p. 343; ibid., *1588–92*, pp 184, 232, 250, 259, 280; Michael MacCarthy-Morrogh, 'The English presence in early

seventeenth-century Munster' in Ciaran Brady and Raymond Gillespie (ed.), *Natives and newcomers: essays on the making of Irish colonial society* (Dublin, 1986), pp 173–5; Bagwell, *Tudors*, iii, 435–6; *Cal. S.P. Ire., 1509–73*, p. 290; Ciaran Brady, 'The framework of government' in Brady and Gillespie (ed.), *Natives and newcomers*, p. 35.

11. J. R. Hale, *Renaissance Europe* (London, 1971), pp 11–46; Barnaby Rich, *A new description of Ireland* (London, 1610), pp 63–4.

12. Kenneth Nicholls, 'Gaelic society and economy in the high middle ages' in *N.H.I.*, ii, 408–10; T. H. Hollingsworth, *Historical demography* (Cambridge, 1976), pp 268–70; Henry Kamen, *European society, 1500–1700* (London, 1984), pp 25–31; Thomas Flynn, *The Irish Dominicans, 1536–1641* (Dublin, 1993), p. 63; Ciaran Brady, 'Political women and reform in Tudor Ireland' in Margaret MacCurtain and Mary O'Dowd (ed.), *Women in early modern Ireland* (Dublin, 1991), p. 69; Lennon, *Lords of Dublin*, p. 66.

13. R. E. Glasscock, 'Land and people, *c.* 1300' in *N.H.I.*, ii, 205–7; F. E. Dixon, 'The weather in old Dublin' in *Dublin Hist. Rec.*, xiii (1953), pp 94–107; xv (1959), pp 65–73; H. H. Lamb, *Climate, past, present and future*, ii: *Climatic history and the future* (London, 1977), pp 8, 460–3; Colm Lennon, 'The great explosion in Dublin in 1597' in *Dublin Hist. Rec.*, xlii (1988), pp 12–13.

14. See, e.g., 'Chronicle of Dublin', *s.a.* (T.C.D., MS 543); Richard Berleth, *The twilight lords* (London, 1978), p. 119; Lennon, 'Great explosion', p. 14; idem, *Richard Stanihurst the Dubliner*, pp 153–6.

15. Katharine Simms, 'Warfare in the medieval Gaelic lordships' in *Irish Sword*, xii (1975–6), pp 98–108; G. A. Hayes-McCoy, *Irish battles: a military history of Ireland* (Belfast, 1989), pp 48ff; Siobhán de hÓir, 'Guns in medieval and Tudor Ireland' in *Irish Sword*, xv (1982–3), pp 76–88; see also Chapter 2 below.

16. F. H. Aalen, *Man and the landscape in Ireland* (London, 1978), pp 109–34; Anngret Simms, 'Core and periphery in medieval Europe: the Irish experience in a wider context' in W. J. Smyth and Kevin Whelan (ed.), *Common ground: essays on the historical geography of Ireland presented to T. Jones Hughes* (Cork, 1988), pp 22–40; Andrews, 'A geographer's view of Irish history'.

17. S. G. Ellis, *Tudor Ireland: crown, community and the conflict of cultures, 1470–1603* (London, 1985), pp 12–17, 33–5; idem, *Reform and revival: English government in Ireland, 1470–1534* (London, 1986); N. P. Canny, *From Reformation to Restoration* (Dublin, 1987), pp 1–14; idem, *Elizabethan conquest*, pp 4–6, 8, 10–23; see also D. B. Quinn and K. W. Nicholls, 'Ireland in 1534' in *N.H.I.*, iii, 1–20.

18. Brendan Bradshaw, *The Irish constitutional revolution of the sixteenth century* (Cambridge, 1979), pp 3–13; Robin Frame, *English lordship in Ireland, 1318–61* (Oxford, 1982), pp 331–5; Ellis, *Reform and revival*, pp 1–11.

19. Frame, *English lordship*, p. 335; Canny, *Reformation to Restoration*, pp 1–6; Ellis, *Reform and revival*, pp 1–11; C. A. Empey, 'The Butler lordship' in *Journal of the Butler Society*, i (1970–71), pp 174–87.

20. Ellis, *Reform and revival*, pp 12–31; idem, *Tudor Ireland*, pp 151–3.
21. Ellis, *Reform and revival*, pp 31–48; idem, *Tudor Ireland*, pp 155–6.
22. Steven Ellis, 'Henry VII and Ireland, 1491–6' in J. F. Lydon (ed.), *Anglo-Irish relations in the later middle ages* (Dublin, 1981), pp 242–9; idem, *Reform and revival*, pp 143–54; idem, 'Parliament and community in Yorkist and Tudor Ireland' in Art Cosgrove and James McGuire (ed.), *Parliament and community: Historical Studies, XIV* (Belfast, 1983), pp 43–68; R. D. Edwards and T. W. Moody, 'The history of Poynings' law, pt I: 1494–1615' in *I.H.S.*, ii (1940–41), pp 415–24.
23. Ellis, *Reform and revival*, pp 67–105; idem, *Tudor Ireland*, p. 154.
24. Ellis, *Reform and revival*, pp 49–66; idem, *Tudor Ireland*, pp 57–9.
25. Ellis, *Reform and revival*, pp 106–32; idem, *Tudor Ireland*, pp 158–61.
26. Ellis, *Reform and revival*, pp 193–200; D. B. Quinn, 'Anglo-Irish local government, 1485–1534' in *I.H.S.*, i (1938–9), pp 354–81.
27. Ellis, *Reform and revival*, pp 183–9; Quinn, 'Anglo-Irish local government'.

Chapter 1: Town and County in the English Part of Ireland, *c.* 1500 (pp 20–40)

1. B. J. Graham, 'The towns of medieval Ireland' in R. A. Butlin (ed.), *The development of the Irish town* (London, 1977), pp 52–5; John Bradley, 'The medieval towns of County Tipperary' in William Nolan (ed.), *Tipperary: history and society* (Dublin, 1985), pp 34–59; W. G. Neely, *Kilkenny: an urban history, 1391–1843* (Belfast, 1989), pp 1–14; Lauro Martines, *Power and imagination: city-states in Renaissance Italy* (London, 1983), pp 94–5.
2. Anthony Sheehan, 'Irish towns in a period of change, 1558–1625' in Brady and Gillespie (ed.), *Natives and newcomers*, pp 93–119; S. G. Ellis, 'Economic problems of the church: why the Reformation failed in Ireland' in *Jn. Ecc. Hist.*, xli (1990), p. 262; Brendan Bradshaw, 'The Reformation in the cities: Cork, Limerick and Galway, 1534–1603', in John Bradley (ed.), *Settlement and society in medieval Ireland: studies presented to F. X. Martin, O.S.A.* (Kilkenny, 1989), p. 468; Lennon, *Lords of Dublin*.
3. Gearóid Mac Niocaill, *Na buirgéisí, xii–xv aois* (2 vols, Dublin, 1984); Geoffrey Martin, 'Plantation boroughs in medieval Ireland, with a handlist of boroughs to c. 1500' in David Harkness and Mary O'Dowd (ed.), *The town in Ireland: Historical Studies, XIII* (Belfast, 1981), pp 23–32; *Holinshed's Irish chronicle*, ed. Liam Miller and Eileen Power, (Dublin, 1979), pp 39–62; Kenneth Nicholls, 'Gaelic society and economy in the high middle ages' in *N.H.I.*, ii, 409–10; Sheehan, 'Irish towns', pp 94–7; cf. H. B. Clarke, review of T. B. Barry, *The archaeology of medieval Ireland* (London, 1988), in *I.H.S.*, xxvi (1989), p. 409.
4. Cf. Bradley, 'Towns of Tipperary', pp 34–5; cf. R. B. Dobson, 'Urban decline in late medieval England' in *Trans. Royal Hist. Soc.*, 5th ser., xxvii (1977), pp 1–22; D. B. Quinn, 'The re-emergence of English policy as a major factor in Irish affairs, 1520–34' in *N.H.I.*, ii, 665; John D'Alton, *The history of Drogheda and its environs* (2 vols, Dublin,

1844), i, 159, 170, 172; John D'Alton and J. R. Flanagan, *The history of Dundalk and its environs*, (Dublin, 1864), pp 81–6; John Bradley, 'The medieval towns of County Meath' in *Ríocht na Midhe*, ix (1988–9), pp 36, 40; William Burke, *History of Clonmel* (Waterford, 1907), pp 29–30; Terence O'Rorke, *The history of Sligo, town and county* (2 vols, Dublin, 1889), i, 79; Gearóid Mac Niocaill, 'Registrum cantariae S. Salvatoris Waterfordensis' in *Anal. Hib.*, xxiii (1966), pp 174–5; Bradshaw, 'Reformation in the cities', pp 448–50.

5. For the development of boroughs see Mac Niocaill, *Na buirgéisí*, ii, 325–37; Bradley, 'Towns of Meath', p. 42; idem, 'Towns of Tipperary', pp 45–8, 52–4; Graham, 'Towns of medieval Ireland'; P. Fitzgerald and J. J. McGregor, *The history, topography and antiquities of the county and city of Limerick* (2 vols, Dublin, 1826–7), ii, 398; Gearóid Mac Niocaill, 'Medieval Galway: its origins and charters' in Diarmuid Ó Cearbhaill (ed.), *Galway: town and gown, 1484–1984* (Dublin, 1984), pp 1–4.

6. See, e.g., Fitzgerald and McGregor, *History of Limerick*, p. 398; William O'Sullivan, *The economic history of Cork from the earliest time to the Act of Union* (Cork, 1937), pp 16–22, 43, 47, 50; D'Alton, *History of Drogheda*, 171–2; J. J. Webb, *Municipal government in Ireland, medieval and modern* (Dublin, 1918), passim; Mac Niocaill, *Na buirgéisí*.

7. Lennon, *Lords of Dublin*, ch. 2; D'Alton, *History of Drogheda*, i, 137; Mac Niocaill, *Na buirgéisí*, ii, 343.

8. Mac Niocaill, *Na buirgéisí*, ii, 338–65; Lennon, *Lords of Dublin*, ch. 2.

9. Lennon, *Lords of Dublin*, ch. 3; Julian Walton, 'The merchant community of Waterford in the sixteenth and seventeenth centuries' in Philippe Butel and L. M. Cullen (ed.), *Cities and merchants: Irish and French perspectives on urban development* (Dublin, 1986), pp 183–92; Mac Niocaill, 'Medieval Galway', pp 5–9; D'Alton, *History of Drogheda*, i, 247–8; Fitzgerald and McGregor, *History of Limerick*, pp 395ff; Neely, *Kilkenny*, pp 28–9; Walton, 'Merchant community of Waterford', p. 185; Mary O'Dowd, *Power, politics and land: early modern Sligo, 1568–1688* (Belfast, 1991), pp 58–9, 144–54; Quinn and Nicholls, 'Ireland in 1534', p. 5.

10. Timothy O'Neill, *Merchants and mariners in medieval Ireland* (Dublin, 1987); *Blake family records, first series: 1300–1599*, ed. M. J. Blake (London, 1902); Lennon, *Richard Stanihurst*, pp 15–16; Neely, *Kilkenny*, pp 57–9; R. H. Rylands, *The history, topography and antiquities of the county and city of Waterford* (London, 1824), p. 136; Mac Niocaill, 'Medieval Galway', p. 8; cf. Lennon, *Lords of Dublin*, ch. 1.

11. Lennon, *Lords of Dublin*, ch. 3; Nuala Burke, 'The making of medieval Dublin' in *Dublin Arts Festival booklet* (Dublin, 1976), pp 17–21.

12. Gearóid Mac Niocaill, 'Socio-economic problems of Irish towns' in David Harkness and Mary O'Dowd, *The town in Ireland: Historical Studies, XIII* (Belfast, 1981), pp 15–18; idem, *Na buirgéisí*, ii, ch. 3.

13 Cf. Bradley, 'Towns of Tipperary'; idem, 'Towns of Meath'; Myles Ronan, 'Lazar-houses of St Laurence and St Stephen in medieval Dublin' in John Ryan (ed.), *Essays and studies presented to Professor Eoin Mac*

Néill (Dublin, 1940); Mac Niocaill, 'Registrum cantariae S. Salvatoris'; Brendan Bradshaw, *The dissolution of the monasteries in the reign of Henry VIII* (Cambridge, 1974), pp 85–6, 121–5; Timothy Corcoran, *State papers in Irish education* (Dublin, 1916); Helga Hammerstein, 'Aspects of the continental migration of Irish students in the reign of Elizabeth I' in *Historical Studies, VIII* (Dublin, 1971), pp 137–53.

14. Myles Ronan, 'Religious customs of Dublin medieval guilds' in *I.E.R.*, 5th ser., xxvi (1925), pp 225–41, 364–85 ; cf. Mervyn James, 'Ritual, drama and social body in the late medieval towns' in *Past and Present*, no. 98 (1983), pp 3–29; P. J. Corish, *The Irish Catholic experience* (Dublin, 1985), p. 54; Lennon, *Lords of Dublin*, pp 128.

15. Mac Niocaill, *Na buirgéisí*, ii, 375–7; J. J. Webb, *The guilds of Dublin* (Dublin, 1929), pp 18–19, 24–8, 31–2, 33–4, 37–8; Henry Berry, 'The records of the Dublin guild of merchants, known as the Guild of Holy Trinity, 1438–1671' in *R.S.A.I.Jn.*, 5th ser., x (1900), pp 44–68.

16. M. D. O'Sullivan, *Italian merchant bankers in Ireland in the thirteenth century* (Dublin, 1962); O'Neill, *Merchants and mariners*, pp 45, 58–9, 77, 78, 85, 101; S. G. Ellis, 'Irish customs administration under the early Tudors' in *I.H.S.*, xii (1980–81), pp 271–7; cf. O'Sullivan, *Economic history of Cork*, pp 61–4.

17. Lennon, *Lords of Dublin*, p. 53; W. A. Childs and Timothy O'Neill, 'Overseas trade' in *N.H.I.*, ii, 498–503; Neely, *Kilkenny*, p. 55.

18. For the social ascendancy of the Dublin patriciate see Lennon, *Lords of Dublin*, ch. 3; for Waterford see Walton, 'Merchant community of Waterford', pp 183–92; for Drogheda see W. Ball Wright (ed.), *Ball family memoirs*, passim; James Lydon, 'The city of Waterford in the late middle ages' in *Decies*, xii (1979), pp 5–15.

19. Childs and O'Neill, 'Overseas trade', pp 501–3; Kevin Down, 'Colonial society and economy in the high middle ages' in *N.H.I.*, ii, 467–9, 473– 81.

20. Down, 'Colonial society and economy', pp 446–50, 461, 470; Canny, *Elizabethan conquest*, pp 12–13; idem, 'Hugh O'Neill and the changing face of Gaelic Ulster' in *Studia Hib.*, x (1971), pp 7–35; C. A. Empey, 'The Norman period' in Nolan (ed.), *Tipperary*, pp 76–84.

21. Down, 'Colonial society and economy', pp 455–9; James Mills, 'Tenants and agriculture near Dublin in the fourteenth century' in *R.S.A.I.Jn.*, xxi (1890–91), pp 54–63; A. J. Otway-Ruthven, 'The organisation of Anglo-Irish agriculture in the middle ages' in *R.S.A.I.Jn.*, lxxxi (1951), pp 1–13.

22. Colmcille Ó Conbhuí, 'The lands of St Mary's abbey, Dublin' in *R.I.A. Proc.*, lxii, sect. C (1961–2), pp 21–84; Otway-Ruthven, 'Anglo-Irish agriculture'; C. A. Empey and Katharine Simms, 'The ordinances of the White Earl and the problem of coign in the later middle ages' in *R.I.A.Proc.*, lxxv, sect. C (1975), pp 178–87; H. F. Hore (ed.), 'The rental book of Gerald, ninth Earl of Kildare, begun in the year 1518' in *Jn. Kildare Arch. Soc.*, v (1858–9), pp 301–9; Down, 'Colonial society and economy', pp 464–7.

23. Mac Niocaill, *Na buirgéisí*, ii, 1–11; Victor Treadwell, 'The Irish customs administration in the sixteenth century' in *I.H.S.*, xx (1977), pp 384–92;

idem, 'The Irish parliament of 1569–71' in *R.I.A. Proc.*, lxv, sect. C (1966–7), p. 79; Lennon, *Lords of Dublin*, pp 35–9; Brendan Bradshaw, 'The opposition to the ecclesiastical legislation in the Irish Reformation parliament' in *I.H.S.*, xvi (1969), pp 285–303.

24. H. F. Hore and James Graves, *The social state of the southern and eastern counties of Ireland in the sixteenth century* (Dublin, 1870), pp 31, 33–4, 36, 44, 50, 58–60; O'Neill, *Merchants and mariners*, pp 119–29; W. P. Burke, *History of Clonmel* (Waterford, 1907), pp 25–9.

25. Hore and Graves, *Southern and eastern counties*, pp 33–4; Ellis, *Reform and revival*, pp 53–4; Empey and Simms, 'Ordinances of the White Earl'.

26. Canny, *Elizabethan conquest*, pp 4–6; O'Sullivan, *Old Galway*, pp 53, 59, 60–1, 108; A. S. Green, *The making of Ireland and its undoing* (London, 1908), pp 168–87; Lydon, 'City of Waterford', pp 5–15.

27. Treadwell, 'Irish parliament of 1569–71'; Canny, *Elizabethan conquest*, p. 9; Lydon, 'City of Waterford'; *Blake family records*, ed. Blake.

28. A. K. Longfield, *Anglo-Irish trade in the sixteenth century* (London, 1929), chs 1–2; Childs and O'Neill, 'Overseas trade', pp 492–500.

29. Longfield, *Anglo-Irish trade*, pp 41–76; O'Neill, *Merchants and mariners*, pp 20–83; Childs and O'Neill, 'Overseas trade', pp 500–9.

Chapter 2: Society and Culture in Gaelic Ireland (pp 42–64)

1. 'St Patrick's Purgatory: Francesco Chiericati's letter to Isabella d'Este' in *Seanchas Ardmhaca*, xii (1986–7), pp 1–10; for later accounts of Gaelic Ireland in the sixteenth century see D. B. Quinn, *The Elizabethans and the Irish* (Ithaca, N.Y., 1966); for an analysis of the impact of these accounts see, e.g., Ciaran Brady, 'Sixteenth-century Ulster and the failure of Tudor reform' in Ciaran Brady, Mary O'Dowd and Brian Walker (ed.), *Ulster: an illustrated history* (London, 1989), pp 80–1.

2. The great monument is Kenneth Nicholls's work in the Gill History of Ireland series: *Gaelic and gaelicised Ireland in the later middle ages* (Dublin, 1972), and he has also made several other significant contributions including *Land, law and society in sixteenth-century Ireland* (N.U.I. O'Donnell lecture, 1976) and 'Gaelic society and economy in the high middle ages' in *N.H.I.*, ii, 397–438; also Katharine Simms, *From kings to warlords: the changing political structure of Gaelic Ireland in the late middle ages* (Suffolk, 1987); Mary O'Dowd, 'Gaelic economy and society' in Brady and Gillespie (ed.), *Natives and newcomers*, pp 120–47; Michelle O'Riordan, *The Gaelic mind and the collapse of the Gaelic world* (Cork, 1991).

3. D. B. Quinn and K. W. Nicholls, 'Ireland in 1534' in *N.H.I.*, iii, 1–20; Nicholls, 'Gaelic society and economy' in *N.H.I.*, ii, 408–10.

4. Spenser's views are cited in Quinn, *Elizabethans and Irish*, pp 53–4; Nicholls, *Gaelic and gaelicised Ireland*, pp 114–19; Hiram Morgan, 'The colonial venture of Sir Thomas Smith in Ulster, 1571–5' in *Hist. Jn.*, xxviii (1985), pp 268, 272; O'Dowd, 'Gaelic economy and society', p. 130.

5. Nicholls, *Gaelic and gaelicised Ireland*, pp 114–16; idem, 'Gaelic society and economy', pp 410–12; Canny, *Elizabethan conquest*, pp 13–14; idem, 'Hugh O'Neill and the changing face of Gaelic Ulster' in *Studia Hib.*, x

(1970), pp 27–8; Katharine Simms, 'Guesting and feasting in Gaelic Ireland' in *R.S.A.I. Jn.*, cviii (1978), p. 79.

6. K. W. Nicholls (ed.), *The O'Doyne manuscript: documents relating to the family of O'Doyne (Ó Duinn) from Archbishop Marsh's Library, Dublin, MS Z 4.2.19: with appendices* (Dublin, 1983); idem, *Gaelic and gaelicised Ireland*, pp 68–71, 116; Canny, *Elizabethan conquest*, pp 10–14; Bernadette Cunningham, 'The Composition of Connacht in the lordships of Clanricard and Thomond, 1577–1641' in *I.H.S.*, xxiv (1984), p. 6.

7. O'Dowd, 'Gaelic economy and society', pp 127–8; Quinn, *Elizabethans and Irish*, pp 70–1.

8. Nicholls, *Gaelic and gaelicised Ireland*, pp 119–22; idem, 'Gaelic society and economy', pp 417–21; Canny, *Elizabethan Ireland*, p. 6; O'Dowd, *Power, politics and land*, pp 76, 86–7, 150, 151; Hiram Morgan, 'The end of Gaelic Ulster: a thematic interpretation of events between 1534 and 1610' in *I.H.S.*, xxvi (1988), pp 21–2; O'Neill, *Merchants and mariners in Ireland*, pp 80, 82–3.

9. Nicholls, *Gaelic and gaelicised Ireland*, pp 57–65; O'Dowd, 'Gaelic economy and society', pp 126–7; idem, 'Land inheritance in early modern Sligo' in *Irish Economic and Social History Journal*, x (1983), pp 5–18; idem, *Power, politics and land*, pp 69–73.

10. Kenneth Nicholls, *Land, law and society in sixteenth-century Ireland* (Dublin, 1976), pp 6–7; idem, 'Gaelic society and economy', pp 430–2; O'Dowd, 'Gaelic economy and society', pp 125–6; idem, *Power, politics and land*, pp 66–9.

11. Nicholls, *Land, law and society*, pp 13–18; idem, *Gaelic and gaelicised Ireland*, pp 65–7; O'Dowd, 'Gaelic society and economy', pp 128–9.

12. Simms, *From kings to warlords*, pp 39–40, 59; Nicholls, *Gaelic and gaelicised Ireland*, pp 21–5, 69–70; idem, *Land, law and society*, pp 15–20; O'Dowd, 'Gaelic economy and society', pp 121–4.

13. Nicholls, *Gaelic and gaelicised Ireland*, pp 10–12, 22–30; Simms, *From kings to warlords*, pp 27–40, 53–9.

14. Nicholls, *Gaelic and gaelicised Ireland*, pp 24–5, 41–3; Simms, *From kings to warlords*, pp 96–115.

15. Simms, *From kings to warlords*, pp 96–115; for the role of the Kildares see Chapter 3, below; O'Dowd, *Power, politics and land*, pp 15–23.

16. Simms, *From kings to warlords*, pp 83–4, 92–6; Nicholls, *Gaelic and gaelicised Ireland*, pp 40–1.

17. Simms, *From kings to warlords*, pp 39–49, 86–7, 131–2, 135–6; Nicholls, *Gaelic and gaelicised Ireland*, pp 31–7; Ciaran Brady, 'The decline of the Irish kingdom' in Mark Greengrass (ed.), *Conquest and coalescence: the shaping of the state in early modern Europe*, (London, 1991), pp 97–8; C. A. Empey and Katharine Simms, 'The ordinances of the White Earl and the problem of coign and livery in the late middle ages' in *R.I.A. Proc.*, lxxv, sect. C (1975), pp 178–87.

18. Simms, *From kings to warlords*, pp 134–6, 139, 141, 146; Nicholls, *Gaelic and gaelicised Ireland*, pp 35–7.

19. Simms, *From kings to warlords*, pp 124–8; *Elizabethans and Irish*, pp 97–8; Lennon, *Richard Stanihurst the Dubliner*, pp 151–3.

20. Katharine Simms, 'Warfare in the medieval Irish lordships' in *Irish Sword*, xii (1975–6), pp 104–7; idem, *From kings to warlords*, pp 94, 120–8; G. A. Hayes-McCoy, *Scots mercenary forces in Ireland, 1565–1603* (Dublin, 1937), pp 33, 36–7.

21. Simms, 'Warfare in the medieval Gaelic lordships', pp 98–108; Siobhán de hÓir, 'Guns in medieval and Tudor Ireland' in *Irish Sword*, xv (1982–3), pp 76–88.

22. Simms, *From kings to warlords*, pp 79, 88–91, 94–5, 142–3; Nicholls, *Gaelic and gaelicised Ireland*, pp 44–57.

23. Simms, *From kings to warlords*, pp 88–92; Nicholls, *Gaelic and gaelicised Ireland*, pp 47–50; Nerys Patterson, 'Gaelic law and the Tudor conquest of Ireland: the social background of the sixteenth-century recensions of the pseudo-historical Prologue to the *Senchus már*' in *I.H.S.*, xxvii (1991), pp 193–215.

24. Kenneth Nicholls, 'Irishwomen and property in the sixteenth century' in Margaret MacCurtain and Mary O'Dowd (ed.), *Women in early modern Ireland* (Dublin, 1991), pp 17–31.

25. Ibid., p. 22; idem, *Gaelic and gaelicised Ireland*, pp 73–7; Katharine Simms, 'The legal position of Irish women in the later middle ages' in *Irish Jurist*, n.s., x (1975), pp 99–101; Art Cosgrove, 'Marriage in medieval Ireland' in idem (ed.), *Marriage in Ireland* (Dublin, 1985), pp 25–34; Margaret MacCurtain, 'Marriage in Tudor Ireland', ibid., pp 51–66.

26. Nicholls, 'Irishwomen and property', pp 18–19; Katharine Simms, 'Women in Gaelic society' in MacCurtain and O'Dowd (ed.), *Women in early modern Ireland*, pp 36–7, 38–9; Ciaran Brady, 'Political women and reform in Tudor Ireland', ibid., pp 76–7; Lennon, *Richard Stanihurst the Dubliner*, p. 150.

27. Nicholls, *Gaelic and gaelicised Ireland*, pp 77–9; Richard Stanihurst, 'A plain and perfect description of Ireland' in *Holinshed's Irish chronicle*, ed. Liam Miller and Eileen Power (Dublin, 1979), p. 113.

28. Nicholls, *Gaelic and gaelicised Ireland*, pp 79–84; J. A. Watt, *The church in medieval Ireland* (Dublin, 1972), pp 193–5; O'Riordan, *The Gaelic mind and the collapse of the Gaelic world*, pp 1–20.

29. Simms, *From kings to warlords*, pp 5–9; Ellis, *Tudor Ireland*, pp 46–7; O'Riordan, *The Gaelic mind and the collapse of the Gaelic world*, pp 62–118.

Chapter 3: The Kildares and their Critics (pp 65–86)

1. For a full account of the battle see G. A. Hayes-McCoy, *Irish battles: a military history of Ireland* (Belfast, 1989), pp 48–67; for the background see Ellis, *Tudor Ireland*, pp 84–9; D. B. Quinn, 'The hegemony of the Earls of Kildare, 1496–1520' in Cosgrove (ed.), *N.H.I.*, ii, pp 638–52.

2. Hayes-McCoy, *Irish battles*, pp 59–67; Ellis, *Tudor Ireland*, p. 94; cf. R. D. W. Edwards and Mary O'Dowd, *The sources for early modern Irish history, 1534–1641* (Cambridge, 1985), pp 85–7.

3. Ciaran Brady, 'Court, castle and country: the framework of government' in Brady and Gillespie (ed.), *Natives and newcomers*, p. 29; Hayes-

McCoy, *Irish battles*, pp 48–50, 55–8, 60; Quinn, 'Hegemony of the Earls of Kildare', p. 652; Quinn and Nicholls, 'Ireland in 1534', pp 5–20; Nicholls, *Gaelic and gaelicised Ireland*, pp 148–9.

4. Quinn, 'Hegemony of the Earls of Kildare', p. 653; Ellis, *Tudor Ireland*, pp 94–8; Laurence McCorristine, *The revolt of Silken Thomas: a challenge to Henry VIII* (Dublin, 1987), pp 21–57.

5. Richard Stanihurst, 'History of Henry VIII's reign' in Miller and Power (ed.), *Holinshed's Irish chronicle*, p. 253; S. G. Ellis, 'Henry VII and Ireland, 1491–6', pp 247–54; Quinn, 'Hegemony of the Earls of Kildare', pp 645–8.

6. Donough Bryan, *The Great Earl of Kildare, 1456–1513* (Dublin, 1933), pp 91–5, 195–7; Quinn, 'Hegemony of the Earls of Kildare', pp 646, 651; Ellis, *Tudor Ireland*, p. 99.

7. Stanihurst, 'Henry VIII's reign', pp 252–3; Bryan, *The Great Earl of Kildare*, pp 31, 83–4.

8. Stanihurst, 'Henry VIII's reign', p. 251–2; Bryan, *The Great Earl of Kildare*, pp 250, 251; Ellis, *Tudor Ireland*, pp 98–9; John Guy, *Tudor England* (London, 1988), pp 76–7.

9. Ellis, *Reform and revival*, pp 57–62; idem, *Tudor Ireland*, pp 65–6; MacCorristine, *Silken Thomas*, pp 8–9.

10. Ellis, *Tudor Ireland*, p. 103; Bryan, *The Great Earl of Kildare*, pp 8–9, 270–4; MacCorristine, *Silken Thomas*, pp 21–3.

11. Ellis, *Reform and revival*, pp 52–5; Bryan, *The Great Earl of Kildare*, p. 144 ; H. F. Hore (ed.), 'The rental book of Gerald Fitzgerald, ninth Earl of Kildare, begun in the year 1518' in *Jn. Kildare Arch. Soc.*, v (1858–9), pp 266–80, 301–10; vii (1862–3), pp 110–37; viii (1864–6), pp 501–18, 525–46.

12. Bryan, *The Great Earl of Kildare*, pp 91–5.

13. Hore (ed.), 'Rental book of Gerald Fitzgerald'.

14. Simms, *From kings to warlords*, pp 16–19; see also p. 11 above.

15. Quinn, 'Hegemony of the Earls of Kildare', p. 646; Ellis, *Tudor Ireland*, pp 85–6; McCorristine, *Silken Thomas*, p. 29.

16. Ellis, *Tudor Ireland*, pp 94–8; Bryan, *The Great Earl of Kildare*, pp 260–1; Simms, *From kings to warlords*, p. 19.

17. Ellis, *Tudor Ireland*, p. 99; Quinn, 'Hegemony of the Earls of Kildare', pp 653–4; Bryan, *The Great Earl of Kildare*, pp 253–65.

18. Ellis, *Tudor Ireland*, pp 100–2; Quinn, 'Henry VIII and Ireland', pp 318–24.

19. Garret Óg emerges as a hero of the narrative in Stanihurst, 'Henry VIII's reign'; Ellis, *Tudor Ireland*, p. 101.

20. For the background to and substance of the case of the Old English reformers see Brendan Bradshaw, *The Irish constitutional revolution of the sixteenth century* (Cambridge, 1979), pp 32–57; see also Ellis, *Tudor Ireland*, pp 102–3.

21. Bradshaw, *Irish constitutional revolution*, pp 4–8, 17–20, 32–44; cf. Bryan, *The Great Earl of Kildare*, pp 18–22.

22. Bradshaw, *Irish constitutional revolution*, p. 24; Ellis, *Reform and revival*, passim.

23. Bradshaw, *Irish constitutional revolution*, pp 49–57; James McConica, *Humanism at the court of Henry VII* (Oxford, 1965).
24. Ellis, *Tudor Ireland*, p. 103.
25. Stanihurst, 'Henry VIII's reign'; Bryan, *The Great Earl of Kildare*, pp 252–3; Edwards and O'Dowd, *Sources for early modern Irish history*, pp 88–91.
26. Bryan, *The Great Earl of Kildare*, pp 268–70; Quinn, 'Hegemony of the Earls of Kildare'; Stanihurst, 'Henry VIII's reign', p. 293.
27. MacCorristine, *Silken Thomas*, p. 153; Ellis, *Tudor Ireland*, p. 71; idem, 'Kildare ascendancy'; cf. Mary Ann Lyons, 'Church and society in early sixteenth-century Kildare, 1500–40' (unpublished M.A. thesis, St Patrick's College, Maynooth, 1991); Stanihurst, 'Henry VIII's reign', p. 293.
28. Quinn, 'Henry VIII and Ireland', p. 322; Ellis, *Tudor Ireland*, pp 103–4.
29. Quinn, 'Henry VIII and Ireland', pp 322–3; Stanihurst, 'Henry VIII's reign', p. 255.

Chapter 4: Kildare Power and Tudor Intervention, 1520–35 (pp 87–112)
1. Quinn, 'Henry VIII and Ireland', p. 326; Ellis, *Tudor Ireland*, pp 108–10.
2. Bradshaw, *Irish constitutional revolution*, pp 58–61, for the background to the Surrey expedition; cf. John Guy, *Tudor England* (Oxford, 1988), pp 106–7.
3. D. B. Quinn, 'The re-emergence of English policy as a major factor in Irish affairs, 1520–34' in *N.H.I.*, ii, 665–6; idem, 'Henry VIII and Ireland', pp 326–76; Ellis, *Tudor Ireland*, pp 108–9; Bradshaw, *Irish constitutional revolution*, pp 72–6.
4. See *S.P. Hen. VIII*, ii, 51–7; Bradshaw, *Irish constitutional revolution*, pp 62–5; Quinn, 'Henry VIII and Ireland', pp 325–7; idem, 'English policy, 1520–34', pp 663–4; Ellis, *Tudor Ireland*, pp 111–13.
5. Bradshaw, *Irish constitutional revolution*, pp 64–6; Ellis, *Tudor Ireland*, pp 114–15; Art Cosgrove, *Late medieval Ireland, 1370–1541* (Dublin, 1981), pp 110–11; Quinn, 'Henry VIII and Ireland', pp 666–7.
6. Ellis, *Tudor Ireland*, pp 110–11, 113–14; Quinn, 'English policy, 1520–34', pp 665–6.
7. Bradshaw, *Irish constitutional revolution*, pp 79–83; Ellis, *Tudor Ireland*, pp 114–15; cf. J. J. Scarisbrick, *Henry VIII* (London, 1968), pp 174–82; Guy, *Tudor England*, pp 107–9; Quinn, 'English policy, 1520–34', p. 668.
8. Cosgrove, *Late medieval Ireland*, pp 111–12; Ellis, *Tudor Ireland*, p. 115; Quinn, 'Henry VIII and Ireland', pp 328–9.
9. Quinn, 'Henry VIII and Ireland', pp 330–1; idem, 'English policy, 1520–34', p. 669; Ellis, *Tudor Ireland*, pp 155–16; C. A. Empey, 'The Butler lordship' in *Journal of the Butler Society*, i (1970–71), pp 184–6.
10. Quinn, 'Henry VIII and Ireland', pp 331–2; idem, 'English policy, 1520–34', pp 669–71; Stanihurst, 'Henry VIII's reign', pp 254–5.
11. Quinn, 'English policy, 1520–34', pp 671–2; idem, 'Henry VIII and Ireland', p. 332; Ellis, *Tudor Ireland*, p. 116.
12. Quinn, 'English policy, 1520–34', p. 672.
13. Ibid., pp 672–3; Ellis, *Tudor Ireland*, pp 117–18; Stanihurst, 'Henry VIII's reign', p. 255.

14. Ellis, *Tudor Ireland*, p. 118; Quinn, 'English policy, 1520–34', pp 674–5.
15. Stanihurst, 'Henry VIII's reign', pp 256–9; Quinn, 'English policy, 1520–34', pp 673–4.
16. Cf. McCorristine, *Silken Thomas*, pp 37–41.
17. 'Chronicle of Dublin', *s.a.* (T.C.D., MS 543); cf. H. F. Hore and James Graves (ed.), *The social state of the southern and eastern counties of Ireland in the sixteenth century* (Dublin, 1870), passim; Quinn, 'English policy, 1520–34', pp 674–5; McCorristine, *Silken Thomas*, pp 38–42.
18. Quinn, 'Henry VIII and Ireland', pp 334–6; idem, 'English policy, 1520–34', pp 675–6; Steven Ellis, 'Tudor policy and the Kildare ascendancy, 1496–1534' in *I.H.S.*, xx (1977) p. 243; idem, *Tudor Ireland*, pp 118–19.
19. Quinn, 'Henry VIII and Ireland', pp 335–8; idem, 'English policy, 1520–34', pp 677–9; Ellis, 'Tudor policy and the Kildare ascendancy', pp 243–4.
20. Stanihurst, 'Henry VIII's reign', p. 260; Quinn, 'Henry VIII and Ireland', pp 338–9; idem, 'English policy, 1520–34', pp 679–80; Ellis, *Tudor Ireland*, p. 119.
21. Stanihurst, 'Henry VIII's reign', p. 277; Quinn, 'Henry VIII and Ireland', pp 338–9; idem, 'English policy, 1520–34', pp 679–81; Ellis, *Tudor Ireland*, pp 119–20.
22. Stanihurst, 'Henry VIII's reign', pp 260–1; Quinn, 'English policy, 1520–34' pp 681–2; Ellis, *Tudor Ireland*, pp 121–2; McCorristine, *Silken Thomas*, pp 40–5; Brendan Bradshaw, 'Cromwellian reform and the origins of the Kildare rebellion, 1533–4' in *Transactions of the Royal Historical Society*, xxvii (1976), pp 69–79.
23. Quinn, 'English policy, 1520–34', pp 682–4; Ellis, *Tudor Ireland*, pp 120–3; Bradshaw, 'Cromwellian reform', pp 69–79; McCorristine, *Silken Thomas*, pp 45–53.
24. Quinn, 'English policy, 1520–34', pp 685–6; Ellis, *Tudor Ireland*, pp 123–4; Bradshaw, 'Cromwellian reform', pp 69–93; cf. idem, *Irish constitutional revolution*, pp 90–104; McCorristine, *Silken Thomas*, pp 51–5.
25. Quinn, 'English policy, 1520–34', pp 685–6; Ellis, *Tudor Ireland*, pp 123–4; Bradshaw, 'Cromwellian reform', pp 69–93; McCorristine, *Silken Thomas*, pp 62–5.
26. McCorristine, *Silken Thomas*, pp 59–74; S. G. Ellis, 'The Kildare rebellion and the early Henrician Reformation' in *Hist. Jn.*, xix (1976), pp 809–16; Bradshaw, 'Cromwellian reform', pp 69–93; cf. Stanihurst, 'Henry VIII's reign', pp 262–6.
27. McCorristine, *Silken Thomas*, pp 67–78; Ellis, 'Kildare rebellion', pp 812–16; Bradshaw, 'Cromwellian reform', pp 69–93.
28. McCorristine, *Silken Thomas*, pp 68, 86, 90–1; Ellis, 'Kildare rebellion'.
29. Stanihurst, 'Henry VIII's reign', pp 271–6; McCorristine, *Silken Thomas*, pp 86–90, 96–7.
30. McCorristine, *Silken Thomas*, pp 97–109; Ellis, *Tudor Ireland*, pp 127–8.
31. Stanihurst, 'Henry VIII's reign' pp 277–83; McCorristine, *Silken Thomas*, pp 109–19; Ellis, *Tudor Ireland*, p. 128.
32. S. G. Ellis, 'Henry VIII, rebellion and the rule of law' in *Hist. Jn.*, xxiv (1981), pp 527–9; idem, *Tudor Ireland*, p. 129; McCorristine, *Silken Thomas*, pp 121–30.

33. Ellis, *Tudor Ireland*, pp 129–31; Bradshaw, *Irish constitutional revolution*, pp 106–17; McCorristine, *Silken Thomas*, pp 131–52.

Chapter 5: Religion and Reformation, 1500–40 (pp 113–143)
1. See R. D. W. Edwards, *Church and state in Tudor Ireland* (Dublin, 1935), pp 49ff.
2. See Brendan Bradshaw, 'George Browne, first Reformation Archbishop of Dublin, 1536–1554' in *Jn. Ecc. Hist.*, xxi (1970), pp 301–26; idem, 'Sword, word and strategy in the Reformation in Ireland' in *Hist. Jn.*, xxi (1978), pp 475–502.
3. For a recent overview see Euan Cameron, *The European Reformation* (Oxford, 1991); for the Irish reform movement see Chapter 2 above.
4. For an example of contemporary criticism see Edmund Spenser, *A view of the present state of Ireland*, ed. W. L. Renwick (Oxford, 1970), and for bad impressions abroad of Irish clergy in the sixteenth century see Lennon, *Richard Stanihurst the Dubliner*, pp 141–4.
5. Canice Mooney, *The church in Gaelic Ireland, thirteenth to fifteenth centuries* in P. J. Corish (ed.), *A history of Irish Catholicism*, ii, 5 (Dublin, 1969); J. A. Watt, *The church in medieval Ireland* (Dublin, 1972), p. 184; Ellis, *Tudor Ireland*, pp 184–5; Katherine Walsh, 'Clerical estate' in John Bradley (ed.), *Settlement and society in medieval Ireland: studies presented to F. X. Martin, O.S.A.* (Kilkenny, 1988), pp 364–71; Art Cosgrove, 'The medieval period' in Réamonn Ó Muirí (ed.), *Irish church history today* (Armagh, 1991), pp 13–26; Brendan Bradshaw, *The dissolution of the religious orders in Ireland under Henry VIII* (Cambridge, 1974), pp 41–2; Benigus Millett, 'Dioceses in Ireland up to the fifteenth century' in *Seanchas Ardmhacha*, xii (1986), pp 15–22; J. A. Watt, 'The church and the two nations in late medieval Armagh' in W. J. Sheils and Diana Wood (ed.), *The churches, Ireland, and the Irish*, Studies in Church History, XXV (Oxford, 1989), pp 37–54.
6. Aubrey Gwynn, *The medieval province of Armagh, 1470–1545* (Dundalk, 1946); J. A. Watt, *The church in medieval Ireland* (Dublin, 1972), pp 106–7, 123–7; idem, 'The church in late medieval Armagh', pp 37–54; Anthony Lynch, 'The church in late medieval Ireland' in *Archiv. Hib.*, xxx (1981); Mary Ann Lyons, 'Church and society in early sixteenth-century Kildare, 1500–40' (unpublished M.A. thesis, St Patrick's College, Maynooth, 1991).
7. James Murray, 'Archbishop Alen, Tudor reform and the Kildare rebellion' in *R.I.A. Proc.*, lxxxix, sect. C (1989), pp 1–16.
8. Ibid.
9. Ibid; J. F. Ferguson, *Remarks on . . . actions bill* (1843) (R.I.A., Haliday pamphlets, 1860/4); Helga Hammerstein, 'Aspects of the continental education of Irish students in the reign of Elizabeth I' in *Historical Studies, VIII* (Dublin, 1971), pp 137–53; S. G. Ellis, 'Economic problems of the church: why the Reformation failed in Ireland' in *Jn. Ecc. Hist.*, xli (1990), pp 247–57; H. F. Berry (ed.), *Register of the wills and inventories of the diocese of Dublin, 1457–83;* Margaret Murphy, 'The high cost of dying: an analysis of *pro anima* bequests in medieval

Dublin' in Sheils and Wood (ed.), *The churches, Ireland and the Irish*, pp 119–22.

10. Berry (ed.), *Register of wills*, p. 9; Bradshaw, *Dissolution of religious orders*; F. X. Martin, 'The Irish friars and the Observant movement of the fifteenth century' in *Proceedings of the Irish Catholic Historical Committee* (Dublin, 1960), pp 10–16; Thomas Flynn, *The Irish Dominicans, 1536–1641* (Dublin, 1993), pp 7–8.

11. Bradshaw, *Dissolution of religious orders*, p. 112.

12. Ibid., pp 8–38; C. A. Empey, 'The sacred and the secular: the Augustinian priory of Kells in Ossory, 1193–1541' in *I.H.S.*, xxix (1984), pp 131–51.

13. Murray, 'Archbishop Alen', pp 12–16; Bradshaw, *Dissolution of religious orders*, pp 82–92.

14. H. G. Leask, *Irish churches and monastic buildings*, iii: *Medieval Gothic, the last phases* (Dundalk, 1960), pp 11–40; L. P. Murray, 'The ancient chantries of County Louth' in *Louth Arch. Soc. Jn.*, ix (1939), pp 181–208; Brendan Bradshaw, 'The Reformation in the cities: Cork, Limerick and Galway, 1534–1603' in Bradley (ed.), *Settlement and society*, pp 448–52; Colm Lennon, 'The chantries in the Irish Reformation: the case of St Anne's Guild, Dublin, 1550–1630' in R. V. Comerford, Mary Cullen, J. R. Hill and Colm Lennon (ed.), *Religion, conflict and coexistence in Ireland: essays presented to Monsignor Patrick J. Corish* (Dublin, 1990), pp 7–11.

15. Murray, 'Chantries of County Louth'; Lennon, 'Chantries in the Irish Reformation', pp 10–11.

16. M. V. Ronan, 'Religious customs of Dublin medieval guilds' in *I.E.R.*, 5th ser., xxvi (1981), pp 225–41, 364–85.

17. Watt, *Church in medieval Ireland*, pp 130–50; Walsh, 'Clerical estate'; Ellis, *Tudor Ireland*, pp 186, 191.

18. Mooney, *Church in Gaelic Ireland*, pp 24–6, 31–2, 59–60; Nicholls, *Gaelic and gaelicised Ireland*, pp 100–1; P. J. Corish, *The Irish Catholic experience* (Dublin, 1985), p. 56.

19. Mooney, *Church in Gaelic Ireland*, pp 59–60; John Watt, 'Gaelic polity and cultural identity' in *N.H.I.*, ii, 334–45; Nicholls, *Gaelic and gaelicised Ireland*, pp 96–7.

20. Mooney, *Church in Gaelic Ireland*, pp 10–20; Nicholls, *Gaelic and gaelicised Ireland*, pp 111–13.

21. Mooney, *Church in Gaelic Ireland*, pp 14–17; K. W. Nicholls, 'Rectory, vicarage and parish in the western Irish dioceses' in *R.S.A.I. Jn.*, ci (1971), pp 53–84.

22. Mooney, *Church in Gaelic Ireland*, pp 54–5; Nicholls, *Gaelic and gaelicised Ireland*, pp 102–5.

23. Kevin Down, 'Colonial society and economy in the high middle ages' in *N.H.I.*, ii, 486; Mooney, *Church in Gaelic Ireland*, p. 17; Nicholls, *Gaelic and gaelicised Ireland*, pp 94–5, 108, 109.

24. Bradshaw, *Dissolution of religious orders*, ch. 1; Martin, 'The Irish friars and the Observant movement', pp 10–16; Flynn, *Irish Dominicans*, pp 68–93.

25. Mooney, *Church in Gaelic Ireland*, pp 22–3, 29–30, 40–1.

26. Watt, *Church in medieval Ireland*, pp 209–14; Mooney, *Church in Gaelic Ireland*, pp 32–45; Gearóid Mac Niocaill, 'Religious literature and practice in late medieval Ireland' (R. I. Best lecture, N.L.I., 17 June 1979).

27. Corish, *Irish Catholic experience*, pp 58–62; Mac Niocaill, 'Religious literature and practice'; John Bossy, *Christianity in the west, 1400–1700* (Oxford, 1985), p. 59; Mooney, *Church in Gaelic Ireland*, pp 28, 32–9, 46–7.

28. Lennon, *Richard Stanihurst the Dubliner*, pp 156–7; Ellis, *Tudor Ireland*, pp 187–8; Gwynn, *Medieval province of Armagh*, p. 203.

29. Lennon, *Richard Stanihurst the Dubliner*, p. 157; Ellis, *Tudor Ireland*, pp 186, 191; Murray, 'Archbishop Alen', pp 1–16.

30. Steven Ellis, 'The Kildare rebellion and the early Henrician Reformation' in *Hist. Jn.*, xix (1976), pp 809–11; R. D. W. Edwards, 'The Irish Reformation parliament of Henry VIII, 1536–7' in *Historical Studies*, VI (London, 1968), pp 59–84.

31. Brendan Bradshaw, 'The opposition to the ecclesiastical legislation in the Irish Reformation parliament' in *I.H.S.*, xvi (1968–9), pp 285–303.

32. Ibid.

33. Edwards, *Church and state*, pp 47ff; Bradshaw, 'Sword, word and strategy in the Reformation'; idem, 'George Browne', pp 305–13.

34. Bradshaw, 'George Browne'; idem, *Dissolution of religious orders*, pp 98–109; Ronan, *Reformation in Dublin*, pp 81–128.

35. Bradshaw, 'George Browne', pp 301–13; Edwards, *Church and state*, pp 47ff; Ronan, *Reformation in Dublin*, pp 98–104, 202–10.

36. Ronan, *Reformation in Dublin*, pp 129–239; Bradshaw, 'George Browne'; idem, *Dissolution of religious orders*, pp 101–2.

37. Bradshaw, 'Opposition to ecclesiastical legislation', pp 285–303; idem, *Dissolution of religious orders*, pp 66–7.

38. Bradshaw, *Dissolution of religious orders*, pp 110ff.

39. Ibid., pp 112–22.

40. Ibid., pp 137–59, 181–205.

Chapter 6: Political and Religious Reform and Reaction, 1536–56 (pp 144–175)

1. Bagwell, *Ireland under the Tudors*, i, 258–60; Bradshaw, *Irish consitutional revolution*, pp 263–5; Ellis, *Tudor Ireland*, p. 139.

2. The fullest discussion of the options for reform is in Bradshaw, *Irish constitutional revolution*, chs 5 and 6; for the career of St Leger in Ireland see Ciaran Brady, 'The government of Ireland, c. 1540–83' (unpublished Ph.D. thesis, Trinity College, Dublin, 1980), pp 71–111.

3. Steven Ellis, 'Henry VIII, rebellion and the rule of law' in *Hist. Jn.*, xxiv (1981), pp 517–27; Bradshaw, *Irish constitutional revolution*, p. 177.

4. Ellis, 'Henry VIII, rebellion and the rule of law', pp 517–27; idem, 'Thomas Cromwell and Ireland, 1532–40' in *Hist. Jn.*, xxiii (1980), pp 497–519; Bradshaw, *Irish constitutional revolution*, pp 98–106.

5. Bradshaw, *Irish constitutional revolution*, pp 147–54, 167–9; idem, 'The opposition to the ecclesiastical legislation', pp 285–303; Edwards, 'Irish Reformation parliament of Henry VIII, 1536–7', pp 59–84.

6. Bradshaw, 'The opposition to the ecclesiastical legislation'; idem, *Dissolution of religious orders*, pp 51–65; Edwards, 'Irish Reformation parliament of Henry VIII, 1536–7', pp 66–80.
7. Bagwell, *Tudors*, i, 199–204, 206–8, 210–14, 222–32, 235–8; Ciaran Brady, 'The decline of the Irish kingdom' in Mark Greengrass (ed.), *Conquest and coalescence: the shaping of the state in early modern Europe* (London, 1991), p. 104; Ellis, *Tudor Ireland*, pp 131–6.
8. Bradshaw, *Irish constitutional revolution*, pp 122–3, 176–7, 193; Ellis, *Tudor Ireland*, p. 136.
9. Bagwell, *Tudors*, i, 238–41; Bradshaw, *Irish constitutional revolution*, pp 174–80; Ellis, *Tudor Ireland*, p. 136.
10. Bradshaw, *Irish constitutional revolution*, pp 194, 210; cf. Stanihurst, 'Henry VIII's reign', p. 298; Ellis, *Tudor Ireland*, pp 135–6.
11. Bradshaw, *Irish constitutional revolution*, p. 193–6; Brady, 'Government of Ireland', pp 71–2.
12. Bradshaw, *Irish constitutional revolution*, pp 202, 222–3; Bagwell, *Tudors*, i, 249–52.
13. Bradshaw, *Irish constitutional revolution*, pp 200–12; Brady, 'Government of Ireland', pp 80–5.
14. Bradshaw, *Irish constitutional revolution*, pp 231–8; Robert Dunlop, 'Some aspects of Henry VIII's Irish policy' in T. F. Tout and James Tait (ed.), *Historical essays* (London, 1902), pp 282–305.
15. Bradshaw, *Irish constitutional revolution*, pp 222–3; P. L. O'Toole, *History of the Clan O'Toole and other Leinster septs* (Dublin, 1890), pp 258–63.
16. Donal Moore, *English action, Irish reaction: the MacMurrough Kavanaghs, 1530–1630* (Maynooth, 1987).
17. Bradshaw, *Irish constitutional revolution*, pp 210–11; Bagwell, *Tudors*, i, 255–6.
18. Bradshaw, *Irish constitutional revolution*, p. 219; Bagwell, *Tudors*, i, 256–7.
19. Bradshaw, *Irish constitutional revolution*, pp 220–1; Bagwell, *Tudors*, i, 262–3.
20. Bradshaw, *Irish constitutional revolution*, pp 208–10, 217–19; Bagwell, *Tudors*, i, 263, 264, 268–70.
21. Ellis, *Tudor Ireland*, pp 143–4; D. G. White, 'Henry VIII's Irish kerne in France and Scotland, 1544–5' in *Irish Sword*, iii (1957–8), pp 213–25.
22. Bradshaw, *Irish constituional revolution*, pp 245–51; Edwards, *Church and state*, pp 117–18.
23. Bradshaw, *Dissolution of religous orders*, pp 181–205; Brady, 'Government of Ireland', pp 87–96.
24. Bradshaw, *Dissolution of religious orders*, pp 181–205, 231–47; Brady, 'Government of Ireland', pp 92–3; Ellis, *Tudor Ireland*, p. 144; Lennon, *Lords of Dublin*, pp 36–9; cf. Stanihurst, 'Henry VIII's reign', p. 310.
25. Bradshaw, *Irish constitutional revolution*, pp 240, 255–7; *Cal. Ormond deeds, 1509–1547*, pp 252–5; Bagwell, *Tudors*, i, 282–7.
26. Bradshaw, *Dissolution of religious orders*, pp 162–80; Ellis, *Tudor Ireland*, pp 145–6; Brady, 'Government of Ireland', pp 71–8.
27. Brady, 'Government of Ireland', pp 99–102; Nicholas Canny, *From Reformation to Restoration: Ireland, 1534–1660* (Dublin, 1987), pp

49–58; D. G. White, 'The reign of Edward VI in Ireland: some political, social and economic aspects' in *I.H.S.*, xiv (1964–5), pp 198–211.

28. White, 'The reign of Edward VI', pp 198–205; Bagwell, *Tudors*, i, 326–9; Canny, *From Reformation to Restoration*, pp 49–50.

29. Brendan Bradshaw, 'The Edwardian Reformation in Ireland' in *Archiv. Hib.*, xxxiv (1976–7), pp 83–93.

30. Bradshaw, 'The Edwardian Reformation', pp 85–93; Lennon, 'The chantries in the Irish Reformation', pp 6–7, 11–13.

31. White, 'The reign of Edward VI', pp 204–6; Brady, 'Government of Ireland', p. 102.

32. Bradshaw, 'The Edwardian Reformation', pp 87–93; idem, 'The Reformation in the cities'.

33. White, 'The reign of Edward VI', pp 204–7; Bagwell, *Tudors*, i, 359–61, 378–9.

34. D. B. Quinn, 'Edward Walshe's "Conjectures" concerning the state of Ireland [1552]' in *I.H.S.*, v (1946–7), pp 309–22; Ellis, *Tudor Ireland*, p. 232.

35. Bradshaw, 'The Edwardian Reformation', pp 92–3; S. G. Ellis, 'John Bale, Bishop of Ossory, 1552–3' in *Journal of the Butler Society*, ii (1984), pp 283–93.

36. Bagwell, *Tudors*, i, 374–7.

37. Michael Dolley, 'The Irish coinage, 1534–1691' in *N.H.I.*, iii, 408–12; Bagwell, *Tudors*, i, 370–2.

38. *Cal. S.P. Ire., 1509–73*, pp 90, 92, 99, 100; Ciaran Brady, 'Conservative subversives: the community of the Pale and the Dublin administration, 1556–86' in P. J. Corish (ed.), *Radicals, rebels and establishments: Historical Studies, XV* (Belfast, 1985), pp 17–18; Lennon, *Lords of Dublin*, p. 102, 104, 116.

39. Ellis, *Tudor Ireland*, p. 233; Bagwell, *Tudors*, i, 384–6, 395–6; Ciaran Brady, 'Thomas, tenth Earl of Ormond' in idem (ed.), *Worsted in the game: losers in Irish history* (Dublin, 1989), p. 51.

40. Brady, 'Government of Ireland', pp 104–7; Canny, *From Reformation to Restoration*, pp 56–8.

41. Brady, 'Government of Ireland', pp 107–10.

42. Ibid., pp 110–11.

Chapter 7: The Pale and Greater Leinster, 1556–88 (pp 177–207)

1. Richard Berleth, *The twilight lords* (London, 1978), pp 157–61; Elizabeth O'Connor, 'The rebellion of James Eustace, Viscount Baltinglass, 1580–81' (unpublished M.A. thesis, St Patrick's College, Maynooth, 1989), pp 117–20.

2. A. P. Smyth, *Celtic Leinster* (Dublin, 1982), p. 109.

3. Brady, 'Government of Ireland', pp 112–17; idem, 'Court, castle and country: the framework of government in Tudor Ireland' in Brady and Gillespie (ed.), *Natives and newcomers*, pp 44–9; idem, 'The decline of the Irish kingdom' in Greengrass (ed.), *Conquest and coalescence*, pp 94–115; Canny, *From Reformation to Restoration*, pp 58–60, 70–1, 91–6, 109–11.

4. Brady, 'Government of Ireland', pp 117–30; Canny, *From Reformation to Restoration*, pp 58–9; Ellis, *Tudor Ireland*, pp 232–8.
5. Bagwell, *Ireland under the Tudors*, i, 399–402; Brady, 'Government of Ireland', pp 145–8; Vincent Carey, 'Gaelic reaction to plantation: the case of the O'More and O'Connor lordships of Laois and Offaly, 1570–1603' (unpublished M.A. thesis, St Patrick's College, Maynooth, 1985); Canny, *From Reformation to Restoration*, pp 59–62.
6. Brady, 'Conservative subversives', pp 18–19; idem, 'Government of Ireland', pp 136–8; Bradshaw, *Irish constitutional revolution*, pp 269–75; Canny, *From Reformation to Restoration*, pp 64–9.
7. Brady, 'Government of Ireland', pp 163–76; Canny, *From Reformation to Restoration*, pp 67–9, 71–3.
8. Canny, *Elizabethan conquest*, pp 45–57; idem, *From Reformation to Restoration*, pp 71–7; Brady, 'Government of Ireland', pp 178–83.
9. Canny, *Elizabethan conquest*, pp 139–41; idem, *From Reformation to Restoration*, pp 85–6; Victor Treadwell, 'The Irish parliament of 1569–71' in *R.I.A. Proc.*, lxv, sect. C (1966), pp 55–89.
10. Canny, *Elizabethan conquest*, p. 68; idem, *From Reformation to Restoration*, pp 86–8; Bagwell, *Tudors*, ii, 156–9, 160–3; for a fresh interpretation of the revolt of Sir Edmund Butler see David Edwards, 'The Butler revolt of 1569' in *I.H.S.*, xxviii (1993), pp 228–55.
11. Ellis, *Tudor Ireland*, pp 264–8; Canny, *Elizabethan conquest*, p. 91; idem, *From Reformation to Restoration*, pp 89–91.
12. Canny, *Elizabethan conquest*, p. 112; idem, *From Reformation to Restoration*, pp 91–2; Brady, 'Government of Ireland', pp 209–22.
13. Brady, 'Government of Ireland', pp 223–7; idem, 'Conservative subversives', pp 20–4; Canny, *From Reformation to Restoration*, pp 94–6.
14. Brady, 'Conservative subversives', pp 24–5; Nicholas Canny, *The formation of an Old English elite in Ireland* (Dublin, 1975), pp 20–5.
15. Canny, *Formation of an Old English elite*, pp 23–5; Bradshaw, *Irish constitutional revolution*, pp 276–8; Ellis, *Tudor Ireland*, pp 246–8; Brady, 'Conservative subversives', pp 24–5, 29–30.
16. Canny, *Formation of an Old English elite*, pp 11–31.
17. Ibid., pp 6–9; Canny, *Elizabethan conquest*, pp 4–5, 11–12, 26–7.
18. Canny, *Formation of an Old English elite*, pp 9–12; Brady, 'Government of Ireland', pp 223–4; Lennon, *Richard Stanihurst the Dubliner*, pp 79–84; idem, *Lords of Dublin*, pp 111–14.
19. Treadwell, 'Parliament of 1569–71', pp 55–89; Anthony Sheehan, 'Irish towns in a period of change' in Brady and Gillespie (ed.), *Natives and newcomers*, pp 111–12, 115; Lennon, *Lords of Dublin*, pp 97–101.
20. Lennon, *Lords of Dublin*, pp 69–70, 77–80; Canny, *Formation of Old English elite*, pp 19–20.
21. See Brian Fitzgerald, *The Geraldines: an experiment in Irish government* (London, 1951); Brady, 'Thomas, tenth Earl of Ormond', p. 56: Lennon, *Lords of Dublin*, pp 29, 34; Colm Lennon, 'Richard Stanihurst (1547–1618) and Old English identity' in *I.H.S.*, xxi (1978–9), pp 121–43; Canny, *Formation of an Old English elite*, pp 25–9.

22. Colm Lennon, 'Reform ideas and cultural resources in the inner Pale in the mid-sixteenth century' in *Stair*, ii (1979), pp 3–10; Canny, *Formation of an Old English elite*, pp 29–31; Helga Hammerstein, 'Aspects of the continental education of Irish students in the reign of Elizabeth I' in *Historical Studies, VIII* (Dublin, 1971), pp 137–53.

23. Brady, 'Conservative subversives', pp 25–8; Canny, *From Reformation to Restoration*, pp 100–3.

24. Smyth, *Celtic Leinster*, pp 21–3, 71–2; Brady, 'Government of Ireland', pp 78–81.

25. Henry Goff, 'English conquest of an Irish barony: the changing patterns of landownership in the barony of Scarawalsh, 1540–1640' in Kevin Whelan and W. J. Smyth (ed.), *Wexford, history and society* (Dublin, 1987), pp 122–49; Moore, *English action, Irish reaction*, pp 10–19; O'Toole, *History of the Clan O'Toole*, pp 232–93.

26. Carey, 'Gaelic reaction to plantation', ch. 4.

27. Ibid., chs 2–3.

28. Ibid., pp 150–210.

29. Ibid., pp 177ff; Ellis, *Tudor Ireland*, pp 233, 260; Kenneth Nicholls, *The O'Doyne manuscript* (Dublin, 1983), pp ix–x.

30. Moore, *English action, Irish reaction*, pp 10–15; Raymond Gillespie and Gerard Moran (ed.), *Longford: essays in county history* (Dublin, 1991), pp 15–17; Carey, 'Gaelic reaction to plantation'; Nerys Patterson, 'Gaelic law and the Tudor conquest of Ireland: the social background of the sixteenth-century recension of the pseudo-historical Prologue to the *Senchus már*' in *I.H.S.*, xxvii (1991), pp 206–14; Goff, 'English conquest of an Irish barony', pp 127–32.

31. Rolf Loeber, *The geography of English colonisation of Ireland from 1534 to 1609* (Dublin, 1990), pp 23–9; Carey, 'Gaelic reaction to plantation', pp 211–60.

32. Brady, 'Government of Ireland', pp 392–419; Goff, 'English conquest of an Irish barony'.

33. Carey, 'Gaelic reaction to plantation', pp 211–60.

34. Lennon, *Lords of Dublin*, pp 69–70, 72, 135–8.

35. Nicholas Canny, *Kingdom and colony: Ireland in the Atlantic world, 1560–1800* (Baltimore, 1988), pp 3–5; idem, 'Identity formation in Ireland: the emergence of the Anglo-Irish' in Nicholas Canny and Anthony Pagden (ed.), *Colonial identity in the Atlantic world, 1500–1800* (Princeton, 1987), pp 159–65; idem, *From Reformation to Restoration*, pp 96–8.

36. A study of the causes and course of the rebellion has recently been completed by Elizabeth O'Connor: 'The rebellion of James Eustace, Viscount Baltinglass, 1580–81' (unpublished M.A. thesis, St Patrick's College, Maynooth, 1989); see also Brady, 'Conservative subversives', pp 26–8.

37. O'Connor, 'Rebellion of Viscount Baltinglass', pp 106–66; Helen Coburn Walshe, 'The rebellion of William Nugent, 1581' in Comerford, Cullen, Hill and Lennon (ed.), *Religion, conflict and coexistence*, pp 26–52.

38. O'Connor, 'Rebellion of Viscount Baltinglass', pp 167–219; Coburn Walshe, 'Rebellion of William Nugent', pp 38–48; Brady, 'Conservative subversives', pp 26–8.

39. Colm Lennon, 'Richard Stanihurst (1547–1618) and Old English ident-
    ity' in *I.H.S.*, xxi (1978–9), pp 121–43; Canny, *Formation of an Old
    English elite*, pp 25–9.
40. Brady, 'Conservative subversives', pp 28–30; Canny, *From Reform-
    ation to Restoration*, pp 109–10, 112, 119–20.
41. Victor Treadwell, 'Sir John Perrot and the Irish parliament of 1585–6'
    in *R.I.A. Proc.*, lxxxv, sect. C (1985), pp 259–308; Brady, 'Conservative
    subversives', pp 28–30.

Chapter 8: Munster: Presidency and Plantation, 1565–95 (pp 208–236)
 1. Bagwell, *Ireland under the Tudors*, ii, 82–8.
 2. Ibid.; Ciaran Brady, 'Faction and the origins of the Desmond rebellion
    of 1579' in *I.H.S.*, xxii (1981), p. 300; Anne Chambers, *Eleanor, Countess
    of Desmond, c. 1545–1638* (Dublin, 1986), pp 33–44.
 3. Canny, *Elizabethan conquest*, pp 47–50, 57; idem, *From Reformation
    to Restoration*, pp 70–3; Ellis, *Tudor Ireland*, p. 252.
 4. Canny, *Elizabethan conquest*, pp 93–9; idem, *From Reformation to
    Restoration*, pp 73, 74, 75–6; Brady, 'Government of Ireland', pp 176,
    186–7; Michael MacCarthy-Morrogh, *The Munster plantation: English
    migration to southern Ireland, 1583–1641* (Oxford, 1986), pp 20–1.
 5. Canny, *Elizabethan conquest*, p. 99; idem, *From Reformation to Restor-
    ation*, pp 74–5, 76–7; Brady, 'Faction and the origins of the Desmond
    rebellion', pp 301–2.
 6. Canny, *Elizabethan conquest*, pp 66–9, 77–84.
 7. Brady, 'Faction and the origins of the Desmond rebellion', pp 304–5;
    Canny, *Elizabethan conquest*, pp 100–2, 143–5, 147–8.
 8. Bagwell, *Tudors*, ii, 163–9; Canny, *Elizabethan conquest*, pp 101–2,
    121–2.
 9. Bagwell, *Tudors*, ii, 185–9, 209–10, 221–5; Canny, *Elizabethan conquest*,
    pp 102–3; Berleth, *Twilight lords*, pp 60–5.
10. Bagwell, *Tudors*, ii, 233–4; Canny, *Elizabethan conquest*, pp 102–3.
11. Brady, 'Faction and the origins of the Desmond rebellion', pp 294,
    302–3, 305–6.
12. Ibid., pp 307–8; Bagwell, *Tudors*, ii, 247–8, 251–4, 263–8.
13. Brady, 'Faction and the origins of the Demond rebellion', pp 303–4;
    Canny, *Elizabethan government*, pp 144–5; Treadwell, 'Parliament of
    1569–71'.
14. Brady, 'Thomas, tenth Earl of Ormond', pp 49–60; Neely, *Kilkenny*, pp
    76–82.
15. Canny, *Elizabethan conquest*, pp 104–6; idem, *From Reformation to
    Restoration*, pp 91–3; Brady, 'Government of Ireland', pp 211–17.
16. Canny, *Elizabethan conquest*, pp 104–6; idem, *From Reformation to
    Restoration*, pp 92–3.
17. Canny, *Elizabethan conquest*, pp 106–8; idem, *From Reformation to
    Restoration*, p. 93; Brady, 'Faction and the origins of the Desmond
    rebellion', pp 296–7.
18. Brady, 'Faction and the origins of the Desmond rebellion', pp 307–11.
19. Ibid., p. 307; Bagwell, *Tudors*, iii, 1–11.

20. Brady, 'Faction and the origins of Desmond rebellion', pp 309–11; Canny, *From Reformation to Restoration*, pp 99–100; Bagwell, *Tudors*, iii, 12–24.
21. Bagwell, *Tudors*, iii, 25–30; Berleth, *Twilight lords*, pp 97–112.
22. Bagwell, *Tudors*, iii, 29–43.
23. Ibid., pp 51–8, 59–78.
24. Ibid., pp 83–90, 91–2, 93–6; MacCarthy-Morrogh, *Munster plantation*, pp 19–20, 25.
25. Bagwell, *Tudors*, iii, 97–8, 104–5; Ellis, *Tudor Ireland*, pp 283–4; MacCarthy-Morrogh, *Munster plantation*, p. 26.
26. Bagwell, *Tudors*, iii, 111–15.
27. MacCarthy-Morrogh, *Munster plantation*, pp 4–5, 21–30.
28. Ibid., pp 4–16.
29. Ibid., pp 16–18, 38–42.
30. Ibid., pp 30–8.
31. Ibid., pp 46–56.
32. Ibid., pp 18–19, 65, 71, 79–80, 93–4; Anthony Sheehan, 'Official reaction to native land claims in the plantation of Munster' in *I.H.S.*, xxiii (1983), pp 300–1.
33. MacCarthy-Morrogh, *Munster plantation*, pp 71–6, 80–4; Sheehan, 'Official reaction to native land claims', pp 300–1.
34. MacCarthy-Morrogh, *Munster plantation*, pp 67–9, 79–80, 82–3, 97–106; Sheehan, 'Official reaction to native land claims', pp 302–13; Canny, *From Reformation to Restoration*, pp 129–31.
35. MacCarthy-Morrogh, *Munster plantation*, pp 107–30.
36. Ibid., pp 107–8, 130–5; Sheehan, 'Official reaction to native land claims', pp 313–17.

Chapter 9: Connacht: Council and Composition, 1569–95 (pp 237–263)
1. Bagwell, *Ireland under the Tudors*, iii, 172–95; Laurence Flanagan, *Ireland's Armada legacy*, pp 16–24; Francesco de Cuellar, 'Account of his adventures', ed. Bernard MacDonagh (Sligo, n.d.).
2. Bernadette Cunningham, 'Political and social change in the lordships of Clanricard and Thomond, 1569–1641' (unpublished M.A. thesis, University College, Galway, 1979), pp 10–14; idem, 'Natives and new-comers in Mayo, 1560–1603' in Raymond Gillespie and Gerard Moran (ed.), *'A various country': essays in Mayo history* (Westport, 1987), pp 24–9; Bagwell, *Tudors*, ii, 82; Canny, *Elizabethan conquest*, pp 23, 34; idem, *From Reformation to Restoration*, p. 70.
3. Bagwell, *Tudors*, ii, 110, 114; Canny, *Elizabethan conquest*, p. 105.
4. Canny, *Elizabethan conquest*, pp 93–9; idem, *From Reformation to Restoration*, p. 74.
5. Bagwell, *Tudors*, ii, 170; Canny, *Elizabethan conquest*, pp 108–9; Ellis, *Tudor Ireland*, p. 262.
6. Bagwell, *Tudors*, ii, 170–2; Canny, *Elizabethan conquest*, pp 146, 152, 156; Ellis, *Tudor Ireland*, p. 263; Donough O'Brien, *History of the O'Briens* (London, 1949), pp 61–5.
7. Bagwell, *Tudors*, ii, 170, 182, 216–19; Canny, *Elizabethan conquest*, pp 112–14, 146; idem, *From Reformation to Restoration*, pp 89–91.

8. Bagwell, *Tudors*, ii, 182; Cunningham, 'Natives and newcomers in Mayo', pp 30–1, 38; Canny, *Elizabethan conquest*, pp 109–12; Brady, 'Government of Ireland', pp 210–13.

9. Brady, 'Government of Ireland', pp 213–22; Canny, *Elizabethan conquest*, pp 112–13; Bagwell, *Tudors*, ii, 317–18; Ellis, *Tudor Ireland*, pp 268, 270; Anne Chambers, *Granuaile: the life and times of Grace O'Malley, c. 1530–1603* (Dublin, 1983), pp 83–4.

10. Bagwell, *Tudors*, ii, 321–3, 338; Canny, *Elizabethan conquest*, pp 113–14; Ellis, *Tudor Ireland*, pp 271–2.

11. Canny, *Elizabethan conquest*, p. 114; Ellis, *Tudor Ireland*, p. 272; Cunningham, 'Lordships of Clanricard and Thomond', pp 68–9.

12. Anne Chambers, *Chieftain to knight: Tibbot Bourke, 1567–1629, first Viscount Mayo* (Dublin, 1983), pp 43, 49, 50, 51, 57; idem, *Granuaile*, pp 96–102; Cunningham, 'Natives and newcomers in Mayo', pp 32–3.

13. Mary O'Dowd, *Power, politics and land: early modern Sligo, 1568–1688* (Belfast, 1991), pp 27–30.

14. Cunningham, 'Natives and newcomers in Mayo', p. 33; idem, 'Lordships of Clanricard and Thomond', pp 85–8; Canny, *From Reformation to Reformation*, pp 110–12, 113.

15. Bernadette Cunningham, 'The Composition of Connacht in the lordships of Clanricard and Thomond, 1577–1641' in *I.H.S.*, xxix (1984), pp 1–14; Canny, *From Reformation to Restoration*, pp 113–17.

16. Cunningham, 'Composition of Connacht', pp 2–5; Canny, *From Reformation to Restoration*, pp 113–14.

17. Cunningham, 'Composition of Connacht', pp 4–5; Ellis, *Tudor Ireland*, pp 288–9.

18. Cunningham, 'Natives and newcomers in Mayo', pp 37–42; Chambers, *Granuaile*, pp 106–8; idem, *Chieftain to knight*, pp 57, 60; O'Dowd, *Power, politics and lands*, pp 32–4, 66–9.

19. Cunningham, 'Composition of Connacht', p. 6; Canny, *From Reformation to Restoration*, p. 115; Ellis, *Tudor Ireland*, p. 289.

20. Cunningham, 'Composition of Connacht', pp 11–12, 13–14; idem, 'Lordships of Clanricard and Thomond', pp 98–103.

21. Cunningham, 'Composition of Connacht', p. 9; Canny, *From Reformation to Restoration*, p. 116; O'Dowd, *Power, politics and land*, pp 34–40; Cunningham, 'Natives and newcomers in Mayo', pp 36–7; Raymond Gillespie, 'Lords and commons in seventeenth-century Mayo' in Gillespie and Moran (ed.), *'A various country'*, p. 47.

22. Bagwell, *Tudors*, iii, 153–6; Cunningham, 'Natives and newcomers in Mayo', p. 40; Chambers, *Granuaile*, pp 108–12; idem, *Chieftain to knight*, pp 60–8.

23. Bagwell, *Tudors*, iii, 156–61, 166–7; Ellis, *Tudor Ireland*, p. 294.

24. Bagwell, *Tudors*, iii, 204–8; Chambers, *Chieftain to knight*, pp 60–8.

25. O'Dowd, *Power, politics and land*, pp 35–40.

26. Ibid., p. 89; Rolf Loeber, *The geography and practice of English colonisation in Ireland from 1534 to 1609* (Athlone, 1991), pp 34–6; Gillespie, 'Lords and commons in Mayo', pp 47–8.

27. O'Dowd, *Power, politics and land*, pp 35–6, 74–6; Gillespie, 'Lords and commons in Mayo', pp 52–3.
28. O'Dowd, *Power, politics and land*, pp 38, 74–5, 95–8; Loeber, *Geography and practice of English colonisation*, pp 35–6; Cunningham, 'Composition of Connacht', p. 5; Chambers, *Granuaile*, p. 102.
29. O'Dowd, *Power, politics and land*, pp 63–87; Cunningham, 'Lordships of Clanricard and Thomond', pp 108–68; idem, 'Natives and newcomers in Mayo', pp 41–3; Canny, *From Reformation to Restoration*, pp 127–33.
30. O'Dowd, *Power, politics and land*, pp 38–9, 70–3, 115–16; Cunningham, 'Natives and newcomers in Mayo', pp 37–40.
31. Bagwell, *Tudors*, iii, 210, 212, 213, 214, 216, 230; Hiram Morgan, 'Extradition and treason-trial of a Gaelic lord: the case of Brian O'Rourke' in *Irish Jurist*, xxii (1987), pp 285–301; O'Dowd, *Power, politics and land*, p. 40.
32. O'Dowd, *Power, politics and land*, pp 40, 41; Bagwell, *Tudors*, iii, 227–8, 235–6; Hiram Morgan, *Tyrone's rebellion: the outbreak of the Nine Years' War in Tudor Ireland* (Dublin, 1993), pp 144–5, 189.
33. O'Dowd, *Power, politics and land*, pp 40–4, 89–91; Morgan, *Tyrone's rebellion*, pp 189–90; Canny, *From Reformation to Restoration*, pp 131–2.

Chapter 10: Ulster and the General Crisis of the Nine Years' War, 1560–1603 (pp 264–302)
1. Bagwell, *Ireland under the Tudors*, iii, 339–42; Ciaran Brady, 'Sixteenth-century Ulster and the failure of Tudor reform' in Ciaran Brady, Mary O'Dowd and Brian Walker (ed.), *Ulster: an illustrated history* (London, 1989), p. 100.
2. Hiram Morgan, 'The end of Gaelic Ulster: a thematic interpretation of events between 1534 and 1610' in *I.H.S.*, xxvi (1988), p. 32.
3. Brady, 'Sixteenth-century Ulster', pp 81–5.
4. Canny, *From Reformation to Restoration*, p. 62; Ellis, *Tudor Ireland*, pp 230–1, 237, 238–9; Bagwell, *Tudors*, ii, 360–1, 377.
5. Morgan, *Tyrone's rebellion*, pp 19–20, 23; Brady, 'Government of Ireland', p. 75.
6. Brady, 'Sixteenth-century Ulster', pp 88–9, 92; Ellis, *Tudor Ireland*, pp 238–9, 249; Bagwell, *Tudors*, ii, 15–22; Canny, *Elizabethan conquest*, p. 6.
7. Bagwell, *Tudors*, ii, 23–30; Brady, 'Government of Ireland', pp 130–2, 152–5; Canny, *From Reformation to Restoration*, pp 65–6.
8. Brady, 'Government of Ireland', pp 154–5, 157; Canny, *From Reformation to Restoration*, p. 66; Bagwell, *Tudors*, ii, 31–40.
9. Bagwell, *Tudors*, ii, 51–7; Nicholas Canny, 'Hugh O'Neill and the changing face of Gaelic Ulster' in *Studia Hib.*, x (1970), pp 28–30; Nicholls, *Gaelic and gaelicised Ireland*, p. 71; Morgan, 'End of Gaelic Ulster', pp 16–17.
10. Brady, 'Government of Ireland', pp 162–4, 168–70; Bagwell, *Tudors*, ii, 61–3, 64–5, 89–100; Ellis, *Tudor Ireland*, pp 240–1.
11. Canny, *Elizabethan conquest*, pp 50–1, 58; Ellis, *Tudor Ireland*, p. 254; Bagwell, *Tudors*, ii, 89–90, 105-7.

12. Bagwell, *Tudors*, ii, 102–11; Canny, *Elizabethan conquest*, pp 58–9; Ciaran Brady, 'The killing of Shane O'Neill: some new evidence' in *Irish Sword*, xv (1982), pp 116–19.
13. Bagwell, *Tudors*, ii, 115–20; Brady, 'The killing of Shane O'Neill', pp 118–23.
14. Brady, 'Sixteenth-century Ulster', pp 89–90; Morgan, *Tyrone's rebellion*, pp 23, 90–1, 94–6; Canny, 'Hugh O'Neill', pp 20–1.
15. Morgan, 'End of Gaelic Ulster', pp 16–17; idem, *Tyrone's rebellion*, pp 119–20, 124; Canny, 'Hugh O'Neill', pp 13–14.
16. Canny, *Elizabethan conquest*, pp 69–77; Brady, 'Government of Ireland', pp 105–6.
17. Canny, *Elizabethan conquest*, pp 77, 85–8; Hiram Morgan, 'The colonial venture of Sir Thomas Smith, 1571–1575' in *Hist. Jn.*, xxviii (1985), pp 261–78.
18. Morgan, 'Sir Thomas Smith', pp 265–6, 271–4.
19. Ibid., p. 264; Canny, *Elizabethan conquest*, pp 88–9.
20. Canny, *Elizabethan conquest*, pp 89–90; Bagwell, *Tudors*, ii, 284–5, 288–301.
21. Bagwell, *Tudors*, ii, 303–6; Canny, *Elizabethan conquest*, pp 90–1, 118–23.
22. Morgan, 'Sir Thomas Smith', p. 272; Canny, *Elizabethan conquest*, p. 139; idem, *From Reformation to Restoration*, pp 83–4.
23. Morgan, 'Sir Thomas Smith', pp 261, 274–8; Canny, 'Hugh O'Neill', pp 25–9.
24. Canny, *Elizabethan conquest*, pp 7, 8–9; Morgan, 'End of Gaelic Ulster', pp 20, 22–3; idem, *Tyrone's rebellion*, p. 34; Tony Canavan, *Frontier town: an illustrated history of Newry* (Belfast, 1989).
25. Morgan, *Tyrone's rebellion*, p. 24; Bagwell, *Tudors*, ii, 120, 305–6.
26. Morgan, *Tyrone's rebellion*, pp 50, 89, 92–3, 95, 96–7; Canny, 'Hugh O'Neill', p. 23.
27. Canny, 'Hugh O'Neill', pp 21–2, 23–4.
28. Morgan, *Tyrone's rebellion*, pp 34–48.
29. Ibid., pp 38–41, 50–1.
30. Ibid., pp 51–4; Brady, 'Sixteenth-century Ulster', pp 84–5, 95–6.
31. Morgan, *Tyrone's rebellion*, pp 40, 41, 42–3; Ciaran Brady, 'The O'Reillys of east Breifne and the problem of surrender and regrant' in *Breifne*, vi (1985), pp 246–8.
32. Bagwell, *Tudors*, iii, 196–7; Brady, 'Sixteenth-century Ulster', pp 95–7; Morgan, *Tyrone's rebellion*, pp 61–2, 71–2, 130; idem, 'Extradition and treason-trial of a Gaelic lord: the case of Brian O'Rourke' in *Irish Jurist*, xxii (1987), pp 285–301.
33. P. J. Duffy, 'The territorial organisation of Gaelic landownership and its transformation in County Monaghan, 1591–1640' in *Irish Geography*, xiv (1981), pp 1–26; Canny, *From Reformation to Restoration*, pp 117–19; Morgan, *Tyrone's rebellion*, pp 61–71.
34. Morgan, *Tyrone's rebellion*, pp 120–2, 123–33; O'Dowd, *Power, politics and land*, pp 40, 41.
35. Morgan, *Tyrone's rebellion*, pp 142–5, 154–5.

36. Morgan, *Tyrone's rebellion*, pp 74–5, 79, 96–7, 102–3, 155–8; Canny, *From Reformation to Restoration*, pp 139, 140.
37. Morgan, *Tyrone's rebellion*, pp 147–53, 163–6; Brady, 'Sixteenth-century Ulster', pp 98–9; Canny, *From Reformation to Restoration*, pp 139–42.
38. Morgan, *Tyrone's rebellion*, pp 169–72; Ellis, *Tudor Ireland*, p. 300.
39. G. A. Hayes-McCoy, 'The army of Ulster, 1593–1601' in *Irish Sword*, i (1950), pp 105–17; idem, 'Strategy and tactics in Irish warfare, 1593–1601' in *I.H.S.*, ii (1941), pp 255–79; Morgan, *Tyrone's rebellion*, pp 179–83; idem, 'End of Gaelic Ulster', pp 18–20; Ellis, *Tudor Ireland*, p. 304.
40. Brady, 'Sixteenth-century Ulster', pp 99–100; Bagwell, *Tudors*, iii, 275–88; Morgan, *Tyrone's rebellion*, pp 179–84, 189–90; Patrick Logan, 'Pestilence in the Irish wars: the early phase' in *Irish Sword*, vii (1966), pp 280–1.
41. Bagwell, *Tudors*, iii, 274–5; G. A. Hayes-McCoy, 'The completion of the Tudor conquest, and the advance of the Counter-Reformation, 1571–1603' in *N.H.I.*, iii, 123–4; Cyril Falls, *Elizabeth's Irish wars* (London, 1950), pp 230–42.
42. Morgan, *Tyrone's rebellion*, pp 181; Colm Lennon, 'The great explosion in Dublin, 1597' in *Dublin Hist. Rec.*, xlii (1988), pp 7–20.
43. Hayes-McCoy, *Irish battles*, pp 106–31.
44. Bagwell, *Tudors*, iii, 302–10; MacCarthy-Morrogh, *Munster plantation*, pp 130–5.
45. Falls, *Elizabeth's Irish wars*, pp 225–47; Hayes-McCoy, 'Tudor conquest and Counter-Reformation', pp 127–9.
46. Hayes-McCoy, 'Tudor conquest and Counter-Reformation', p. 129; Hiram Morgan, 'Hugh O'Neill and the Nine Years' War in Tudor Ireland' in *Hist. Jn.*, xxxvi (1993), pp 1–17; idem, 'End of Gaelic Ulster', p. 32.
47. Falls, *Elizabeth's Irish wars*, pp 253–91.
48. J. J. Silke, *Kinsale: the Spanish intervention in Ireland at the end of the Elizabethan wars* (Liverpool, 1970), pp 103–52.
49. Falls, *Elizabeth's Irish wars*, pp 319–39.
50. Nicholas Canny, 'The treaty of Mellifont and the reorganisation of Ulster, 1603' in *Irish Sword*, ix (1969–70), pp 249–62; idem, 'Hugh O'Neill', pp 7–12.

Chapter 11: From Reformation to Counter-Reformation, 1560–1600 (pp 303–324)

1. Edwards, *Church and state*, pp 117–18.
2. Henry Fitzsimon, *Words of comfort . . . to persecuted Catholics*, ed. Edmund Hogan (Dublin, 1891), pp 174–5.
3. Bradshaw, *Irish constitutional revolution*, pp 245–51; idem, 'The Edwardian Reformation in Ireland' in *Archiv. Hib.*, xxxiv (1976–7), pp 83–93.
4. Ellis, *Tudor Ireland*, pp 209–10.
5. Bradshaw, 'Edwardian Reformation', p. 96; Helen Coburn Walshe, 'Enforcing the Elizabethan settlement: the vicissitudes of Hugh Brady,

Bishop of Meath, 1563–84' in *I.H.S.*, xxvi (1989), pp 358–9; Colm Lennon, 'The chantries in the Irish Reformation: the case of St Anne's Guild, Dublin, 1550–1630' in Comerford, Cullen, Hill and Lennon (ed.), *Religion, conflict and coexistence*, pp 11–12.

6. H. A. Jefferies, 'The Irish parliament of 1560: the Anglican reforms authorised' in *I.H.S.*, xxvi (1988), pp 128–41.

7. Ibid.; Ellis, *Tudor Ireland*, pp 214-15; Edwards, *Church and state*, pp 187–90.

8. Lennon, *Lords of Dublin*, pp 46, 138–9; Ellis, *Tudor Ireland*, p. 218; Victor Treadwell, 'The Irish parliament of 1569–71' in *R.I.A.Proc.*, lxxxv, sect. C (1985), pp 73ff.

9. Colm Lennon, 'Reform ideas and cultural resources in the inner Pale in the mid-sixteenth century' in *Stair*, ii (1979), pp 3–10; R. D. W. Edwards, 'Ireland, Elizabeth I and the Counter-Reformation' in S. T. Bindoff, Joel Hurstfield and C. H. Williams (ed.), *Elizabethan government and society* (London, 1961), pp 315–39; Alan Ford, 'The Protestant Reformation in Ireland' in Brady and Gillespie (ed.), *Natives and newcomers*, pp 55, 59–62.

10. Aidan Clarke, 'Varieties of uniformity: the first century of the Church of Ireland' in Sheils and Wood (ed), *The churches, Ireland and the Irish*, p. 111; Steven Ellis, 'Economic problems of the church: why the Reformation failed in Ireland' in *Jn. Ecc. Hist.*, xli (1990), pp 253–6; Coburn Walshe, 'Enforcing the Elizabethan settlement', pp 360–3.

11. Clarke, 'Varieties of uniformity', pp 113–14; Ellis, 'Economic problems of the church', pp 245–57; Ford, 'Protestant Reformation', pp 52–3.

12. S. G. Ellis, 'John Bale, Bishop of Ossory, 1552–3' in *Journal of the Butler Society*, ii (1984); Nicholas Canny, 'Why the Reformation failed in Ireland: une question mal posée' in *Jn. Ecc. Hist.*, xxx (1979); Lennon, *Lords of Dublin*, pp 137–8.

13. Edwards, *Church and state*, pp 226–31.

14. Lennon, *Richard Stanihurst the Dubliner*, p. 22; Elizabeth O'Connor, 'The rebellion of James Eustace, Viscount Baltinglass, 1580–81' (unpublished M.A. thesis, St Patrick's College, Maynooth, 1989), pp 35–43; Seán Ó Mathúna, *An tAthair William Bathe, C.I.: ceannrodaí sa teangeolaíocht* (Dublin, 1980), pp 39–41; David McNally, 'Sir John Plunkett of Dunsoghly' (unpublished B.A. thesis, St Patrick's College, Maynooth, 1987).

15. Ford, 'Protestant Reformation', pp 52–3.

16. Ibid.; Ellis, 'Economic problems of the church', pp 255–6; Helen Coburn Walshe, 'Responses to the Protestant Reformation in sixteenth-century Meath' in *Ríocht na Midhe*, vii (1987), pp 97–109; idem, 'Enforcing the Elizabethan settlement', pp 362–3; J. F. Ferguson, *Remarks on . . . actions bill* (1843) (R.I.A., Haliday pamphlets, 1860/4).

17. Lennon, *Lords of Dublin*, pp 134, 138; Donald Jackson, *Intermarriage in Ireland, 1550–1650* (Montreal, 1970); Coburn Walshe, 'Responses to the Protestant Reformation', pp 97–109; Brendan Bradshaw, 'The Reformation in the cities: Cork, Limerick and Galway, 1534–1603' in Bradley (ed.), *Settlement and society in medieval Ireland*, pp 465–76.

18. Colm Lennon, 'The Counter-Reformation in Ireland, 1542–1641' in Brady and Gillespie (ed.), *Natives and newcomers*, pp 85–6; F. M.

Jones, 'The Counter-Reformation' in P. J. Corish (ed.), *A history of Irish Catholicism*, iii, 3 (Dublin, 1967), pp 13–35.

19. O'Connor, 'Rebellion of Viscount Baltinglass'; Helen Coburn Walshe, 'The rebellion of William Nugent, 1581' in Comerford, Cullen, Hill and Lennon (ed.), *Religion, conflict and coexistence*, pp 26–52; Brady, 'Conservative subversives', pp 26–8; Lennon, 'Counter-Reformation', pp 85–6; Edwards, *Church and state*, pp 268–70.

20. Lennon, *Lords of Dublin*, pp 152–7; Brady, 'Conservative subversives', pp 28–30.

21. Ellis, *Tudor Ireland*, pp 219–20; Brendan Bradshaw, 'Sword, word and strategy in the Reformation in Ireland' in *Hist. Jn.*, xxi (1978), pp 475–502; Canny, *From Reformation to Restoration*, pp 104–5, 134–6.

22. Bradshaw, 'The Reformation in the cities', pp 465–8; Canny, *From Reformation to Restoration*, pp 135–6; Lennon, *Lords of Dublin*, pp 163–4; David Rothe, *Analecta*, ed. P. F. Moran (Dublin, 1884), pp 491–2; Bagwell, *Tudors*, ii, 213–14; Thomas Flynn, *The Irish Dominicans, 1536–1641* (Dublin, 1993), p. 73.

23. Nicholas Canny, 'Identity formation in Ireland: the emergence of the Anglo-Irish' in Nicholas Canny and Anthony Pagden (ed.), *Colonial identity in the Atlantic world, 1500–1800* (Princeton, 1987), pp 159–65; idem, *From Reformation to Restoration*, pp 133–5; Ford, 'Protestant Reformation', pp 61–3; Colm Lennon, '"The bowels of the city's bounty": the municipality of Dublin and the foundation of Trinity College' in *Long Room*, no. 37 (1992), pp 10–16.

24. Helga Hammerstein, 'Aspects of the continental education of Irish students in the reign of Elizabeth I' in *Historical Studies, VIII* (Dublin, 1971), pp 137–53.

25. Lennon, *Lords of Dublin*, pp 161–3, 212–14; P. J. Corish, *The Catholic community in the seventeenth and eighteenth centuries* (Dublin, 1985), pp 91–5.

26. Lennon, 'Chantries in the Irish Reformation', pp 13–20; Brady, 'Conservative subversives', pp 29–30.

27. Jones, 'The Counter-Reformation', pp 41–5; J. J. Silke, 'The Irish appeal of 1593 to Spain: some light on the genesis of the Nine Years' War' in *I.E.R.*, 5th ser., xcii (1959), pp 279–90, 362–71; Hiram Morgan, 'Hugh O'Neill and the Nine Years' War in Tudor Ireland' in *Hist. Jn.*, xxxvi (1993), pp 1–17; idem, *Tyrone's rebellion*, pp 139–43.

28. Gráinne Henry, *The Irish in the Netherlands* (Dublin, 1992), pp 114–44; Lennon, *Richard Stanihurst the Dubliner*, pp 45–56.

29. Morgan, 'Hugh O'Neill'; Lennon, *Richard Stanihurst the Dubliner*, pp 62–4; Aidan Clarke, 'Colonial identity in early seventeenth-century Ireland' in T. W. Moody (ed.), *Nationality and the pursuit of national independence: Historical Studies, XI* (Belfast, 1978), pp 57–72; Corish, *Catholic community*, pp 105–11.

Bibliographical Guide

A. General

Edwards, R. D. W., and O'Dowd, Mary, *Sources for early modern Irish history, 1534–1641* (Cambridge, 1985) is the best guide to documentary evidence for the period. For a chronology and lists of leading figures and officials see *A new history of Ireland*, ix (Oxford, 1984). Aspects of Richard Bagwell, *Ireland under the Tudors* (3 vols, London, 1885–90) are revised in the following modern surveys:

Canny, Nicholas, *From Reformation to Restoration: Ireland, 1534–1660* (Dublin, 1987)

Collins, M. E., *Ireland, 1477–1610* (Dublin, 1980)

Cosgrove, Art (ed.), *A new history of Ireland*, ii: *Medieval Ireland 1169–1534* (Oxford, 1987)

Ellis, Steven, *Tudor Ireland: crown, community and the conflict of cultures, 1470–1603* (London, 1985)

Moody, T. W., Martin, F. X., and Byrne, F. J. (ed.) *A new history of Ireland*, iii: *Early modern Ireland, 1534–1691* (Oxford, 1976)

The following works help to provide an interpretative framework for the events of the period:

Andrews, K. R., Canny, N. P., and Hair, P. E. H. (ed.), *The Westward Enterprise: English activities in Ireland, the Atlantic and America, 1480–1650* (Liverpool, 1978)

Bradshaw, Brendan, *The Irish constitutional revolution of the sixteenth century* (Cambridge, 1979)

Brady, Ciaran, 'The government of Ireland, c. 1540–83' (unpublished Ph.D. thesis, Trinity College, Dublin, 1980)

—— and Gillespie, Raymond (ed.), *Natives and newcomers: essays on the making of Irish colonial society, 1534–1641* (Dublin, 1986)

B. Introduction

Aalen, F. H., *Man and the landscape in Ireland* (London, 1978)

Andrews, J. H., 'A geographer's view of Irish history' in T. W. Moody and F. X. Martin (ed.), *The course of Irish history* (Cork, 1967)

—— *Plantation acres: an historical study of the Irish land surveyor and his maps* (Belfast, 1985)

Brady, Ciaran, 'Court, castle and country: the framework of government in Tudor Ireland' in Brady and Gillespie (ed.), *Natives and newcomers*

Dunlop, Robert, 'Sixteenth-century maps of Ireland' in *English Historical Review*, xx (1905)

Ellis, Steven, *Reform and revival: English government in Ireland, 1470–1534* (London, 1986)

—— *The Pale and the far north: government and society in two early Tudor borderlands* (Galway, 1988)

Empey, C. A., 'The Butler lordship' in *Journal of the Butler Society*, i (1970–71)

Frame, Robin, *English lordship in Ireland, 1318–61* (Oxford, 1982)

Hayes-McCoy, G. A., *Irish battles: a military history of Ireland* (Belfast, 1989)

Hore, H. F. and Graves, James (ed.), *The social state of the southern and eastern counties of Ireland in the sixteenth century* (Dublin, 1870)

Quinn, D. B., 'Ireland and the sixteenth-century European expansion' in *Historical Studies*, i (1958)

Simms, Anngret, 'Core and periphery in medieval Europe: the Irish experience in a wider context' in Smyth and Whelan (ed.), *Common ground*

Simms, Katharine, 'Warfare in medieval Irish lordships' in *Irish Sword*, xii (1975–6)

Smyth, A. P., *Celtic Leinster* (Dublin, 1982)

Smyth, W. J., and Whelan, Kevin (ed.) *Common ground: essays on the historical geography of Ireland presented to T. Jones Hughes* (Cork, 1988)

C. Chapter 1: Town and County in the English Part of Ireland, c. 1500

Barrett, George, *History of Bandon and the west Cork towns* (Cork, 1869)

Bradley, John, 'The medièval towns of County Tipperary' in William Nolan, (ed.), *Tipperary: history and society* (Dublin, 1985)

—— 'The medieval towns of County Meath' in *Riocht na Midhe*, ix (1988–9)

Canavan, Tony, *Frontier town: an illustrated history of Newry* (Belfast, 1989)

Canny, Nicholas, 'From the Reformation to the penal laws' in Diarmuid Ó Cearbhaill, (ed.), *Galway: town and gown, 1484–1984* (Dublin, 1984)

Childs, W. A., and O'Neill, Timothy, 'Overseas trade' in *N.H.I.*, ii

Corbett, William, and Nolan, William (ed.), *Thurles: the cathedral town* (Dublin, 1989)

D'Alton, John, *The history of Drogheda with its environs* (2 vols, Dublin, 1844)

—— and O'Flanagan, J. R., *The history of Dundalk and its environs* (Dundalk, 1864)

Down, Kevin, 'Colonial society and economy in the high middle ages' in *N.H.I.*, ii

Empey, C. A., and Simms, Katharine, 'The ordinances of the White Earl and the problem of coign in the later middle ages' in *Proceedings of the Royal Irish Academy*, lxxv, sect. C (1975)

Fitzgerald, P., and McGregor, J. J., *The history, topography and antiquities of the county and city of Limerick* (2 vols, Dublin, 1826–7)

Hore, H. F., and Graves, James (ed.), *The social state of the southern and eastern counties of Ireland in the sixteenth century* (Dublin, 1870)

Lennon, Colm, *The lords of Dublin in the age of reformation* (Dublin, 1989)

Lydon, James, 'The city of Waterford in the later middle ages' in *Decies*, xii (1979), pp 5–15

Mac Niocaill, Gearóid, *Na buirgéisí, xii–xv aois* (2 vols, Dublin, 1964)

—— 'Socio-economic problems of the late medieval Irish town' in David Harkness and Mary O'Dowd (ed.), *The town in Ireland: Historical Studies, XIII* (Belfast, 1981)

Martin, Geoffrey, 'Plantation boroughs in medieval Ireland, with a handlist of boroughs to *c.* 1500' in Harkness and O'Dowd (ed.), *The town in Ireland*

Neely, William, *Kilkenny: an urban history, 1391–1843* (Belfast, 1989)

Nolan, William (ed.), *Tipperary: history and society* (Dublin, 1985)

O'Neill, Timothy, *Merchants and mariners in medieval Ireland* (Dublin, 1987)

O'Sullivan, William, *The economic history of Cork from the earliest time to the Act of Union* (Cork, 1973)

O'Sullivan, M. D., *Old Galway: the history of a Norman colony in Ireland* (Cambridge, 1942)

O'Rorke, Terence, *The history of Sligo, town and county* (2 vols, Dublin, 1889)

Ryland, R. H., *The history, topography and antiquities of the county and city of Waterford* (London, 1824)

Sheehan, Anthony, 'Irish towns in a period of change, 1558–1625' in Brady and Gillespie (ed.), *Natives and newcomers*

Seoighe, Mainchín, *The story of Kilmallock* (Limerick, 1987)

Walton, Julian, 'The merchant community of Waterford in the sixteenth and seventeenth centuries' in Philippe Butel and L. M. Cullen (ed.), *Cities and merchants: Irish and French perspectives on urban development* (Dublin, 1986)

D. Chapter 2: Society and Culture in Gaelic Ireland

Butler, W. F. T., *Gleanings from Irish history* (London, 1925)

Nicholls, Kenneth, *Gaelic and gaelicised Ireland in the sixteenth century* (Dublin, 1972)

—— *Land, law and society in sixteenth-century Ireland* (Dublin, 1976)

—— (ed.), *The O'Doyne manuscript: documents relating to the family of O'Doyne (Ó Duinn) from Archbishop Marsh's Library, Dublin* (Dublin, 1983)

—— 'Gaelic landownership in Tipperary in the light of the surviving Irish deeds' in Nolan (ed.), *Tipperary: history and society*

—— 'Gaelic society and economy in the high middle ages' in *N.H.I.*, ii

—— 'Irishwomen and property in the sixteenth century' in MacCurtain and O'Dowd (ed.), *Women in early modern Ireland*

O'Dowd, Mary, *Power, politics and land: early modern Sligo, 1568–1688* (Belfast, 1991)

—— 'Land inheritance in early modern Sligo' in *Irish Economic and Social History Journal*, x (1983), pp 5–18

—— 'Gaelic society and economy' in Brady and Gillespie (ed.), *Natives and newcomers*

—— and Margaret MacCurtain (ed.), *Women in early modern Ireland* (Edinburgh, 1991)

O'Riordan, Michelle, *The Gaelic mind and the collapse of the Gaelic world* (Cork, 1991)

Patterson, Nerys, 'Gaelic law and the Tudor conquest of Ireland: the social background of the sixteenth-century recension of the pseudo-historical Prologue to the *Senchus már*' in *I.H.S.*, xxvii (1991)

Quinn, D. B., *The Elizabethans and the Irish* (Ithaca, N.Y., 1966)

Simms, Katharine, *From kings to warlords: the changing political structure of Gaelic Ireland in the late middle ages* (Suffolk, 1987)

—— 'Warfare in late medieval Gaelic lordships' in *Irish Sword*, xii (1975–6)

—— 'The medieval kingdom of Lough Erne' in *Clogher Record*, ix (1977)

—— 'Guesting and feasting in Gaelic Ireland' in *Journal of the Royal Society of Antiquaries of Ireland*, cviii (1978)

—— 'Women in Gaelic Ireland' in O'Dowd and MacCurtain (ed.), *Women in early modern Ireland*

—— 'Bardic poetry as a historical source' in Tom Dunne (ed.), *The writer as witness: literature as historical evidence* (Cork, 1987)

E. Chapter 3: The Kildares and their Critics, 1500–20
  Chapter 4: Kildare Power and Tudor Intervention, 1520–35

Bradshaw, Brendan, 'Cromwellian reform and the origins of the Kildare rebellion, 1533–4' in *Transactions of the Royal Historical Society*, 5th ser., xxvii (1977)

Bryan, Donough, *Gerald Fitzgerald, the Great Earl of Kildare, 1456–1513* (Dublin, 1933)

Ellis, Steven, 'Tudor policy and the Kildare ascendancy, 1496–1534' in *I.H.S.*, xx (1977)

—— 'Henry VII and Ireland, 1491–6' in James Lydon (ed.), *England and Ireland in the late middle ages* (Dublin, 1981)

—— 'The Kildare rebellion and the early Henrician Reformation' in *Historical Journal*, xix (1976)

—— 'Thomas Cromwell and Ireland, 1532–40' in *Historical Journal*, xxiii (1980)

—— 'Henry VIII, rebellion and the rule of law' in *Historical Journal*, xxiv (1981)

Hore, H. F. (ed.), 'The rental book of Gerald Fitzgerald, ninth Earl of Kildare, begun in the year 1518' in *Journal of the Kildare Archaeological Society*, v (1858–9), vii (1862–3), viii (1864–6)

—— and Graves, James (ed.), *The social state of the southern and eastern counties of Ireland in the sixteenth century* (Dublin, 1870)

McCorristine, Laurence, *The revolt of Silken Thomas: a challenge to Henry VIII* (Dublin, 1987)

Quinn, D. B., 'The hegemony of the Earls of Kildare, 1496–1520' in *N.H.I.*, ii

—— 'The re-emergence of English policy as a major factor in Irish affairs, 1520–34' in *N.H.I.*, ii

—— 'Henry VIII and Ireland, 1509–34' in *I.H.S.*, xii (1960–61)

—— and Nicholls, Kenneth, 'Ireland in 1534' in *N.H.I.*, iii

Stanihurst, Richard, 'History of Henry VIII's reign' in *Holinshed's Irish chronicle*, ed. Liam Miller and Eileen Power (Dublin, 1979)

F. Chapter 5: Religion and Reformation, 1500–40

Bottigheimer, Karl, 'Why the Reformation failed in Ireland: une question bien posée' in *Journal of Ecclesiastical History*, xxxvi (1985)

Bradshaw, Brendan, 'The opposition to the ecclesiastical legislation in the Irish Reformation parliament' in *I.H.S.*, xvi (1968–9)

—— 'George Browne, first Reformation Archbishop of Dublin' in *Journal of Ecclesiastical History*, xxi (1970)

—— *The dissolution of the religious orders under Henry VIII* (Cambridge, 1974)

—— 'Sword, word and strategy in the Reformation in Ireland' in *Historical Journal*, xxi (1978)

—— 'The Reformation in the cities: Cork, Limerick and Galway, 1534–1603' in John Bradley (ed.), *Settlement and society in medieval Ireland: studies presented to F. X. Martin, O.S.A.* (Kilkenny, 1988)

Corish, P. J., *The Irish Catholic experience* (Dublin, 1985)

Empey, C. A., 'The sacred and the secular: the Augustinian priory of Kells in Ossory, 1193–1541' in *I.H.S.*, xxiv (1984)

Edwards, R. D. W., *Church and state in Tudor Ireland* (Dublin, 1935)

—— 'The Reformation parliament of Henry VIII, 1536–7' in *Historical Studies, VI* (Dublin, 1968)

Ellis, Steven, 'Economic problems of the church: why the Reformation failed in Ireland' in *Journal of Ecclesiastical History*, xli (1990)

Flynn, Thomas, *The Irish Dominicans, 1536–1641* (Dublin, 1993)

Gwynn, Aubrey, *The medieval province of Armagh, 1470–1545* (Dundalk, 1946)

Lennon, Colm, 'The sixteenth century' in Réamonn Ó Muirí (ed.), *Irish church history today* (Armagh, 1990)

—— 'The chantries in the Irish Reformation: the case of St Anne's Guild, Dublin, 1550–1630' in R. V. Comerford, Mary Cullen, J. R. Hill and Colm Lennon (ed.), *Religion, conflict, and coexistence: essays presented to Monsignor Patrick J. Corish* (Dublin, 1991)

Lynch, Anthony, 'The church in late medieval Ireland' in *Archivium Hibernicum*, xxx (1981)

Mooney, Canice, *The church in Gaelic Ireland, thirteenth to fifteenth centuries* in P. J. Corish (ed.), *A history of Irish Catholicism*, ii, 5 (Dublin, 1969)

Murray, James, 'Archbishop Alen, Tudor reform and the Kildare rebellion' in *Proceedings of the Royal Irish Academy*, lxxxix, sect. C (1989)

Murray, Laurence, 'The ancient chantries of County Louth' in *Journal of the Louth Archaeological Society*, ix (1939)

Nicholls, Kenneth, 'Rectory, vicarage and parish in the western Irish dioceses' in *Journal of the Royal Society of Antiquaries of Ireland*, ci (1971)

Ronan, Myles, *The Reformation in Dublin, 1536–58* (London, 1926)

—— 'Religious customs of Dublin medieval guilds' in *Irish Ecclesiastical Record*, 5th ser., xxvi (1925)

Walsh, Katherine, 'Clerical estate' in John Bradley (ed.), *Settlement and society*

Watt, J. A., *The church in medieval Ireland* (Dublin, 1972)

—— 'Gaelic polity and cultural identity' in *N.H.I.*, ii

—— 'The church and the two nations in medieval Armagh' in W. J. Sheils and Diana Wood (ed.), *The churches, Ireland, and the Irish*, Studies in Church History, XXV (Oxford, 1989)

G. Chapter 6: Political and Religious Reform and Reaction, 1536–56
Besides the general surveys and interpretative essays referred to Section A above, the following should be consulted:

Bradshaw, Brendan, 'The Edwardian Reformation in Ireland' in *Archivium Hibernicum*, xxxiv (1976–7)

Brady, Ciaran, 'Conservative subversives: the community of the Pale and the Dublin administration, 1556–86' in P. J. Corish (ed.), *Radicals, rebels and establishments: Historical Studies, XV* (Belfast, 1985)

—— 'Thomas, tenth Earl of Ormond' in Ciaran Brady (ed.), *Worsted in the game: losers in Irish history* (Dublin, 1989)

—— 'The decline of the Irish kingdom' in Mark Greengrass (ed.), *Conquest and coalescence: the shaping of the state in early modern Europe* (London, 1991)

Dolley, Michael, 'The Irish coinage, 1534–1691' in *N.H.I.*, iii

Dunlop, Robert, 'Some aspects of Henry VIII's Irish poilicy' in T. F. Tout and James Tait (ed.), *Historical essays* (London, 1902)

Ellis, S. G., 'John Bale, Bishop of Ossory, 1552–3' in *Journal of the Butler Society*, ii (1984)

Moore, Donal, *English action, Irish reaction: the MacMurrough Kavanaghs, 1530–1630* (Maynooth, 1987)

O'Toole, P. L., *History of the Clan O'Toole and other Leinster septs* (Dublin, 1890)

Quinn, D. B., 'Edward Walshe's "Conjectures" concerning the state of Ireland [1552]' in *I.H.S.*, v (1946–7)

White, D. G., 'Henry VIII's Irish kerne in France and Scotland, 1544–5' in *Irish Sword*, iii (1957–8)

—— 'The reign of Edward VI in Ireland: some political, social and economic aspects' in *I.H.S.*, xiv (1964–5)

H. Chapter 7: The Pale and Greater Leinster, 1556–88
Besides the general surveys and interpretative essays in A and several studies in G above, the following works are important:

Berleth, Richard, *The twilight lords* (London, 1978)

Brady, Ciaran, 'Court, castle and country: the framework of government in Tudor Ireland' in Brady and Gillespie (ed.), *Natives and newcomers*

Canny, Nicholas, *The formation of an Old English elite in Ireland* (Dublin, 1975)

—— *The Elizabethan conquest of Ireland: a pattern established, 1565–1576* (Hassocks, 1976)

—— *Kingdom and colony: Ireland in the Atlantic world, 1560–1800* (Baltimore, 1988)

—— 'Identity formation in Ireland: the emergence of the Anglo-Irish' in Nicholas Canny and Anthony Pagden (ed.), *Colonial identity in the Atlantic world, 1500–1800* (Princeton, 1987)

Carey, Vincent, 'Gaelic reaction to plantation: the case of the O'More and O'Connor lordships of Laois and Offaly, 1570–1603' (unpublished M.A. thesis, St Patrick's College, Maynooth, 1985)

Coburn Walshe, Helen, 'The rebellion of William Nugent, 1581' in Comerford, Cullen, Hill and Lennon (ed.), *Religion, conflict and coexistence*

Edwards, David, 'The Butler revolt of 1569' in *I.H.S.*, xxviii (1993)

Fitzgerald, Brian, *The Geraldines: an experiment in Irish government* (London, 1951)

Goff, Henry, 'English conquest of an Irish barony: the changing patterns of landownership in the barony of Scarawalsh, 1540–1640' in Kevin Whelan and W. J. Smyth (ed.), *Wexford: history and society* (Dublin, 1987)

Lennon, Colm, 'Richard Stanihurst (1547–1618) and Old English identity' in *I.H.S.*, xxi (1978–9)

—— 'Reform ideas and cultural resources in the inner Pale in the mid-sixteenth century' in *Stair*, ii (1979)

—— *Richard Stanihurst the Dubliner, 1547–1618* (Dublin, 1979)

Loeber, Rolf, *The geography and practice of English colonisation of Ireland from 1534 to 1609* (Dublin, 1990)

O'Connor, Elizabeth, 'The rebellion of James Eustace, Viscount Baltinglass, 1580–81' (unpublished M.A. thesis, St Patrick's College, Maynooth, 1989)

Sheehan, Anthony, 'Irish towns in a period of change' in Brady and Gillespie (ed.), *Natives and newcomers*

Treadwell, Victor, 'The Irish parliament of 1569–71' in *Proceedings of the Royal Irish Academy*, lxv, sect. C (1966)

—— 'Sir John Perrot and the Irish parliament of 1585–6' in *Proceedings of the Royal Irish Academy*, lxxxv, sect. C (1985)

I. Chapter 8: Munster: Presidency and Plantation, 1565–95

Brady, Ciaran, 'Faction and the origins of the Desmond rebellion of 1579' in *I.H.S.*, xxii (1981)

Butler, George, 'The battle of Affane' in *Irish Sword*, viii (1967–8)

Chambers, Anne, *Eleanor, Countess of Desmond, c. 1545–1638* (Dublin, 1986)

MacCarthy-Morrogh, Michael, *The Munster plantation: English migration to southern Ireland, 1583–1641* (Oxford, 1986)

—— 'The English presence in early seventeenth-century Munster' in Brady and Gillespie (ed.), *Natives and newcomers*

Sheehan, Anthony, 'Official reaction to native land claims in the plantation of Munster' in *I.H.S.*, xxiii (1983)

—— 'The overthrow of the plantation of Munster, October 1598' in *Irish Sword*, xv (1982–3)

J. Chapter 9: Connacht: Council and Composition, 1569–95

Chambers, Anne, *Granuaile: the life and times of Grace O'Malley, c. 1530–1603* (Dublin, 1983)

—— *Chieftain to knight: Tibbot Bourke, 1567–1629, first Viscount Mayo* (Dublin, 1983)

Cuellar, Francesco de, 'Account of his adventures', ed. Bernard MacDonagh (Sligo, n.d.)

Cunningham, Bernadette, 'Political and social change in the lordships of Clanricard and Thomond, 1569–1641' (unpublished M.A. thesis, University College, Galway, 1979)
—— 'The Composition of Connacht in the lordships of Clanricard and Thomond, 1577–1641' in *I.H.S.*, xxix (1984)
—— 'Natives and newcomers in Mayo, 1560–1603' in Raymond Gillespie and Gerard Moran (ed.), *'A various country': essays in Mayo history* (Westport, 1987)
Flanagan, Laurence, *Ireland's Armada legacy* (Dublin, 1988)
Gillespie, Raymond, 'Lords and commons in seventeenth-century Mayo' in Gillespie and Moran (ed.) *'A various country'*
Morgan, Hiram, 'Extradition and treason-trial of a Gaelic lord: the case of Brian O'Rourke' in *Irish Jurist*, xxii (1987)
—— *Tyrone's rebellion: the outbreak of the Nine Years' War in Tudor Ireland* (Dublin, 1993)
O'Brien, Donough, *History of the O'Briens* (London, 1949)
O'Dowd, Mary, *Power, politics and land: early modern Sligo, 1568–1688* (Belfast, 1991)

K. Chapter 10: Ulster and the General Crisis of the Nine Years' War, 1560–1603
Brady, Ciaran, 'The killing of Shane O'Neill: some new evidence' in *Irish Sword*, xv (1982)
—— 'The O'Reillys of east Breifne and the problem of surrender and regrant' in *Breifne*, vi (1985)
—— 'Sixteenth-century Ulster and the failure of Tudor reform' in Ciaran Brady, Mary O'Dowd and Brian Walker (ed.), *Ulster: an illustrated history* (London, 1989)
Canavan, Tony, *Frontier town: an illustrated history of Newry* (Belfast, 1989)
Canny, Nicholas, 'Hugh O'Neill and the changing face of Gaelic Ulster' in *Studia Hibernica*, x (1970)
—— 'The treaty of Mellifont and the reorganisation of Ulster 1603' in *Irish Sword*, ix (1969–70)
Duffy, P. J., 'The territorial organisation of Gaelic landownership and its transformation in County Monaghan, 1591–1640' in *Irish Geography*, xiv (1981)
Falls, Cyril, *Elizabeth's Irish wars* (London, 1950)
Hayes-McCoy, G. A., 'Strategy and tactics in Irish warfare, 1593–1601' in *I.H.S.*, ii (1941)
—— 'The army of Ulster, 1593–1601' in *Irish Sword*, i (1950)
—— 'The completion of the Tudor conquest, and the advance of the Counter-Reformation, 1571–1603' in *N.H.I.*, iii
Lennon, Colm, 'The great explosion in Dublin, 1597' in *Dublin Historical Record*, xlii (1988)
Logan, Patrick, 'Pestilence in the Irish wars: the early phase' in *Irish Sword*, vii (1966)
Morgan, Hiram, 'The colonial venture of Sir Thomas Smith, 1571–1575' in *Historical Journal*, xxviii (1985)

—— 'The end of Gaelic Ulster: a thematic interpretation of events between 1534 and 1610' in *I.H.S.*, xxvi (1988)

—— *Tyrone's rebellion: the outbreak of the Nine Years' War in Tudor Ireland* (Dublin, 1993)

—— 'Hugh O'Neill and the Nine Years' War in Tudor Ireland' in *Historical Journal*, xxxvi (1993)

Silke, J. J., *Kinsale: the Spanish intervention in Ireland at the end of the Elizabethan wars* (Liverpool, 1970)

L. Chapter 11: From Reformation to Counter-Reformation, 1560–1600

Canny, Nicholas, 'Why the Reformation failed in Ireland: une question mal posée' in *Journal of Ecclesiastical History*, xxx (1979)

Clarke, Aidan, 'Colonial identity in early seventeenth-century Ireland' in T. W. Moody (ed.), *Nationality and the pursuit of national independence: Historical Studies, XI* (Belfast, 1978)

—— 'Varieties of uniformity: the first century of the Church of Ireland' in Sheils and Wood (ed.), *The churches, Ireland and the Irish*

Coburn Walshe, Helen, 'Responses to the Protestant Reformation in sixteenth-century Meath' in *Riocht na Midhe*, vii (1987)

—— 'Enforcing the Elizabethan settlement: the vicissitudes of Hugh Brady, Bishop of Meath, 1563–84' in *I.H.S.*, xxvi (1989)

Corish, P. J., *The Catholic community in the seventeenth and eighteenth centuries* (Dublin, 1985)

Edwards, R. D. W., 'Ireland, Elizabeth I and the Counter-Reformation' in S. T. Bindoff, Joel Hurstfield and C. H. Williams (ed.), *Elizabethan government and society* (London, 1961)

Fitzsimon, Henry, *Words of comfort . . . to persecuted Catholics*, ed. Edmund Hogan (Dublin, 1891)

Ford, Alan, 'The Protestant Reformation in Ireland' in Brady and Gillespie (ed.), *Natives and newcomers*

Henry, Gráinne, *The Irish in the Netherlands* (Dublin, 1992)

Jackson, Donald, *Intermarriage in Ireland, 1550–1650* (Montreal, 1970)

Jefferies, H. A., 'The Irish parliament of 1560: the Anglican reforms authorised' in *I.H.S.*, xxvi (1988)

Jones, F. M., 'The Counter-Reformation' in P. J. Corish (ed.), *A history of Irish Catholicism*, iii, 3 (Dublin, 1967)

Lennon, Colm, 'Reform ideas and cultural resources in the inner Pale in the mid-sixteenth century' in *Stair*, ii (1979)

—— 'The Counter-Reformation in Ireland, 1542–1641' in Brady and Gillespie (ed.), *Natives and newcomers*

—— '"The bowels of the city's bounty": the municipality of Dublin and the foundation of Trinity College' in *Long Room*, no. 37 (1992)

McNally, David, 'Sir John Plunkett of Dunsoghly' (unpublished B.A. thesis, St Patrick's College, Maynooth, 1987)

Ó Mathúna, Seán, *An tAthair William Bathe, C.I.: ceannrodaí sa teangeolaíocht* (Dublin, 1980)

Rothe, David, *Analecta*, ed. P. F. Moran (Dublin, 1884)

Silke, J. J., 'The Irish appeal of 1593 to Spain: some light on the genesis of the Nine Years' War' in *Irish Ecclesiastical Record*, 5th ser., xcii (1959)

Index

absentees, 34, 71, 103
Act of Absentees, 1536, 140, 147
Act of Appeals, 1536, 135
Act of Faculties, 1537, 135
Act of First Fruits, 1536, 135
act of kingly title, 1541, 154–5
Act of Slander, 1536, 134, 135
act of subsidy, 1536, 147
Act of Supremacy, 1536, 113–14, 134,
   135, 307
  opposition to, 113
Act of Uniformity, 307, 308
acts of attainder, 230–31
Acts of Succession, 134, 135
administration. see also Irish council;
  reform movement
  Bagenal's influence, 286
  chief office-holders, 13
  church-papistry, 313–14
  description of, 11–18
  English viceroys preferable, 112
  functions of, 15–16
  income and expenditure, 15
  influence of, 80–81
  New English in, 201–2
  and Nine Years' War, 294–6
  and Reformation, 166–7, 311
  reforms, 302
  revenue deficit, 164, 171–2, 174–5,
    181–2
  revenue of, 91–2, 147–8
  'secret council', 101–2
adventurers, 184
advowsons, 119, 122, 162, 311, 314,
  315, 318, 321
Affane, Co. Waterford
  battle of, 208, 209, 210
Agard, Sir Francis, 195, 200
Agard, Thomas, 141, 153, 161
agriculture, 171, 190, 200
  changing systems, 10–11, 197–8

English influence, 156
Gaelic, 44–6
in Kildare earldom, 71–2
manors, 33–4
and planters, 235
principal crops, 45–6
social divisions, 49–50
in Ulster, 281–2, 293
Alen, John, Archbishop of Dublin,
  Lord Chancellor, 101, 102, 103,
  108, 140
  reform movement, 117, 121–2,
  133–4
Alen, John, Lord Chancellor, 104,
  140, 150, 201
  monastic grants, 141, 148
  opposes St Leger, 161, 163
All Hallows, Dublin, 121, 140, 141
Anglican church. see Reformation
anglicisation, 296
  Connacht, 241, 252–3, 259–60
  Ulster, 291–2
Anglo–Norman earldoms. see
  Desmond; Kildare; Ormond
Anglo–Norman lordships
  anglicisation, 209–10
  burden of cess, 181–2
  Cromwellian policy, 146–7
  economic conditions, 189–90, 192
  and Elizabethan policy, 178
  encroached upon, 184
  freeholders' rights, 266–7, 286–7
  gaelicisation, 80
  reaction to colonists, 213
  resented by towns, 219
annals, 66, 248
Annals of Ulster, 76, 126, 131
Antrim, County, 169, 291
  garrison, 183
  held by MacDonnells, 280
  Nine Years' War, 300

Antrim, County *continued*
    settlers, 277, 278–9
    woodlands, 3
aos dana, 76
Apsley, Captain, 242
architecture, 26
    castellated houses, 192
    'Irish Gothic', 131
    and planters, 235
    religious, 120–21, 122–3
Ardee, Co. Louth, 21, 26, 123
    attacked, 151
    monastery, 122
Ardnaree, battle of, 254–5
Ards, Co. Down, 277, 278, 280
Argyll, Earl of, 92, 275
aristocracy, cult of, 83–4
Armagh, County, 171, 291
    settlers, 277, 280
    Tyrone prevents shiring, 292, 293
Armagh archdiocese, 62, 115, 117,
    126, 170, 308, 309, 310
    friaries, 130
Armagh town, 267, 282, 296, 300
    Burgh recaptures, 294
    garrison, 169
    garrison withdrawn, 271
army. *see* troops
Arnold, Sir Nicholas, 182, 210, 272
Arthur, Prince, 83
Arthur family, 25
Askeaton, Co. Limerick, 97, 217, 224
Athassel monastery, Co. Tipperary,
    121
Athclynt, Co. Monaghan, 264–5, 298
Athenry, Co. Galway, 67, 120, 240,
    242, 245
    attacked, 245
    burnt, 243
    Dominican *studia*, 131
Athlone, Co. Westmeath, 165–6, 171,
    239, 241, 245, 257
    burnt, 243
Athy, Co. Kildare, 190, 296–7
    charter, 84
    raided, 197
Augustinian Order, 120, 137, 141, 142
Aylmer, Sir Gerald, 154, 173, 175

Babe family, 315
Baculum Jesu, 138

Bagenal, Sir Henry, 296
    defeats Maguire, 290
    and Tyrone, 290–91, 292
Bagenal, Mabel, 290
Bagenal, Sir Nicholas, 165, 169, 267,
    282
    opposes Perrot, 286
Bale, John, Bishop of Ossory, 170–71,
    173, 305–6, 311–12
Ball, Margaret, 312, 317, 321
Ball, Walter, 312, 317
Ball family, 25, 320
Ballinafad castle, 261, 262
Ballyboggan, Co. Meath, 138, 140,
    148, 161
Ballymote, Co. Sligo, 258, 261, 262, 290
Ballyshannon castle, 57, 294
Baltinglass, Viscount. *see* Eustace
Baltinglass abbey, 140, 313
Baltinglass rebellion, 1580, 194, 202–5,
    206, 225–6, 318, 319
    battle of Glenmalure, 177, 203, 317
Bann river, 4, 276
    fisheries, 159
bards, 2
Barnewall, John, 66, 96
Barnewall, Sir Patrick, 122
    and monastic dissolutions, 135–6,
    140, 141
    and Reformation, 313
Barrett, Richard, Bishop of Killala, 126
Barrow river, 3, 4, 5, 100
Barry, David, Viscount Buttevant,
    226, 298
    and O'Neill rebellion, 23
Barry, James, Lord, 162, 212, 214, 216,
    218, 226
    composition rent, 221–2
    Desmond rebellion, 225
Bathe, James, 161, 313–14
Beacon, Richard, 319
Bective abbey, Co. Meath, 140, 161
Bellahoe, ford of, 151
Belleek castle, 261, 290, 291, 294
Bellingham, Sir Edward, 195, 199
    fortresses, 178
    Lord Deputy 1548–9, 164–8, 267
    and purveyance, 172–3
    and Reformation, 305
Benet, Nicholas, 122
Berkeley, Edward, 232

Bermingham, Lord, 162
Bermingham, Sir Patrick, 90, 101, 103
Bermingham, Thomas de, 120
Bermingham family, 71
betaghs, 34–5
biataigh, 54
billeting, 186
  Connacht, 243, 244
  Dublin, 102, 191, 295
  expanded by O'Neill, 275
  resentment of, 150, 181, 184
  of Scots mercenaries, 283
  Ulster, 287
  used by Bingham, 262
Bingham, Captain George, 262, 292
Bingham, Sir George, 254, 255, 256,
  258, 262
Bingham, John, 254
Bingham, Sir Richard, 46, 260, 287,
  290, 294
  Burke rebellion, 254–5
  Connacht president, 238, 248–9,
  252–63
  income of, 253
  in Sligo, 257–8, 289
Bingham, Sir William
  Burke rebellion, 1589, 255–6
Birr castle, 105
Black Death, 7
'black rents', 37, 75, 77, 98, 102
  abolition, 156
Blackwater fort, 292, 294, 296, 300, 301
Blackwater river, 4, 279, 290
Blake family, 25, 40, 48
Blount, Charles. *see* Mountjoy, Lord
Bodkin, Christopher, Archbishop of
  Tuam, 308, 313
bogland, 3–4
Boleyn, Anne, 100, 103, 134, 137
Boleyn, Margaret, 85
Boleyn, Mary, 100
Boleyn, Sir Thomas, 94, 100, 102
bonaght, 55
Book of Common Prayer
  First, 166, 168, 305
  Second, 171, 307
Book of Howth, 66
Book of Reformation, 166
booleying, 44
boroughs, 20, 21, 22, 29, 81, 84. *see
  also* towns

administration of, 24–5
autonomy of, 23–4
grants to, 23
manorial rights, 34–5
Borrow, Captain Thomas, 277
Bosher, Jasper, 199
bothaigh, 49
Bourchier, Sir George, 232
Boyle, Co. Roscommon, 254, 258, 261
  abbey, 129, 258
  Sidney in, 240
Boyne river, 4
Boys, Richard, 120
Brabazon, Sir William, 140, 141, 148,
  167, 174
  campaign against O'Connor, 163
  and Grey, 150
  monastic grants, 161
  and St Leger, 153
Brackland castle, 149
Brady, Hugh, Bishop of Meath, 308,
  309, 310, 314
brehon law, 57–62, 75, 76, 200
  banned in Munster, 216
  and plantations, 234
brehons, 57–8, 198
Breifne, 171, 285
Brereton, Sir Andrew, 165, 168, 267,
  272
Brethren of the Common Life, 132
Brett, Jerome, 278
brewing industry, 30, 32
bridges, 5
Bristol, 40, 172
Brittany, 5, 40, 48
Brody, William, 110
Broet, Fr Pascal, 303
Brotherhood of Arms, 15, 72, 73, 83
Browne, George, Archbishop of
  Dublin, 113, 114, 160
  and Grey, 150
  and king's supremacy, 136, 137
  and monastic dissolutions, 141
  and Reformation, 138–9, 153,
  166–7, 168
  removed on marriage, 173, 306
Browne, John, 255, 257
Browne, Sir Valentine, 229–30, 234
Browne, Captain Thomas, 277
Browne family, 235
Bryan, Sir Francis, 167

buannacht, 55
Bundrowes castle, 57, 261, 289
Burgh, Thomas Lord, 295
  Lord Deputy 1597, 294
Burghley, Lord, 229, 231, 280
Burgundy, 70, 83
Burke, Edmund (MacWilliam), 254-5
Burke, John, Sheriff of Galway, 243
Burke, John ('Mac an Iarla'), of
  Clanricard, 240, 243, 245-6
Burke, Richard MacShane
  (MacWilliam), 240
Burke, Richard, 2nd Earl of
  Clanricard
  Connacht presidency, 243
  marriages, 60
  and presidency, 244
  and sons, 245
  and Shane O'Neill, 269
  Thomond succession dispute, 240
Burke, Richard-in-Iarainn, 247, 259
Burke, Richard MacOliverus
  (MacWilliam), 247, 250, 254
Burke, Richard MacRickard ('Devil's
  Hook'), 254-5, 256
Burke, Shane MacOliverus
  (MacWilliam), 244, 245, 247
Burke, Tibbott na Long, 256
Burke, Ulick, 262
Burke, Ulick, 1st Earl of Clanricard,
  149, 157-8, 162, 168
Burke, Ulick, 3rd Earl of Clanricard
  ('Mac an Iarla'), 240, 243, 245-6,
  249, 250, 257, 259
  Nine Years' War, 294, 297
Burke, Ulick Finn, of Clanricard, 73, 77
  battle of Knockdoe, 65-7
Burke, Walter na Mully, 256
Burke, William ('Blind Abbot'), 256
Burke, William (MacWilliam), 254
Burke (Clanricard) lordship, 23, 65-7,
  171
Burke (MacWilliam) lordship, 17, 66
  inter-family strife, 247
  and O'Donnell, 262
  and presidency, 244
  revolt, 1570, 243
  succession dispute, 253, 254-5
Burkes of Clanwilliam, 224
Burkes of Mayo, 259, 297
Burnell, Sir John, 108, 109, 111, 122

Burnell family, 26
Butler, Sir Edmund, brother of 10th
  Earl Ormond, 184, 196, 197, 208,
  214, 216, 219
Butler, Edward, brother of 10th Earl
  Ormond, 208, 214, 216, 219
Butler, James, brother of 10th Earl
  Ormond, 208, 214, 216, 219
Butler, James, 9th Earl of Ormond,
  34, 94, 95, 97, 100-101, 103, 136,
  149, 151, 162-3
  and Reformation, 136, 137
  and St Leger, 154, 157, 161
Butler, lord of Dunboyne, 101
Butler, Piers Roe, Earl of Ossory, 55,
  69, 85, 90, 96, 136, 157
  death of, 151
  and Fitzgerald rebellion, 108, 110
  Kildare feud, 96-7, 104
  Lord Deputy, 1522, 94-6
  Lord Deputy, 1528, 98, 100-101
  marries Kildare's daughter, 61, 73
  model factories, 30
  and Reformation, 134
  restored to Ormond, 149
  and Skeffington deputyship, 102-3
Butler, Sir Thomas, 157
Butler, Thomas, son of Piers Roe, 104
Butler, Thomas, 7th Earl of Ormond,
  85
Butler, Thomas, 10th Earl of
  Ormond, 173, 192, 197
  cess protest, 187
  Desmond feud, 182, 208-9, 210
  and Desmond rebellion, 225, 226-7
  and FitzMaurice rebellion, 214,
  219-20
  and Fitzwilliam, 216
  Munster lord general, 1583, 228
  and Munster presidency, 211-12,
  220, 230, 232
  Nine Years' War, 295-6, 297, 299
  and Shane O'Neill, 269, 270
  and St Leger, 174, 175
  and Thomond, 215, 240, 242-3
Butler family, 28, 29-30

Cahir, Lord, 219
Cahir castle, 157
Calais, 146
Callan river, 296
Calvinism, 318
Campbell, Lady Agnes, 60-61, 275
Campion, Edmund, 82, 309

Cannon, Thomas, 106
Capuchin Order, 322
Carbury, Co. Kildare, 71
Carew, Sir George, 299, 300, 301
Carew, Sir Peter, 184, 185, 195–6, 199,
  200, 214, 299
  Munster settlement, 213
Carlingford, 21, 26, 69, 269
Carlow, County, 5, 43, 71, 72, 195
  absentees' lands, 103
  Gaelic lordships, 10
  Grey in, 149
  seneschals, 200
  surrender and regrant, 156
Carlow town, 170, 197
Carmelite Order, 120, 322
Carrickfergus, Co. Antrim, 21, 95,
  266, 267, 278
  decayed, 280
  garrison, 169
  under O'Neill pressure, 282
Carrigaline castle, 213, 214
Carrigogunnell castle, 149
Carter, Arthur, 223
Casey, William, Bishop of Limerick,
  168
Cashel, Co. Tipperary, 215
Cashel diocese, 170
castellated houses, 26
Castle Chamber, Court of, 16
Castlebar, Co. Mayo, 258
Castlemaine castle, 215, 216, 217
Castlemartyr castle, 214, 217
castles, 9, 57, 81, 192, 235
Câteau-Cambrésis, peace of, 267
Cathach, 133
cattle raising, 44–5
Cavan, County, 285, 286–7
Cavan town, 47, 282
Cecil, Sir William, 270, 272, 276
cess, 173, 181–2, 184, 186, 198, 206, 244
  Connacht, 243
  Perrot accused of, 255
  resistance campaigns, 187, 189, 190
  used by Bingham, 262
Challoner, John, 312
Challoner, Luke, 312
Challoner family, 320
chancery law, 59–60
Chapuys, Eustace, 106, 107
charities, 27–8

Charles V, Emperor, 88, 101, 104, 106,
  107, 110
charters, 22, 23, 81, 123
  increase in, 84
  and trade, 35–6
Chatterton, Thomas, 276–7, 278, 280
Cheevers, Sir Christopher, 184
Chichester, Sir Arthur, 300, 301
Chiericati, Francesco, 42
Christ Church, Dublin, 120, 138
Christian humanism, 81, 88, 114, 310
chronometry, 6–7
Church of Ireland, 303, 308
  financial problems, 310–11
Cistercian Order, 124, 140, 141–2
citizenship, 23
Clancarty, Earl of. *see* MacCarthy
  More, Donal
Clancy, Boetius, 237, 251
Clandeboye, lordship of, 44, 171, 275,
  282
  deserted, 280
  settlers, 277
  surrendered, 279
Clandonnell family, 245, 247, 254, 256
Clangibbon family, 247, 256
Clanmalier, Viscounts (O'Dempseys),
  156, 196
Clanricard, earldom of, 239, 240, 291.
  see also Burke
  composition indenture, 251, 253
  and Composition of Connacht, 259
  and Connacht presidency, 238,
    241–2, 248–9
  Mac an Iarlas' revolt, 243
  taxation reform, 244
Clare, County, 239, 257, 262
  raided, 297
  shired, 241, 242
  Spanish Armada, 237
Clare Island, 237
Clement VIII, Pope, 299, 322
clergy
  coarbs and erenaghs, 127
  friary training, 131
  Gaelic priests in Pale benefices, 119
  lack of education, 119, 128–9,
    308–9, 311
  lay patrons of, 123–4
  and Reformation, 138–9, 167
Clifford, Sir Conyers, 294, 297–8

climate, 7–8, 99
clocks, 6–7
Clonfert diocese, 311
Clonmel, Co. Tipperary, 20, 21, 36, 39, 208, 319
burnt, 22
Clontibret, battle of, 292–3
coarbs, 127
coastal travel, 5–6
coign and livery, 54–5, 74–5, 79, 197, 209
arrests for, 212
banned, 184, 211, 216, 220, 241, 244
burden of, 190
complaints of, 192
composition, 186, 249
effect on markets, 37
and freeholding, 233–4
Kildare earldom, 72, 95
used by seneschals, 200
used by Surrey, 92
Colmcille, St, 133
colonies. see plantations
Common Pleas, Court of, 16
communications, 5–6, 7–8
Composition of Connacht, 238, 249–54, 257–8, 258–9, 289
native reactions to, 260–61
composition rents, 186–7, 203, 205, 206, 209–10
Connacht, 244–5, 248
Munster, 221–2
Ulster, 285, 287, 290, 292
used by presidencies, 220
Connacht, 12, 17, 236, 300. see also Composition of Connacht 1569–95, 237–63
agriculture, 44, 46
Croft in, 171
Desmond rebellion, 224
friaries, 130–32, 163
'great freedoms', 252–3
invaded by Shane O'Neill, 269
Kildare in, 1526, 96
mercenaries, 55–6
Nine Years' War, 294, 297
overlordship in, 53
presidency, 179, 183, 185–6, 210, 238, 239–49
rebellion, 1589, 255–6
Reformation in, 319

regional council, 186
religious orders, 124
shiring, 245
'slantyaght', 74
St Leger in, 153, 156–8
Thomond rebellion, 1570, 242–3
trade, 48
urbanisation, 21
constables, 81
Conton family, 122
Cork town, 20, 85, 169, 215, 220
'black rent', 37
Cork–London post, 6
dominant families, 25, 47
famine conditions, 227–8
Gaelic trade, 39
and Geraldine overlordship, 219
powers of, 22
St Leger in, 157
staple port, 29
Cork, County, 38
agriculture, 11
clans, 43
Desmond rebellion, 223, 225
famine conditions, 227–8
plantation, 231
ports defended, 169
Sidney in, 214
surrender and regrant, 210–11
woodlands, 3
corporations, 190–91
Corpus Christi Guild, Dublin, 124, 139
Cosby, Sir Francis, 177, 200
'coshery', 55
Costello barony, Co. Mayo, 259
council. see Irish council; Privy Council
Council of the North, 146
Council of Trent, 193, 313, 315, 320
Counter-Reformation, 60, 133, 193, 194, 203, 207, 217, 306, 315. see also Roman Catholicism
and Desmond rebellion, 225
early weaknesses, 312–14
education abroad, 320–21
and FitzMaurice, 222–3
Jesuit missions, 303–4
and Munster revolt, 213–14
in the Pale, 316–18
and Tyrone, 298–9
'country disease', 9, 91
county sheriffs, 17

Court of Chancery, 16
Court of High Commission, 308, 312, 316, 318
Court of King's Bench, 16
Courtenay, Sir William, 232
courts of justice, 16–17
Cowley, Robert, 84, 141, 163
Cowley, Walter, 163, 170
coyne and livery. *see* coign
craft guilds, 28–9, 30
Craik, Alexander, Bishop of Kildare, 308, 311
Creagh, Richard, Archbishop of Armagh, 313
Creagh family, 25
creaghts, 44, 281
Crean family, 25, 47, 49, 260
Croft, Sir James, 164, 178, 195
    Lord Deputy, 1551, 169–73, 267
    and Reformation, 305
Cromer, George, Archbishop of Armagh, 103, 106, 118, 138, 160
Cromwell, Thomas, 89, 103–4, 137
    administrative reform, 106, 145, 146–7
    downfall of, 151
    intelligence network, 104–5, 140
    Irish policy, 112, 151–2
'cuddies', 55
currency, 36–7, 172, 295
    sterling alignment rejected, 148
Curwin, Hugh, Archbishop of Dublin, 173, 306, 308, 309, 311
Cusack, Anna, 321
Cusack, George, 258
Cusack, Mary, 141
Cusack, Sir Thomas, 105, 106, 141, 142, 144, 175, 210
    and Arnold, 182
    caretaker administration, 173
    circuit of west and north, 171
    land grants, 161–2
    and Shane O'Neill, 269, 271
    and St Leger, 154
Cusack family, 122
customs revenues, 15, 17, 29–30, 53, 191, 206
crown resumes, 135, 136, 147–8

Daingean castle, 149, 163
Dalkey, Co. Dublin, 26

Daly, Robert, Bishop of Kildare, 308
Darcy, lord of Platten, 66
Darcy, Sir William, 73, 79, 84, 90, 96, 98
Darcy family, 73
Davells, Henry, 223, 224
de la Pole, Richard, 97
De rebus in Hibernia gestis (Stanihurst), 324
dead, cult of, 132
Decies, Viscount. *see* Fitzgerald, Sir Maurice
deforestation, 10
del Águila, Don Juan, 300
Delahide, Christopher, 104
Delahide, James, 106
Delvin, Baron of, 66, 96, 98, 101, 122
Denton, Dr James, 95–6
Derry, 273, 291, 299, 319
Desmond, earldom of, 12, 16, 218
    demesne exploitation, 35
    liberties of, 17
    and plantation, 233–4, 236
Desmond, earls of. *see* Fitzgeralds
Desmond, Katharine Countess of, 9
Desmond rebellion, 210, 222–7, 223, 228, 291, 316
    acts of attainder, 230–31
    aftermath, 226–7
    costs of, 229
    Smerwick massacre, 226
d'Este, Isabella, Duchess of Mantua, 42
Devereux, Abbot Alexander, 122
Devereux, Stephen, 122
Devlin clan, 56, 58
devotional practices, 124, 132–3, 139, 322
    shrines closed, 137–8
Dillon, Bartholomew, 104
Dillon, Luke, 206
Dillon, Robert, 204, 206, 241, 258
Dillon, Theobald, 254, 258–9
Dillon, Thomas, 258
disease, 8–9, 27, 91, 295
divorce, 60
Docwra, Sir Henry, 299–300, 301
Dominican Order, 120, 131, 142, 242, 319, 322
Donamona castle, 247
Donegal, County, 261, 273, 289, 319
    friary, 130–31

Donegal town, 282
Dorset, Marquis of, 93, 95
Dorsey (Darcy) family, 47
Douai University, 193, 320
Dowdall, George, Archbishop of
    Armagh, 160, 168, 305, 306
  critical of cess, 181
  defects to Rome, 170
  and Reformation, 167
  restored as, 173
Dowdall family, 122, 124, 315
Down, County, 3, 277, 278
Drake, Sir Francis, 278, 279
Drogheda, Co. Louth, 5, 21, 22, 23,
    67, 109, 190
  corporation, 23–4
  dominant families, 25, 32
  friary, 119, 130
  guilds, 124
  housing, 192
  militias, 72
  parliament in, 14
  purveyance, 173
  regalia, 24
  staple port, 29, 40
  trading zone, 32
Drury, Sir William, 193, 316, 319
  Munster president, 219, 220–22, 224
Dublin, 20, 22, 25, 67, 102, 109, 178,
    190, 216, 240, 258, 286
  architecture, 26
  Baltinglass rebellion, 203
  clocks, 6–7
  corporation, 23–4
  county borough status, 162
  disease, 8
  Dominican *studia*, 131
  Dublin–London correspondence, 6
  explosion, 1597, 295
  fee-farm rent, 24
  Fitzgerald rebellion, 106–7, 141
  friars, 119, 120, 130
  garrison supplies, 191
  guilds, 30, 124
  housing, 192
  Howard enters, 87
  Jesuit mission, 303–4
  Kilmainham pattern, 139
  liberties, 17
  map, early 16th c., 31
  merchant families, 5, 25, 32, 47, 201

militias, 72
mint, 172
monastic dissolutions, 140–41, 142
mortality rates, 7
mystery plays, 28, 139
Nine Years' War, 295
parliament in, 14
printing-press, 168
purveyance, 173
Reformation in, 312
regalia, 24
schools, 28
shrines closed, 137–8
trade, 29, 32, 40, 48
Dublin, County, 11, 121, 190
Dublin archdiocese, 117, 118, 121–2,
    309
Dublin Castle, 6, 22, 187, 203–4, 286,
    313
  attacked by Thomas Fitzgerald,
    108–9
  O'Donnell escapes, 289
  O'Neill's head sent to, 274
  ruinous, 87
  single combat, 197
Dublin corporation, 141
Dudley, Lord Robert, 182
Duiske abbey, Co. Kilkenny, 140
Duke, Sir Henry, 287, 292
Dún an Óir, Smerwick, 224–5
Dunboy castle, 301
Dunboyne, Lord, 219
Dunbrody abbey, Co. Wexford, 122,
    140
Dundalk, Co. Louth, 5, 21, 137, 151,
    282
  blockaded by Shane O'Neill, 269
  burnt, 22
  council session, 291
Dungannon, Co. Tyrone, 151, 294
Dungarvan, Co. Waterford, 169, 223
Dunluce castle, 285
Dunsany, Baron of, 66
Dunsany, Co. Meath, 73, 122

education, 27–8, 62–4, 166–7, 194,
    314. *see also* university schemes
  for clergy, 308–9
  continental universities, 119
  English universities, 81, 194
  in monasteries, 131
  of women, 61

Edward VI, King, 113, 164, 166, 171–3, 180, 306, 307
Egerton, Sir Ralph, 95–6
Egerton, Thomas, 231
Elizabeth I, Queen, 182, 185, 190–91, 202, 204, 208, 222, 240, 264, 277
  composition rent to, 250
  death of, 6, 301
  and Desmond, 217, 224, 226–7
  and Essex plan, 278–9
  excommunicated, 315–16
  and FitzMaurice revolt, 214
  and Gaelic lords, 218
  and 2nd Earl Essex, 297, 298
  and Ormond, 212, 219, 228
  O'Rourke surrendered to, 261
  and Shane O'Neill, 269, 270, 272–3, 276
  and Thomond rebellion, 242–3
  and Tyrone, 292
  and Ulster settlements, 277, 278
  and university, 320
emigration, 3
England
  Counter-Reformation, 324
  foreign policy, 205
  impropriated benefices, 314
  Kildare recalled to, 97–100
  trade with, 40, 201
English lordship. *see also* Gaelic Ireland; Old English
  administration of, 53
  and brehon law, 58–9
  description of, 10–18
  gaelicisation, 79, 80
  growing power of magnates, 80–81
  increasing size of, 80–81
  maps, 19, 176
  town and country in, 20–40
Ennis friary, 131
Enniskillen, Co. Fermanagh, 292
environment, natural, 1–10
erenaghs, 126, 131, 133
Erne river, 4, 294
Essex, 1st Earl of, 185, 277, 280, 281, 282
  Antrim plans, 278–9
  supported by Hugh O'Neill, 279, 283
Essex, 2nd Earl of, 177, 264, 265, 288, 299

Athclynt meeting, 298
  governor of Ireland, 297–8
Eustace, Dame Genet, 110
Eustace, James, Viscount Baltinglass, 194, 316. *see also* Baltinglass rebellion
Eustace, Roland, 187, 313
Eustace, Thomas, Viscount Baltinglass, 148, 161
Eustace family, 123, 148, 190, 194, 202
exchequer, 15, 16

faculties, commission for, 147
Fagan family, 313
fairs. *see* markets
famine, 8, 227–8, 295
Farney barony, 149, 288
fasting, 133
fee-farm rent, 17, 23, 24, 37
Fenton, Geoffrey, 229
Fermanagh, County, 261, 268, 291
  invaded by Shane O'Neill, 270
  Maguire lordships, 51, 52
  shired, 285
Fernandez, Gonzalo, 101
Fertagh, Niall MacBrian, 278
festivals, 7, 28–9, 124, 132
feudalism, 10, 11, 53, 80, 221
  'bastard feudalism', 75, 146, 157
Fews, the, 52
Field, Fr Richard, S.J., 322
Field of the Cloth of Gold, 83
Finglas, Sir Patrick, 90, 104, 139
Finglas, Thomas, 105, 106
firearms, 9, 57, 65, 72–3, 293
fisheries, 33, 40, 46
Fitton, Sir Edmund, 232
Fitton, Sir Edward, 185–6, 244
  Connacht president, 238, 241–3, 247
  and Reformation, 312, 319
  Thomond rebellion, 242–3
FitzEdmond, John, of Cloyne, 228
FitzEustace, Alice, 71
FitzEustace, Roland, 73
FitzEustace family, 73
Fitzgerald, Alice, daughter of 9th Earl of Kildare, 98
Fitzgerald, Edward Fitzgibbon, 222
Fitzgerald, Eleanor, 61, 73–4, 150
Fitzgerald, Eleanor, Countess of Desmond, 221, 226–7, 228

Fitzgerald, Eustacia, 73
Fitzgerald, Garret Mór, 8th Earl of
  Kildare ('Great Earl'), 62, 82–3,
  84, 87, 149
  accepted as overlord, 75–7
  battle of Knockdoe, 65–7
  career of, 68–73
  daughters' marriages, 61, 73–4
  death of, 77–8
Fitzgerald, Garret Óg, 9th Earl of
  Kildare, 69, 72, 75, 83, 89–90,
  118, 123, 145
  death of, 108
  debate with Wolsey, 98–9
  description of, 82–4
  imprisoned in London, 105–7
  Lord Deputy 1513–19, 78–9, 85–8
  Lord Deputy 1524–8, 96–100
  Lord Deputy 1532–4, 103–6
  rivalry with Ormond, 94–6
  and Skeffington, 102–3
  Surrey seeks return of, 92
Fitzgerald, Gerald, 15th Earl of
  Desmond, 213, 247, 319. *see also*
  Desmond rebellion
  and Baltinglass rebellion, 206
  death of, 228, 229
  and Fitzgerald rebellion, 107
  imprisoned, 212, 216
  in London, 1562–4, 210
  and Munster presidency, 211–12,
  217–18, 221–2
  Ormond feud, 182, 208–9
  and Shane O'Neill, 269
  and Thomond, 239–40
Fitzgerald, Gerald, 11th Earl of
  Kildare, 111, 141, 145, 149, 150,
  154, 180, 194, 197
  1554, exacts kin-slaying fine, 58
  arrested, 1574, 185
  asserts position, 174
  and Baltinglass rebellion, 203
  cess protest, 187
  command upgraded, 182–3
  death of, 192
  Grey's collusion alleged, 151
  restored, 173
  and Shane O'Neill, 269, 270, 271
  and Sussex, 181
Fitzgerald, Henry, son of Garret Mór,
  62, 66, 67, 73, 75–6

Fitzgerald, Sir James, brother of
  Garret Óg, 73, 95, 96, 110, 111
Fitzgerald, Sir James, of Desmond, 223
Fitzgerald, James FitzJohn, 14th Earl
  of Desmond, 151, 154, 159, 162,
  168
  lordship confirmed, 169
  and St Leger, 157, 163
Fitzgerald, James FitzMaurice, of
  Desmond, 217, 226, 238, 243,
  299, 324
  rebellion, 1569, 213–15, 242, 243,
  316
  rebellion, 1579, 193–4, 203, 222–4,
  316, 322
Fitzgerald, James FitzMaurice, 10th
  Earl of Desmond, 99
  raids on Ormond, 1524, 97
  Spanish contacts, 101
Fitzgerald, James FitzMaurice, rival
  13th Earl of Desmond, 151
Fitzgerald, James FitzThomas, rival
  16th Earl of Desmond (Súgán
  Earl), 236, 297, 298, 299
Fitzgerald, John FitzThomas, rival
  13th Earl of Desmond, 97
Fitzgerald, Sir John, of Desmond, 203,
  212, 215, 223–4, 225–6, 227, 230
Fitzgerald, John FitzEdmund, of
  Imokilly, 208, 214, 216, 222, 231
Fitzgerald, John, Knight of Kerry, 208
Fitzgerald, Margaret, 61, 73
Fitzgerald, Sir Maurice, Lord Decies,
  208–9, 214, 216, 225
  and presidency, 222
Fitzgerald, Maurice, 10th Earl of
  Desmond, 68, 69, 85, 88, 89
Fitzgerald, Maurice, uncle of 9th Earl
  of Kildare, 86
Fitzgerald, Richard, uncle of 10th Earl
  of Kildare, 110, 111
Fitzgerald, Sir Thomas, of Kildare,
  97–8
Fitzgerald, Thomas, 12th Earl of
  Desmond, 101, 102
Fitzgerald, Thomas, 7th Earl of
  Kildare, 73
Fitzgerald, Thomas, 10th Earl of
  Kildare ('Silken Thomas'). *see
  also* Kildare rebellion
  act of attainder, 147
  execution of, 150

Fitzgeralds. *see* Desmond, earldom of;
　Kildare, earldom of
Fitzgibbon, Edmund, 11th White
　Knight, 222, 228
Fitzgibbon, John Oge, 10th White
　Knight, 208, 214
Fitzgibbon, Maurice, 6th White
　Knight, 73
Fitzherbert, Sir Anthony, 95–6
Fitzmaurice, Thomas, Baron of
　Lixnaw, 227
Fitzmaurice, Lord, 162
FitzMaurice rebellion, 1569, 213–15,
　242–3, 316
FitzMaurice rebellion, 1579, 193–4,
　203, 222–4, 316, 322
Fitzpatrick, Sir Barnaby, 201
Fitzsimon, Fr Henry, 303–4
Fitzsimon, Michael, 319
Fitzsimon, Nicholas, 258
Fitzsimon, William, 203
Fitzwalter, Lord, 175
Fitzwilliam, Sir William, 174–5, 180,
　292
　and Hugh O'Neill, 290–91
　Lord Deputy 1571–5, 184–5, 216,
　219, 243
　Lord Deputy 1588–94, 155, 256,
　260–61
　and Ulster, 266
　and Ulster colonies, 277–9
　Ulster policy, 287–91
Flanders, 5, 43, 104, 323
Flattisbury, Philip, 69, 82–3
Fleming, Christopher, 288
Fleming family, 73, 123, 281
Ford of the Biscuits, 5, 292
forests, 3–4
　deforestation, 10
　timber trade, 39, 48, 198
'form of the beads', 113, 137, 139
Fort Governor, King's County. *see*
　Philipstown
Fort Protector, Queen's County. *see*
　Maryborough
fosterage, 61–2, 75–6, 201
France, 5, 43, 169, 210, 316
　allied with Scotland, 267
　and Counter-Reformation, 303
　and Fitzgerald rebellion, 107
　FitzMaurice in, 222–3

invasion of, 92
　and Ulster, 167
　war with England, 159
Francis I, King of France, 88, 97
Franciscan Order, 119–20, 130, 131,
　138, 242, 322
　monastic dissolutions, 142
　Third Order Regular, 131–2
freeholders, 34
friars, 119–20, 130–32, 138–9, 150

Gaelic church, 124–34, 160, 319
　buildings, 130–31
　devotional literature, 131–2
　devotions, 132–3
　dioceses, 115–17
　hereditary succession, 125–7, 129
　lack of infrastructure, 126–7
　lay involvement, 129–30
　and Reformation, 305
　relations with Rome, 124–5, 126,
　128, 133
　role of bishops, 125–7
Gaelic Ireland, 11, 42–64, 94, 148, 187,
　209–10. *see also* English lordship;
　Gaelic church; surrender and
　regrant
　administration of lordships, 53–5
　anglicisation policy, 145, 146, 162,
　194, 198–9, 288. *see also* reform
　movement
　chieftains' submissions, 90
　coexistence with English, 67–8
　and Counter-Reformation, 317, 318
　and Desmond rebellion, 225
　dynastic succession, 51–2
　and Elizabethan policy, 178
　'Gaelic recovery', 10
　Gaelic system banned, 37–8, 216,
　217, 242, 250, 251, 253
　Grey's approaches to, 149–50
　guerrilla warfare, 177–8
　Henry VIII's policy, 90–91, 112
　and Henry's sovereignty, 144, 154–5
　hereditary service families, 53–4
　history and genealogy, 62–3
　inheritance, 48, 260
　inter-sept rivalry, 195
　internal migration, 46–7
　and Kildare, 84, 111
　and Kildare earldom, 74–7

Gaelic Ireland *continued*
   land grants, 196
   land tenure, 11, 81
   learning, 62–4, 76
   legal system, 57–62
   lordships, 50–57
   and New English, 199, 201
   and Old English, 188, 189, 193
   and plantations, 180–81, 213, 214,
     231–2, 234–5
   and presidencies, 239, 247
   raids, 96, 150
   social system, 43–50
   status of women, 59–61
   and towns, 20, 26–7
   trade, 39
   tributes, 54–5, 74–5
   and Ulster colonies, 279–81
   warfare in, 9, 195
gairm sluaigh, 55–6
Gallagher, Sir John, 287
Gallen, Co. Leix, 197
galloglas. *see* troops, Irish
Galway town, 21, 22, 40, 65, 136, 149,
   157, 239, 241, 245
   architecture, 26
   attacked, 243
   battle of Knockdoe, 67
   dominant families, 25, 47–8
   dress codes, 38
   and Dublin administration, 80
   Gaelic trade, 39
   merchants, 260
   monastic dissolutions, 142
   Reformation in, 312
   seventy hanged, 254
   Sidney visits, 240, 245
Galway, County, 239, 257, 262, 300
   agriculture, 45
   settlers, 258
   shired, 241, 243, 245
Gardiner, William, 295
gavelkind, 48, 59–60
gavillers, 34
Geese, John, Bishop of Lismore and
   Waterford, 115
geography, 1–10
   and settlement patterns, 9–10
Gerald of Wales, 1, 2, 80
Geraldine League, 141, 150
Geraldines. *see* Desmond, earls of;
   Kildare, earls of

Gerardus Mercator, 2–3
Germany, 132
Gherardini family, 82–3
Gilbert, Humphrey, 214–15, 218, 224,
   238, 242, 273, 276
Giraldus Cambrensis, 1, 2, 80
Glen of Aherlow, 215, 224, 228
Glenmalure, battle of, 177, 203, 317
Glens of Antrim, 267, 274, 285
Glenshesk, battle of, 272, 274
Glin, Knight of, 230
Goldsmith, John, 153–4
Goodacre, Hugh, Archbishop of
   Armagh, 170, 305
Gormanston, Lord, 66, 187
governors
   correspondence with London, 6
   illness among, 9
   itineration, 14
   responsible for defence, 15–16
   role of, 12–13
   travel improvements, 4–5
Grace Dieu, Dublin, 120, 142, 313
Graney nunnery, Co. Kildare, 161
great councils, 14, 162
Greatconnell, Co. Kildare, 117, 120,
   141
Gregory XIII, Pope, 203, 222–3, 226,
   316
Grenville, Sir Richard, 213, 214, 233
Grey, Elizabeth, 78, 84, 93, 95, 105,
   145, 149
Grey, Lord Leonard, 5, 110–13, 144,
   156, 178
   downfall of, 151–2
   granted monastic land, 140
   Lord Deputy 1536–40, 145–52
   military expeditions, 147–9
   monastic grants, 148
   and Reformation, 136, 139
Grey de Wilton, Arthur Lord, 229,
   319
   and Baltinglass rebellion, 203–5
   battle of Glenmalure, 177, 203
   and Desmond rebellion, 226, 227,
   228
   Lord Deputy 1580, 177
Grey family, 102
'grey merchants', 37–8, 47, 162, 190
guardianship, 235
Guild of St Anne, Dublin, 123, 322

Guild of St George. *see* Brotherhood of Arms
Guild of the Blessed Virgin, Blessed Trinity and St Katherine, 123–4
guilds, 28–9, 36, 38–9. *see also* religious guilds
guns. *see* firearms

harbours, 5
Harrington, Sir Henry, 200, 297
Hartpole, Robert, 197, 200
Hatton, Sir Christopher, 232
Henry II, King of France, 167
Henry VII, King of England, 65, 87, 98
    and Garret Mór, 68–9, 70, 77
Henry VIII, King of England, 58, 78, 101–2, 303
    called King of Ireland, 144–5, 154–5
    and Cromwell, 103–4
    death of, 164
    and Earl of Tyrone, 158–9
    Fitzgerald rebellion, 107–12
    Howard as Deputy, 86, 87
    and Irish administration, 77–8
    and Irish church, 133
    and Kildare, 82, 97–100
    and Ormond dispute, 85
    Ossory as Deputy, 93–4, 100–101
    plans for Gaelic Ireland, 90–91, 153
    policy of retrenchment, 112–13
    Reformation, 134–43
    summons Kildare and Ossory, 1533, 105–6
    supremacy promulgated, 113–14
    wars of, 159–60
Herbert, Sir Edward, 287, 292
Herbert, Sir William, 232, 233, 235, 319
Heron, Nicholas, 180, 195, 200
hides, trade in, 40, 45, 198
highway robbery, 36
holidays, public, 7
Holles, Denzil, 233
Holy Cross abbey, 129
Holy Cross shrine, Ballyboggan, 138
Holy Trinity cathedral, Dublin, 124, 141
holy wells, 124
horses, 45

Horsey, Captain, 273
hospitals, 9, 27
housing, 47, 192. *see also* castles
Hovendon family, 201, 275, 283
Howard, Thomas, Earl of Surrey, 94, 95, 100, 152
    expedition, 1520, 89–93
    Lord Deputy 1519–22, 86, 87, 91–3
    supports Skeffington, 102
Howth, Baron of, 66, 187
Humphrey, Fr James, 113–14, 138

Idrone, Co. Carlow, 184, 196, 213
Ignatius of Loyola, St, 303
Inchiquin, Baron of, 251, 294
industry, manufacturing, 30, 32
infant mortality, 9
Inge, Hugh, 78
'Injunctions', 166
Inns of Court, London, 16, 316
Ireland. *see* English lordship; Gaelic Ireland
Irish council, 13–14, 78, 101, 104–5
    caretaker administration, 1552, 173
    complaints by Bagenal, 291
    Cromwell downgrades, 146–7, 147
    Fitzgerald rebellion, 107, 108–9, 111
    and Garret Óg, 79
    and Grey, 149–50
    Kildare–Ossory feud, 104–5
    losing policy-making power, 188
    monastic suppressions, 140–41
    and Reformation, 135–7
    role of, 13–14
    and St Leger, 153–4
Irish language, 138, 192, 270, 308
    Gaelic typeface, 312
Italy, 5, 43, 107, 226

James VI, King of Scotland, 261, 301
Jerpoint abbey, Co. Kilkenny, 120, 142
Jobson, Francis, 229–30
Jones, Thomas, Bishop of Meath, 318, 319
Joyce family, 254

Katharine of Aragon, 103, 104, 134
Kavanagh, Brian MacCahir, 194, 195, 196, 198
Kavanagh, Cahir MacArt, 153, 156, 163, 195

Kavanagh, Cahir MacInnyCross, 156
Kavanagh, Donal Spainneach, 195
Kavanagh family, 3, 10, 149, 170, 195
  Baltinglass rebellion, 203
  and Bellingham, 165
  Idrone claim, 184
  pacified by St Leger, 153
  raids, 190, 197
  and seneschals, 200
  surrender and regrant, 155, 156, 174
Kearney, John, 312
Kells, Co. Meath, 22, 142
kerne. *see* troops, Irish
Kerry, County
  Desmond rebellion, 223
  and Dublin administration, 80
  famine conditions, 227–8
  liberties, 17
  plantation, 229, 231, 233, 235
  surrender and regrant, 211
  woodlands, 3
Kerry, Knight of, 208
Kerry palatinate, 217, 229
Kerrycurrihy barony, Co. Cork, 211,
  213, 222, 233
Kildare, County, 11, 70, 72, 196
  absentees' lands, 103
  Baltinglass rebellion, 203
  coign and livery, 190
  liberties, 82
  monastic dissolutions, 148, 161
  pacified, 146
Kildare, earldom of, 57, 218
  administration, 71–2
  coign and livery, 190
  collapse of hegemony, 111–12
  demesne exploitation, 35
  development of, 68–70
  dynastic marriages, 73–4
  and Gaelic Ireland, 74–7
  levies payable to, 55
  military strength, 72–3
  protection payments to, 53
  records preserved, 82
  wealth of, 70–72
Kildare, earls of. *see* Fitzgeralds
Kildare diocese, 84, 117, 309, 310
Kildare earldom, 12
  household troops, 15
  liberties of, 17
  role of governor, 13

Kildare rebellion, 1534, 103, 105–11,
  118, 134, 135, 138
  aftermath, 146, 147
  costs of, 140–41
  executions, 111, 150
Kildare town, 72, 190
  charter, 84
Kilkenny town, 20, 30, 97, 137, 171,
  173, 190, 221
  anti-Gaelic trade laws, 38
  architecture, 26
  besieged, 1569, 214
  building in, 192
  coign and livery, 190
  dominant families, 25
  Fitzgerald rebellion, 109
  growth of, 219
  Kavanagh raids, 195
  mystery plays, 28, 124, 139
  river transport, 36
  schools, 28
  Statutes of, 11
Kilkenny, County, 94, 101–2, 305
  commissioners, 16–17
  monastic dissolutions, 142
Kilkenny castle, 94
Kilkenny diocese, 310
Killeen, Baron of, 66
Kilmallock, Co. Limerick, 157, 214,
  215, 218, 224, 316
King's County
  created, 180–81
kingship, 52–3, 76
Kinsale, Co. Cork, 169, 215
  battle of, 300–301
  and Geraldine overlordship, 218
Kite, John, 78
Knights Hospitaller of St John,
  Kilmainham, 306
Knockdoe, battle of, 1504, 65–7, 70,
  73, 75, 77
Knollys, Sir Francis, 272–3

Lacy, Hugh, Bishop of Limerick, 313
Lagan river, 4
Lambert, Matthew, 317
Lancaster, Bishop, of Kildare, 173,
  306
land ownership, 192, 199
  Connacht, 253, 260
  English–Gaelic conflict, 195–6

Gaelic, 48–50, 61
  succession rights, 59–60
Lane, Edmund, Bishop of Kildare,
  117
Lane, Sir Ralph, 261, 289
law courts, 16–17
Lawrence, St, 124
Lea castle, 71
learned classes
  and religious orders, 131
Lecale, 165, 168, 267, 272, 280
Lee, river, 4
legal system, 192, 198–9
  chancery law, 59–60
  Gaelic, 57–61
Leicester, Earl of, 182, 242, 270, 272,
  291, 309
Leighlin Bridge, 5, 165, 170, 195, 197
Leinster, 10, 57
  1556–88, 177–207
  Bellingham campaigns, 165–6
  Carew land claim, 184, 185, 195–6,
    213
  clans, 43
  composition tax, 186–7
  Fitzgerald rebellion, 107, 108
  Gaelic areas under threat, 112
  Grey sorties, 149
  Nine Years' War, 294
  peace unstable, 163–4
  recusancy, 319
  'slantyaght', 74
  St Leger sorties, 153, 155
  submissions to Garret Mór, 75
  surrender and regrant, 155–6
  towns, 21
  unrest, 1577, 187
Leitrim, County, 252
  Burke rebellion, 256
  settlement, 287
  shired, 261
  Spanish Armada, 237
Leix, 195, 199. *see also* Queen's
  County
  Fort Protector, 165–6, 178
  Gaelic land grants, 196
  Gaelic lordships, 10
  plantation planned, 168, 169–70,
    179, 180
  plantations, 180–81, 182, 183–4
  surveys, 4

Lennox, Earl of, 160
leper-houses, 27
Lestrange, Sir Thomas, 255, 258
Leverous, Thomas, Bishop of Kildare,
  173, 306, 308
liberties, 16, 17, 82, 85
  dismantling of, 146
  enlarged, 173
  Ormond–Desmond feud, 209
life expectancy, 7
Liffey river, 4
Lifford, Co. Donegal, 272, 273, 279,
  282, 294
Limerick, 5, 22, 136, 149, 215, 240
  attacked, 214
  'black rent', 37, 77
  Desmond rebellion, 224
  dominant families, 25
  and Dublin administration, 80
  Gaelic trade, 38, 39
  Geraldine overlordship, 218
  monastic dissolutions, 142
  Oath of Supremacy, 139
  parliament in, 157
  Reformation in, 312
  regalia, 24
  staple port, 29
Limerick, County, 97
  Desmond rebellion, 223, 225
  famine conditions, 227
  Nine Years' War, 297
  plantation, 235
  Sidney in, 214
  survey of, 230
Lisbon Irish College, 320
Lismullin convent, Co. Meath, 122,
  141
literature, devotional, 131–2
Lixnaw, Lord, 228
local government, reform of, 146–7
Loftus, Adam, Archbishop of Dublin,
  205, 206, 295, 308, 309, 312, 316
  financial problems, 310
  on recusancy, 317–18
Loftus, Captain Adam, 297
Lombard, Peter, 299, 324
London
  correspondence with, 6
  Fitzgerald executions, 111
  Kildare in, 97–100, 103
  merchants' colonies, 213

London *continued*
  mint, 172
  Shane O'Neill in, 270
Longford, County, 142
Lord Lieutenant
  role of, 13
  title of, 87
Lords Deputy. *see* governors
Lough Derg, 1, 132
Lough Foyle, 273, 296, 299
Louth, County, 11, 108, 115, 314, 315
  castellated houses, 192
  coign and livery, 190
  friary, 161
  monastic dissolutions, 141
  wayside crosses, 124
Louth, Lord. *see* Plunket
Louvain University, 119, 193, 320
Low Countries, 3, 205, 320
Luttrell, Thomas, 154
Luttrell family, 313, 315
Lyon, Bishop, of Cork, 46

MacArt, Cahir, 149
MacArt, Fearganainm, 149
MacBrady, Siobhán, 126
MacBrady, Thomas, Bishop of
  Kilmore, 125, 126
MacBrady family, 47
MacBrien family, 158
MacCann family, 283
MacCarthy, Sir Cormac MacTaidhg,
  218
MacCarthy, Cormac Óg, of
  Muskerry, 89, 97
MacCarthy, Sir Dermot, of Muskerry,
  212, 214
MacCarthy, Florence, 298, 299
MacCarthy clan, 216
MacCarthy More, Donal, Earl of
  Clancarty, 55, 210–11, 214–15,
  218, 236
  and Munster plantation, 233–4
MacCarthy More lordship, 51, 169
MacCarthy Reagh, 61, 74, 150
MacCarthy Reagh, Donal, 89
MacCarthy Reagh, Donough, of
  Carbery, 218, 221
MacCarthy Reagh, Eleanor, 111
MacClancy clan, 58, 237
MacCoghlan clan, 58
MacCongail, Donal, Bishop of
  Raphoe, 313

MacCostello clan, 254, 259
MacDavid family, 129
MacDermott clan, 66, 74, 245
MacDonagh clan, 53, 258
MacDonnell, Alaster MacRandal Boy,
  272
MacDonnell, Alexander Óg, 274
MacDonnell, Angus, 272, 285
MacDonnell, Catherine, 271
MacDonnell, Finola, 'Iníon Dubh',
  60–61, 275–6, 289
MacDonnell, James, 169, 267, 271,
  272, 275
MacDonnell, Sorley Boy, 272, 274,
  280, 285
MacDonnell clan, 169, 171, 254–5
  defensive alliance, 281
  raids, 284–5
  and Shane O'Neill, 269, 272, 274
MacEgan family, 58
MacEvilly clan, 247
MacGeoghegan, Brian, 204
MacGeoghegan, Melaghlin, 75
MacGeoghegan, Morirte, 75
MacGeoghegan clan, 74
MacGibbon, Maurice, Archbishop of
  Cashel, 214, 316
MacGillapatrick, of Upper Ossory,
  156, 219
MacKenraghty, Maurice, 319
Mackworth, Captain, 197
MacLean, Catherine, Dowager
  Countess of Argyll, 61, 268–9, 271
MacLean clan, 284
MacMahon, Brian MacHugh Óg, 288
MacMahon, Hugh Roe, 288
MacMahon, Sir Ross, 287–8
MacMahon family, of Oriel, 54, 67,
  74, 149, 171, 266, 273, 281
  backs Hugh O'Neill, 284
  settlement, 287–8
  and Shane O'Neill, 268, 272
  surrender and regrant, 285
MacManus clan, 54
MacMurrough clan, 74, 108
MacNamara, MacCon, 130
MacNamara clan, 66, 158, 239, 251
MacQuillan clan, 159, 267
MacQuin, Fergal, 75
MacRennall clan, 74
MacSheehy clan, 230

MacSweeney family, Fanad, 55
MacTaidhg, Sir Cormac, 225
MacWilliam Burke. *see* Burke
Magauran, Cormac, Bishop of
    Ardagh, 126
Magauran, Cormac, Bishop of
    Kilmore, 126
Magauran, Edmund, Archbishop of
    Armagh, 261, 290, 323
Magennis, Prior Glaisne, Iveagh, 129
Magennis, Sir Hugh, of Iveagh, 282,
    286, 290
Magennis clan, 171, 266, 281, 285
Magennises of Iveagh, 67
Magrath, Miler, Archbishop of
    Cashel, 7
Maguire, Cathal Óg MacManus, Dean
    and Canon, 126
Maguire, Conor Roe, 290
Maguire, Hugh, Lord of Fermanagh,
    262, 291, 323
    and Earl of Tyrone, 289–90
    Nine Years' War, 296, 299
    siege of Enniskillen, 292
Maguire, Nicholas, Bishop of
    Leighlin, 125
Maguire, Philip, 52
Maguire, Shane, 272
Maguire, Thomas, 126
Maguire clan, 51, 261–2, 266, 273
    backs Hugh O'Neill, 284
    clerical families, 126
    hereditary service families, 54
    hosting obligation, 56
    and Shane O'Neill, 268
    surrender and regrant, 285
Mainwaring, Edmund, 232
Malachy, St, 126
Malby, Sir Nicholas, 224, 257, 277,
    278, 280
    Connacht president, 238, 246–8,
    252, 257
    and Mac an Iarlas, 245–6
Malone family, 47
manors
    commercial exploitation, 35
    links with markets, 32–40
    peasant communities, 34–5
maoir, 53–4
maps, 2–3
marches, 10–11, 34, 99, 101

Grey's campaigns, 149
'march law', 58–9
towns, 26
trade, 39
markets, 20, 29
    manorial links, 32–40
    problems with, 36–8
    threatened by disorder, 100
marriage
    age, 7
    of clergy, 126–7, 129
    dynastic, 73–4
    Gaelic, 60
    Gaelic–English intermarriage, 259
    intermarriage forbidden, 148
    of planters, 232
marshals, Gaelic, 53–4
Mary I, Queen, 170, 173, 179, 305, 308
Maryborough (Fort Protector),
    Queen's County, 165–6, 169–70,
    178, 181, 183, 198, 200–201
Masterson, Thomas, 195, 199, 200
Maynooth, Co. Kildare, 70, 72, 82
    castle, 109, 110
    collegiate chapel, 83, 123
Mayo, County, 247, 260
    Burke rebellion, 255–6
    composition tax, 251
    and presidency, 239
    rebellion, 1589, 263
    settlers, 254, 257, 259
    shired, 245
mayor, role of, 24
Meath, County, 11
    agriculture, 10–11
    church-building, 122
    economic conditions, 190
    monastic dissolutions, 140, 141,
    148, 161
    Nugent conspiracy, 204
    Reformation in, 319
    shrines closed, 137–8
    urbanisation, 21
Meath diocese, 117, 119, 309
medical knowledge, 9
Meelick castle, 181
Mellifont, Co. Louth
    abbey, 122, 124, 141, 161
    peace of, 6, 301–2
mendicant friars, 119–20, 130–32, 137,
    138–9

Mendoza, Don Pedro de, 237
merchant families, 25–6, 32, 47
    map of, 41
merchant guilds, 21, 25–6, 29, 32,
    190–91
merchants, 5, 172–3, 184
meteorology, 8
middlemen, 49–50
migration, internal, 46–7
millenarianism, 133
Mitchelstown castle, 214
Monaghan, County, 261, 268
    settlement, 287–8, 291
    shired, 285
    support for Tyrone, 291
    Sussex sortie, 269
Monaghan town, 290
monasteries
    dissolution of, 120–22, 139–43,
        148, 190, 305, 314
    dissolution opposed, 135–6
    education in, 131
    exactions, 121
    in Gaelic church, 129–30
    lay leases, 122
    St Leger and dissolutions, 160–62
Monasternenagh, battle of, 224
Money family, 320
Moore, Sir Edward, 201
More, Thomas, 103
Moret castle, 71
mortality rates, 7–9
mortgages, 234, 235, 260
Mountjoy, Lord
    Lord Deputy, 1600, 299–302
Moyne friary, Co. Mayo, 131
Mullaghmast, Co. Kildare
    massacre, 1577, 187, 197
Mullingar, Co. Westmeath, 25, 190
Mulryan, Abbot Matthew, 129
municipalities, 17
Munster, 48, 96, 173, 174, 183, 214–15,
    278
    1565–95, 208–36
    Carew president, 299
    clans, 43
    commission, 1588, 234
    Desmond lordship confirmed, 169
    Desmond rebellion, 223–8, 291
    Essex circuit of, 297
    famine, 227–8

feudalism in, 10
Fitzgerald rebellion, 107, 108, 193–4
FitzMaurice rebellion, 213–15, 316
Gaelic raids, 5
Grey sorties, 149, 150
lordships, 12, 51
mercenary troops, 57
Nine Years' War, 297, 301
Oath of Supremacy, 138
Ormond–Desmond feuds, 182
peace unstable, 167
plantation, 210, 212–13, 229–36, 280
plantation destroyed, 235–6
plantation plans, 184
presidency, 179, 185, 211–13,
    215–18, 242, 245
rebellion, 1598, 235–6
Reformation in, 319
regional council, 186
'slantyaght', 74
St Leger in, 153, 156–8
surrender and regrant, 218
survey of, 229–30, 233
murage, 17, 23
musicians, hereditary, 63
mystery plays, 28, 124, 132, 139

Naas, Co. Kildare, 26, 82, 190
    fee-farm rent, 24
    guilds, 123–4
    raided, 197
Nangle, Richard, Bishop of Clonfert,
    138
Navan, Baron of, 66
Navan, Co. Meath, 22, 151, 162
Neale, Co. Mayo, 255, 257
Nenagh, Co. Tipperary, 165–6
Netherlands, 132, 255, 286, 316, 323
Netterville, George, 204, 317
Netterville, Richard, 187
New English, 188–9, 193
    and composition plan, 249
    Connacht settlers, 253–4, 257–8,
        260, 261
    criticism of administration, 191–2
    and Gaelic Irish, 195, 199
    influence of, 178
    and Old English, 161–2, 194, 202
    and plantations, 229–36
    planters, 169
    and presidencies, 248

and Reformation, 319–20
religion of, 304, 312
'New Injunctions', 137, 139
Newry, Co. Down, 165, 267, 270, 277,
  292, 294, 300
  development of, 282
  garrison, 183
news, transmission of, 6
Nicholls, Kenneth, 21
Nine Years' War, 5, 238, 253, 259,
  264–5, 266, 292–302
  costs of, 295, 302
  and Counter-Reformation, 322–3
  Spanish troops, 300
Nore river, 4
Norfolk, Thomas Howard, 4th Duke
  of, 242. *see also* Howard,
  Thomas, Earl of Surrey (later 2nd
  Duke of Norfolk)
Normans, 9–10, 11
Norris, Sir John, 229, 279, 294, 319
Northumberland, Lord, 164, 182
Nugent, Nicholas, 204
Nugent, Richard. *see* Delvin, Baron of
Nugent, William, 203–4, 317, 319
Nugent family, 190, 194

Ó Faoláin, Eugene, 129
Ó hUiginn, Pilib Bocht, 131
Ó Maolchonaire, Urard, 131
Oath of Supremacy, 136, 137, 138,
  207, 308
O'Brien, Conor, 3rd Earl of
  Thomond, 239–40
  rebellion, 1570, 242–3
O'Brien, Conor, of Thomond, 107, 149
O'Brien, Donal, of Thomond, 239–40,
  242
O'Brien, Donough, 2nd Earl of
  Thomond, 158, 239
  and FitzMaurice revolt, 215
  succession dispute, 239–40
O'Brien, Donough, 4th Earl of
  Thomond, 249, 250, 257, 259
  Nine Years' War, 294, 297
O'Brien, Finola, 130–31
O'Brien, Matthew, Bishop of
  Kilmacduagh, 126
O'Brien, Murrough, 1st Earl of
  Thomond, 157–8, 163, 167, 168
O'Brien, Ranelt, 126
O'Brien, Sir Tadhg MacMurrough, 242

O'Brien, Turlough, Bishop of
  Killaloe, 126
O'Brien, Sir Turlough, of Corcomroe,
  251
O'Brien, Turlough Donn, of
  Thomond, 66, 77, 126
O'Brien clan
  Desmond supporters, 208
O'Brien's Bridge, 5, 77, 149
O'Briens of Thomond, 23
  assist Desmond, 97
  dynastic politics, 77
  raids, 5
Observant friars, 60, 62, 119–20, 131
  and Reformation, 138–9
O'Byrne, Feagh MacHugh, 177, 194,
  195, 200, 294
  battle of Baltinglass, 203
  raids, 187
O'Byrne, Hugh, 200
O'Byrne, Phelim MacFeagh, 297
O'Byrne clan, 74, 170
  Baltinglass rebellion, 203
  and Bellingham, 165
  Fitzgerald rebellion, 108
  growing assimilation, 194
  raids, 197
  surrender and regrant, 155, 156
O'Byrne lordship, 10, 45
O'Cahan, Donal, 302
O'Cahan clan, 159, 274
O'Callaghan clan, 48
O'Carroll, Sir Charles, of Ely, 298
O'Carroll, Fearganainm, 105
O'Carroll of Ely, 10, 66, 74, 90, 149,
  156, 219
O'Connolly family, 54
O'Connor, Brian, 98, 110, 149, 153,
  165
O'Connor, Cahir, 165
O'Connor, Conor MacCormac, 187,
  196, 197
O'Connor, Donal, 252
O'Connor, Donough, 181
O'Connor, Rory Caoch, 194
O'Connor, Tadhg MacGillapatrick,
  197
O'Connor clan, 10, 45, 67, 74, 90, 149,
  163, 167, 195, 196, 200
  Baltinglass rebellion, 203
  'black rents', 102

O'Connor clan *continued*
    Desmond supporters, 208
    Fitzgerald rebellion, 108
    land grants, 196
    Mullaghmast massacre, 187
    Nine Years' War, 296
    pacified by St Leger, 153
    and plantation, 170, 181, 182, 201
    raids, 164, 190
    rebellions, 196–7
    surrender and regrant, 155, 156
    transplanting, 229
O'Connor Don, 245
O'Connor Faly, 71, 98, 107
O'Connor Roe, 66
O'Connor Sligo, Brian, 57
O'Connor Sligo, Donal, 240, 247–8,
    250, 256
O'Connor Sligo, Donough, 256, 298
O'Connor Sligo clan, 53, 150, 260, 262
    O'Donnell feud, 287
O'Crean, Andrew, Bishop of Elphin,
    313
O'Dempsey, Owen MacHugh, 196
O'Dempsey, Sir Terence, 196
O'Dempsey clan, 156, 194
O'Devlins, 283
O'Doherty, Sir John, 287
O'Donnell, Calvagh, 61, 272, 273
    and Shane O'Neill, 268, 270
O'Donnell, Donal, 287, 289
O'Donnell, Hugh Dubh (d. 1537),
    102, 131
O'Donnell, Hugh Dubh (d. 1600), 248,
    252, 268–9, 273–4, 276, 282, 289
    supports Hugh O'Neill, 284
    surrender and regrant, 285
O'Donnell, Hugh Óg, 77
O'Donnell, Hugh Roe (d. 1505), 66,
    75–6, 130
O'Donnell, Hugh Roe (d. 1602), 239,
    262, 284, 286, 287, 289–90, 291,
    323
    death of, 301
    and MacWilliam Burke succession,
        297
    Nine Years' War, 296, 298, 299, 300
    siege of Enniskillen, 292
O'Donnell, Manus, 53, 61, 73, 89, 131,
    150, 151, 159, 160, 169, 303
    and Kildare, 96
O'Donnell, Niall Garbh, 299, 301

O'Donnell, Rory, 301, 302
O'Donnell lordship, Tyrconnell, 53,
    55, 62, 168, 247–8
    aggrandisement, 275–6
    castles, 57
    confrontation with Fitzwilliam, 289
    defensive alliance, 281
    and Essex, 279
    and Kildare, 73–4
    O'Connor Sligo feud, 287
    Scottish raids, 284–5
    shired, 285
    support for Tyrone, 291
O'Donnelly clan, 54, 62, 284
O'Donoghue More, 234
O'Doran family, 198–9
O'Dowds, 248, 259, 262
O'Driscolls, 38, 40
O'Dunne clan, 55, 156
O'Dwyer, Abbot William, 129
O'Dwyer clan, 74
O'Fallon, Donal, Bishop of Derry, 125
O'Farrell, Brian, of Annaly, 74
O'Farrell, William, Bishop of Ardagh,
    126
O'Farrell clan, 67, 74, 171, 198
Offaly, 149, 165–6, 178, 195. see also
        King's County
    agriculture, 45
    Gaelic land grants, 196
    Gaelic lordships, 10
    Grey in, 178
    plantation planned, 168, 169–70,
        179, 180
    plantations, 180–81, 182, 183–4
    surveys, 4
Offaly, Thomas, Lord, 89
O'Fihely, Maurice, 125
O'Flaherty, Donal an Chogaidh, 244
O'Flaherty, Donal Crone, 244
O'Flaherty, Murrough na Doe, 240,
    244, 251, 255, 256
O'Flaherty, Owen, 251
O'Flaherty clan, 237, 247
O'Gallagher, Redmund, Bishop of
        Derry, 323
O'Gara clan, 53, 259, 260
O'Grady clan, 126
O'Hagan clan, 56, 274, 283, 290
O'Hanlon clan, 67, 171
O'Hara clan, 53, 248, 260

O'Harte, Eugene, Bishop of Achonry, 9, 313, 323
O'Harte clan, 256
O'Healy, Patrick, Bishop of Mayo, 224, 316
O'Hedian, John, 125
O'Hedian, Richard, Archbishop of Cashel, 115
O'Hely, James, Archbishop of Tuam, 261, 323
O'Hurley, Dermot, Archbishop of Cashel, 205, 317, 318
Oireacht Uí Chatháin, 275
O'Keeffe clan, 214
O'Kelly, Melaghlin, 66
O'Kelly clan, 126
O'Kennedy clan, 66, 219
Old English, 88, 93, 103–4, 192. *see also* reform movement
and Anglo–Normans, 226–7
Baltinglass rebellion, 194, 202–5
and composition, 249
Connacht colonists, 253–4, 257, 258–9
Desmond rebellion, 230
Fitzgerald rebellion, 112
and Gaelic Irish, 193
monastic dissolutions, 135–6, 140–41
and New English, 161–2, 202
number of retainers, 95–6
and Perrot, 206
and plantations, 234–5
planters, 169, 231
and presidency scheme, 210
religion of, 115, 193, 304–5, 317, 318, 319, 321
and Sidney, 187–9
and St Leger, 153–4, 157, 161–2, 164
and Surrey, 92
and Sussex, 270, 272
Tyrone appeals to, 298–9
ollaimh, 63
O'Loughlin clan, 243, 251
O'Mahon clan, 243, 251
O'Malley, Dubhdarach Roe, 237
O'Malley, Gráinne (Grace), 59, 60–61, 256, 259
O'Malley clan, 245, 247, 254
O'Meara clan, 219
O'More, Conal, 181

O'More, MacGillapatrick, 165
O'More, Owney MacRory, 5, 236, 296–7
O'More, Rory Óg, 185, 187, 195, 198, 200
raids, 196, 197
O'More clan, 10, 74, 89, 102, 167, 195, 200
Baltinglass rebellion, 203
Fitzgerald rebellion, 108
land grants, 196
Mullaghmast massacre, 187, 197
Nine Years' War, 296, 299
plantation planned, 170
and plantations, 181, 182, 201
raids, 164, 190
rebellions, 196–7
surrender and regrant, 155, 156
transplanting, 229
O'Moriarty clan, 228
O'Mulryan clan, 62
O'Neill, Sir Art, 286, 299
O'Neill, Art MacBaron, 292
O'Neill, Art Óg, 76
O'Neill, Brian, Baron of Dungannon, 268, 270
O'Neill, Sir Brian MacPhelim, 44, 269, 277–8, 279, 280, 281
O'Neill, Conn Bacach, 1st Earl of Tyrone, 53, 98, 108, 160, 283, 303
accepts paternity of Matthew, 61
bears sword of state for Kildare, 96
and Brereton, 168
and Croft, 169
and Fitzgerald rebellion, 107
and Geraldine League, 150
and Grey, 151
and MacDonnells, 267
and St Leger, 158–9, 163, 268
submits to Skeffington, 102
treaty with Surrey, 89
O'Neill, Conn MacNeill Óg, 290
O'Neill, Cormac MacBaron, 291, 292
O'Neill, Donnell, 76
O'Neill, Hugh, 2nd Earl of Tyrone, 201, 265–6, 268, 270, 281, 286, 289
Athclynt meeting, 1599, 264–5, 298
and Bagenal, 290
and Catholic faith, 298–9
and Counter-Reformation, 322–3, 324

O'Neill, Hugh, 2nd Earl of Tyrone
  continued
  family connections, 290–91
  made Baron of Dungannon, 274–5
  Nine Years' War, 292–302
  peace of Mellifont, 301–2
  rebellion, 236
  rise of, 283–92
  supports Essex, 279
O'Neill, Hugh Gavelagh MacShane, 291
O'Neill, Hugh MacNeill Mór, of the Fews, 274
O'Neill, Matthew, Baron of Dungannon, 61, 159, 169, 268, 270, 274
O'Neill, Niall Conallach, 133
O'Neill, Shane, 159, 169, 171, 265, 276, 280, 281, 283, 313
  aims of, 270–71
  campaign against, 183
  fostered by O'Donnellys, 62
  in London, 270
  MacShanes, 274, 284, 291
  raids, 181, 182
  struggle with Sussex, 267–72
  treaty with, 271–2
O'Neill, Shane Óg, 284
O'Neill, Turlough Brasselagh of the Fews, 274, 284
O'Neill, Turlough Luineach, 265, 270, 271, 291, 299
  defensive alliance, 281
  and Essex, 279
  illness, 1579, 284
  to occupy north Tyrone, 285–6, 290
  as The O'Neill, 274–5
  terms agreed, 282–3
  and Ulster settlers, 278
O'Neill, Turlough MacHenry of the Fews, 284
O'Neill lordship (Tyrone), 45, 51, 67, 247
  hereditary service families, 54
  hereditary troops, 55–6
  succession disputes, 274–5, 284
  surrender and regrant, 174
O'Neill lordship (Clandeboye), 52, 171, 267
  attacked by Kildare, 95
O'Neill lordship (of the Fews), 52, 284
Oneilland barony, 283, 290

O'Neills of Dungannon, 73, 76
O'Quinns, 283, 290
Ordinances for the government of Ireland, 105
O'Reilly, Eamonn, 287
O'Reilly, Sir John, 287
O'Reilly, Maolmórdha, 268, 272
O'Reilly, Pilib, 286, 287
O'Reilly clan, 47, 67, 74, 168, 171, 266, 273, 281, 282
  Perrot settlement, 286–7
  and Shane O'Neill, 270
  surrender and regrant, 285
Ormond, Joan, Countess of, 209
Ormond, Margaret, Countess of, 95
Ormond, earldom of, 12, 26, 61, 73, 219. *see also* Butler family
  coign and livery, 190
  defence of, 16
  demesne exploitation, 35
  fosterage, 62
  hereditary brehons, 58
  levies payable to, 55
  liberties of, 17
  monastic dissolutions, 141, 160–61
  and presidency, 221
  prisage rights, 18
  title dispute, 85, 88, 89–90, 95
  title granted to Boleyn, 100
O'Rourke, Brian, 204, 250, 255, 257, 261, 287, 319
  submits, 245
O'Rourke, Brian Óg, 287, 290, 323
O'Rourke clan, 74, 237, 252, 259
Ortelius, Abraham, 2–3
O'Shaughnessy clan, 45, 158, 239, 240
Ossory diocese, 170
O'Sullivan Beare, lordship of, 40, 216, 218, 235, 301
  and FitzMaurice revolt, 214
  standing army, 56
O'Sullivan More, lordship of, 216, 218
  and FitzMaurice revolt, 214
O'Toole, Brian, 155, 163
O'Toole, Turlough, 153, 155, 163
O'Toole, Turlough MacShane, 155, 163
O'Toole clan, 10, 71, 74, 102, 195
  and Bellingham, 165
  Fitzgerald rebellion, 109
  growing assimilation, 194
  pacified by St Leger, 153
  surrender and regrant, 155, 174

Oughtred, Sir Henry, 235
Our Lady of Trim shrine, 137–8
Oxford University, 119, 125, 309

palatinates, 17, 209, 217
    and presidencies, 211, 212
Palatyne, Walter, 167
Pale, the, 11, 79, 103, 153
    1556–88, 177–207
    administrative reform, 12
    agriculture, 33
    Bellingham campaigns, 165–6
    billeting complaints, 179
    church-building, 122–3
    coign and livery, 92
    Counter-Reformation in, 316–17
    defences of, 15, 69, 98, 99–100, 150
    economic problems, 189–90
    English–Gaelic land disputes, 195–6
    Fitzgerald rebellion, 108, 111
    Gaelic lordships within, 10
    Gaelic raids, 94, 96, 151
    migration to, 46
    monastic dissolutions, 139–40, 141,
        142, 148, 160–61
    and Nine Years' War, 295, 299
    Oath of Supremacy, 138
    pacified by Skeffington, 145–6
    peace with Gaelic lords, 162
    raids, 164, 174
    recusancy in, 317–18
    Reformation in, 308
    seneschals, 165
    shrines closed, 137–8
    surrender and regrant, 155–6
    trading zone, 32
Palmerstown rectory, 122
Paris, George, 167
Paris University, 119
Parker, John, 153, 161, 175
parliament, Irish, 11, 12, 93, 103, 156,
    190, 306
    Act of Supremacy, 113
    Cromwellian legislation, 147–8
    ecclesiastical bills, 134–6, 147
    Henry titled King of Ireland,
        144–5, 154–5
    judicial role, 16
    in Limerick, 1542, 157
    members' rights disputed, 184
    mercantilist bills, 191, 218

monastic suppressions, 140
Old English dominant, 206–7
    under Perrot, 206–7
    religious reform acts, 307–8
    role of, 14
    under Sidney, 183–4, 188, 191
    under St Leger, 162–3
    subsidy bill fails, 1531, 102–3
    under Surrey, 92
    trading legislation, 37–8
    in Trim, 1542, 159
Pass of the Plumes, 5
Patrick, St, 324
Paul III, Pope, 303
Paul IV, Pope, 305
Peachey, Sir John, 92
Pelham, Sir William, 193, 224, 225, 227
Perrot, Sir John, 179, 185, 261, 266
    Composition of Connacht, 249–50
    dispute with Bingham, 255
    Lord Deputy 1584, 205–7, 229,
        248–9
    Munster presidency, 215–16,
        217–20, 238
    and O'Donnells, 289
    and Ormond, 219
    and Reformation, 317
    Ulster policy, 284–6
Pettit family, 25
petty custom, 30
philanthropy, 27–8
Philip II, King of Spain, 214, 222, 290,
        305, 316. *see also* Spanish Armada
    and Tyrone, 291
Philipstown (Fort Governor), King's
        County, 165–6, 170, 178, 181,
        183, 198, 200–201
physicians, hereditary, 63
Piers, Captain William, 267, 274, 279
pilgrimages, 1, 132
Pipho, Robert, 200
piracy, 5–6, 36, 172
Pius V, Pope, 315–16
plague, 8, 27, 87
plantations, 169–70, 179, 207, 209,
        213, 280. *see also* Leix; Offaly
    attacks on, 196–7, 297
    'chargeable lands', 233–4
    colonies in Ulster, 276–83
    commission, 1588, 234
    'intermixers', 233

plantations *continued*
    Leinster, 200–201
    Munster, 210, 212–13, 229–36
    planning and practice of, 229–36
    reactions to, 185
    St Leger plans, 168, 170
    Surrey plans, 91
Plunket, Oliver, Lord Louth, 161
Plunket, Sir John, of Dunsoghly, 313
Plunkets of Dunsoghly, 66
Plunkett, Sir Christopher, 122
Plunkett, Edward, 122
Plunkett family, 122
Plunketts of Dunsany, 73, 124
pluralism, 119, 128, 129
poets, Gaelic, 2, 62–4, 216
Pole, Cardinal, 306
political environment, 10–18
Polydore Vergil, 2, 11
Popham, John, 231
population, 4
    internal migration, 46–7
    manorial, 33–4
    mortality rates, 7–9
    urban, 21, 22
port towns, 135, 136, 209
Portlester, Co. Meath, 71, 72, 73
portolan charts, 2, 5
ports, 39–40, 84, 169
Portugal, 5
post-boats, 5–6
poundage, 30
Power, Lord, 208
Power family, 17
Powerscourt castle, 71
Poynings, Sir Edward, 82
Poynings' Law, 1494, 14, 68, 147, 188, 206
presidency councils, 179, 183, 185, 209, 210
    Connacht, 238, 239–49
    costs of, 243–4
    Munster, 211–13, 217–18
    Ulster, 282
primogeniture, 51, 75, 155, 156, 158, 184, 251, 267, 288
printing, 168, 312
prisage, 18, 29–30
Privy Council, 13–14
    censures Grey de Wilton, 204
    complaints concerning Kildare, 79
    and Essex plan, 278
    Irish policy, 173
    and Ormond–Desmond feud, 210, 212
    and plantations, 231, 234
    and Sidney's Ulster plans, 276
    and St Leger, 163
    and Tyrone, 283, 291
Protestantism. *see* Reformation
purgatory, 166
Puritanism, 318
purveyance, 37, 54, 172–3, 179

Queen's County
    created, 180–81
Quin, John, Bishop of Limerick, 168
Quin friary, Co. Clare, 130, 131
Quinn clan, 56

Radcliffe, Sir Henry, 180, 181, 201
Radcliffe, Thomas, Lord Fitzwalter.
    see Sussex, Earl of
Raleigh, Sir Walter, 226, 229, 232, 297
Randolph, Captain, 319
Randolph, Colonel Edward, 273
Ratcliffe, Robert, 5–6
Rathlin Island, 169, 279, 280
Rawson, John, 78, 101, 103
Recalde, Admiral, 237
Red Book of Kildare, 82
Redman, Mr, 27
'redshanks', 57, 275
reform movement, 79–82, 84–5, 88, 92–3, 100, 193. *see also* Reformation
    1536–40, 144–5
    failure of, 199
    Grey's efforts, 145–52
    moves against Kildare and Ossory, 106
    religious, 114, 133–4, 164
Reformation, 28, 60, 83, 89, 113–15, 134–43, 241–2, 303, 304, 315. *see also* monasteries
    attitudes of clergy, 138–9
    attitudes of laity, 139–40
    and Bellingham, 166–7
    course of, 305–11
    and Croft, 170–71
    ecclesiastical commissions, 308
    evangelisation, 318–20
    legislation, 147

liturgical changes, 308
and New English, 304
number of impropriated benefices, 314–15
and Perrot, 205–6
profits, 314–15
Protestantism, 164, 193, 201, 305, 307
recusancy, 193, 202, 205, 207, 312, 316, 317–18, 320–21
responses to, 311–15
shrines closed, 137–8
and St Leger, 164, 168, 173
structural weaknesses, 305–7
religion, 108. *see also* clergy; Counter-Reformation; Gaelic church; Reformation
Catholicism restored, 1553, 306
church buildings, 120–21, 122–3, 314–15
dioceses, 115–17
English control reasserted, 89
financial problems, 310–11
fragmented authority, 117–18
Henry head of church, 136–7
influence of, 62
jurisdiction problems, 160
lay involvement in church, 121–4, 311
map of dioceses, 116
marriage law, 60
of Old English, 189
and political identity, 315–24
pre-Reformation church, 115–24
role of bishops, 117
religious devotions, 124, 132–3, 139, 322
shrines closed, 137–8
religious guilds, 28–9, 123–4, 167, 315, 318
survival of, 321–2
religious orders, 28, 119–20, 125–6
in Gaelic church, 129–32
Renaissance, 72, 83
Rice, James, 26, 27
Rich, Barnaby, 7, 319
Richard II, King, 177
Richmond, Duke of, 101, 105
river transport, 4, 36
roads, 36
Robbins, Arthur, 229–30

Roche, David, Viscount, 212, 214, 218
Desmond rebellion, 225
Roche, Maurice, 162
Rochford, Robert, S.J., 203, 316–17
Rokeby, Sir Ralph, 241, 243
Rokeby, William, 78
Roman Catholicism
Baltinglass rebellion, 203–4
and Old English, 193, 205
restored, 170, 173
retained, 202
Ronayne family, 47
Rookes, Edward, 110
Roscommon, County, 257, 260, 300
attacked by Maguire, 290
and presidency, 239
settlers, 258
shired, 241, 245
Roscommon castle, 257
Roscommon town, 258
Ross town, 36, 39
Rothe family, 25
Route, the, 267, 274
rural communities, 34–5
Russell, Sir William
Lord Deputy 1594–7, 292–4

St Audoen's, Dublin, 113, 114, 123, 138, 139, 322
St David's, Naas, 123–4
St Doulagh's well, Co. Dublin, 124, 313
St John, Elizabeth, 69
St John's, Newgate, 27, 122, 140
St Katharine's monastery, Waterford, 121
St Lawrence, Thomas, 122
St Lawrence family, 66, 122–3
St Leger, Anne, 85
St Leger, Sir Anthony, 53, 150, 182, 195, 211, 240, 266, 268
Desmond opposes, 163
financial administration, 174–5
heads royal commission, 135, 148
land grants, 161, 178
Lord Deputy 1540–47, 144–5, 152–63
Lord Deputy 1553–6, 173–5
Lord Deputy 1550–51, 167–9
monastic dissolutions, 142
purveyance, 172

St Leger, Sir Anthony *continued*
  and Reformation, 303, 305–6
  surrender and regrant, 155–9, 194
St Leger, George, 73
St Leger, Sir Warham, 183, 211–12,
  213, 214, 227–8, 233
St Loe, Sir William, 148, 165
St Mary's, Howth, 122–3
St Mary's abbey, Dublin, 120, 142
St Mary's abbey, Trim, 124, 161
St Mary's church, Maynooth, 83, 117
St Mary's well, Mulhuddart, 313
St Patrick's Cathedral, Dublin, 6, 113,
  144, 206, 306, 309, 310
St Patrick's Purgatory, Lough Derg, 1,
  132
St Saviour's, Waterford, 28
St Sepulchre, liberty of, 17
St Thomas's abbey, Dublin, 161
St Wolstan's, Co. Kildare, 140, 148, 201
Salamanca College, 320
Salmeron, Alfonso, 303
San Giuseppe, Bastiano di, 226
Sanders, Dr Nicholas, 223, 224, 225–6,
  316
Savage clan, 278
scholars, Gaelic, 62–4
Scotland, 169. *see also* Scots
  mercenaries
  Argyll invasion threat, 92
  Counter-Reformation, 324
  English war with, 159–60
  expulsion planned, 180
  Gaelic contacts with, 43
  and Geraldine League, 150
  trade with, 5, 40, 48
  and Ulster, 167, 265
  Ulster settlements, 169, 253, 266,
    267, 272, 274, 276, 279, 280
Scots mercenaries, 9, 55–6, 241, 246,
  249, 271, 273, 285
  massive expansion, 275–6
  and O'Donnell succession dispute,
    289
  settlement of, 56–7
  used by Burke, 254–5
  used by O'Neills, 284, 292, 293
  used by Turlough Luineach
    O'Neill, 282–3
Scurlock, Barnaby, 187
sea transport, 5–6
Sebastian, King of Portugal, 223

Sedgrave, Walter, 203
Sedgrave family, 25
seneschals, 165, 184, 185, 195–6, 197,
  207, 223, 288
  cessing, 198
  role of, 199–200
servitors, 195, 202
settlement patterns, 9–10
Seymour, Jane, 134
Shannon river, 4, 5, 77, 149
Shee family, 25
sheriff's courts, 16–17
Sherlock family, 25
Shillelagh, 165
shiring, 16–17, 241, 245, 285–6
Shrewsbury, Earl of, 17, 34, 85
Shrule castle, 243, 247
Sidney, Sir Henry, 6, 179, 180, 193,
  195, 197, 202, 205, 242, 275
  arrests Desmond, 212
  and cess, 190
  composition rents, 244–5
  FitzMaurice revolt, 214
  Kavanagh agreement, 198
  Lord Deputy 1565–71, 182–4
  Lord Deputy 1575–8, 185–7, 219–21
  Mac an Iarla revolts, 243, 245–6
  and Old English, 187–9
  O'Neill peerage, 282–3
  presidency councils, 209, 211–13,
    215, 238, 240–41
  and seneschals, 199
  and Shane O'Neill, 272–4
  in Ulster, 276–7, 280, 282
  university scheme, 309
siege warfare, 9, 57, 73, 108–9, 110
Simms, Dr Katharine, 76
Simnel, Lambert, 73
simony, 119, 129
Skeffington, Sir William
  Fitzgerald rebellion, 108, 109–10
  Lord Deputy 1534–5, 105, 106,
    109–12
  Pale pacified by, 145–6
  and Reformation, 134
  sent to Ireland, 101–3
Slane, Baron of, 66
Slane, Co. Meath, 73, 123
Slaney river, 3, 4
'slantyaght', 74–5, 100
slánuigheacht, 74

Sligo, County, 260
  Burke rebellion, 256
  composition rents, 251–2
  friary, 131
  Maguire raids, 261–2, 290
  O'Rourke raids, 257
  and presidency, 239, 247–8
  rebellion, 1589, 263
  settlers, 257–8, 259
  shired, 245
  Spanish Armada, 237, 256
  surrender and regrant, 248
Sligo castle, 257, 261, 289, 292
Sligo town, 21, 240, 258
  attacked, 261
  burnt, 22
  customs paid to O'Donnell, 53
  dominant families, 25, 47, 49, 260
Smerwick Harbour, Co. Kerry, 223,
  225–6
Smith, George, 278
Smith, Thomas, 44, 277–8, 281, 283
Smith, Thomas (younger), 277, 278, 279
Society of Jesus, 303–4, 312, 322
soldiers. *see* troops
Somerset, Protector, 164, 166, 167
Spain, 43, 83, 132, 286, 293, 320
  and Counter-Reformation, 303,
    304, 316, 322–3
  and Fitzgerald rebellion, 107, 109
  invasion feared, 231
  and Nine Years' War, 265, 266,
    298–9, 299, 300–301
  and Shane O'Neill, 270
  trade, 5, 40, 48
  troops at Smerwick, 226
  and Tyrone, 296
Spanish Armada, 237–8, 255, 256, 259,
  261, 263, 287
Spenser, Edmund, 44, 228, 297, 319
Stanihurst, James, 313
Stanihurst, Nicholas, 161–2
Stanihurst, Richard, 82, 324
Stanihurst family, 25
Stanley, Sir George, 180
Stanley, Sir William, 177, 323
staple ports, 29–30, 38
Staples, Edward, Bishop of Meath, 119
  and Reformation, 136–7, 138, 166–7
  removed on marriage, 173, 306
  and St Leger, 153, 160

Statutes of Kilkenny, 11, 80
Stile, Sir John, 87, 92
Strabane, Co. Tyrone, 282, 283, 286
Strong, Anastasia, 321
studia particularia, 125
Stukely, Thomas, 223, 316
subsidy tax, 14–15, 184
succession law, 51–2
Suir river, 3, 4
surrender and regrant, 155–9
  agricultural improvement, 198
  Connacht, 239, 240–41, 248
  ecclesiastical, 160
  failure of, 194–5
  Munster, 210–11
  in Munster, 218
  Perrot's plan, 205
  and Sussex, 179, 180
  terms revised, 174
  Ulster, 266, 285
Surrey, Earl of. *see* Howard,
  Thomas
surveys, 4
suspension bill, 206
Sussex, Earl of, 173, 183, 187, 195,
  205, 216
  Lord Deputy 1556–63, 179
  presidencies, 210
  and seneschals, 199
  and Ulster, 267–72

Taaffe, William, 259
Taaffe family, 315
Talbot, Robert, 95
Tallow, Co. Waterford, 235, 297
tanistry, 51, 59, 156, 184, 239, 271
tanning industry, 30, 40, 45
Tara, Co. Meath, 151
taxation, 14–15, 23, 147, 238, 272. *see
  also* cess; composition rents;
  coign and livery
  ecclesiastical, 137
  increases proposed, 135, 136
  land tax, 148
  Old English opposition to, 188–9
  in Pale, 181
  and plantations, 231
  subsidy, 14–15
Teeling, John, 110
Thomond, earldom of, 245, 291. *see
  also* O'Briens

Thomond, earldom of *continued*
  composition indenture, 250–51, 252, 253
  and Composition of Connacht, 259
  and presidency, 221, 238, 248–9
  settlers, 258
  succession disputes, 173, 174, 182, 239–40
  surrender and regrant, 180, 240–41
  taxation reform, 244
Thurles, Co. Tipperary, 22, 26
time, measurement of, 6–7
Tintern Abbey, Co. Wexford, 140
Tipperary, County, 94, 149, 214, 215, 300
  agriculture, 11
  clans, 43
  Desmond rebellion, 223
  monastic abuses, 120
  monastic dissolutions, 142
  Ossory rules, 101–2
  plantation, 231
  woodlands, 3
Tipperary palatinate, 212, 230
tithes, 128, 311, 314
Tobin, Margaret, 60
Topographia Hiberniae (Gerald of Wales), 1
tower-houses, 47
Tower of London, 187, 212, 295, 313
towns, 71–2, 100, 191. *see also* markets; urbanisation
  administration, 24–5, 26, 80
  Connacht, 240
  cultural and economic functions, 27–32
  definition of, 21–2
  dominant families, 25–6
  economic conditions, 190–92
  in English Ireland, 20–40
  festivals, 28–9
  and Gaelic Ireland, 20, 47
  and Gaelic society, 26–7, 47–8
  industry, 30, 32
  'Irishtowns', 38
  municipal courts, 24
  New English *versus* Old English, 202
  and plantations, 235
  and presidency, 245
  regalia, 24
  revenues of, 24
  ruling groups, 22–7
  and St Leger, 162
  trade, 32, 35–40
  Ulster, 282
trade, 162, 200
  agricultural, 33–4
  by-laws, 38
  charts, 2
  control of, 38–9
  difficulties of, 36–8
  English and Welsh, 201
  with Gaels, 47–8
  imports and exports, 40, 190
  international, 5–6, 39–40
  mercantilist bills, 191
  and merchant guilds, 29–30
  money shortages, 36–7
  in the Pale, 190
  reforms, 184
  towns, 22, 35–40
  in Ulster, 282
transport, 4–5, 36, 190
travellers, accounts by, 1–2, 42
Tremayne, Edmund, 185–6, 219
Trim, Co. Meath, 26, 124
  castle, 109
  mendicant friars, 130
  parliament, 1542, 159
  shrine closed, 137–8
Trimblestown, Lord. *see* Barnewall, John
Trinity College, Dublin, 310, 312, 320
Trinity Guild, 124
troops. *see also* billeting; coign and livery; purveyance
troops, English, 93. *see also* seneschals
  atrocities by, 197
  costs of, 15
  levies burdensome, 99–100
  marchland campaigns, 149
  military posts, 196
  numbers of, 92, 171, 181, 269, 273, 294, 299
  presidential, 219–20
  problems with, 89
troops, Irish, 9, 54, 55–7, 56, 65, 72, 89, 240, 270. *see also* Scots mercenaries
  bonaghts, 55, 275
  cavalry, 56
  in English wars, 159–60, 160
  hereditary, 247

hosting obligations, 15–16, 55–6
Kildare's military strength, 72–3
'masterless' men punished, 216,
    220, 221, 242
retinues reduced, 163
serving abroad, 323–4
standing armies, 56
supplied as tribute, 74
as tribute, 74
tuarastal, 52–3
Tyrone's army, 293
used by New English, 201
Troy, Abbot, 124
Tuam archdiocese, 62, 115, 126, 130
tuarastal, 52–3
Tullaghogue, 301
Tullow castle, 108
Tyrconnell. *see* O'Donnells
Tyrone, County, 46, 270, 271, 273,
    283, 284
agriculture, 45
divided, 286
surrender and regrant, 180
Tyrone prevents shiring, 292, 293
Tyrone, earldom of, 267. *see also*
    O'Neills
Sidney's plans for, 276
strength of, 266–7
succession disputes, 173, 174, 268,
    270
Tyrone, lordship of, 282
Tyrrell, Captain Richard, 297

Ulster, 11, 12, 38, 115, 169, 183, 257,
    261, 273. *see also* Nine Years'
    War; Scots mercenaries
1560–1603, 264–302
agriculture, 44
clans, 43
colonial schemes, 276–82
composition rent, 285
Essex as governor, 185
friaries, 130–31, 131–2
Grey sorties, 151
Jesuit mission, 303
and Kildare, 67, 69, 75–6, 95
lack of towns, 282
monastic dissolutions, 163
O'Donnell revolt, 262
O'Neill connections, 290–91
peace unstable, 167–8

Perrot's policy, 284–6
plantation, 184, 213
port rights, 84
presidency council, 179, 210
rebellion, 1598, 235–6
Reformation in, 319
religious orders, 124
Scottish trade, 48
settlers, 288
Shane O'Neill's rebellion, 267–74
St Leger in, 153, 158–9
survey, 288
urbanisation, 21
undertakers, 231–2, 233, 234–5
university schemes, 28, 128, 193,
    229
Archbishop Browne, 166–7, 309
Counter-Reformation, 312–13
Elizabethan, 309–10
Garret Mór, 83
Loftus, 320
Perrot, 206, 310
Upper Ossory, Baron of, 197
urbanisation, 10, 17–18
Ussher, James, 324
Ussher, John, 312
Ussher family, 320

Valla, Lorenzo, 83
Verdon family, 123, 315
viceroy. *see* governor
Viking foundations, 10, 20, 22

Wafer, Nicholas, 110
wakes, 132
Wales, 146, 182, 201, 211, 314, 324
influence of, 10
trade with, 40
Wallop, Sir Henry, 205, 206, 229–30,
    318
Walsh, Nicholas, 206, 207
Walsh, William, Bishop of Meath,
    173, 306, 308
Walshe family, 25
Walsingham, Francis, 229, 231
warfare
costs of, 164, 181–2, 201, 295, 302
extent of, 9
Gaelic troops, 55–7
guerrilla warfare, 177–8, 280
Tyrone's army, 293

Waterford town, 5, 20, 21, 22, 85, 169,
   208, 324
   architecture, 26
   attacked, 214
   citizenship in, 23
   craft guilds, 30
   dominant families, 17, 25, 32
   Fitzgerald rebellion, 109
   Gaelic trade, 38, 39
   Geraldine overlordship, 218
   mendicant friars, 130
   monastic dissolutions, 142
   regalia, 24
   river transport, 36
   schools, 28
   staple port, 29
Waterford, County, 298
   commissioners, 16–17
   monastic dissolutions, 142
   plantation, 231
   survey of, 230
Waterford, Dean of, 27
Waterford diocese, 310–11
Waterhouse, Sir Edward, 226
Wauchop, Robert, Archbishop of
   Armagh, 160, 168, 305
Wellesley, Walter, Bishop of Kildare,
   117, 141
Westmeath, County, 171
   Baltinglass rebellion, 203
   coign and livery, 190
   monastic dissolutions, 142
   Nugent conspiracy, 204
Weston, Robert, 311
Wexford town, 5, 22, 36
   liberties, 17, 85
Wexford, County, 5, 108, 149, 195,
   199, 310
   'black rent' abolished, 156
   castellated houses, 192
   clans, 43
   coign and livery, 190

   monastic dissolutions, 148
   seneschals, 200
   surrender and regrant, 156
White, Edward, 251
White, Sir Nicholas, 206
White, Rowland, 200
White, Victor, 319
White family, 267
Wicklow, County, 10, 155, 194, 297
   absentees' lands, 103
   agriculture, 45, 198
   clans, 43
   seneschals, 200
   woodlands, 3, 39
Willis, Captain Humphrey, 288, 289,
   290, 319
Wiltshire, Earl of. *see* Boleyn, Sir
   Thomas
Wingfield, Sir Jacques, 177, 180, 213
Winter, Admiral Sir William, 226
Wise, Sir Andrew, 174
Wolfe, Fr David, S.J., 312–13
Wolsey, Cardinal Thomas, 78, 82, 86,
   88, 94, 101, 103, 133
   debate with Kildare, 98–9
   fall of, 102, 117
   and Kildare–Ormond feud, 95
women
   and Counter-Reformation, 321
   in Gaelic law, 59–61
woollen industry, 30, 40, 45, 93, 190,
   191

Yellow Ford, battle of the, 296
Youghal, Co. Cork, 169, 215
   attacked, 214, 225
   friary, 131
   Gaelic trade, 39
   Geraldine overlordship, 218

Zouche, Elizabeth, 69, 78
Zwinglianism, 166